CORPORATE PERSONHOOD

The topic of corporate personhood has captured the attention of many who are concerned about the increasing presence, power, and influence of corporations in modern society. Recent Supreme Court cases like *Citizens United*, *Hobby Lobby*, and *Masterpiece Cakeshop* – which solidified the free speech and religious liberty rights of corporations and their owners – have heightened the controversy over treating corporations as persons under the law. What does it mean to say that the corporation is a person, and why does it matter? In CORPORATE PERSONHOOD, Susanna Kim Ripken addresses these questions and highlights the complexity of the corporate personhood concept. Using a broad, interdisciplinary framework – incorporating law, economics, philosophy, sociology, psychology, organizational theory, political science, and linguistics – this highly original work explores the complex, multidimensional nature of corporate personhood and its implications for corporate rights and duties.

Susanna Kim Ripken is a Professor of Law at Chapman University, Fowler School of Law, with a joint appointment in the Wilkinson College of Arts, Humanities, and Social Sciences. She teaches business law courses and has published several articles on corporate law, corporate personhood, and securities regulation. She is a graduate of Stanford University and UCLA Law School.

Corporate Personhood

SUSANNA KIM RIPKEN
Chapman University, Fowler School of Law

CAMBRIDGE
UNIVERSITY PRESS

CAMBRIDGE
UNIVERSITY PRESS

University Printing House, Cambridge CB2 8BS, United Kingdom

One Liberty Plaza, 20th Floor, New York, NY 10006, USA

477 Williamstown Road, Port Melbourne, VIC 3207, Australia

314–321, 3rd Floor, Plot 3, Splendor Forum, Jasola District Centre, New Delhi – 110025, India

79 Anson Road, #06–04/06, Singapore 079906

Cambridge University Press is part of the University of Cambridge.

It furthers the University's mission by disseminating knowledge in the pursuit of education, learning, and research at the highest international levels of excellence.

www.cambridge.org
Information on this title: www.cambridge.org/9781108416528
DOI: 10.1017/9781108241366

First published 2019

Printed and bound in Great Britain by Clays Ltd, Elcograf S.p.A.

A catalogue record for this publication is available from the British Library.

ISBN 978-1-108-41652-8 Hardback
ISBN 978-1-108-40392-4 Paperback

For Randy and Kai

Contents

Acknowledgments

Writing a book is a group effort. I know that now. I could not have completed this book without the help and generosity of so many people.

I thank my colleague and accomplished author, Lan Cao, who first inspired me to believe that I could write a book like this one. It was through my conversations with Lan that I learned about the book writing and publication process. I am grateful for her guidance, advice, and mentoring during the earliest stages of this project.

Sherry Leysen, the Associate Director of the Law Library at Chapman University, Fowler School of Law, provided invaluable research assistance. Her research and editing contributions to this book cannot be overstated. Her knowledge and expertise, her ability to find the obscurest of sources, and her unflagging good cheer were instrumental in advancing this book project from its inception. I owe a debt of gratitude to her and the superb, dedicated staff of the Law Library.

My thanks go to Daniel Bogart, John Eastman, Donald Kochan, and Celestine McConville who graciously took the time to provide me with insightful comments on draft chapters. I also thank my former students, Sarvnaz (Sam) Torabi and Susan Nikdel, for their exceptional research assistance and kindness. Both Sam and Susan generously volunteered their time, even after they had graduated from law school, to provide critical research support.

I am grateful to Cambridge University Press and especially senior editor Matt Gallaway who first saw value in this book project. I also want to thank four anonymous Cambridge peer reviewers who provided helpful critiques and suggestions that sharpened my thinking on the scope and direction of the book. Content managers Becky Jackaman and Laura Bayne at Cambridge ably shepherded the book through the publication process, Helen Kitto provided superb copyediting of the manuscript, and Karthik Orukaimani at Integra skillfully managed the final production.

Some of the ideas presented in this book were first discussed in law review articles that I published in prior years. They include *Characteristics of Soulless Persons: The Applicability of the Character Evidence Rule to Corporations*, 2000 University of Illinois Law Review 763 (2000); *Corporations Are People Too:*

A Multi-Dimensional Approach to the Corporate Personhood Puzzle, 15 FORDHAM JOURNAL OF CORPORATE & FINANCIAL LAW 97 (2009); *Corporate First Amendment Rights After* Citizens United*: An Analysis of the Popular Movement to End the Constitutional Personhood of Corporations*, 14 UNIVERSITY OF PENNSYLVANIA JOURNAL OF BUSINESS LAW 209 (2011); and Citizens United, *Corporate Personhood, and Corporate Power: The Tension Between Constitutional Law and Corporate Law*, 6 UNIVERSITY OF ST. THOMAS JOURNAL OF LAW & PUBLIC POLICY 285 (2012). I want to recognize these excellent law journals and their very capable staffs.

Most of all, my family members deserve my deepest gratitude for their unending support, patience, and prayers. I thank my parents who never stop encouraging and inspiring me. They immigrated to the United States fifty years ago with the hope of providing the greatest possible opportunities for their family. Their life journey is a moving and inspirational tale of hope and faith, setbacks and sacrifices, resilience and triumph, and unwavering love for their family. All of my accomplishments are theirs. I thank my siblings and their families for their encouragement, and especially my sister for devoting many hours to cataloging sources and helping with the research for this project. Finally, to my husband and son, who are the light of my life, who daily give me reasons to rejoice, and who endured the long process of my writing this book, thank you.

Table of Cases

Abrams v. United States, 250 U.S. 616 (1919).
Adarand Constructors, Inc. v. Pena, 515 U.S. 200 (1995).
A.H. Emp. Co. v. Fifth Third Bank, No. 11 C 4586, 2012 WL 686704 (N.D. Ill. 2012).
Amber Pyramid, Inc. v. Buffington Harbor Riverboats, 129 F. App'x 292 (7th Cir. 2005).
Austin v. Mich. State Chamber of Commerce, 494 U.S. 652 (1990).
Autolube Grp. LLC v. Delfin Grp. USA LLC, No. 2:13–2422-PMD, 2014 WL 5488400 (D.S.C. 2014).
Bains LLC v. Arco Products Co., 405 F.3d 764 (9th Cir. 2005).
Bank of Augusta v. Earle, 38 U.S. (13 Pet.) 519 (1839).
Bank of the U.S. v. Deveaux, 9 U.S. (5 Cranch) 61 (1809).
Barrows v. Jackson, 346 U.S. 249 (1953).
Braunfeld v. Brown, 366 U.S. 599 (1961).
Brown v. Bd. of Educ., 347 U.S. 483 (1954).
Buckley v. Valeo, 424 U.S. 1 (1976).
Burwell v. Hobby Lobby Stores, Inc., 134 S. Ct. 2751 (2014).
Calderon v. Sw. Bell Mobile Sys., LLC, 390 F. Supp. 2d 714 (N.D. Ill. 2005).
Carnell Constr. Corp. v. Danville Redev. & Hous. Auth., 745 F.3d 703 (4th Cir. 2014).
Cent. Hudson Gas & Elec. v. Pub. Servs. Comm'n of N.Y., 447 U.S. 557 (1980).
Chicago, Burlington & Quincy R.R. v. Chicago, 166 U.S. 226 (1897).
Chicago, Milwaukee & St. Paul Ry. Co. v. Minnesota, 134 U.S. 418 (1890).
Cholla Ready Mix, Inc. v. Civish, 382 F.3d 969 (9th Cir. 2004).
Citizens United v. FEC, 558 U.S. 310 (2010).
City of Boerne v. Flores, 521 U.S. 507 (1997).
City of Richmond v. J.A. Croson Co., 488 U.S. 469 (1989).
Coleman & Williams, Ltd. v. Wis. Dep't Workforce Dev., 401 F. Supp. 2d 938 (E.D. Wis. 2005).
Conestoga Wood Specialties Corp. v. Sebelius, 917 F. Supp. 2d 394 (E.D. Pa. 2013).

Conestoga Wood Specialties Corp. v. Sec'y of U.S. Dep't of Health & Human Servs., 724 F.3d 377 (3d Cir. 2013).
Conn. Gen. Life Ins. Co. v. Johnson, 303 U.S. 77 (1938).
Consol. Edison Co. v. Pub. Serv. Comm'n, 447 U.S. 530 (1980).
Contemporary Pers., Inc. v. Godiva Chocolatier, Inc., No. 09–00187, 2009 WL 2431461 (E.D. Penn. 2009).
County of San Mateo v. S. Pac. R.R. Co., 13 F. 722 (C.C.D. Cal. 1882).
Covington & Lexington Tpk. Rd. Co. v. Sandford, 164 U.S. 578 (1896).
Craig v. Masterpiece Cakeshop, Inc., 370 P.3d 272 (Colo. App. 2015).
Des Vergnes v. Seekonk Water Dist., 601 F.2d 9 (1st Cir. 1979).
Dodge v. Ford Motor Co., 170 N.W. 668 (Mich. 1919).
Domino's Pizza, Inc. v. McDonald, 546 U.S. 470 (2006).
Emp't Div. v. Smith, 494 U.S. 872 (1990).
FCC v. AT&T, Inc., 562 U.S. 397 (2011).
FEC v. Nat'l Right to Work Comm., 459 U.S. 197 (1982).
FEC v. Wis. Right to Life, Inc., 551 U.S. 449 (2007).
First Nat'l Bank of Boston v. Bellotti, 435 U.S. 765 (1978).
Florence Urgent Care v. Healthspan, Inc., 445 F. Supp. 2d 871 (S.D. Ohio 2006).
Gersman v. Grp. Health Ass'n, Inc., 931 F.2d 1565 (D.C. Cir. 1991).
Gifford v. McCarthy, 23 N.Y.S. 3d 422 (N.Y. App. Div. 2016).
Gilardi v. U.S. Dep't of Health & Human Servs., 733 F.3d 1208 (D.C. Cir. 2013).
Guides, Ltd. v. Yarmouth Grp. Prop. Mgmt., Inc., 295 F.3d 1065 (10th Cir. 2002).
Gulf, Colorado & Santa Fe Ry. Co. v. Ellis, 165 U.S. 150 (1897).
Hale v. Henkel, 201 U.S. 43 (1906).
Hobby Lobby Stores, Inc. v. Sebelius, 870 F. Supp. 2d 1278 (W.D. Okla. 2012).
Hobby Lobby Stores, Inc. v. Sebelius, 723 F.3d 1114 (10th Cir. 2013).
Holland/Blue Streak v. Barthelemy, 849 F.2d 987 (5th Cir. 1988).
Howard Sec. Servs., Inc. v. Johns Hopkins Hosp., 516 F. Supp. 508 (D. Md. 1981).
Hudson Valley Freedom Theater, Inc. v. Heimbach, 671 F.2d 702 (2d Cir. 1982).
John & Vincent Arduini Inc. v. NYNEX, 129 F. Supp. 2d 162 (N.D.N.Y. 2001).
Jones v. Culver Franchising Sys., Inc., 12 F. Supp. 3d 1079 (N.D. Ill. 2013).
Kasky v. Nike, Inc., 45 P.3d 243 (Cal. 2002).
Louis K. Liggett Co. v. Lee, 288 U.S. 517 (1933).
Louisville, Cincinnati, & Charleston R.R. Co. v. Letson, 43 U.S. (2 How.) 497 (1844).
Lynch v. Donnelly, 465 U.S. 668 (1984).
Major Tours, Inc. v. Colorel, 799 F. Supp. 2d 376 (D.N.J. 2011).
Masterpiece Cakeshop, Ltd. v. Colorado Civil Rights Comm'n, 138 S. Ct. 1719 (2018).
McConnell v. FEC, 540 U.S. 93 (2003).
Minneapolis & St. Louis Ry. Co. v. Beckwith, 129 U.S. 26 (1889).

NDN Drywall, Inc. v. Custom Drywall, Inc., No. Civ. 04-CV-4706DSDSRN, 2005 WL 1324056 (D. Minn. 2005).
N.Y. Cent. & Hudson River R.R. Co. v. United States, 212 U.S. 481 (1909).
New Louisiana Holdings, LLC v. Arrowsmith, No. 11 C 5031, 2012 WL 6061710 (N. D. Ill. 2012).
Noble v. Union River Logging R.R. Co., 147 U.S. 165 (1893).
Obergefell v. Hodges, 135 S. Ct. 2584 (2015).
Org. of Minority Vendors, Inc. v. Ill. Cent. Gulf R.R., 579 F. Supp. 574 (N.D. Ill. 1983).
Oti Kaga, Inc. v. S.D. Hous. Dev. Auth., 342 F.3d 871 (8th Cir. 2003).
Pac. Gas & Elec. Co. v. Pub. Utils. Comm'n, 475 U.S. 1 (1986).
Paul v. Virginia, 75 U.S. (8 Wall.) 168 (1868).
Pembina Consol. Silver Mining & Milling Co. v. Pennsylvania, 125 U.S. 181 (1888).
Perez v. Abbott Labs., No. 94 C 4127, 1995 WL 86716 (N.D. Ill. 1995).
Prestige Rests. & Entm't, Inc. v. Bayside Seafood Rest., Inc., No. 09–23128-CIV, 2010 WL 680905 (S.D. Fla. 2010).
Regents of the Univ. of Cal. v. Bakke, 438 U.S. 265 (1978).
Roberts v. U.S. Jaycees, 468 U.S. 609 (1984).
Rosales v. AT&T Info. Sys., Inc., 702 F. Supp. 1489 (D. Colo. 1988).
Ross v. Bernhard, 396 U.S. 531 (1970).
Russick v. Hicks, 85 F. Supp. 281 (W.D. Mich. 1949).
Safety Sols., Inc. v. City of Chicago, No. 11 C 1305, 2011 WL 3652446 (N.D. Ill. 2011).
San Mateo v. S. Pac. R.R. Co., 13 F. 722 (C.C.D. Cal. 1882).
Santa Clara v. S. Pac. R.R. Co., 118 U.S. 394 (1886).
Searcy v. Hous. Lighting & Power Co., 907 F.2d 562 (5th Cir. 1990).
Sec. & Data Techs., Inc. v. Sch. Dist. of Phila., 145 F. Supp. 3d 454 (E.D. Pa. 2015).
Shaffer & Munn v. Union Mining Co., 55 Md. 74 (1880).
Shah v. Am. Bottling Co., No. 07–1042, 2008 WL 718435 (C.D. Ill. 2008).
Sherbert v. Verner, 374 U.S. 398 (1963).
State v. Arlene's Flowers, Inc., 389 P.3d 543 (Wash. 2017).
Stormans, Inc. v. Selecky, 854 F. Supp. 2d 925 (W.D. Wash. 2012).
Stormans, Inc. v. Wiesman, 794 F.3d 1064 (9th Cir. 2015).
Sullivan v. Little Hunting Park, Inc., 396 U.S. 229 (1969).
Telescope Media Grp. v. Lindsey, 271 F. Supp. 3d 1090 (D. Minn. 2017).
Thinket Ink Info. Res., Inc. v. Sun Microsystems, Inc., 368 F.3d 1053 (9th Cir. 2004).
Triad Assocs., Inc. v. Chi. Hous. Auth., 892 F.2d 583 (7th Cir. 1989).
Trs. of Dartmouth Coll. v. Woodward, 17 U.S. (4 Wheat.) 518 (1819).
Ultimax Transp., Inc. v. British Airways, PLC, 231 F. Supp. 2d 1329 (N.D. Ga. 2002).
United States v. Martin Linen Supply Co., 430 U.S. 564 (1977).
Unites States v. Morton Salt Co., 338 U.S. 632 (1950).
United States v. White, 322 U.S. 694 (1944).

Va. State Bd. of Pharmacy v. Va. Citizens Consumer Council, Inc. 425 U.S. 748 (1976).
Village of Arlington Heights v. Metro. Hous. Dev. Corp., 429 U.S. 252 (1977).
Wheeling Steel Corp. v. Glander, 337 U.S. 562 (1949).
Wisconsin v. Yoder, 406 U.S. 205 (1972).
Witte v. Zoological Soc'y of Phila., No. 06–3878, 2007 WL 433473 (E.D. Penn. 2007).
Woods v. City of Greensboro, 855 F.3d 639 (4th Cir. 2017).
Ziegler v. City of Warren, No. 4:04CV1248, 2007 WL 509764 (N.D. Ohio 2007).

Introduction

If you picked up this book, opened it to this page, and started reading this sentence, chances are you are a person.

My assumption in writing this book is that its readers would be persons, i.e., human beings, actual flesh and blood people. I figured you might be a student, a professor, a lawyer, a business executive, a policymaker, an activist, or any other person who is interested in the role of corporations in our society today. What I did not contemplate is that the reader of this book would be a corporation.

Yet corporations are people too, or so the law says. As legal persons, they can conduct activities in and out of the marketplace in much the same way human individuals do. Corporations can enter into contracts, buy and sell property, sue and be sued, and make claims to some of the most fundamental rights guaranteed to all persons under the Constitution. Why shouldn't I assume that a corporation as a person can pick up this book and absorb its contents? A corporation cannot *read*, you reply; it is not a real person, its personhood under the law is a metaphor. But the corporation can *speak*, according to the United States Supreme Court. Indeed, its speech is entitled to First Amendment protection. And herein lies one of the most perplexing dilemmas in American law. The corporation is not a flesh and blood person, but it nonetheless seeks to be regarded as a person with all the legal rights that pertain to personhood. Courts over time have allowed corporations to be treated in much the same manner as human persons, but the justifications for doing so have not always been consistent nor clearly articulated, revealing a deep ambiguity over the idea that corporations are fellow persons in the eyes of the law.

The personhood of corporations has always been a vexing puzzle for legal scholars, but in the last few years the dilemma over corporate personhood has moved well beyond academic circles and has become a controversial topic among wide swaths of the American public. Perhaps the surge of interest in the subject can be attributed to recent Supreme Court decisions that have extended corporate political speech and religious exercise rights in unprecedented directions. For example, in 2010, the Court in *Citizens United v. Federal Election Commission* upheld the First Amendment right of corporations to use unlimited corporate funds to support or oppose candidates in political elections.[1] In 2014, the Court in *Burwell v. Hobby Lobby Stores, Inc.* held that it is a violation of a corporation's right to religious freedom to require the company to provide employees with access to contraceptive methods that the corporation finds morally objectionable based on its religious principles.[2] Most recently, in 2018, the Court in *Masterpiece Cakeshop, Ltd. v. Colorado Civil Rights Commission* upheld on very narrow grounds the right of a bakery business owner to refuse to bake a wedding cake for a same-sex couple because of his religious objections to same-sex marriage.[3] The nation engaged in heated debate over these cases, questioning whether corporate entities can and should have the same status as human individuals to claim fundamental free speech and religious exercise rights.

The very notion that corporations can be persons under the Constitution has sparked outrage among a significant portion of the general public that believes corporations should not share the same constitutional rights of human beings. When former presidential candidate Mitt Romney famously stated, "Corporations are people," at the Iowa State Fair during his 2011 campaign, he found himself in the center of the corporate personhood controversy.[4] Someone in the audience immediately shouted back, "No, they're not!" Romney replied, "Of course they are. Everything corporations earn ultimately goes to people. Where do you think it goes?" Romney's point was not that corporations themselves are persons, but that corporations are essentially collections of human individuals whose financial interests are always at stake. Nonetheless, his statement drew widespread ridicule and scorn from opponents who accused him of equating corporations with real persons and presumably revealing his bias in favor of large corporations.

As the Romney incident demonstrated, the concept of corporate personhood has touched a nerve for many people who question the legitimacy of corporations' status as persons under the law. When the Occupy Wall Street movement began to pick up momentum in late 2011, angry protesters waved banners that read "End Corporate Personhood" and "Corporations Are Not People."[5] These slogans symbolized deep discontent over social and economic inequalities perceived to be the result of the

1 Citizens United v. FEC, 558 U.S. 310 (2010).

2 Burwell v. Hobby Lobby Stores, Inc., 134 S. Ct. 2751 (2014).

3 Masterpiece Cakeshop, Ltd. v. Colorado Civil Rights Comm'n, 138 S. Ct. 1719 (2018).

4 Philip Rucker, *Mitt Romney Says 'Corporations Are People,'* Wash. Post (Aug. 11, 2011), www.washingtonpost.com/politics/mitt-romney-says-corporations-are-people/2011/08/11/gIQABwZ38I_story.html [https://perma.cc/6LF6-BE5C].

5 Joel Bakan, *Psychopaths, Inc.: On Corporate Personhood, in* The Occupy Handbook 353, 354 (Janet Byrne ed., 2012) (noting sign at an Occupy protest reading "We the People, Not We the Corporations"); Jim Hightower, *Organize in 2012*, Other Words (Jan. 9, 2012), https://otherwords.org/organize_in_2012/ [https://perma.cc/W332-PL99] (displaying photo of Occupy Wall Street sign reading "Revoke Corporate Personhood"); Mark Trumbull, *Can 'Occupy Wall Street' Really Get Money out of Politics?*, Christian Sci. Monitor (Oct. 14, 2011), www.csmonitor.com/USA/Politics/2011/1014/Can-Occupy-Wall-Street-really-get-money-out-of-politics [https://perma.cc/A2XT-D8UJ] (displaying photo of protester holding a sign reading "End Corporate Personhood").

growing dominance of corporate power. Many people began to connect corporate personhood with the corrupting influence of money in politics and the widening gap between the "haves" and the "have nots." Several activist organizations launched a popular movement to amend the Constitution to establish that the expenditure of corporate money is not equivalent to political speech and that human beings, not corporations, are the only persons entitled to constitutional rights.[6] Numerous federal and state lawmakers, responding to pressures by their constituents, have openly expressed support for such a constitutional amendment to abolish the personhood of corporations. It is abundantly clear that corporate personhood is a significant issue that no longer occupies the attention of legal scholars alone, but has become a topic of considerable concern for many average Americans who decry "big business" and the overbearing influence of "corporate America."

My interest in the concept of corporate personhood began almost twenty years ago when I wrote a law review article on a federal rule of evidence called the character evidence rule. Under that rule, evidence of a person's character generally is not admissible in court to show that the person acted in conformity with that character on a particular occasion.[7] It is deemed unfair, for example, to present evidence of a person's prior misdeeds to prove that the person has a bad character and therefore must have committed the crime for which he is currently being tried. I wondered whether the character evidence rule applied to corporations in the same way it applies to individuals. I questioned first whether the corporation is even a "person" capable of having character for purposes of the character evidence rule, and second, even if the corporation could be regarded as a person, whether it could actually possess a "character" of its own, independent of the individual members of the corporation. After considerable research and thought, I answered both of those questions in the affirmative, but I ultimately concluded that the character evidence rule should not apply with equal force to corporations because they do not have the same moral status as human beings.[8] My ideas were tentative at the time. I recognized even then that corporate personhood is complicated and that clear-cut conclusions about its implications were elusive.

For me, the inquiry I entertained in that law review article was the start of a decades-long interest in understanding more broadly what it means to say that a corporation is a person and why it matters. Over the years, I have learned how intractable the debate over corporate personhood is, largely due to the multidimensional nature of the topic. In the past, the subject of corporate personhood was of interest mainly only to a small group of legal academics who argued about the essential nature of corporate bodies.

6 *Move to Amend's Proposed 28th Amendment to the Constitution*, MOVE TO AMEND, https://movetoamend.org/wethepeopleamendment [https://perma.cc/5AFB-5KVM]; *The Amendment*, FREE SPEECH FOR PEOPLE, https://freespeechforpeople.org/the-amendment/ [https://perma.cc/YG7H-YMLP].

7 *See* FED. R. EVID. 404(a).

8 *See* Susanna M. Kim, *Characteristics of Soulless Persons: The Applicability of the Character Evidence Rule to Corporations*, 2000 U. ILL. L. REV. 763, 804–08.

However, with corporations playing an increasingly more visible and influential role in our global society, I have watched as the corporate personhood topic has entered the public consciousness and become the source of dismay among growing numbers of people. Some of the most provocative issues today arise in cases involving the corporation and free speech rights, corporate religious freedoms, and corporate racial identity. To the extent a corporation can be considered a person, how far will we go to say that the corporation then has its own speech, religion, and race, all of which are entitled to some measure of respect? These are pressing issues that defy easy answers. From the United States Supreme Court's sharp 5–4 division in many of the most significant recent corporate constitutional rights cases, it is clear that the Court is as divided as the rest of us on these contentious topics surrounding the legal status of corporations.

Mainstream presentations of corporate personhood tend to be binary and fairly simplistic. People have a tendency to jump quickly into "for" or "against" camps. If you favor corporate personhood, you are regarded as pro-corporation: you accept and embrace the expansion of corporate rights and the exercise of corporate power in society. If you oppose corporate personhood, you are viewed as anti-corporation: you lament the dominating presence of corporations in society and you demand greater corporate accountability rather than broad corporate rights. These simplistic interpretations and binary positions do not take into account the nuances and complexity of corporate personhood. If pressed, most people would likely say they want corporations to be treated as persons in some situations, but not in all. Yet if we are willing to call someone or something a person in one context, on what grounds can we conclude that that person is suddenly no longer a person when the context changes? It would help to understand what corporate personhood means and why it can or should be relevant in certain circumstances.

One of the reasons it is so difficult to make sense of corporate personhood is because the concept combines two terms that themselves are extraordinarily complex: "corporation" and "personhood." The "corporation," or the "corporate-ness" of the object, refers to the collective nature of the firm. The root of the word "corporation" comes from the Latin word *corpus*, which means "body." The company represents the unified body of human individuals who together compose the collective association operating as one. This idea of many people coming together to form one person has always created tension and dichotomies in the law. We struggle to define exactly what a corporate body is. Is it simply the aggregate of individuals who contract with each other to utilize the firm for their mutual benefit? Or is it an entity, once created and thriving, that becomes something larger than the sum of its parts, taking on an identity and force of its own? If the corporation is merely the aggregation of its human participants, then the "rights and duties of an incorporated association are in reality the rights and duties of the persons who compose it,"[9] and

[9] 1 Victor Morawetz, A Treatise on the Law of Private Corporations 3 (Boston, Little, Brown, & Co. 2d ed. 1886). Morawetz wrote that it is "self-evident that a corporation is not *in reality* a person or

the law should be structured to protect their individual rights and hold them directly accountable. If, however, the corporation is an independent entity, separate and apart from the individual shareholders and employees (who can come and go without changing the structure and identity of the corporation), then the rights and duties of the corporation may be fundamentally different in kind from those of its individual members.[10] In that case, the law should allow the entity itself to exercise certain rights in pursuing its own goals and likewise be held accountable for its actions.

This tension between the "aggregate-ness" and the "separate-ness" of the corporation exists in all situations involving collective groups, including nation states. When we refer to "America," do we mean the sum total of all individual Americans, or do we mean the national entity that has its own global identity? Can an America exist without individual Americans to act as its members?[11] By the same token, can there be individual Americans without an America existing a priori?[12] The corporate nature of any association of human beings poses a conundrum whenever we must decide whether the collective should possess rights or bear duties that go beyond those of the individuals who compose the collective.

At bottom, these two opposing positions represent the perennial clash between individualist and collectivist conceptions of human beings and their group associations. The individualist approach maintains that the individual is the only appropriate unit of social, political, legal, and economic analysis. The premise is that "society is constituted of autonomous, equal, units, namely separate individuals, and that such individuals are more important, ultimately, than any larger constituent group."[13] Individuals are always primary; ontologically they exist prior to any group or collective entity. Groups are secondary; their existence and significance arise out of the freely contracted arrangements of their human constituents. This reductionist viewpoint asserts that all group actions are reducible to and redescribable as individual actions. From this perspective, the corporation cannot exist or act without its human members. Those human beings alone are accountable for corporate actions, and they alone are entitled to claim any rights. The individualist approach extols

a thing distinct from its constituent parts. The word 'corporation' is but a collective name for the corporators or members who compose [it]." *Id.* at 2.

10 Otto Gierke: Associations and Law: The Classical and Early Christian Stages 7 (George Heiman ed. & trans., 1977) ("The association, or group, is a living entity ... Every group has a real and independent communal life, a conscious will, and an ability to act that are distinct from the lives and wills of its individual members.").

11 *Cf.* Patricia H. Werhane, Persons, Rights, and Corporations 51 (1985) ("Corporations have no reality over and above their constituents, because they are created by and function only because of them.").

12 *Cf.* Peter F. Drucker, Concept of the Corporation 21 (rev. ed. 1972) ("The corporation is permanent, the shareholder is transitory. It might even be said without much exaggeration that the corporation is really socially and politically a priori whereas the shareholder's position is derivative.").

13 Alan Macfarlane, The Origins of English Individualism 5 (1978); *see also* May Brodbeck, *Methodological Individualisms: Definition and Reduction, in* Readings in the Philosophy of the Social Sciences 280 (May Brodbeck ed., 1968).

individual autonomy, self-realization, and responsibility. It suggests that corporations are nothing more than the aggregate of their individual participants, and corporations' status as independent entities is merely a convenient fiction.[14]

In contrast, the collectivist conception embraces a social model of human activity. It asserts that human beings are inherently social. Individuals from the moment they are born are first members of families and groups, and it is in these settings that they learn to identify themselves in terms of their positions and roles vis-à-vis others.[15] Individuals are always embedded in social contexts and derive their meaning from community. Groups are primary; they are an essential part of society. They are naturally occurring human institutions that arise out of the compelling human tendency to socialize and associate with others. People are continually absorbed into large and small groups of all kinds throughout their lifetime, and these groups are basic components of society that are themselves appropriate units of analysis. An organization as a whole can be greater than the sum of its parts; it can have an identity, a presence, and a life of its own. There are irreducible group level properties and processes that explain group phenomena in terms that cannot be redescribed solely as individual actions.[16] Under this view, corporations are real and separate entities in their own regard. They can have rights and duties that apply to them on an organizational basis. The collectivist viewpoint suggests that corporations' independence and autonomy demand a measure of respect and restraint from the state.

The tension between the individualist model and the collectivist model of human activity is one of many dichotomies or dualities that are inherent in the corporate form. The conflict reveals the problem with trying to define the corporation in unitary terms. When individuals join together in collective arrangements, the group can be described as both a cause and a result of individual intention and activity. The continual paradox of the corporation as both the aggregate of its individual members and a separate entity with its own identity reflects the multidimensional nature of the corporation as a person. Thus, the "corporate" component of corporate personhood is complex and resistant to simplistic interpretations of its meaning.

The "personhood" component of corporate personhood is equally complex. What exactly does it mean to be a person? The origin of the word "person" comes from the Latin word *persona*, which originally referred to the masks worn by actors on a theatrical stage. The one wearing the mask took on a *persona* and played an identifiable role. Anyone can don the mask. So long as the mask is in place, the wearer is deemed by others to be the character he is playing. Persona thus signified an outward disguise, or shell, an empty slot that anyone can fill. In legal terminology,

14 *See* Christian List & Philip Pettit, GROUP AGENCY: THE POSSIBILITY, DESIGN, AND STATUS OF CORPORATE AGENTS 3, 74 (2011) (also referring to this individualist paradigm as "eliminativism" or "singularism").

15 *See* Robert C. Solomon, ETHICS AND EXCELLENCE: COOPERATION AND INTEGRITY IN BUSINESS 77–79 (1992).

16 *See* Deborah Perron Tollefsen, GROUPS AS AGENTS 4, 138 (2015); Andreas Georg Scherer, *Modes of Explanation in Organization Theory, in* THE OXFORD HANDBOOK OF ORGANIZATION THEORY 310, 326–27 (Haridimos Tsoukas & Christian Knudsen eds., 2003).

a legal person is anyone the law deems fit to act under the law and to play a particular role in the legal process. From this perspective, legal personhood is an empty slot into which the law can drop any object, including a corporation, in order to assign it various rights and duties.[17] Many statutes, including the federal Dictionary Act, define the term "person" to include corporations, partnerships, and other associations, as well as individuals.[18]

Determining who or what should fit within the legal definition of person has not always been a simple endeavor. It is often mired in controversy and conflict because deciding who counts as a person is inevitably influenced by considerations that go beyond legal expediency. Philosophers and psychologists consider personhood to be the exclusive privilege of those with essential traits such as the capacity for reason, rational thought, free will, self-awareness, or phenomenal consciousness. Religious and moral conceptions of personhood emphasize the importance of possessing an inner conscience and the capacity to discern between right and wrong. Persons are often described as ends in themselves,[19] having autonomy and moral rights that must be respected, as well as moral responsibilities for which persons must be held accountable. Political, social, and cultural assumptions and expectations also contribute to an understanding of persons as citizens who have a social and civic identity. They carry the capacities, rights, and duties that foster their meaningful participation in the political process and in the life of the community. All combined, our "notion of person, now bearing both a conscience and a civic identity, [has become] the foundation of modern political, social and legal institutions."[20]

Given the complexity of personhood, what sorts of living and non-living beings should qualify for personhood status? Debates over the personhood of fetuses, animals, artificial intelligence, and corporate bodies all raise strongly held beliefs and intuitions about the nature of personhood. In these situations, defining personhood is deeply controversial and is closely tied to legal, political, biological, and social conceptions of life, identity, autonomy, citizenship, and equality. To say that a corporation can be classified as a person arguably implies that it carries a certain

17 Richard Tur, *The 'Person' in Law*, *in* PERSONS AND PERSONALITY: A CONTEMPORARY INQUIRY 116, 121 (Arthur Peacocke & Grant Gillett eds., 1987); *see also* John Finnis, *Corporate Persons II: Persons and Their Associations*, *in* 63 PROC. ARISTOTELIAN SOC'Y, SUPP. VOL. 267, 274 (1989) (noting that the concept of *persona* as mask corresponds to "the law's carefree attribution of legal personality to *anything* that figures as the subject of legal relations"); Andrew Vincent, *Can Groups Be Persons?*, 42 REV. METAPHYSICS 687, 700 (1989) ("The term *persona* was "easily adaptable for use in the courts of law for those who were 'playing' particular roles (such as, plaintiff) in the legal process.").

18 *See* 1 U.S.C. § 1 (2012). The American Law Institute defines "person" broadly to include an individual, a corporation, partnership, government agency, any form of association, or any other legal or commercial entity. *See* PRINCIPLES OF CORPORATE GOVERNANCE: ANALYSIS AND RECOMMENDATIONS § 1.28 (AM. LAW INST. 1994).

19 Immanuel Kant, FOUNDATIONS OF THE METAPHYSICS OF MORALS 53 (Robert Paul Wolff ed., Lewis White Beck trans., Bobbs-Merrill Co. 1969) (1785).

20 THE CATEGORY OF THE PERSON: ANTHROPOLOGY, PHILOSOPHY, HISTORY at viii (Michael Carrithers et al. eds., 1985).

elevated status and is entitled to claim the legal and moral rights that belong to persons. This triggers difficult ethical and moral questions that the law alone does not satisfactorily resolve. Sophisticated philosophical theories of the meaning and value of persons provide insights into these issues but create yet another layer of complexity. Moral philosophers have puzzled over the extent to which a corporation can be considered a moral person such that it can be held ethically and morally responsible for its actions, apart from any legal liability under the law. If it is a moral person subject to duties to act morally and ethically, then by logical extension, would it not be entitled to the moral rights belonging to all persons, including the right to be treated as an end in itself?

Perhaps there is no reason to entertain any of these questions because the corporation should be viewed simply as a form of property, not a person. The corporation is owned by shareholders who are persons, but the corporation itself is merely a thing, a tool, an instrument through which real people pursue their financial interests. To view the corporation as a person is simply an exercise in anthropomorphism. Human beings have a natural tendency to anthropomorphize objects. We like to attribute human characteristics to pets, machines, moving shapes, and, of course, groups.[21] But we should take care not to press the personhood analogies too far.

All the same, the corporation does not quite fit neatly or exclusively in the category of property either. It may arguably be owned by shareholders as their property, but at the same time the corporation as an independent person owns its own property. Scholars who view corporations as social actors argue that corporations are persons with the ability to act intentionally in pursuit of corporate goals, and that corporations can form their own identity and character separate from that of their individual participants. The two competing conceptions of the corporation as person and as property present another dichotomy within the corporation.[22] The corporation plays dual roles, and as we shall see, this duality causes tension when trying to determine the appropriate scope of corporate rights and duties.

There is also a duality involving the public versus private orientation of the corporation. On the one hand, the corporation can be viewed as the product of the private initiative, private contracts, and private property arrangements of its human members. They are the ones who voluntarily come together to form the corporation and to utilize it to advance their personal interests. The purpose of the corporation is to further the goals of the individual members. They retain

[21] *See* Steven J. Sherman & Elise J. Percy, *The Psychology of Collective Responsibility: When and Why Collective Entities Are Likely to Be Held Responsible for the Misdeeds of Individual Members*, 19 J. L. & Pol'y 137, 165 (2010).

[22] *See* Katsuhito Iwai, *Persons, Things and Corporations: The Corporate Personality Controversy and Comparative Corporate Governance*, 47 Am. J. Comp. L. 583, 592–93 (1999); Ngaire Naffine, *Who Are Law's Persons? From Cheshire Cats to Responsible Subjects*, 66 Mod. L. Rev. 346, 347 (2003); Jeffrey Nesteruk & David T. Risser, *Conceptions of the Corporation and Ethical Decision Making in Business*, 12 Bus. & Prof. Ethics J., no. 1, Spring 1993, at 73, 76–77.

the prerogative to decide whether to continue the activities of the corporation or terminate them at any time. This viewpoint invites a measure of deference to the preferences of the private actors who make up the corporation. Individuals should be free to choose their own values and enter into mutual exchanges without government intervention. The law should support the contract and property rights of these private parties and avoid interfering with their consensual actions. The private oriented approach eschews heavy government regulation of corporate activities and relations in favor of the free market and private ordering. Private businesses and associations are not government enterprises and should not be subject to state control in the pursuit of their lawful private objectives.

On the other hand, it is also possible to describe corporations in public oriented terms. Individuals who wish to incorporate their businesses can do so only through state incorporation statutes that authorize the legal formation of corporations. Thus, a corporation is a creature of statute. It is a concession of the government. The corporation cannot exist and function without the permission of the state. Private activity and free markets always operate within a framework of legal rules that are publicly enforced by the state. These legal rules are enacted because they are deemed to have some social and public utility. Private individuals must rely on state law to afford them the advantageous features that accompany the corporate form, including limited liability for shareholders. Historically, the government permitted these features and selectively granted corporate charters only because early corporations had a public purpose and served the public interest, such as constructing a public road or canal. The public dimension of corporations justifies greater regulation of their activity for the common good. Since the corporation exists by the good graces of the state, the corporation is subject to the state's supervision of its operations, and the state may define the rights and duties of the corporation in the public interest.

These dueling perspectives regarding the private and public aspects of the corporation assume that the world can be divided into two separate and mutually exclusive realms of activity, but that distinction is unrealistic. Corporations have both private and public attributes combined.[23] The two contrasting orientations are not necessarily irreconcilable. To exist and operate effectively, corporations require the contributions and arrangements of private individuals as well as the authorization and infrastructure of state law. In recent years, the line between the private and public character of corporations has become significantly blurred as many private and government institutions have become increasingly integrated. With greater frequency, the state has allowed private organizations to perform what were traditionally public functions, including running prisons, providing military services and

[23] For a thorough discussion of the "public/private distinction" constituting "two faces of the business enterprise," see Eric W. Orts, Business Persons: A Legal Theory of the Firm 109–31 (2013).

security, collecting garbage, and supplying education.[24] Moreover, the operations of private corporations can have considerable social consequences that affect the public welfare. The public and private dimensions can never be completely separated in practice. Considerations of both are needed to make meaningful determinations regarding the permissible scope of corporate activity and the appropriate delineation of corporate rights and duties.

This leads to a related point about the role and purpose of the corporation, or to put it differently, the justification for its existence. A private oriented view emphasizes the primacy of those who are deemed to be the owners of the corporation, i.e., the shareholders. For them, the main purpose of the business corporation is to create wealth and maximize their returns. That is the reason why the corporation exists. Proponents of the shareholder primacy model argue that the predominant role of the corporation is to pursue profits for the benefit of the owners. In contrast, a public oriented approach envisions a broader role for the corporation. It is more than merely a vehicle for shareholders to further their self-interests. It is a social entity that serves many important public purposes as well.[25] It supplies goods and services to satisfy consumer needs, provides job opportunities to workers, fosters economic growth and development, offers avenues for entrepreneurship that give non-wealthy individuals opportunities for upward social mobility, and even contributes to a sense of community through philanthropic corporate actions. Under this view, the corporation exists to benefit the interests of a variety of stakeholders, all of whom have a stake in the prosperity of the corporation.[26] The purpose of the corporation should not be narrowly construed to advantage only its private owners, but to promote the welfare of the larger public community that contributes to and benefits from its success.[27]

One of the challenges with trying to isolate the main purpose of the corporation is that corporations can have multiple purposes simultaneously. They can further private interests and conduct activities that benefit the public as well. Moreover, there are many different types of entities that fit within the category of corporations,

24 *See id.* at 116–17; Carl J. Mayer, *Personalizing the Impersonal: Corporations and the Bill of Rights*, 41 Hastings L.J. 577, 659 (1990); Christopher D. Stone, *Corporate Vices and Corporate Virtues: Do Public/Private Distinctions Matter?*, 130 U. Pa. L. Rev. 1441, 1446–48 (1982).

25 *See* William T. Allen, *Our Schizophrenic Conception of the Business Corporation*, 14 Cardozo L. Rev. 261, 265 (1992).

26 *See* R. Edward Freeman, *A Stakeholder Theory of the Modern Corporation*, *in* Ethical Theory and Business 56 (Tom L. Beauchamp & Norman E. Bowie eds., 6th ed. 2001).

27 "Discourses of responsibility, citizenship, and commitments to serve public welfare ... are the very ontological root of the corporation and its legal justifications for existence." Joshua Barkan, Corporate Sovereignty: Law and Government under Capitalism 113 (2013). In reply, shareholder primacy proponents argue that maximizing profits for shareholders is not incompatible with these public welfare goals. By maximizing profits, which creates wealth for the entire economy and promotes efficient resource allocation, the corporation ultimately benefits all of its constituencies and society as a whole. *See* Michael E. DeBow & Dwight R. Lee, *Shareholders, Nonshareholders and Corporate Law: Communitarianism and Resource Allocation*, 18 Del. J. Corp. L. 393, 416–19 (1993).

all of which have their own unique purposes and objectives. The large, multinational publicly held oil company is certainly a corporation. But so is the small, family-owned, local flower shop on the corner. When discussing corporations, we typically mean business entities that are formed for economic purposes, but the list of organizations that bear the corporate label is much more diverse. The earliest forms of corporations included guilds, townships, churches, and universities. Today, commercial businesses, nonprofit organizations, social clubs, trade unions, political parties, religious organizations, and media companies are all forms of corporations. Some organizations are large, some are small. Some are profit-oriented, some are not. Some are formed to promote specific values or pursue various educational, social, political, or religious objectives. Others exist mainly to advance the financial interests of their founders. Certain entities, such as "B corporations" or "benefit corporations," have hybrid goals to pursue profits while simultaneously producing a material positive impact on society and the environment. Some corporations are highly structured, formalized, complex entities with thousands of employees and clearly defined group decision-making systems and procedures. They may be so large and have so much wealth that their power is likened to that of political states. Others are simply the alter ego of a single individual owner who performs all the work and calls all the shots, and whose firm is largely just an extension of himself. The wide range of entities that operate under the corporate form exist along a continuum with many different dimensions and purposes.[28] The extent to which some or all of these entities can be categorized as persons may depend in part on the type of corporations they are.

The plurality of organizations that can be classified as corporations is what often makes society's debate over the appropriate status of corporations so difficult to resolve. People's reactions to questions about the acceptable nature and role of corporations, as well as the appropriate scope of corporate rights and duties, differ considerably when speaking about large public corporations versus small mom and pop shops, or about for-profit companies versus nonprofit associations. Much of the controversy over corporate personhood, corporate rights, and corporate responsibilities tends to involve for-profit business enterprises, and this book will focus attention on that type of corporation the most. But at relevant points the book will also consider the range of various corporate entities in order to effectively explore the many aspects of the potential personhood of corporate bodies.

In the context of the business corporation, economic analysis of the nature and function of the corporation has often taken center stage. Theorists have long tried to develop a coherent theory of the corporate firm, and the discipline of economics has made some of the most significant contributions in this regard. In fact, for several decades economic theories of the firm, including the model of the corporation as a "nexus of contracts" rather than a separate person, have dominated legal academic

[28] *See* Orts, *supra* note 23, at 215–22.

thinking about the corporation.[29] Under this model, the corporate person is a fiction that serves as the center of a web of contracts between all the firm's constituents who gather together to gain the benefit of their bargains with each other. The primary objective of this corporate contractual arrangement is to maximize profits. From this perspective, no independent, real corporate entity exists. Scholars have utilized these economic theories both positively and normatively to explain the nature of the firm and its appropriate purposes and obligations.

The economic model is influential, having stood as the standard academic paradigm for analyzing the corporation for many years. But it is insufficient and incomplete. It offers too narrow a focus, too simplistic a response to the question, what is a corporation? By emphasizing the private contractual elements of corporate enterprises, the economic approach describes only one aspect of the corporate entity. It does not give significance to the many other legal, social, political, cultural, philosophical, and moral aspects of the corporation.

The corporation is not just an economic institution. It is also a legal actor and a participant in the political system; it is an artifact and product of our culture; it has a social presence and identity in our consumer world; it is a potential moral agent whose actions may be subject to moral praise or condemnation. We could try to restrict the corporation to being viewed solely as an economic tool for the mutually beneficial exchanges of its participants, but the complexity of the corporation defies such a narrow classification. There are many faces of the corporate person, and each is visible when viewed through the appropriate lens. The disciplines of law, economics, political science, anthropology, sociology, psychology, organizational theory, philosophy, moral theory, and even religious studies all have their own unique lenses through which they see the corporation. From their respective angles, they highlight different sides of the entity. Each has validity, but each in itself is inadequate to provide a comprehensive view. Taken together, they reveal a more complete and meaningful picture of the corporation and its role in society.[30]

A primary premise of this book is that corporate personhood is complicated because it is multidimensional. Discussions of corporate personhood are often impoverished because they focus on only a single or narrow aspect of the corporate person, and they fail to bring other important social science contributions into the conversation. This has often been the case in scholarly treatments of the economic model of the corporation or in analyses of the legal theories of the corporation.

29 *See* Michael C. Jensen & William H. Meckling, *Theory of the Firm: Managerial Behavior, Agency Costs and Ownership Structure*, 3 J. FIN. ECON. 305, 311 (1976).

30 I have previously argued that an interdisciplinary analysis provides a more accurate and useful view of the multidimensional nature of the corporate person. *See* Susanna K. Ripken, *Corporations Are People Too: A Multi-Dimensional Approach to the Corporate Personhoood Puzzle*, 15 FORDHAM J. CORP. & FIN. L. 97 (2009). The "corporation has been reified as an economic actor. And it has not been given sufficient attention as a social, cultural, and political one." Kenneth Lipartito & David B. Sicilia, *Introduction: Crossing Corporate Boundaries, in* CONSTRUCTING CORPORATE AMERICA: HISTORY, POLITICS, CULTURE 1, 3 (Kenneth Lipartito & David B. Sicilia eds., 2004).

While economic and legal theories are both important and necessary, they do not by themselves or in combination adequately account for the myriad other aspects of the nature and function of the corporation in the modern world. Corporate personhood is an intricate knot. Economic and legal theorists have been pulling on only one or two of the many threads of corporate personhood in their attempts to untangle it. The key is to loosen and engage more of the threads in order to unravel the cluster.

This book offers a more comprehensive study of corporate personhood by utilizing multiple disciplines to analyze the corporation, including philosophy, moral theory, organizational behavior, sociology, psychology, and linguistics among others. The objective is to illuminate other dimensions of corporate personhood that are often overlooked. It is useful to examine other discipline's conceptualizations of organizations and personhood because no single approach can fully address all of the intersecting issues that surround the topic of corporate personhood. There is wisdom in approaching the topic in an integrative fashion, incorporating many different perspectives rather than privileging just a few. Part of the difficulty with analyzing corporate personhood is that it is not just a discrete concept, but the heart of a family of concepts that implicate identity, autonomy, citizenship, and moral standing. To fully understand these and other related concepts requires explication from disciplines outside of economics.[31] While the various theories may at times appear to be competing or in conflict, they are in fact complementary; they emphasize different facets of the corporation and represent different ways of understanding its personhood. They are all pieces in the corporate personhood puzzle. When joined, they display a more holistic image. We can expect to see and learn more about corporations than would be possible were we to employ a single theory or point of view.

A central theme of this book is that corporate personhood, much like individual personhood, is complex, textured, and dynamic, continually changing with changing societal views. Personhood need not be an all-or-nothing proposition. The wide spectrum of entities that can be categorized as corporations could possibly coincide with different degrees of personhood that lie along a continuum. An acknowledgment of the many facets of corporate personhood requires us to refrain from making categorical, inflexible conclusions about corporate personhood when confronted with difficult choices about the status, rights, and obligations of corporate entities.

The goal of this interdisciplinary anthology on corporate personhood is to stimulate deeper thinking about the topic by gathering in one place a variety of ideas about the nature of the corporation as a person and revealing the many ways it can be

[31] Even those who study individual human personhood maintain that "[p]ersonhood is a necessarily interdisciplinary subject." It is "an irreducibly holistic" concept that "applies across the physical sciences, social sciences, and humanities." Jack Martin & Mark H. Bickhard, *Introducing Persons and the Psychology of Personhood, in* The Psychology of Personhood: Philosophical, Historical, Social-Developmental, and Narrative Perspectives 1, 2 (Jack Martin & Mark H. Bickhard eds., 2013).

analyzed from different vantage points. My aim is to provide a platform and pathway that allows all those who are interested in the role and status of corporations to gain a deeper understanding of the meaning of corporate personhood and to facilitate ongoing informed conversations about its implications. Thus, this book is intended for a broad audience. It is directed toward all readers, whether trained in the law or not, who are looking for a resource that unpacks the corporate personhood concept in a broad, informative, and accessible way.

My engagement with this topic is not tied to any favoritism toward or opposition to corporate interests. I endeavor to provide a fair and balanced account of the major theories and issues surrounding the personhood of corporations. I hope to show the importance of entertaining a range of ideas about what corporations are, how they operate, and why they can or cannot be regarded as persons. By thoroughly and objectively laying out the different sides of the debate over corporate personhood, the analysis in the book will attempt to equip readers to make their own decisions regarding the important controversies involving the status of corporations as persons. Where I hold certain opinions about the plausibility of various arguments, I point out their strengths and weaknesses in an effort to provide helpful critique. But in doing so, I seek to educate, not to preach or persuade. My objective is to highlight the complexity of corporate personhood, and to lay aside categorical, black and white, pro versus con statements about the corporation in favor of a more nuanced dialogue about the nature of the corporation and its role in society.

While I strive to be thoughtful and thorough in my analysis, a project of this size requires difficult choices as to its scope, lest it become so expansive and unwieldy that it loses its utility. Each of the chapters of this book easily merits its own book-length treatment. Space limitations prevent me from supplying an exhaustive review of the literature in any given chapter. Instead, I provide a focused discussion of the main themes and key resources related to the issues at hand. Tackling the multi-dimensional nature of corporate personhood within the confines of a single book is an ambitious undertaking that will invariably be subject to criticism for leaving out certain considerations or disciplinary contributions. I recognize that there are other disciplines as varied as cultural anthropology and theology that offer significant insights into the personhood of the corporation, but I cannot feasibly include an exploration of all of them. Instead, the book presents a detailed examination of what I regard as most of the relevant disciplinary theories and research to give the reader a good interdisciplinary overview of the contours of personhood as it relates to corporate entities.

Chapter 1 begins with the legal dimension of corporate personhood. The corporation is considered a person under the law with the capacity to act in ways that have legal significance. Historically, three different theories emerged to justify the corporation's personhood status: the artificial/fictional person theory, the aggregate theory, and the real/natural entity theory. Under the first theory, the corporation is viewed as an artificial or fictional person created by the state that grants its charter.

Depending entirely on state law for its existence, the corporation does not belong to the physical world of fact but the abstract world of intangible legal concepts. In contrast, the second theory focuses on the human individuals who make up the corporation. Viewing the corporation as the collection, or aggregate, of the natural persons who participate in the enterprise, the aggregate theory maintains that the corporate person has no existence or identity that is independent of these individuals. This viewpoint eventually served as the basis for the development of the highly influential economic contractual model of the corporation. The final theory makes the claim that the corporation is an undeniably real entity, not an abstraction. It exists as something much more than the aggregation of its individual participants and much more than an approved charter document from the state. The real entity theory recognizes the corporation as an independent collective body with the capacity for group intentions and actions that are qualitatively different in kind from those of its human members.

These traditional legal theories shaped and were shaped by the growth of corporations in America during the nineteenth and twentieth centuries. Each conception of the corporate person had its own normative implications for how corporate rights and duties should be assigned under the law. The legal theories will serve as important reference points throughout the book as other disciplinary perspectives are discussed. In subsequent chapters, the theories will provide a framework for analyzing corporations' status to claim certain fundamental constitutional rights.

The competing legal theories of corporate personhood have not always been determinative of the rights and duties that have been established for corporations. Courts have not consistently relied on any one theory to make determinations about corporate standing in legal cases. Well-known legal realist John Dewey cautioned against reliance on any particular legal or non-legal theories about personhood to make such determinations because he believed any theory could be invoked at any time to support any result one wanted. Dewey instead favored the use of pragmatic considerations to determine whether it is sensible to extend specific rights and duties to corporations based on the consequences of doing so.[32] While Dewey's indeterminacy thesis had merit, like all the other legal theories of the corporation, standing on its own, his view was also incomplete. In response to Dewey's position, Chapter 1 defends the idea that it is valuable to consider legal and non-legal conceptions of the corporation. A multidimensional approach to corporations provides a useful, richer understanding of the corporation. Theories of the corporate person may be indeterminate at times, but they are not irrelevant. The mental schemas we have regarding corporations, and the language we use to talk about them, can have effects on what corporations become. The legal language that is employed to describe corporations can have significant symbolic, expressive, and constitutive effects that can animate and reinforce the

[32] *See* John Dewey, *The Historic Background of Corporate Legal Personality*, 35 YALE L.J. 655 (1926).

personhood of corporations. The importance of language is a theme that is introduced in Chapter 1 and revisited in subsequent chapters of the book.

Chapter 2 turns to philosophical conceptions of corporate personhood. Philosophers have long theorized over what it means to be a person and what traits are essential for one to be classified as a person. Philosophical theories emphasize a host of characteristics and capacities that range from rationality and intentionality to consciousness and emotional vulnerability. The point of identifying the essential properties of personhood is to justify differential treatment of persons and non-persons for both legal and moral purposes. Whether collective entities like corporations can be categorized as persons is a difficult philosophical question that has been the subject of intense debate. The topic raises thorny questions about individual and group ontology as well as the exclusive nature of personhood.

A related philosophical issue involves the moral personhood of individuals and groups. What is required for someone or something to be a moral person, i.e., the subject of moral rights and moral responsibilities that go beyond legal entitlements and legal accountability? Articulating the necessary and sufficient conditions for moral personhood is particularly challenging in the context of corporate bodies. If a corporation intentionally commits an act that wreaks devastating harm on a community or the environment, is the corporation subject to moral blame or condemnation? Does it make sense for people to be morally outraged by the corporation's faulty intentions and actions, or to say that the corporation itself bears moral responsibility above and beyond that borne by its individual human decision-makers? On the one hand, we might argue that the corporation is not a person with moral responsibilities because it has no real conscience or soul. On the other hand, it may be plausible to place moral blame on the corporation for some magnified collective acts and intentions that cannot sensibly be attributed to any particular human member.

If the corporation is a person capable of making moral choices and distinguishing between right and wrong, then we would be justified in expecting it to abide by its moral duties to other persons. If the corporation has moral duties, would it then also be entitled to claim moral rights? Some philosophers would prefer to draw a line at this point, acknowledging the personhood of corporations for purposes of owing moral responsibilities, but denying such status to corporations for claiming moral rights. As Chapter 2 explains, the variety of philosophical theories both for and against corporate personhood underscores the challenge of differentiating between individual versus collective activity for purposes of moral standing. The ideas that emerge from philosophical inquiry into the nature of persons reveal the complicated philosophical and moral dimensions of the corporation. Chapter 2 suggests that personhood may exist along a spectrum with corporations having a unique form of moral personhood. Our philosophical understanding of corporate personhood ultimately contributes to the way we shape the legal rules that apply to corporations.

Other dimensions of the corporation's personhood can be viewed through the lenses of additional social science disciplines that are discussed in Chapter 3, including organizational studies, psychology, sociology, linguistics, and political science. Each of these disciplines identifies the corporation as an organizational reality that itself is an object of study and evaluation. Organizational theory conceptualizes the corporation as an independent decision-making entity that is purposeful and intelligent, having the ability to learn and apply new knowledge to accomplish its goals. The corporation is viewed as a living, active entity that is capable of profoundly affecting and interacting with its environment, with the human individuals who are its members, and with the world of people who are external to its operations. The manifestations of personhood that are often associated with organizations mirror those of human persons, including such concepts as life cycles, identity, personality, character, image, reputation, citizenship, and social influence.

The corporate person has the capacity to form a corporate ethos, culture, and belief system that can significantly affect the individuals within it. Group level phenomena in corporations have significant psychological effects on those who are members of the group. Research findings highlight the power of a corporation's culture and climate to influence and direct individual behavior in the corporation. To the extent individuals' values and principles are shaped by their corporate environment, the individuals are in some sense creatures of the corporation, rather than the other way around.

As social institutions that cultivate a specific brand identity in society, corporations can have a recognizable persona. Corporations create social bonds with people through their products and advertising. They substantially influence people's attitudes and behavior. Our regular interactions with corporations and the way we personify them in our ordinary discourse reinforces our tendency to regard them as separate persons. In fact, careful analysis of the words and grammar we use in speaking about corporations reveals that their perceived personhood is woven into the fabric of our language. The vocabulary we utilize to characterize corporations affects the way we relate to them as persons in the community.

The social dimensions of the corporation's personhood raise important normative questions about the corporation's appropriate role as a functioning member of society. Should the corporation operate predominantly to maximize shareholder profits or should it carry broader social obligations to other sectors of society? How should the corporation balance or prioritize its many constituent interests? To whom should the corporation owe its greatest loyalty? The corporation's membership in society as a person is complicated and demanding because we expect it to fill multiple social functions simultaneously.

In addition, the corporation acts as a relevant participant in the political community. Theories of political pluralism emphasize the distinctiveness and significance of organizations in society. Certain political philosophies envision organizations as mediating institutions that act as important buffers between individuals and the state. Under this view, the corporation as a powerful private institution can become a substantial countervailing force to protect individuals from potentially oppressive government power. At the same time, corporations with their vast resources and power can also resemble state authority and can pose a potential danger to individuals who are no match for corporate power. Corporations are prominent players in the political system. They insert themselves and their money in the political arena and consequently have influence over government officials, policies, and regulation. Whether the corporation's role in the polity is a good or bad thing depends on one's normative vision of the ideal political state, and there is sharp disagreement on that topic.

What apparently seems incontrovertible is that the corporation's role in society is not unidimensional, but rich and complex. It is a member of the larger community, but it is a community in itself as well. The corporation's presence in society carries considerable social, economic, political, and cultural significance. That so many social science disciplines each have distinct and substantive insights into the corporation not only confirms the many dimensions of the corporation as a person, but also underscores the deep interdependence of corporations and individuals in the modern world.

Building on the concepts discussed in the prior chapters, the next two chapters address the corporation's constitutional personhood, i.e., its standing as a person to claim fundamental constitutional rights. The United States Constitution contains no explicit reference to corporations, but the Supreme Court has held that corporations are persons entitled to claim an extensive array of constitutional rights. The support for these rights has developed implicitly from the many different and evolving conceptions of the corporation as a legal, moral, economic, social, and political actor. Chapter 4 provides an overview of the historical development of corporate constitutional rights. It explains how corporations came to be regarded as persons who are entitled to equal protection rights, due process rights, and many other constitutional protections. The analysis then focuses on three of the most controversial arenas today for legal battles on corporate constitutional personhood: (1) corporate free speech rights; (2) corporate religious exercise rights; and (3) corporate racial equality rights.

Chapter 4 examines the extent to which corporations can and should be considered persons whose speech is entitled to protection under the First Amendment. The chapter critically analyzes the cases and theories establishing that corporate persons, like natural persons, have the right to voice their opinions and contribute to the marketplace of ideas. The Supreme Court has held that the expenditure of corporate funds in the political sphere is itself a form of speech and worthy of protection. The Court's opinion in *Citizens United* confirming the speech rights of corporations to spend money in political elections intensified the debate over corporate First Amendment rights. The analysis in this chapter breaks down the conflicting arguments regarding corporate free speech rights in light of the diversity of entities that utilize the corporate form, the wide range of goals pursued by these organizations, and the many disparate reasons for different corporations to engage in speech acts. The chapter suggests that different types of corporate persons could be eligible for different levels of speech protection.

The multidimensional nature of corporations complicates not only the debate over corporate free speech rights, but also, as Chapter 5 explains, the heated conflicts over other recent expansions of corporate rights, including the right of religious freedom. How plausible is it to think the corporation itself can possess and exercise religious beliefs? While it may be acceptable for a church or religious organization to possess certain religious rights, is it equally sensible for a large public company to claim a right to freely exercise its religion? In the Supreme Court's highly controversial *Hobby Lobby* case, the Court held that corporations are persons entitled to statutory protection for the exercise of their religious beliefs. As discussed in this chapter, the various arguments for and against corporate religious liberty rights reflect competing and complementary aspects of the corporate person.

If corporations are persons who can produce their own speech for purposes of free speech rights, and who can form their own religious identity for purposes of religious liberty rights, might they also be capable of possessing their own racial identity for purposes of racial equality rights? There has been significant public discussion about corporate free speech and corporate religion, but a lesser known emerging topic involves the issue of corporate race. The extent to which corporate persons may be described as having a race has become an important issue as society becomes increasingly more diverse and race relations grow more complex. Various courts have held that corporations may acquire a specific racial identity that would allow them to assert racial discrimination claims. Chapter 5 explains how corporate persons can be described as having a race that would entitle them to object to racially discriminatory treatment. The chapter discusses at least four different theories that can potentially be utilized to assign racial identities to corporations, or alternatively, to grant standing to corporations to assert discrimination claims even when the corporation is "racially neutral."

The debates over corporate race, religion, and speech all seek to determine the extent to which the corporate person can and should be treated like a natural person. As corporate rights have steadily expanded, many people have turned a critical eye toward the idea that the corporation is a person entitled to many of the same rights that are afforded to individuals. Concerns about the consolidation of corporate rights and corporate power have caused some people to argue that the concept of corporate personhood has gone too far. They believe that viewing the corporation as a person with claims to the same rights that belong to human individuals is fundamentally wrong and gives corporations an elevated status they do not deserve. The increasing dissatisfaction with the idea that corporations are persons for purposes of certain inalienable rights has galvanized a popular movement to revoke the personhood status of corporations under the law.

A book about corporate personhood would not be complete without some analysis of the popular effort to abolish it entirely. Chapter 6 addresses this important aspect of the corporate personhood debate. Recent years have seen dramatic growth among activist groups and community associations that want to amend the United States Constitution to establish that the only persons who have constitutional rights are human beings, not corporations. Hundreds of grassroots organizations have successfully worked to adopt resolutions at the state and local levels calling for such a constitutional amendment. Activists have made corporate personhood the main target of their reform efforts. They argue that corporate power will be significantly reduced if corporations are stripped of their standing to claim any constitutional rights.

Chapter 6 critically analyzes the objectives, arguments, and achievements of this anti-corporate personhood movement. It is unclear whether the movement will be successful in its drive for a constitutional amendment declaring that corporations are not persons under the Constitution. However, in the process of trying, movement organizers are starting and continuing a public conversation about corporate personhood that is relevant. By zeroing in on corporate personhood, they have brought into sharper focus a concept that was largely of interest only to legal scholars for many years. Some of those scholars dismissed the corporate personhood concept as being indeterminate and irrelevant. But corporate personhood is a concept that has tremendous significance, whether justified or not, for many people who worry about the scope and exercise of corporate power in the modern world. The movement to amend the Constitution has sparked important discussions about the meaning of corporate personhood and created a broader need for books like this one to explain and analyze its contours. In this regard, the movement has contributed to the important discourse surrounding corporate personhood and corporate power.

The book concludes with some closing observations regarding the complexity of the personhood of corporations. It identifies the need to balance various perspectives in deciding how we should view corporations, how they should be treated, and how they should treat us.

1

Legal Theories of the Corporate Person

Perhaps the most powerful act of law is to make and define a legal person. A legal person is the subject of legal rights and duties.[1] Only those who are legally recognized as persons have the capacity to participate in legal relations. Legal personhood has never been a self-evident classification that applies only to living human beings. In fact, one's status as a human being is neither necessary nor sufficient to be a person in the eyes of the law. Non-human organizational entities are treated as legal persons for some purposes, while human beings like infants and mentally impaired individuals are not regarded as full-fledged legal persons for other purposes.

Corporations have long been viewed as persons under the law, capable of entering into legal relations, exercising legal rights, and bearing legal obligations. As a person, the corporation has the ability to enter into contracts, to sue and be sued, to own property in the corporate name, and to claim many fundamental constitutional rights. The theoretical and practical justifications for treating the corporation as a person are varied and have changed over time, reflecting historical changes in the form, purpose, and scale of corporate enterprise. This chapter describes the main legal theories of corporate personhood and explains how these theories shaped and have been shaped by the growing presence of corporations in society. As we will see, different legal theories of the corporation have cycled in and out of favor as political and economic climates for business have shifted.

The differing conceptions of the corporation are analytical but also ideological; they are simultaneously descriptive and prescriptive. To subscribe to a particular theory of the corporation – to say that the corporation is *x*, and not *y* – often reflects a particular political attitude about corporate activity and correspondingly implies that corporations should be treated in a certain way. Although the various depictions of the corporation often seem to contradict each other, each one plays a complementary role in highlighting essential aspects of the multidimensional corporate person.

[1] John Chipman Gray, The Nature and Sources of the Law 27 (Roland Gray ed., Macmillan Co. 2d ed. 1921) (1909).

CORPORATION AS AN ARTIFICIAL AND DEPENDENT PERSON

One of the earliest theories of the corporate person, the artificial person theory, viewed the corporation as an artificial construct of the law.[2] According to this theory, the corporate person is simply an abstract legal fiction, created by law and human beings for the practical purpose of facilitating economic activity. It has no real, independent ontological existence of its own. It has no body, mind, or soul. The corporation's personhood is purely instrumental; it is a legal invention designed to enable human beings to engage usefully in commercial relationships. This conception of the corporation has two important components: (1) the fictional element, and (2) the dependence element.

The fictional element emphasizes that the corporate person exists in only an imaginary way, quite different from the way in which natural persons exist. As an invisible, intangible abstraction of law, "the corporate body is but a name, a thing of the intellect."[3] It has no substantive nature. It does not belong to the physical world of fact but the artificial world of legally created concepts. The "law calls forth the corporation out of nothing, that is, no extra-legal entity exists prior to the sovereign's act."[4] In this sense, anything can be deemed a legal person because legal personhood is simply assigned or defined into existence. It is an "empty slot" into which the law can drop any object, whether real or fictitious, in order to give it rights and duties.[5] The object need not have any measurable philosophical, moral, empirical, social, or political content, nor does it need to carry any resemblance to a natural person. The law can simply extend legal personhood to anything, including a corporation, when there are good reasons for doing so.[6] In the case of the corporation, its legal personhood serves the practical business purpose of allowing the corporation independently to enter into binding legal relations, to exercise rights and to incur obligations, without the continual involvement of every human member of the entity. "So it is that for one purpose and another, it becomes convenient, if not indeed necessary, to let the individual participants fade out of the picture and to look upon the organization as a unit."[7] The fictional nature of corporate personhood thus

[2] Paul Vinogradoff, *Juridical Persons*, 24 COLUM. L. REV. 594, 600–01 (1924). This theory has been called by many different names, including the state grant theory, the fictitious personality theory, the artificial personality theory, the concession theory, and the hierarchical theory. Ron Harris, *The Transplantation of the Legal Discourse on Corporate Personality Theories: From German Codification to British Political Pluralism and American Big Business*, 63 WASH. & LEE L. REV. 1421, 1424 (2006).

[3] John Dewey, *The Historic Background of Corporate Legal Personality*, 35 YALE L.J. 655, 667 (1926).

[4] Note, *Constitutional Rights of the Corporate Person*, 91 YALE L.J. 1641, 1645 n.24 (1982).

[5] Richard Tur, *The 'Person' in Law*, *in* PERSONS AND PERSONALITY: A CONTEMPORARY INQUIRY 116, 121 (Arthur Peacocke & Grant Gillett eds., 1987).

[6] *See id.* at 121 (referring to a case where an Indian idol was given legal personality); *see also* Arthur W. Machen, Jr., *Corporate Personality*, 24 HARV. L. REV. 347, 350 (1911) (noting that purely inanimate objects may be personified, e.g., the estate of a deceased person, a jury, or a community).

[7] Bryant Smith, *Legal Personality*, 37 YALE L.J. 283, 288–89 (1928).

serves as an abbreviation, a convenient shortcut, to apply the rules for natural persons by way of analogy to corporate organizations. It is clearly a fiction, but it is a valuable one that makes economic enterprise easier for the real persons who are involved.

The dependence element of the corporation focuses on the corporation's dependence on the law to create and sustain its personhood. The corporation cannot exist nor have any sort of power without the law's consent. Also known as the "concession theory," it emphasizes that corporations are formed when the government grants approval of their charters, and therefore, the personhood of corporations can be described as a grant or concession from government.[8] The classic statement of this view is found in Chief Justice Marshall's description of the corporation in 1819 in *Trustees of Dartmouth College v. Woodward*: "A corporation is an artificial being, invisible, intangible, and existing only in contemplation of law. Being the mere creature of law, it possesses only those properties which the charter of its creation confers upon it."[9] From this perspective, the corporation is a creation of the state. It does not have an inherent essence. We cannot locate the source of its life and power by looking within the corporation. Rather, we must look to the law that exists outside the corporation as the originator of its personhood. The corporation is completely dependent on a force external to itself, i.e., the state, to create and recognize it.

The state also defines the scope of the corporation's rights and duties. The only powers the corporation possesses are those that are granted by the state. "A corporation has no inherent or natural rights like a citizen. It has no rights but those which are expressly conferred upon it, or are necessarily inferable from the powers actually granted, or such as may be indispensable to the exercise of such as are granted."[10] Of course, any rights the state can give to the corporation, the state can also take away. The same is true for duties. Any legal obligations the corporation possesses, it possesses by reason of the legal rules that create those duties. This means that every element of the corporation's collective being, including every right and duty, is continually dependent for its very existence on the law that constitutes it. In the final analysis, corporations are whatever the law says they are, and corporations have whichever rights and obligations the law says they have.

This theoretical view of the corporation was consistent with the dominating political role of the sovereign that existed at the time the earliest modern corporations were formed.[11] In seventeenth-century England, the corporate charter was used as a technique by the Crown not only to authorize and recognize corporate entities,

8 The concession theory represents a "top-down" approach that sees the corporation as the subordinate subject of law and of the government that charters or otherwise recognizes it. Eric W. Orts, Business Persons: A Legal Theory of the Firm 9–13 (2013).

9 17 U.S. (4 Wheat.) 518, 636 (1819).

10 Shaffer & Munn v. Union Mining Co., 55 Md. 74, 79 (1880).

11 Historical antecedents to the corporate form can be traced back to the ancient Roman Republic. *See* Max Radin, The Legislation of the Greeks and Romans on Corporations (Tuttle, Morehouse &

but also to utilize their power for the benefit of the sovereign. Granting incorporation was the principal device by which royal power was administered and expanded in the polity. Corporate charters were gifts of immunity from the sovereign to encourage corporations to organize and manage hospitals, universities, religious orders, towns, imperial trade, and colonies. Through these operations, corporations helped the state to maintain order in the community, to care for the population, and to foster the wealth, stability, welfare, and security of the state.[12] Corporate charters were granted by special grace of the sovereign, on an individual basis, and only upon a showing that the corporation's proposed project would serve a public purpose or further the interests of the sovereign state.

Obtaining a charter was deemed a significant gift because charters came with substantial privileges, including certain tax exemptions, monopoly rights, rights to land, and perpetual succession. England and other European countries chartered large trading companies, such as the East India Company, the Dutch East India Company, the Royal African Company, and the Hudson Bay Company, to develop foreign trade and colonize foreign lands. Corporations were granted territorial control over specific geographic regions and trade routes, all for the purpose of returning wealth, resources, and power back to the chartering country.[13] The status of these corporations resided in their dependence on the sovereign power that created them. Corporations were essentially an extension of the state. They were artificial instruments owing their existence to the will of the sovereign. It was one such corporation, the Virginia Company of London, that established the first English settlement in Jamestown, Virginia, thereby bringing the corporate form to America. Many of the original American colonies, including Massachusetts, Connecticut, and Georgia among others, were corporations chartered by the Crown.

In colonial America, corporations obtained charters by grants from colonial governors or legislatures, thereby continuing the tradition of viewing the corporation as an artificial person created by law as a concession of the government.[14] Once America gained its independence, corporate charters were granted by special acts of state legislatures.[15] States typically approved charters on a case-by-case basis for corporate enterprises that served a public function and met specific social needs, e.g., public utilities, banks, insurers, transportation services, and water works.

Taylor Press 1910); Ronald J. Colombo, THE FIRST AMENDMENT AND THE BUSINESS CORPORATION 30–32 (2015); Henry Hansmann et al., *Law and the Rise of the Firm*, 119 HARV. L. REV. 1333, 1356–64 (2006). During the Middle Ages, forerunners of the corporation existed in the form of churches, guilds, municipalities, and educational institutions, all of which required charters that were granted by the sovereign. *See* Ron Harris, INDUSTRIALIZING ENGLISH LAW: ENTREPRENEURSHIP AND BUSINESS ORGANIZATION, 1720–1844, at 16–19 (2000).

12 Joshua Barkan, CORPORATE SOVEREIGNTY: LAW AND GOVERNMENT UNDER CAPITALISM 20–30 (2013).

13 *Id.* at 31–35.

14 James Willard Hurst, THE LEGITIMACY OF THE BUSINESS CORPORATION IN THE LAW OF THE UNITED STATES 1780–1970, at 15–17 (1970).

15 Lawrence M. Friedman, A HISTORY OF AMERICAN LAW 188–201 (2d ed. 1985).

The "corporate privilege was granted sparingly; and only when the grant seemed necessary … to procure for the community some specific benefit otherwise unattainable."[16] From the state's perspective, the corporation was a tool of the government to further the public welfare, and this was the only satisfactory justification for the corporation's existence. As Chief Justice Marshall emphasized in the *Dartmouth College* case: "The objects for which a corporation is created are universally such as the government wishes to promote. They are deemed beneficial to the country; and this benefit constitutes the consideration, and, in most cases, the sole consideration of the grant."[17] With the charter, states often granted to corporations special privileges, monopolies, and exclusive rights in order to encourage and reward corporations that undertook large and costly public projects, such as building a bridge or a canal.[18]

At the same time, state legislatures imposed limits on corporate activity in order to protect the public. Early charters and state laws contained specific provisions designed to prevent corporations from engaging in potentially abusive corporate practices. For example, states strictly regulated banking activity through limited powers granted in bank charters and through strict construction of those charters by the courts.[19] Corporations were often limited in how large they could become, how much property they could hold, and how long they could exist. Sometimes legislatures required corporations to give equal voting power to smaller investors, provide favorable treatment to the poor, or ensure that investors and managers could be personally liable for corporate debts. Occasionally, states even regulated the prices that corporations could charge and the rate of return that investors could earn.[20] Courts developed the *ultra vires* doctrine, which prohibited corporations from acting beyond the specified powers given to them in their charters. State legislatures reserved the power to amend or repeal corporate charters in order to retain control over corporate activity.

This framework for corporate enterprise was consistent with the belief that incorporation was a unique privilege or concession awarded by the state. The corporation was viewed as a creature of law, possessing only the rights and duties that the law allowed it to have. This conception of the corporation was not incompatible with the expectation that investors would earn profits from the business. Organizers of early corporations were willing to engage in large and financially risky corporate projects precisely because investors sought to make money from the enterprise. However, the profit goal could not overshadow the idea that corporations

16 Louis K. Liggett Co. v. Lee, 288 U.S. 517, 549 (1933) (Brandeis, J., dissenting).

17 Trs. of Dartmouth Coll. v. Woodward, 17 U.S. (4 Wheat.) 518, 637 (1819).

18 Barkan, *supra* note 12, at 51; Herbert Hovenkamp, *The Classical Corporation in American Legal Thought*, 76 Geo. L.J. 1593, 1609–10 (1988).

19 Gregory A. Mark, Comment, *The Personification of the Business Corporation in American Law*, 54 U. Chi. L. Rev. 1441, 1444 (1987).

20 Martha T. McCluskey, *The Substantive Politics of Formal Corporate Power*, 53 Buff. L. Rev. 1453, 1476, 1478 (2006).

were given legal status to serve the ends of government. From a normative standpoint, the artificial person theory supported a public-oriented view of corporate activity. If the corporation is an artificial construction that derives its existence from the state, the logical result is that the corporation is subservient to the state and subject to state regulation in the public interest. The very laws that create corporations can and should also constrain them to act in ways that benefit, or at least do not harm, the public.

The artificial person theory of the corporation dominated American thinking about corporate personhood until the mid-nineteenth century. At around that time, states began to eliminate the practice of chartering corporations on a case-by-case basis via special acts of the state legislature. The special chartering process fostered perceptions of political favoritism and corruption as certain businesses were granted charters while others were rejected. Many people believed the entire chartering structure favored wealthy, well-connected business people at the expense of new entrepreneurs. The system was regarded as inherently unfair, tainted by legislative bribery and monopolistic practices.[21] It was also inefficient and unwieldy, requiring the state legislature formally to act to approve each individual charter. In response, states adopted general incorporation statutes allowing entrepreneurs to incorporate their businesses freely without individualized grants from the legislature. This legislative change equalized the opportunity for any and all who wished to incorporate their business. "It was cheap and easy to incorporate under general laws – a few papers filed, a few forms and signatures; the privilege of incorporation lay open to whoever wanted it."[22] The act of incorporation became merely a formality of filing and played little role in the personhood of corporations. The notion that corporations existed only as a result of state concession and only for the purpose of benefiting the public gave way to the belief that the corporation actually owed its existence to the individuals who formed the corporation to further their own private financial interests.

The liberalization of the charter system was a factor in loosening the close tie that had previously existed between the corporation and the state. Corporate charters that had previously contained specific restrictions on corporate structure and activity were replaced with standard charters that authorized corporations to engage generally in any lawful acts. By making the charter freely available, states gave up their demand that the corporation directly provide for the public good. The charter was no longer the strict tool of regulation it had

[21] Harry G. Henn & John R. Alexander, Laws of Corporations and Other Business Enterprises 25 (3d student ed. 1983); Hurst, *supra* note 14, at 120. "[L]egislative discretion over access to the corporate form enabled incumbent firms and their politically powerful owners to block entry by new firms." Eric Hilt, *Early American Corporations and the State, in* Corporations and American Democracy 37, 72 (Naomi R. Lamoreaux & William J. Novak eds., 2017).

[22] Friedman, *supra* note 15, at 512.

previously been. *Ultra vires* claims contending that corporations were acting beyond their specified powers virtually ceased by the late-nineteenth century because corporations were legally free to do anything an individual could do. With these changes, the artificial person theory of the corporation diminished in relevance since corporations no longer appeared to be mere fictions that were entirely dependent on the state to define the scope of their existence, purpose, and activities. The corporation looked less like an arm of the state and more like a vehicle for individuals to pursue economic ends. The law allowed for limited shareholder liability and perpetual duration of the business. This solidified the appeal of utilizing the corporate form for entrepreneurial endeavors that required large amounts of capital and risk.

While the artificial person theory of the corporation correctly describes important aspects of the legal basis for corporate personhood, some scholars believe it lacks viability today.[23] It was an idea that was good for its time, but it envisions a critical level of state involvement that is absent now that incorporation is essentially an administrative formality. "The difficulty with viewing the corporation simply as a creature of the state is that the state no longer functions as the dominant force in the development of a corporation's form and character."[24]

The artificial person theory may have fallen from dominance, but the normative and political implications of the theory continue to strike a chord with many who want to see the law regain greater control over the corporation. The idea that corporations should be more socially responsible and subject to stricter regulation resonates with those who believe corporations today have been permitted to gain too much financial and political power. The artificial person theory has never been formally renounced, and it is plausible that legislative and judicial authorities could invoke it today to justify limits on corporate activity.[25]

Opponents of corporate constitutional rights often revert to the artificial person theory to argue that corporations, as mere concessions of the state, should have no legitimate claim to constitutional rights such as freedom of speech or religion. Under this approach, the government "could easily reassert legal control over the structural make-up of corporations" and alter "one or more core attributes of

[23] *See* Henry N. Butler & Larry E. Ribstein, THE CORPORATION AND THE CONSTITUTION, at ix (1995) ("This theory had its origin in the early history of the corporation, when corporations were, in fact, created by special charter. The theory has no relevance today, when corporations are freely formed by making a simple filing under general corporation laws."); Colombo, *supra* note 11, at 99 ("[C]oncession theory has long been abandoned by the vast majority of corporate law scholars and commentators."); Michael J. Phillips, *Corporate Moral Personhood and Three Conceptions of the Corporation*, 2 BUS. ETHICS Q. 435, 442 (1992) ("[T]he theory ceased to reflect social reality over a century ago, and . . . few legal scholars who theorize about corporations take it seriously today.").

[24] Jeffrey Nesteruk, Bellotti *and the Question of Corporate Moral Agency*, 1988 COLUM. BUS. L. REV. 683, 687 n.23.

[25] *See* Lyman Johnson, *Law and Legal Theory in the History of Corporate Responsibility: Corporate Personhood*, 35 SEATTLE U. L. REV. 1135, 1148–49 (2012) (describing the potential viability of this argument).

corporate personhood" to limit corporate power and to increase corporate responsibilities.[26] The switch to general incorporation statutes may have made incorporation virtually automatic for anyone who wants it, but incorporation still requires a charter from the state, and states' authority to grant a charter is concomitant with their authority to deny or revoke it. Indeed, efforts have been made to revive the artificial person theory by petitioning state attorney generals to revoke the charters of corporations accused of serious environmental crimes and human rights violations.[27] Although these petitions have not been successful, they represent an earnest attempt to reinvigorate the conception of the corporation as a fictional person or government concession that can be terminated just as easily as it can be created. Even so, revoking charters and dissolving corporations are perceived as such extreme measures that states are unlikely to utilize them even if the artificial person theory regains some persuasive force.

The conception of the corporation as an artificial legal fiction that is dependent on the state for recognition is not an erroneous depiction of the corporation, but it is an incomplete one. It is true that the corporation has no status as a legal person unless it has an effective charter approved by the state. In this sense, the corporation is a creature of the law, reliant on the state for legal recognition and permission to operate. The law endows the corporate form with special legal attributes such as limited shareholder liability and perpetual duration. The law is essential to defining the corporate person, as well as its rights, powers, and duties. Thus, the personhood of corporations is tied to the state. Yet that does not mean that corporations are extensions of the state. While the corporation may be a government-sanctioned entity, the corporation is not *only* that. Its identity as a creature of law is one aspect of its personhood, but as we shall see, there are many other aspects of its personhood that are equally elemental. The artificial person theory is helpful to a point, but "taken alone, is too authoritarian with respect to the business enterprise"[28] and fails to accommodate other important dimensions of the corporation, including social and moral dimensions. It is understandable that the artificial person model declined as theorists expanded their view to focus on additional facets of corporate personhood that went beyond merely its legal origins.

[26] *Id.* at 1151–52, 1158. Professor Lyman Johnson skillfully explains that the "existence of unexercised [state] power over corporations means the fully emergent corporate 'person' need not be in either rights or responsibilities legally identical to humans, and corporations likewise need not simplistically be equated to the institution of business more generally." *Id.* at 1152.

[27] *See* Robert W. Benson, *How Many Strikes Do Big Corporations Get? The Petition to Revoke UNOCAL's Corporate Charter*, 55 Guild Prac. 113 (1998); Thomas Linzey, *Petition to Attorney General of Delaware to Revoke Corporate Charters of WMX Technologies and Chemical Waste Management Inc.*, 52 Guild Prac. 116 (1995); Thomas Linzey, *Awakening a Sleeping Giant: Creating a Quasi-Private Cause of Action for Revoking Corporate Charters in Response to Environmental Violations*, 13 Pace Envtl. L. Rev. 219 (1995).

[28] Orts, *supra* note 8, at 21.

CORPORATION AS AN AGGREGATE PERSON

By the end of the nineteenth century, it was clear that the artificial person theory offered too narrow a description of the corporation, and a shift in thinking about corporate personhood began to take place. At this time, general incorporation statutes had completely displaced the method of specialized legislative chartering. With the simplification of the incorporation process, the number of corporations increased dramatically. In 1800, there were 335 corporations in the United States.[29] By the time of the first federal income tax in 1916, there were more than 300,000 active corporations.[30] Many of these corporations were small- and medium-sized firms formed by individuals who sought the advantages associated with doing business in the corporate form. Because general incorporation laws allowed anyone easily to incorporate a business without the heavy state scrutiny that had previously existed, the focus shifted from the state as the authority and originator of the corporation to the human individuals who incorporated the business for profit. The corporation looked less like a concession of government designed to serve a public purpose, and more like an arrangement between private individuals to pursue their own personal gain. An alternative view of the corporation arose during this time that looked past the formality of creating a legal fiction and identified the real source of the business: profit-seeking entrepreneurs. From this point of view, the corporation was not so much a creature of the state but the product of individual initiative and enterprise.

This new approach formed the aggregate theory of the corporate person. While the artificial person theory holds that corporations cannot exist without the state, the aggregate theory emphasizes that the corporation cannot be formed without the action and agreement of the human persons behind the business. In fact, no corporate acts would ever occur if not for the individuals who make up the corporate entity. It is "owned, managed, and administered by *people*" and "[i]ts so-called actions are but manifestations of actions by real persons."[31] The corporation is seen as a collection, or aggregate, of individuals who contract with each other to utilize the corporation for their mutual benefit. The corporate person has no existence or identity that is separate and apart from these natural persons. It is "self-evident that a corporation is not *in reality* a person or a thing distinct from its constituent parts. The word 'corporation' is but a collective name for the corporators or members who compose [it]."[32] All of the actions and intentions of the corporation

29 2 Joseph Stancliffe Davis, Essays in the Earlier History of American Corporations, no. IV, at 24 tbl.1 and surrounding text (Lawbook Exch. 2006) (1917).

30 Naomi R. Lamoreaux, *Partnerships, Corporations, and the Limits on Contractual Freedom in U.S. History: An Essay in Economics, Law, and Culture*, *in* Constructing Corporate America: History, Politics, Culture 29, 34 (Kenneth Lipartito & David B. Sicilia eds., 2004).

31 Donald R. Cressey, *The Poverty of Theory in Corporate Crime Research*, *in* 1 Advances in Criminological Theory 31, 36 (William S. Laufer & Freda Adler eds., 1989).

32 1 Victor Morawetz, A Treatise on the Law of Private Corporations 2 (Boston, Little, Brown, & Co. 2d ed. 1886).

are always reducible to the actions and intentions of the individuals within the organization. This model of the corporate person is grounded in methodological individualism, the principle that the individual, not the group, is the appropriate starting point for any legal, political, or social theory. "Every complex social situation, institution, or event is the result of a particular configuration of individuals," and the only way to reach "rock-bottom explanations" of large-scale social phenomena is to boil them down to the "dispositions, beliefs, resources, and inter-relations of individuals."[33]

The aggregate theory retains the fictional element of the artificial person theory; the corporate person is seen as an artificial construct or fiction that is used as a convenient legal shortcut to facilitate economic enterprise. Neither theory suggests that the corporation has a real and distinct ontological existence of its own. Where the aggregate and artificial person theories differ is with regard to the dependence element of the corporation. The aggregate theory rejects the notion that corporations are entirely dependent on the state legislature for their creation; rather, the corporation relies on its human members for its organization and ongoing activity. The source and impetus for the corporation are the individuals who agree to aggregate their talent and resources within the corporate framework to pursue their joint ends. The corporation's origin is traced to these people and their private contractual arrangements with each other, not the state. A corporation cannot "be formed by law without the action of the corporators; for the legislature has not the power to create the mutual consent, which is essential to every contractual relation."[34]

In this way, the aggregate theory reframes the role of the corporate charter. Rather than characterizing the charter as a government grant, the aggregate model sees the charter as a contract among the individuals who combine to form the business, much like a partnership agreement. When the charter is filed with the state, it is only an ex post registration with the state registrar, not an ex ante plea for a grant of sovereign approval. This new line of thinking made a lot of sense when the era of free incorporation began in the late-nineteenth century. With the adoption of general incorporation laws, chartering ceased to be a significant legislative affair and instead became a perfunctory procedural one. Incorporation was viewed more as a matter of individual entitlement than state privilege. Corporations appeared to be self-organized firms, created by and for their participants. The state's recognition of the corporate person was really just an affirmation of people's natural desire and right to come together to accomplish economic tasks in partnership with each other. From this view, the

[33] J. W. N. Watkins, *Methodological Individualism and Social Tendencies*, *in* Readings in the Philosophy of the Social Sciences 269, 270–71 (May Brodbeck ed., 1968).

[34] Victor Morawetz, A Treatise on the Law of Private Corporations other than Charitable 11 (Boston, Little, Brown, & Co. 1882).

corporation is "a creature of free contract among individual shareholders, no different, in effect, from a partnership."[35]

The aggregate theory, also called the contractual or associational theory, is rooted in the right of individuals to associate with one another, to form voluntary groups, to strike mutually beneficial bargains, and to otherwise freely relate to each other in ways that fulfill their own private interests. These concepts resonate with an "inherence theory" of corporations that suggests that "men have a natural right to form a corporation by contract for their own benefit, welfare, and mutual self-interest."[36] One aspect of this model involves the right to partner together contractually to form beneficial business structures that allow individuals to achieve joint economic goals and pursue pecuniary profits. Another branch of this model involves a more political core: the right of political and social association. There has always been a deep American belief in the sanctity of association. People have always formed voluntary groups and organizations with like-minded people to pursue shared interests. Corporations, as collections of individuals, can be analogized to other political and social groups in society that are created to enhance the lives, voices, and powers of individual members, such as churches, clubs, and political parties. These groups form naturally out of individuals' private social, political, and economic relationships. The collective entity consolidates and represents the interests and values of its constituents.

To determine any rights or duties of the organization, the aggregate theory requires us to look past the organizational form to the individual members themselves. Because the corporate person is really just the sum total of all those individuals, it is not possible to distinguish meaningfully between the interests of a corporation and those of its human constituents. The "rights and duties of an incorporated association are in reality the rights and duties of the persons who compose it, and not of an imaginary being."[37]

The United States Supreme Court implicitly relied on this view in *Santa Clara County v. Southern Pacific Railroad* when it declared that a railroad corporation is a person for purposes of the Fourteenth Amendment, and thus its property cannot be taxed differently from the property of individuals.[38] The underlying reasoning was that the corporation's property was essentially the property of the individual shareholders who owned the corporation and therefore should be protected in the same manner. Morton Horwitz explained that the Court's decision relied on the aggregate theory arguments of the railroad company, and on Justice Stephen Field's reasoning

35 Morton J. Horwitz, Santa Clara *Revisited: The Development of Corporate Theory*, 88 W. Va. L. Rev. 173, 184 (1985).

36 Robert Hessen, In Defense of the Corporation 22 (1979).

37 1 Morawetz, *supra* note 32, at 3; *see also* Henry O. Taylor, A Treatise on the Law of Private Corporations Having Capital Stock, at iv (Philadelphia, Kay & Brother 1884) ("By dismissing this fiction [of the legal person] a clearer view may be had of the actual human beings interested, whose rights may then be determined without unnecessary mystification.").

38 118 U.S. 394 (1886).

in his circuit court opinion in a companion case.[39] Justice Field had questioned why individuals' interests in their property should suddenly terminate if they decide to join together and form a corporation. He wrote: "It would be a most singular result if a constitutional provision intended for the protection of every person against partial and discriminating legislation by the states, should cease to exert such protection the moment the person becomes a member of a corporation."[40] To avoid this unfair result, the corporation must be entitled to the same constitutional protection that its human members would have if acting in their individual capacity. The property of the corporation ultimately belongs to the shareholders. "To deprive the corporation of its property ... is, in fact, to deprive the corporators of their property ... [T]he courts will look through the ideal entity and name of the corporation to the persons who compose it, and protect them."[41] From this perspective, the law must uphold corporate rights to protect the rights of the natural persons behind the corporation.

Certain normative implications flow from the aggregate paradigm of the corporation and its focus on individuals. It suggests not only that corporations should be regarded as the product of private initiative and natural market forces, but also that corporations reflect forms of private property and private contract, and that corporate law should be viewed as private law, not public law. The purpose of the corporation is to serve as a vehicle for investors to pursue their own interests, to maximize their wealth, and to accomplish their self-defined goals. Entrepreneurs do not form corporations to have them act as extensions of the state to promote generalized public or community purposes. Corporate "participants who invest their own wealth, time, labor, and knowledge in a business enterprise ... see firms as representing, derivatively, their own interests and expectations, rather than those of a sponsoring government."[42] Unlike the artificial person theory, the aggregate model supports a hands-off, anti-regulatory approach to corporate activity. Rather than interfering with private parties' consensual corporate actions or restricting their property rights, the law should support the financial interests of corporate owners, and it should protect their rights to enter into beneficial contractual relations. This pro-business approach seeks to minimize regulation of business corporations because it encroaches on individuals' property rights and infringes on their freedom to contract in ways that best serve their own interests.

The aggregate theory remains a dominant paradigm in modern conceptions of the corporation. It serves as the foundation for the modern economic theory of the firm, the nexus of contracts model. As will be discussed later in the section of this chapter on the economic theory of the corporate person, this economic model has shaped

39 *See* County of San Mateo v. S. Pac. R.R. Co., 13 F. 722 (C.C.D. Cal. 1882); Horwitz, *supra* note 35, at 177–78.

40 *County of San Mateo*, 13 F. at 744.

41 *Id.* at 747–48.

42 Orts, *supra* note 8, at 10. The aggregate theory represents a "bottom-up" approach that prioritizes the interests of the human members of the corporation over those of the state. *Id.*

academic discourse about corporate law for decades. Moreover, as we will see in Chapters 4 and 5, the Supreme Court has often relied on the aggregate view to support the extension of constitutional rights to the corporation. The establishment of corporate constitutional rights is regarded as necessary to protect the constitutional rights of the individuals within the corporation.

While the aggregate theory has been extremely influential, it too offers only a partial picture of the corporate person. Not all actions of corporations can be redescribed as individual actions.[43] Organizations have certain properties that are truly products of the organization itself; they come about because of the way individuals behave *together*.[44] As the size of the corporation grows, the aggregate theory loses some of its practicability, and some perplexing questions arise. Which individuals are the relevant ones for purposes of the aggregation: the original individuals who started the corporation (perhaps a handful of people), or the individuals who currently own the corporation's stock (perhaps hundreds of people)? Would it be more sensible to include the corporation's employees, creditors, and suppliers in the aggregation of individuals who compose the corporate organization? If so, does this not begin to blur the line between the corporation and the rest of society as the aggregation necessarily expands with the growth of the corporation? If the corporation is merely the sum of its individual members, how can the corporation remain the same person when some or all of its individual members change or depart?

By the early-twentieth century, as corporations grew dramatically in size and scope, the difficulty with answering these questions became increasingly more apparent. At that time, dispersed shareholder ownership and immense growth in the size of corporations revealed a deep separation of ownership and control in large corporations.[45] Widely scattered shareholders of giant corporations were passive investors with small individual holdings who did not control the corporation in any meaningful sense. The board of directors and officers managed the business on the shareholders' behalf. The large corporation appeared to take on its own identity as a functioning organization, separate from the individual shareholders and employees who came and went without changing the fundamental nature of the organization's operations. The corporation had a longevity, a perpetual existence, that its individual members did not. Because the aggregate theory was not an entirely

43 Patricia H. Werhane, PERSONS, RIGHTS, AND CORPORATIONS 51–52 (1985).

44 Michael Keeley, A SOCIAL-CONTRACT THEORY OF ORGANIZATIONS 230 (1988).

45 Adolf A. Berle, Jr. & Gardiner C. Means, THE MODERN CORPORATION AND PRIVATE PROPERTY 119–25 (1932). A shift from democratic voting rights (one vote per person) to plutocratic voting rights (one vote per share) may have been a key factor in this separation of ownership and control, turning the many smaller shareholders into passive investors and enabling the few larger shareholders to control and further empower the board. *See* Colleen A. Dunlavy, *From Citizens to Plutocrats: Nineteenth-Century Shareholder Voting Rights and Theories of the Corporation*, *in* CONSTRUCTING CORPORATE AMERICA, *supra* note 30, at 66, 72–87.

satisfactory description of the corporate person, a new theory, the real entity theory, emerged to explain the personhood of corporations.

CORPORATION AS A REAL AND INDEPENDENT PERSON

As corporations grew increasingly larger near the end of the nineteenth century, many of them were no longer owned and controlled by a small group of founding investors. Rather, the stock was held by numerous shareholders who allowed managers to run the company for the shareholders' benefit. Many small- and medium-sized businesses merged into very large corporate consolidations during the great merger movement that occurred at that time.[46] The massive growth of corporate organizations was at odds with the idea that corporations were simply associations, or aggregates, of the people who formed the corporation. The analogy to partnerships was no longer persuasive. "The reality of the corporation apart from its members was becoming clearer as the relationship of the shareholders to the operations of the business became increasingly distant."[47] Large corporations began taking on a character, reputation, personality, brand, and social identity of their own, distinct from the attributes of their human constituents.[48]

An outpouring of scholarly analysis on corporate personhood accompanied these changes in the structure and operations of corporations. Its origins were largely in the work of Otto Gierke, a German political theorist whose writings on the historical development of Germanic associations and communities were translated into English and promoted by legal scholars Frederic Maitland and Ernst Freund.[49] Gierke observed that human beings naturally form and function in groups, whether it be in families, clans, guilds, or nations. Groups are not created by the state; rather, they are natural, spontaneously formed, timeless entities that preexist the state. Gierke argued that associations were real entities with an autonomous existence stemming from the necessity of group life: "The association, or group, is a living entity ... Every group has a real and independent communal life, a conscious will, and an ability to act that are distinct from the lives and wills of its individual members."[50] In the United States, Freund drew on some of Gierke's ideas to conceptualize the corporation as an autonomous entity with its own will. He argued: "The law does not create the corporate person, but finding it in existence invests it

46 Naomi R. Lamoreaux, THE GREAT MERGER MOVEMENT IN AMERICAN BUSINESS, 1895–1904, at 1–2 (1985).

47 Mark, *supra* note 19, at 1472.

48 Margaret M. Blair, *Corporate Personhood and the Corporate Persona*, 2013 U. ILL. L. REV. 785, 810.

49 Otto Gierke, POLITICAL THEORIES OF THE MIDDLE AGE (Frederic William Maitland trans., Lawbook Exch. 2002) (1900).

50 OTTO GIERKE: ASSOCIATIONS AND LAW: THE CLASSICAL AND EARLY CHRISTIAN STAGES 7 (George Heiman ed. & trans., 1977). "In fact, the group and the individual human could be viewed as two species within the genus of real persons." Andrew Vincent, *Can Groups Be Persons?*, 42 REV. METAPHYSICS 687, 708 (1989) (discussing Gierke's view of groups).

with a certain legal capacity. The corporation ... is not identical with [its human members], for out of the association of the individuals the new personality arises, having a distinct sphere of existence and a will of its own."[51]

Many scholars and jurists began to embrace the idea that corporations exist in their own distinct way. An alternative theory of the corporate person took shape. The real entity theory, also called the natural entity theory, arose to overshadow the aggregate model of the corporation. The real entity theory maintains that the corporation's existence is in many ways independent of the individuals who compose the corporation, as well as independent of the state that legally recognizes its form.

In contrast to the artificial person theory, the real entity theory views the corporation as an undeniably real and non-imaginary person. That which is said to be artificial can still be quite real. As one scholar argued, "an artificial lake is not an imaginary lake," it is something very real that we can see and touch.[52] Although corporate legal personality can be regarded as a fiction, the entity that is personified is certainly not fictional. It is a full-fledged, actual reality that exists as an objective fact and has a real presence in society.

The real entity theory rejects the artificial person theory's view of the corporation as a concession of the state. Rather than viewing the corporation as dependent on the state for its existence, the real entity theory contends that the corporation exists prior to the state. The state merely recognizes the corporation and gives it legal status once the corporation is already formed. Just as the state may record the birth of every baby, or the sale of every parcel of land, so the state records the formation of every corporation via a charter.[53] This corporate formation occurs by virtue of agreement of the private parties who constitute the business, not by virtue of any state action. The state merely adds "legal legitimacy" to the corporation by its public recognition of the entity, but it has nothing to do with the actual creation of the corporation.[54] "What really happens is that the state finding certain persons standing in a certain

[51] Ernst Freund, THE LEGAL NATURE OF CORPORATIONS 13 (Chicago, Univ. of Chi. Press 1897).

[52] Arthur W. Machen, Jr., *Corporate Personality*, 24 HARV. L. REV. 253, 257 (1911). Machen continued: "[A] corporation cannot possibly be imaginary or fictitious and also composed of natural persons. Neither in mathematics nor in philosophy nor in law can the sum of several actual, rational quantities produce an imaginary quantity." *Id.* He argued that the corporation's reality is evident in the tangible results of its operations in the world: "[corporations] bridge rivers, pierce mountains, unite cities, cross seas, control commerce, and accomplish all manner of other visible and tangible results." *Id.* at 267. Machen was also critical of the reductionism that marked the aggregate model of the corporation: "If a corporation is fictitious, the only reality being the individuals who compose it, then by the same token a river is fictitious, the only reality being the individual atoms of oxygen and hydrogen." *Id.* at 261.

[53] *See* Robert Hessen, Editorial, *Creatures of the State? The Case Against Federal Chartering of Corporations*, BARRON'S NAT'L BUS. & FIN. WKLY., May 24, 1976, at 7.

[54] Roger Pilon, *Corporations and Rights: On Treating Corporate People Justly*, 13 GA. L. REV. 1245, 1305 (1979). In fact, if the state suddenly ceased to recognize an existing corporation as a legally viable institution, the corporation would not cease to exist in an objective sense. "[I]t is not the law, with its fiction of juristic personality, that supplies the life blood and beating heart of these vast [corporations].

relation to each other and acting as a unit, upon a request from them, authorizes the group to embark upon a certain course of activity."[55]

The real entity model views the corporation as distinct from the individuals who participate in the corporate enterprise. When several people come together to form an association for some shared purpose, the group entity is larger than and different in kind from the members themselves. Thus, an army, a university, and a church are all distinct units with an identity that is separate from the various individuals who are associated with them. New members may join and old ones may depart, but the entity retains its singularity. Likewise, a corporation is an independent entity whose existence and identity remain the same, even if its membership of individuals changes over time or is in a constant state of flux.[56] This is because one of the distinguishing features of large corporations is their continuity. "[O]rganizations can persist for several generations ... without losing their fundamental identity as distinct units, even though all members at some time come to differ from the original ones."[57] The life of a firm can transcend the lives of the individuals engaged in it.

Under the real entity view, a corporation can have its own will and pursue its own goals in a manner that cannot be equated with the will and goals of its human members. The corporation has a collective consciousness, or collective will, that results from discussion and compromise among the individual members, and may not reflect the preferences of any one person. Actions of the corporation are qualitatively different from those of its individual constituents, who each may have contributed some part to the act, but no one person can be said to be responsible for the unified corporate action.[58] Corporations can initiate and be responsible for their

If the law ... declared that they did not exist, the entities would be found to be not fictitious, but factual ... The huge machine would keep right on rolling. This is of the essence of an institution, and not of a legalistic creation." Adolf A. Berle, Jr., THE 20TH CENTURY CAPITALIST REVOLUTION 18–19 (1954).

55 George F. Deiser, *The Juristic Person*, 57 U. PA. L. REV. 300, 304 (1909).

56 *See* Peter A. French, COLLECTIVE AND CORPORATE RESPONSIBILITY 19–30 (1984); W. Jethro Brown, *The Personality of the Corporation and the State*, 21 LAW Q. REV. 365, 366–67 (1905). Some scholars have argued that corporations can exist for periods of time, with all of their rights and duties, despite having no members whatsoever. Roger Scruton, *Corporate Persons, in* 63 PROC. ARISTOTELIAN SOC'Y, SUPP. VOL. 239, 246 (1989); *see also* Meir Dan-Cohen, RIGHTS, PERSONS, AND ORGANIZATIONS: A LEGAL THEORY FOR BUREAUCRATIC SOCIETY 41–45 (2d ed. 2016) (telling an allegory of the "Personless Corporation" to show that one may "strip the corporation of all individuals and yet preserve, both conceptually and legally, the identity of [the corporation]").

57 Peter M. Blau & W. Richard Scott, FORMAL ORGANIZATIONS: A COMPARATIVE APPROACH 1 (1962). In a complete reversal of the aggregate approach, it could be argued that the role of the shareholder is dependent on the corporation's prior existence, rather than the other way around. *See* Peter F. Drucker, CONCEPT OF THE CORPORATION 21 (rev. ed. 1972) ("The corporation is permanent, the shareholder is transitory. It might even be said without much exaggeration that the corporation is really socially and politically a priori whereas the shareholder's position is derivative.").

58 Susanna M. Kim, *Characteristics of Soulless Persons: The Applicability of the Character Evidence Rule to Corporations*, 2000 U. ILL. L. REV. 763, 790–91 (discussing ways in which the acts of the corporation sometimes may not sensibly be reduced to the actions of individuals within the organization).

own actions and intentions. Indeed, corporate criminal liability emerged at the turn of the twentieth century, about the time the real entity theory arose, to hold corporations independently responsible for their actions. Jurists began to perceive that a corporation itself could be convicted of a crime, due to its own organizational acts and culpable intent, independent of any criminal liability of specific individuals within the corporation.[59]

Support for the real entity theory grew out of the belief that the corporation was a natural outgrowth of people's tendency to join together for shared economic purposes. Far from being an artificial construction of the state, the corporation was viewed as a naturally formed entity that obligates the law to respect and officially recognize it. The law does not create the corporation but instead acts simply as "a device for facilitating and registering the obvious and the inevitable."[60] Real entity proponents argued that the theories of the corporation as artificial and fictional creatures were irrelevant because corporations are real, naturally occurring entities whose "bodies existed and were recognized before a theory was invented to explain their existence and recognition."[61]

In its most extreme form, the real entity theory suggested that group organizations are real living organisms with a body and a will. There was a sense in which groups could take on an animating life force that gave them their own metaphysical ontological status. They were viewed as having a transcendent reality and organic permanence that went beyond the individuals engaged in it.[62] This organicist conception led to metaphysical speculations and anthropomorphist ideas about the corporate entity that were bizarre and unhelpful. The doctrine at times was carried to "grotesque lengths," likening the corporation to a biological organism possessing "senses," "organs," and "gender."[63] This anthropomorphism made little substantive sense when applied to corporate legal transactions. It was too incredulous to think that the creation of a wholly owned subsidiary would mean the creation of a "living being" to serve as an owned "slave," and a contract for one company to merge into another would be "a promise to commit suicide."[64] Critics subsequently argued that extreme notions of the real life of associations, including the state, served as the basis for political theories that became associated with totalitarianism. The more prudent use of the real entity theory was to avoid excessive organicist extensions and focus more specifically on the idea that the corporation was more

59 *See* N.Y. Cent. & Hudson River R.R. Co. v. United States, 212 U.S. 481 (1909) (seminal case recognizing corporate criminal liability).

60 Edward S. Mason, *Introduction*, *in* THE CORPORATION IN MODERN SOCIETY 1, 1 (Edward S. Mason ed., 1959).

61 W. M. Geldart, *Legal Personality*, 27 LAW Q. REV. 90, 96 (1911).

62 *See* Christian List & Philip Pettit, GROUP AGENCY: THE POSSIBILITY, DESIGN, AND STATUS OF CORPORATE AGENTS 73–74 (2011); Michael J. Phillips, *Reappraising the Real Entity Theory of the Corporation*, 21 FLA. ST. U. L. REV. 1061, 1068–69 (1994) (referring to the real entity theory's organicist characteristics that analogized groups to biological organisms).

63 Machen, *supra* note 52, at 256.

64 Martin Wolff, *On the Nature of Legal Persons*, 54 LAW Q. REV. 494, 501 (1938).

than just a fictional entity and more than the mere sum of its parts. The corporation could be viewed as a real person, similar to a natural person, but not identical to a human being.

Two contrasting normative visions of the corporation proceed from the real entity theory. On the one hand, if the corporation is a real and natural being, much like an individual person, the corporation should be entitled to many of the same rights and privileges that are afforded to natural persons. Under the real entity approach, corporations are viewed as private institutions, not public entities, and therefore should be treated like private citizens. They should be free from government interference and overbearing regulation of their activities. They are no more in need of legal regulation than individuals are. If the corporation is a product of private entrepreneurial initiative and natural market tendencies toward economic consolidation, then the corporation should be left alone to do what it is naturally formed to do and what it is best at doing, i.e., furthering the shared interests of private individuals. It is not a creature of the state and thus should not be beholden to the state to foster specific public interests.

On the other hand, a slightly different interpretation of the real entity theory implies a more public-oriented normative view of corporations. If the corporation is a real person in society, it should have the same sorts of moral, ethical, and social responsibilities that individuals have. As a citizen of a larger community, it enjoys certain rights and privileges, but it should also bear the corresponding duties of a citizen to be sensitive to the impact of its activities on others. Its operations affect not only its investors, but also its employees, customers, creditors, and the larger community in which it exists. The corporation may be a private institution, but its business is not just a matter of private concern because everything it does is bound to affect the public in significant ways. From this perspective, the corporation has certain public-oriented obligations. The corporation should strive to be a contributing and responsible member of society, and at the very least, should avoid affirmatively harming others as it pursues its interests. The real entity theory embraces a stronger regulatory environment for corporations and supports greater tort and criminal liability for corporate persons who violate the law. The state should regulate corporations to use their powers not merely to maximize profits for their shareholders, but also to consider other participants in the corporation and to facilitate the greater good of society.

With these two very different normative visions of the corporation, the real entity theory represented a balance between the artificial person and aggregate theories. The aggregate view emphasized the role and rights of private shareholders so heavily that it gave the corporation too many rights vis-à-vis the state, while the artificial person theory focused so strongly on the role of the state as the creator of the corporation that it gave the state too much power to regulate corporations. The real entity view appeared to be "the most congruent with business realities as well as the one most suited to some balance between corporations and the state."[65]

Some scholars suggest that the real entity model retains its viability today because it seems to fit best with modern perceptions of corporations.[66] Large corporations are not commonly viewed as state-created entities or extensions of the government. Nor are they regarded as mere clusters of individuals, or as abstract fictional concepts. Corporations are perceived as being real entities that people can see and interact with, yet they are not individuals themselves. They are in a category of their own, different from human beings, and separate from the government. The real entity theory adopts a more holistic view of the corporate person than is described by the artificial person and aggregate theories alone.

INDETERMINACY OF THE LEGAL THEORIES OF THE CORPORATE PERSON

As a historical matter, the debate over which legal theory of the corporation was most accurate continued until the late 1920s when a pragmatic view of the legal treatment of corporations emerged. John Dewey, in his influential 1926 article, *The Historic Background of Corporate Legal Personality*, convincingly argued that the competing theories of the corporate person were indeterminate.[67] One could invoke any of the corporate personhood theories to support whatever result one wanted. Each model could be utilized to justify either limiting corporate power or enlarging it. Dewey observed that all of the theories were manipulable: "[e]ach theory has been used to serve the same ends, and each has been used to serve opposing ends."[68] The outcomes of contested legal issues involving corporate rights and duties appeared to be dependent on political considerations, not on consistent application of the personhood theories. Dewey argued that the use of the word "person" when discussing the corporation was ultimately meaningless. It does not really matter what we call the corporation or which model we use to describe its essence. Instead of labeling it a person, we could just as easily refer to it as a "right-and-duty-bearing unit" and assign it whichever rights and obligations that we feel are prudent from a political standpoint.[69] It becomes merely "a verbal matter whether we call [corporations] all 'persons,' or whether we call some of them persons and not others – or

[65] Reuven S. Avi-Yonah, *The Cyclical Transformations of the Corporate Form: A Historical Perspective on Corporate Social Responsibility*, 30 DEL. J. CORP. L. 767, 798 (2005).

[66] *See id.* at 812–13; Elizabeth Pollman, *Reconceiving Corporate Personhood*, 2011 UTAH L. REV. 1629, 1662; Thomas A. Smith, *The Use and Abuse of Corporate Personality*, 2 STAN. AGORA 69, 70–72 (2001) (arguing that some legal theories, as descriptions of the world, are "better and truer" than others, and the natural entity theory "comes closest in its broad overall outlines to the truth").

[67] Dewey, *supra* note 3.

[68] *Id.* at 669. Dewey argued that the various theoretical corporate personhood concepts were simply being used after the fact as "rationalizations" for positions held by debating parties. *Id.* at 665.

[69] *Id.* at 656.

whether we abandon the use of the word entirely."[70] In other words, the personhood designation is not determinative and is arguably irrelevant.

Dewey's opinion about the indeterminacy of the corporate personhood theories had validity. This indeterminacy has been illustrated in the Supreme Court's jurisprudence on the constitutional rights of corporate entities. The Court has sporadically used the artificial person, aggregate, and real entity theories to support its decisions, sometimes invoking multiple theories in a single case. In *Hale v. Henkel*, for example, the Court relied on the artificial person theory to hold that corporations are not entitled to the Fifth Amendment privilege against self-incrimination.[71] The Court stated that "the corporation is a creature of the State . . . presumed to be incorporated for the benefit of the public."[72] In the same opinion, the Court used the aggregate theory to hold that corporations are protected by the Fourth Amendment from unreasonable searches. The rationale was that the "corporation is, after all, but an association of individuals under an assumed name,"[73] and their individual property rights were entitled to protection. Utilizing different theories, the same case both supported and rejected the personhood of the corporation at the same time for purposes of analyzing different rights under the Constitution.

Over the years, the corporate personhood designation and the underlying legal theories have been selectively applied in constitutional law cases, producing seemingly incoherent results. An example of this is found in the Supreme Court's Fifth Amendment decisions. The Supreme Court has held that corporations, as creatures of the state, are not persons entitled to the Fifth Amendment privilege against self-incrimination, since that privilege "is essentially a personal one, applying only to natural individuals."[74] However, the Court has also held that corporations are persons entitled to the Fifth Amendment protection against double jeopardy because the corporation, much like a natural person, has the same interests as an individual in avoiding "embarrassment, expense and ordeal," not to mention "liv[ing] in a continuing state of anxiety and insecurity."[75] The Court has never clearly explained why a corporation is a person for purposes of the double jeopardy clause of the Fifth Amendment, but not for purposes of the self-incrimination clause of the same amendment. The use of the term "person" in both clauses is analytically indistinguishable. The self-incrimination clause follows immediately after and is grammatically part of the double jeopardy clause. Yet the Court has used different conceptions of the corporate person to support the differing results, underscoring

70 *Id.* at 662.

71 Hale v. Henkel, 201 U.S. 43, 70 (1906).

72 *Id.* at 74.

73 *Id.* at 76.

74 United States v. White, 322 U.S. 694, 698 (1944).

75 United States v. Martin Linen Supply Co., 430 U.S. 564, 569 (1977) (quoting Green v. United States, 355 U.S. 184, 187 (1957)).

Dewey's argument that the paradigms are easily manipulable to rationalize conclusions that are politically determined.

Scholars have argued that the personhood of corporations under the Constitution has not been consistently controlled by personhood terminology or theories, but by an almost ad hoc approach to corporate rights. At times, the Supreme Court has utilized conflicting theories of corporate personhood to support particular results, rather than as guiding principles to help reach them.[76] From this standpoint, Dewey had a point in observing that the term "person" signifies whatever the "law makes it signify."[77] Although Dewey downplayed the relevance of the legal theories of the corporation, his statement about the power of the law to determine the contours of the term "person" resonates with the artificial person theory. It suggests that the corporation is dependent on the state, through legislation and the courts, to define what the corporate person is and what rights and duties it should have. Dewey, however, ostensibly urged a pragmatic approach to dealing with issues of corporate rights and duties, i.e., dropping the theoretical debates about the source of the corporation's personhood and focusing instead on the practical consequences of assigning certain rights and duties to the corporation. He rejected the idea that in order for the corporation to be called a person it must possess certain intrinsic properties that are characteristic of what we define metaphysically as a person. The relevant question was not what corporations are, but what corporations do, and whether treating them as legal persons and giving them particular rights or duties will produce beneficial or detrimental consequences.[78] The legal realists like Dewey who favored this approach believed that resolving these issues about the scope of corporate power must involve practical political judgments, not abstract theoretical or philosophical ones.

This legal realist view of the corporation dampened the debate over the various legal theories of corporate personhood. Dewey's assertion about their indeterminacy became conventional wisdom, and the controversy over the nature of the corporate person lost its fervor. To theorize over the concept of corporate personhood was deemed an exercise in "transcendental nonsense."[79] The goal was no longer to search for an inhering essence of the corporation but to analyze concrete facts to identify and evaluate the effects of calling the corporation a person. This was a shift toward a pragmatic instrumentalist approach to law under which legal rules can be justified by assessing the practical consequences of utilizing those rules as

76 Phillip I. Blumberg, *The Corporate Entity in an Era of Multinational Corporations*, 15 Del. J. Corp. L. 283, 318 (1990).

77 Dewey, *supra* note 3, at 655. Dewey argued that the corporate personhood concept has constantly displayed "chameleon-like change," and the effect on legal doctrine has been to "generate confusion and conflict." *Id.* at 658.

78 *Id.* at 660–61.

79 *See* Felix S. Cohen, *Transcendental Nonsense and the Functional Approach*, 35 Colum. L. Rev. 809 (1935). Cohen argued that abstract concepts that cannot be defined in terms of actual experience are meaningless. *Id.* at 826.

instruments to serve chosen ends.[80] From this perspective, whether a corporation should be treated as a person depends on the facts and circumstances and may vary from case to case, depending on the issues at stake. Dewey's pragmatic treatment of the corporation's legal status continues to find support among modern legal scholars who prefer to avoid analysis of what the corporation is, and instead focus on the effects of granting corporations certain rights and duties.[81]

Not everyone agrees with Dewey's indeterminacy thesis. Some scholars have argued that legal conceptions of the corporation are not perpetually manipulable but have in fact influenced the determination of certain legal outcomes. While the legal theories have not necessarily dictated results, they have had a role in "tilting" or shaping our views of the corporation and their treatment under the law.[82] In this regard, legal theories matter, ideas have consequences, and different conceptualizations of the corporation can and do influence the resolution of certain corporate legal issues. While Dewey's indeterminacy thesis had merit, like all the other legal theories of the corporation, standing on its own, his view of corporate personhood was also incomplete. As will be discussed later in the section of this chapter on the language of corporate personhood, Dewey rejected the value of integrating non-legal frameworks into our legal understanding of the corporation, and he did not account for the lasting power and influence of language to form our perceptions of corporate personhood.

ECONOMIC THEORY OF THE CORPORATE PERSON

Although interest in the theoretical basis for calling the corporation a person languished for many decades after Dewey's work, the topic was revived in the 1980s when legal scholars began to draw upon ideas originating in the fields of economics and finance to form a new theory of the corporation. The theory focused on the contractual relations among the corporation's participants. Bolstered by the law and economics movement in legal scholarship, the contractual theory became extremely influential in the legal academy.[83] It has served as the dominant paradigm of the corporation for several decades.

This view of the corporate person relies on a contract model rooted in neoclassical economic theory. Under this paradigm, the corporation is merely a fiction that

80 *See* Robert S. Summers, *Pragmatic Instrumentalism in Twentieth Century American Legal Thought – A Synthesis and Critique of Our Dominant General Theory About Law and Its Use*, 66 Cornell L. Rev. 861 (1981).

81 *See, e.g.*, Richard Schragger & Micah Schwartzman, *Some Realism About Corporate Rights*, *in* The Rise of Corporate Religious Liberty 345, 347 (Micah Schwartzman et al. eds., 2016); Pollman, *supra* note 66, at 1631, 1675.

82 *See* Horwitz, *supra* note 35, at 175–76.

83 *See* Steven M. Teles, The Rise of the Conservative Legal Movement: The Battle for Control of the Law 216 (2008) ("Simply measured in terms of the penetration of its adherents in the legal academy, law and economics is the most successful intellectual movement in the law of the past thirty years, having rapidly moved from insurgency to hegemony.").

serves as a "nexus of contracts" among the firm's various individual participants.[84] These contracts are not all formal contracts as defined by law, but the economist's notion of contracts as reciprocal arrangements involving mutual expectations between parties. The human parties are defined according to the economist's notion of rational self-interested actors who freely contract according to their own utility calculations. Market forces bring shareholders, managers, creditors, employees, suppliers, consumers, and others together to seek the benefit of their mutual bargains. Their web of interrelated contracts is what constitutes the corporation. From this perspective, no independent, real corporate entity exists. The idea of a separate corporate person is only a convenient fiction. The corporate entity itself has no precise boundaries, and "it makes little or no sense to try to distinguish between those things which are 'inside' the firm … from those things that are 'outside' of it."[85] In fact, some proponents of the model prefer the term "contractarian theory" over "nexus of contracts" because the latter might imply the corporation exists on its own as an entity apart from the contracts among its participants. There is no conceptual justification for reifying the mass of intertwined contracts that compose the corporate form. As a result, the concept of the distinct corporate person tends to disappear.[86]

Ownership of the firm also disappears as a meaningful concept.[87] Since the organization decomposes into a group of identifiable participants who negotiate an equilibrium position among themselves, no one class of participants, not even the shareholder class, has a right to regard itself as the owner of the corporation. The shareholders are just one group of inputs whose rights are determined by the many interrelated contracts making up the corporation. That said, the managers are considered the agents of the shareholder principals who agree to bear the residual risk if the firm is not successful. In return, the managers' role is to act to maximize shareholder interests. The managers are obliged to serve at the behest of the shareholders. The risk that managers will fail to do so generates agency costs that must be constrained by internal and external market forces if the corporation is to produce gains for all of its constituent parties and ultimately for the shareholders as residual claimants.

According to the contractarian model, the corporation springs up naturally as a product of private, voluntary actions by people who are free to contract in their own

84 *See* Michael C. Jensen & William H. Meckling, *Theory of the Firm: Managerial Behavior, Agency Costs and Ownership Structure*, 3 J. FIN. ECON. 305, 311 (1976). Jensen & Meckling's article was one of the key foundational works on this theory. Others include Armen A. Alchian & Harold Demsetz, *Production, Information Costs and Economic Organization*, 62 AM. ECON. REV. 777 (1972) and Eugene F. Fama & Michael C. Jensen, *Separation of Ownership and Control*, 26 J. L. & ECON. 301 (1983).

85 Jensen & Meckling, *supra* note 84, at 311; *see also* Oliver Hart, *An Economist's Perspective on the Theory of the Firm*, 89 COLUM. L. REV. 1757, 1764 (1989).

86 *See* William W. Bratton, Jr., *The "Nexus of Contracts" Corporation: A Critical Appraisal*, 74 CORNELL L. REV. 407, 420 (1989).

87 Eugene F. Fama, *Agency Problems and the Theory of the Firm*, 88 J. POL. ECON. 288, 289–90 (1980).

self-interest. The corporation is not a metaphysical entity with its own ontological standing, nor is its existence a privilege bestowed by the state. It is a private undertaking by individual citizens. The contractarian model constitutes a modern variant of the aggregate theory of corporate personhood that, as previously discussed, says the corporation is nothing more than the collection of individuals who choose to join together to conduct their business in corporate form. The contractarian theory similarly holds that the corporation is merely the sum of its contractual parts.

The foundational concepts of the contractarian theory are not necessarily novel. Although the theory is regarded as a modern-day economics-based theory, early-twentieth century thinkers about the corporate form also made use of contractual concepts when discussing corporate personhood. For example, in 1911, W. M. Geldart's discussion of the legal personality of corporations utilized language that, in hindsight, resonates with the modern contractual model:

> If we are going to get nearer to the facts, we must at least add the notion of contract to that of co-ownership, a contract made by every shareholder with every other, limiting his right of ownership to a right to share in profits and to vote at shareholders' meetings, contracts between each shareholder and the directors, between each shareholder and every person who supplies a ton of coals or steel rails; innumerable contracts to the making of which he has not given a moment's thought. To escape from the fictitious person we have fallen into the arms of the fictitious contract.[88]

The combination of all these explicit and implicit contracts is at the heart of the corporate enterprise. The contractarian theory is thus immensely reductionist, decomposing the firm into its many contractual pieces.

As a normative matter, the contractarian theory not only describes corporations as the center of interrelated contracts between freely contracting individuals, but also asserts that corporations should be allowed to function freely in that manner. The private individuals who voluntarily enter into these contracts should be given wide discretion to order their affairs in whatever way they choose. Corporate property is private property. Under this model, the most important laws are those that protect private property rights and enforce contracts. The law should provide only a set of non-mandatory default rules that the parties can change by voluntary agreement if they desire.[89] There should be no government policing of their relationships and contracts; rather, the state should yield to freedom of contract and freedom of association principles. The contractarian approach implies a preference for minimizing the regulation of business and eliminating restrictions on corporate activity.

88 Geldart, *supra* note 61, at 97–98.

89 *See* Frank H. Easterbrook & Daniel R. Fischel, The Economic Structure of Corporate Law 15 (1991); Lucian Arye Bebchuk, *Foreword: The Debate on Contractual Freedom in Corporate Law*, 89 Colum. L. Rev. 1395, 1396–97 (1989); Henry N. Butler, *The Contractual Theory of the Corporation*, 11 Geo. Mason U. L. Rev., no. 4, Summer 1989, at 99, 100.

From this standpoint, corporations should be afforded the latitude to do what they do best, generate profits for shareholders. Under the shareholder primacy and profit maximization principles, the interests of other constituencies must be subordinate to the corporation's primary concern for maximizing shareholder wealth.[90] Non-shareholder interests can all contract for their own protections. By maximizing profits, the corporation creates wealth for the broader economy, which ultimately benefits all of its constituents and society as a whole. According to this model, the more profits a company makes, the more those profits feed back into the system, providing jobs for workers, goods and services for consumers, prosperity for communities, and strong capital markets for the continuous economic growth of society.[91] This does not mean that corporations owe any legal, moral, or social responsibility to promote the public interest. Unlike the artificial person theory, the contractarian theory rejects the idea that the corporation possesses public-oriented duties toward the state or society. The mass of contracts that make up the corporation is a private endeavor among private citizens who each seek to benefit financially from the arrangement. Thus, the corporation's main purpose should be to increase the returns to its participants, and the law should be structured to avoid distracting corporations from that goal.

Because the firm is not regarded as a real or separate entity, it does not make sense to speak of such things as the entity's independent will, intent, or social or moral responsibilities, apart from those of its individual participants. Like the aggregate theory, the contractarian model reflects a strong adherence to methodological individualism wherein individuals are always the primary unit of analysis and groups can never be explained apart from their individual members. As a result, issues are analyzed from the vantage point of the individuals with an emphasis on their interests and obligations as the relevant contracting parties.

The economic contractarian theory of the corporation has had a commanding presence in legal academic thought for many decades. Yet it remains subject to considerable criticisms. Some argue that the theory assumes perfect, complete, and purposive contracting by rational economic actors, but in the real world, human beings' bounded rationality and limited problem-solving abilities make such perfect contracting an illusion.[92] The contractarian theory warns against the dangers of reification of the corporate enterprise, but "the equal and opposite sin to reification

90 *See* David Millon, *The Single Constituency Argument in the Economic Analysis of Business Law, in* LAW & ECONOMICS: TOWARD SOCIAL JUSTICE 43, 45 (Dana L. Gold ed., 2009).

91 *See* Easterbrook & Fischel, *supra* note 89, at 38; Mark J. Roe, *The Shareholder Wealth Maximization Norm and Industrial Organization*, 149 U. PA. L. REV. 2063, 2065–66 (2001) (describing the utilitarian basis for maximizing shareholder wealth).

92 William W. Bratton, *The Economic Structure of the Post-Contractual Corporation*, 87 NW. U. L. REV. 180, 183–84 (1992); Bratton, *supra* note 86, at 448–49. In response, contractarians may counter that the theory does not contemplate true contracts as used in the conventional legal sense, but only an "analogy to contract." Easterbrook & Fischel, *supra* note 89, at 15. But then this is like an "analogy to persons," which is what the other theories of corporate personhood arguably entail.

is reductionism."[93] The corporation might be reduced to a nexus of contracts, but those contracts can be reduced to a nexus of expectations, which in turn can be reduced to nexuses of perceptions, and so on. At some point, deconstructive measures blind us to the reality of the bigger picture.[94]

Critics also see a problem with the contractarian theory's emphasis on private contracting and economic markets. It fails to acknowledge that such private ordering operates against a backdrop of public law, and it is the law that provides the mechanism for creating and enforcing private contracts.[95] By focusing so intently on the private interests of shareholders to pursue profit maximization, the contractarian model loses sight of the public-oriented aspects of the firm that are integral to its successful functioning. While economic market forces are important, the contractarian theory does not account for other powerful forces, both political and social, that shape what corporations are and what they do.

The theory has made important contributions to our understanding of the firm by pointing out that the corporation has significant contractual aspects. Standing on its own, however, the theory is incomplete. The contractarian paradigm does not fully explain the empirical reality of the relations among members within the corporation as well as the relations between the corporation and the broader society. It does not give significance to the social, moral, political, and institutional aspects of the corporate person. The economic model ultimately provides a very narrow conception of a much more complicated reality.

This complaint, however, can be lodged against any one of the personhood theories of the corporation discussed in this chapter. By itself, no one theory of the corporate person can adequately and comprehensively explain the nature, role, and purpose of the corporation. The personhood of corporations is multidimensional. Each theory looks at the corporation from a different angle and highlights a different side of the entity. The economic contractarian theory of the corporation is an especially useful tool because it focuses our attention on critical contractual aspects of the corporation. But it is only one tool, and there are many others. Those who favor the economic theory believe no other theory of the firm presents a credible alternative to the unitary nexus of contracts model. However, that belief assumes we must have a single theory that can adequately define the corporation and justify policy decisions about the legal treatment of corporate activity. If we must choose

93 Marc Galanter, *Planet of the APs: Reflections on the Scale of Law and Its Users*, 53 BUFF. L. REV. 1369, 1371 (2006).

94 The denial of the existence of a real and separate corporate entity does not necessarily have to follow from a reductionist approach. A related formulation of the contractual model asserts that the contractual arrangements combine to create an entity that is not reducible to the collective rights and duties of shareholders. Frederick Pollock & Frederic W. Maitland, *Corporation and Person, in* ANTHROPOLOGY AND EARLY LAW 300, 303 (Lawrence Krader ed., 1966) (corporation created through contract becomes indivisible unit comparable to human being).

95 For an excellent discussion of the importance of law in the creation and maintenance of corporate persons, see generally Orts, *supra* note 8.

one or the other, the argument goes, the contractarian model is better than all others. But it is not clear why such a choice needs to be made at all. It is not necessary or even beneficial to settle on an agreement that, at bottom, the corporation is *essentially* a nexus of contracts, or *essentially* a legal fiction, or *essentially* an aggregate of individuals. The multidimensional nature of the corporate person defies unitary classification. The corporation is a complex reality, and to understand its nature and role in the world, we should be open to seeing it from many different vantage points.

THE LANGUAGE OF CORPORATE PERSONHOOD AND A RESPONSE TO DEWEY

To say that no one single theory of the corporation can capture the full picture of the corporate person does not mean that we should abandon theorizing about the corporation and simply adopt the exclusively pragmatic instrumentalist approach advocated by John Dewey in 1926. Because the corporate theories seem so indeterminate and manipulable, Dewey argued that the term "person" meant very little and the concept of corporate personhood was ultimately irrelevant. He disfavored the merging of popular and philosophical notions of personhood with the legal application of corporate personhood, and instead he preferred a practical, consequences-oriented conception of the corporation as the bearer of legal rights and duties. If Dewey's views maintain some of their sensibility today, one might wonder why we should continue to take corporate personhood seriously in light of Dewey's critique.

Although Dewey would like us to drop the whole matter, the reality is, even after all these years, the controversy over the personhood of corporations refuses to be swept away by the proof that corporate personhood theories are indeterminate. People still care deeply about it and want to talk about it. Indeed, the terminology of corporate personhood has become the center of a national debate over what the corporation is and how it should be treated in modern society. The battle has moved beyond theoretical arguments among scholars. The battle appears in sharply divided Supreme Court cases holding that a corporation is a person for purposes of exercising its statutory rights to religious freedom (*Hobby Lobby*) and its free speech rights to donate to political campaigns (*Citizens United*). The battle appears in the angry protests of anti-corporate activists waving banners that read "End Corporate Personhood" and "Corporations Are Not People." It appears in the growing popular movement to amend the Constitution to declare that only human beings, not corporations, are persons entitled to constitutional rights. In spite of Dewey's insistence that the terminology of personhood is meaningless, the act of calling the corporation a person today is loaded with meaning, and that meaning is rooted in significant moral, social, political, and legal values.

It is not enough to dismiss the controversy over the nature of the corporation as Dewey did by asserting that all conceptions of the corporation are indeterminate and that personhood is an empty term. The problem is much more complicated. In the law, concepts have a force of their own because of their ability ex ante to influence our thinking and their use ex post to justify our conclusions about how things should be structured in our society. The fact that we talk about corporations in the language of personhood is not insignificant.[96] In an important sense, law is meaningful in the way that language is meaningful: "How we describe something [in our choice of words] is an important part of how we perceive it."[97] Language as a system of discourse conditions the way people think about things and interpret the world around them. Beyond merely *reflecting* societal views and values, legal language actually helps *form* prevailing judgments and understandings. When the law endorses and promotes certain theories of the corporate entity, the law affects our perceptions of the corporation and nudges us to view it in a particular light.[98] By calling the corporation a person, we tend to think of it as a being that has the attributes and the moral status of a natural person. This contributes to a propensity to treat the corporation with similar considerations that ground the rights of individual human beings. The personhood designation is more than an arbitrary, indeterminate label; it commands a measure of inviolability that is difficult to square with the idea that the entity is merely a tool to achieve an economic purpose. The vocabulary that we use to characterize corporations influences the manner in which we see and relate to them. The legal language of personhood has symbolic, expressive, and constitutive functions that animate and reinforce the personhood of corporations.

Language does more than merely describe a state of affairs. Through its ability to influence thought and discussion, it can help bring about that state of affairs. This is because "[i]nstitutions are very much dependent on language: what we cannot imagine and express in language has little chance of becoming a sociological reality."[99] This creative aspect of legal language is interesting. The law not only

96 Contrary to Dewey's assertion that the term "person" has no substantive meaning and is used only for legal convenience, linguists have utilized linguistic evidence to demonstrate that our usage of the term "person" reflects and shapes our view of corporations as beings that are capable of intelligence, intention, and other qualities associated with human personhood. *See* Sanford A. Schane, *The Corporation Is a Person: The Language of a Legal Fiction*, 61 TUL. L. REV. 563 (1987) (utilizing linguistic analysis to refute Dewey's claim that the term "person" is arbitrary and indeterminate).

97 Ellen A. Peters, *Reality and the Language of the Law*, 90 YALE L.J. 1193, 1195 (1981). Language has a labeling function that is an integral feature of law as language. *Id.*; *see also* Ian Hacking, REWRITING THE SOUL: MULTIPLE PERSONALITY AND THE SCIENCES OF MEMORY 238 (1995) (discussing the concept of "semantic contagion," whereby the description of an action or behavior can shape its moral consequences).

98 "It is vital not to discount the role that language plays in this context ... The problems of law are problems of political language in the largest sense." The "verbal construct" of the image of the corporation "channels the thinking about corporations and in turn controls the material relations [of individuals and collectivities] themselves." Mark, *supra* note 19, at 1467 n.70; *see also* Tamara R. Piety, *Why Personhood Matters*, 30 CONST. COMMENT. 361, 385 (2015) (Calling the corporation a person matters a great deal because the "personhood language exploits our impulse to reject as discriminatory distinctions between *human* persons and extends it to distinctions between human beings and corporations.").

99 Robert N. Bellah et al., THE GOOD SOCIETY 15 (1991).

reflects and incorporates pre-existing social conditions and relations. It also has the capacity to establish new ones.[100] It is an active discourse that creates the social world.[101] In this regard, the law creates truth, or makes things true in the eyes of the law.[102] Law is "constitutive" in the sense that it forms the mental frames, categories, and schema individuals use to comprehend and construct the social world.[103] Legal labeling can not only create cognitive categories but can also "produce behavior that confirms the law's cognitive categories ..."[104] The ability to shape people's perceptions and understandings of the world around them, including their view of corporations, is one of the most important forms of power that legal language possesses. Although the utilization of the corporate personhood designation may seem indeterminate at times, it is not immaterial. Law does matter, and language matters too. "Each of us is partly made by our language, which gives us the categories in which we perceive the world ... and in remaking our language we contribute to the remaking of our characters and lives."[105]

To focus so acutely on an analysis of language and its effects may strike some as engaging in needless semantics. This is a valid concern, and the intent of this discussion is not to engage in semantic arguments over the use of the personhood term. Rather, the goal is to highlight the critical role that language plays in how we evaluate corporate claims. Those who prefer Dewey's pragmatic approach to corporate personhood eschew extended discussions of the use of legal statements and terminology. Some scholars argue that ontological and semantic claims about legal statements are the wrong sorts of considerations for answering what they believe boil down to moral questions about corporate entitlements.[106] Instead, they contend that common sense morality moral theories, and our moral beliefs are what tell us whether corporate entities should or should not have certain legal entitlements. While this analysis is instructive, the question still remains, how are those moral theories and moral beliefs formed? What contributes to the development of common sense

100 Jeffrey Nesteruk, *Law and the Virtues: Developing a Legal Theory for Business Ethics*, 5 Bus. Ethics Q. 361, 362 (1995) (book review).

101 Pierre Bourdieu, *The Force of Law: Toward a Sociology of the Juridical Field*, 38 Hastings L.J. 814, 839 (1987); Laurence H. Tribe, *The Curvature of Constitutional Space: What Lawyers Can Learn from Modern Physics*, 103 Harv. L. Rev. 1, 7–8, 20 (1989) (describing the continually active and interactive role of law in recreating society).

102 Jack M. Balkin, *The Proliferation of Legal Truth*, 26 Harv. J.L. & Pub. Pol'y 5, 6 (2003). Law helps to define reality by "selectively interpreting and therefore selectively reinforcing part of the status quo, thereby helping to reformulate or reconstruct reality." Warren J. Samuels, *The Idea of the Corporation as a Person: On the Normative Significance of Judicial Language*, *in* Corporations and Society: Power and Responsibility 113, 122 (Warren J. Samuels & Arthur S. Miller eds., 1987).

103 Richard H. McAdams, *The Expressive Power of Adjudication*, 2005 U. Ill. L. Rev. 1043, 1045 n.4.

104 Mark C. Suchman, *On Beyond Interest: Rational, Normative and Cognitive Perspectives in the Social Scientific Study of Law*, 1997 Wis. L. Rev. 475, 492.

105 James Boyd White, Justice as Translation: An Essay in Cultural and Legal Criticism 2[illegible] (1990).

106 *See, e.g.*, Steven Walt & Micah Schwartzman, *Morality, Ontology, and Corporate Rights*, [illegible] Law & Ethics Hum. Rts. [illegible] (2017).

morality? I contend that language, both legal and cultural, plays a role in shaping moral beliefs and values. What we learn and believe, we acquire in part through language. To be sure, our common sense morality has a role in shaping the laws we create and the legal language that we use to govern society. At the same time, law influences the formation of prevailing values and understandings. There is a dynamic, reciprocal relationship between law and moral belief, with each informing and helping to create the other. It is important to think carefully about this connection and its application in the law and language of corporate personhood. We should acknowledge that "legal developments affect our moral judgments about corporations, including our conception of their moral status."[107] In this respect, language and the expression of law do have significance beyond semantics. Dewey's dismissal of the relevance of the legal terminology of personhood does not seem to do justice to the bigger picture.

Part of the reason why the personhood designation is so controversial is due to the power of language and law to send signals about society's value judgments. When the law announces that a corporation is a person, with many of the same rights and duties of a human person, it sends a message about how society values corporations and how they should be treated. Law as language has an expressive function: it makes statements, and it expresses certain beliefs and attitudes about societal values.[108] For example, sentencing laws that punish criminal behavior express society's moral condemnation of certain acts, making a statement about the kinds of conduct the community views as reprehensible.[109] Government policies that appear to endorse a particular religion violate the Establishment Clause, in part because they signal to non-adherents that they are outsiders and that their differing beliefs are unwelcome in the political community.[110] Laws that previously legalized racial segregation in schools were invalidated under the Fourteenth Amendment because, among other things, they communicated the

[107] Jeffrey Nesteruk, *The Moral Status of the Corporation: Comments on an Inquiry*, 2 Bus. Ethics Q. 461, 463 (1992).

[108] Alex Geisinger, A *Belief Change Theory of Expressive Law*, 88 Iowa L. Rev. 35, 40 (2002); Cass R. Sunstein, *On the Expressive Function of Law*, 144 U. Pa. L. Rev. 2021, 2024 (1996). In asserting that the legal language of personhood matters, I do not seek to argue, as H. L. A. Hart did, that the meaning of expressions is performative, i.e., that the meaning of an expression is its use to perform particular types of acts within a set of rules. *See* H. L. A. Hart, Essays in Jurisprudence and Philosophy 3–4, 275–76 (1983); *see also* Walt & Schwartzman, *supra* note 106, at 8–9 (describing Hart's views). Instead, I wish to draw upon the substantial body of scholarship dealing with the expressive function of legal language to make statements about our value judgments and to send signals about our underlying moral beliefs. *See, e.g.*, Richard H. McAdams, The Expressive Powers of Law: Theories and Limits 136–37 (2015); Mark D. Rosen, *Establishment, Expressivism, and Federalism*, 78 Chi.-Kent L. Rev. 669, 682–83 (2003).

[109] *See* Samuel W. Buell, *The Blaming Function of Entity Criminal Liability*, 81 Ind. L.J. 473, 498 (2006); Dan M. Kahan, *Social Influence, Social Meaning, and Deterrence*, 83 Va. L. Rev. 349, 362 (1997); Sunstein, *supra* note 108, at 2023.

[110] Lynch v. Donnelly, 465 U.S. 668, 688 (1984) (O'Connor, J., concurring).

harmful message that minority groups were inferior, disfavored members of society.[111] Law by its nature has expressive elements, and we are affected by the social and symbolic meaning of legal language, doctrines, and decisions.

Law makes important statements about the intrinsic and relative value of things. In the context of corporate personhood, for example, the law communicates who counts as a legal person and tells us whether corporations should hold the same place as individuals in our legal system. By upholding corporate rights under the First Amendment, the law arguably sends the message that corporate speech and individual speech have the same worth and are deserving of the same protections. Thus, legal language signals the value we as a society place on people, corporations, and certain actions such as speech. When law uses the term "person" to categorize an object, it "acts as a vehicle for expressing beliefs and values about persons, both legal and natural."[112] When people perceive that law and legal language send the wrong message, there is backlash and resistance as evolving societal values conflict with the signals of the law. In the corporate personhood context, we have witnessed some of that backlash as some citizens believe the law of corporate personhood sends the dubious message that corporate activity and individual activity are of equal value and merit.

This is an indication of the intricate relationship between legal language and our system of beliefs. Law is a social product. As our social and cultural beliefs change over time, they affect and shape the development of law and legal doctrine. At the same time, as discussed above, the law plays a role in shaping our beliefs and our conception of reality. There is a reciprocal, dynamic quality to the formation of legal language and evolving societal beliefs. At times, legal language is the force that drives new thinking and perceptions; at other times, our beliefs and values force the development of new legal terminology and doctrine. It is a two-way street. Our language and our beliefs are dependent upon one another, continually affecting and being affected by each other.[113]

Dewey did not embrace this connection between our belief system and our legal system. In fact, he warned against entertaining ideas from other non-legal disciplines to inform our analysis of legal personhood because he believed they only confuse and complicate matters. He viewed the legal concept of corporate personhood as pure artifice, a tool for practical legal use. He criticized the tendency to look outside

111 Brown v. Bd. of Educ., 347 U.S. 483 (1954); Elizabeth S. Anderson & Richard H. Pildes, *Expressive Theories of Law: A General Restatement*, 148 U. PA. L. REV. 1503, 1542–44 (2000) (discussing the expressive dimensions of *Brown v. Bd. of Educ.*).

112 Note, *What We Talk About When We Talk About Persons: The Language of a Legal Fiction*, 114 HARV. L. REV. 1745, 1761 (2001).

113 Margaret Radin has similarly observed that as concepts change and develop, they can cause social and cultural transformations; likewise, social and cultural developments can drive conceptual transformations. Margaret Jane Radin, *Reflections on Objectification*, 65 S. CAL. L. REV. 341 (1991); *see also* David Millon, *Theories of the Corporation*, 1990 DUKE L.J. 201, 241–47 (demonstrating how legal rules have shaped new thinking about corporations, and vice versa, how theoretical beliefs about corporations have shaped the formation of new legal doctrine).

the law for guidance on what it means to be a person worthy of recognition under the law. Dewey argued that "popular, historical, political, moral, philosophical, metaphysical and … theological" theories of personhood should not influence judgments about what the legal concept of personhood should entail.[114] To avoid confusion and conflict, Dewey urged us to keep the legal concept separate from any social and cultural notions of personhood. In his view, law is a self-enclosed system that does not and should not need to look elsewhere for its meaning.

The difficulty with this approach, however, is that legal concepts are inherently a reflection of and connected with our broader system of beliefs. Law cannot divorce itself from our culture, history, politics, moral beliefs, and social norms. These non-legal factors contribute to our vision of what makes a person, and the legal concept of personhood is unavoidably infused with this vision. Even when trying to determine the legal personhood of human beings, the analysis is necessarily a larger non-legal question involving metaphysical, cultural, social (and not just biological) understandings of what it is to be a whole and proper person.[115] Dewey strongly urged us not to clutter the practical determination of legal personhood with non-legal considerations because of the messy results, but as much as we might try, the law cannot be insulated from these broader aspects of our existence. Dewey preferred to ignore the constantly shifting popular and philosophical notions of personhood, but in some respects, we are "unable to avoid speculation about what it is to be a person [as] the legal term is constantly contaminated by non-legal moral meanings and may even be unintelligible without them."[116]

Dewey was concerned that using these non-legal theories makes personhood an indeterminate and muddled concept because the theories are constantly changing with the times. But determinacy and precision are not necessarily superior values. In some situations, certain moral, ethical, and social concerns may emerge that call for a more adaptable, open-ended approach. There is value in acknowledging the many facets of the corporation, as viewed through different disciplinary lenses, even

114 Dewey, *supra* note 3, at 655.

115 Ngaire Naffine, *Who Are Law's Persons? From Cheshire Cats to Responsible Subjects*, 66 MOD. L. REV. 346, 359–61 (2003). This analysis is raised, for example, when determining the personhood of a fetus or a mentally impaired individual. In our predominantly liberal legal culture, we regard a person as an autonomous being who can stand alone, independently of others, individuated and separated from one's mother, and capable of exercising reason and intelligent thought. These considerations are a product of our cultural, philosophical, political, and social views of personhood. "[W]e see how a particular cultural understanding of who and what is to count as an integrated and autonomous being, who is therefore susceptible to personification, shapes what we as lawyers often take to be brute biology. There is a metaphysics here that is rarely addressed." *Id.* at 361.

116 *Id.* at 349. In certain respects, Dewey's views are consistent with my own thesis about the dynamic nature of personhood. He notes that "the history of western culture shows a chameleon-like change" in the various philosophical and popular notions of personhood. Dewey, *supra* note 3, at 658. While Dewey argues that these shifting notions should not affect the legal conception of the corporation, he does not dismiss them as entirely irrelevant. In fact, he acknowledges that these various non-legal considerations "express struggles and movements of immense social import, economic and political." *Id.* at 664.

though we know the various disciplinary theories are bound to matter in different ways for different issues over time.

Dewey preferred to abandon theoretical discussions of personhood and instead focus pragmatically on hard facts and consequences in evaluating legal issues. From his point of view, it does not matter how we conceptualize corporations; all that matters is evaluating the facts and then resolving conflicts by weighing the practical consequences of competing resolutions.

While it is always critical to engage in comprehensive and honest assessments of facts and circumstances when faced with any legal controversy, it is also important not to jettison theory entirely from the analysis. It is error to assume that theory and practice are necessarily separate inquiries. Practice without theory lacks perspective and direction; it results in an admixture of intuitive reactions to specific factual situations. Theory without a connection to practice is hollow and lacks relevance in the face of real world problems; it results in "an intellectual game only vaguely connected to the very phenomena it is supposed to understand and explain."[117] Theoretical and practical analyses go hand in hand and are deeply related. "When we think carefully about practical issues, we are impelled to theorize – although that does not mean that we merely 'apply' a theory."[118] It means that we reflect on how specific cases are connected, how they fit into the big picture, and how they can be resolved to build a more just society. For this reason, it is important to engage in discussions of the various theoretical conceptions of the corporation. We cannot effectively evaluate corporate rights and responsibilities unless we also think about the moral status of corporations. We need analysis of theory as well as practice to decide how best to deal with complicated corporate issues.

MULTIDIMENSIONAL MODEL OF CORPORATE PERSONHOOD

All of the legal theories of corporate personhood offer a partial glimpse into the nature of the corporation. Each one correctly describes but one of the many aspects of the corporate totality. The corporation's existence and functionality depend on individuals, on contractual relationships, on state law and charters, and on social recognition of its identity and presence. The corporation is a legal fiction, but it is a real entity with which we engage daily in a very practical way. All of the legal theories of corporate personhood, and the various features of the corporation that they accentuate, cannot be fully appreciated without an understanding of their interrelationship, and their relationship to the entity as a whole. While the different theories each seek independently to explain the essence of the corporation, the theories in fact are dependent upon each other and upon their integrated roles to provide a comprehensive description of the corporate person.

[117] Hugh LaFollette, *Introduction, in* The Oxford Handbook of Practical Ethics 1, 8 (Hugh LaFollette ed., 2003).

[118] *Id.* at 8.

This book favors a "multidimensional" analysis of the corporation that encompasses the many different conceptions of the corporation.[119] This approach recognizes that all the various legal and non-legal theories of the corporation play a part in describing the full essence of the corporate person. An adequate account of the corporation requires us to view the entity broadly, focusing on its varied roles and multiple purposes. The corporation is a constantly evolving entity that shapes and is shaped by society's shifting views of the nature of corporate life. A multidimensional approach recognizes that the personhood of corporations is dynamic, textured, and ever-evolving. It is an ongoing project that involves continual reflection and adaptation. Rather than embracing one particular theory of the corporate person, a multidimensional approach maintains a broader outlook and integrates the respective contributions made by the various interdisciplinary conceptions of the corporation.[120]

There is no single theory of the corporation that will permanently and neatly solve the legal, moral, philosophical, political, and social issues that surround corporate activity. Our circumstances, our economy, our political structures, our laws, our belief systems, our language, and our culture change over time, and with them, our view of corporations. If we are to resolve important questions about the acceptable role of corporations in our society, it would be helpful to have a richer understanding of the many facets of corporate personhood. A multidimensional approach acknowledges that the concept of the corporate person stems from a mass of legal and non-legal considerations, all of which contribute to our positive and normative view of corporate personhood.[121]

Legal rules and public policies should be sensitive to the multifaceted nature of the corporation. Recognizing both the public and private interests involved in corporate activity, we can acknowledge that both the government and individual business participants have valid claims and expectations that merit attention. Multidimensional analysis allows for the careful balancing of different interests and values to decide important issues involving corporate rights and responsibilities. This may mean continual case-by-case, issue-by-issue, substantive interdisciplinary discussions over significant corporate controversies, which is admittedly burdensome, but increasingly necessary as corporate persons coexist with human persons in the global community. At times, certain personhood concepts, theories, and values

[119] I first proposed and discussed this multidimensional approach to analyzing corporate personhood about a decade ago. *See* Susanna K. Ripken, *Corporations Are People Too: A Multi-Dimensional Approach to the Corporate Personhood Puzzle*, 15 Fordham J. Corp. & Fin. L. 97, 167–74 (2009).

[120] *See id.* at 168. Eric Orts has similarly argued in favor of an "institutional theory" of the firm that skillfully combines elements from the main legal theories of the firm to provide a moderate "middle ground" between extremes. Orts, *supra* note 8, at 12–19. This approach is also consistent with non-legal views of the firm originating in "philosophical and sociological" discourses. *Id.* at 15.

[121] *See* Ripken, *supra* note 119, at 169. In the context of corporate power, Joshua Barkan has similarly observed that an understanding of corporate power "requires investigating the multiple modes of thought and practice that have attempted to define these institutions" and that "these forces are multiple and heterogeneous rather than linear and unified." Barkan, *supra* note 12, at 15.

will take precedence over others for resolving certain issues. A consideration of the practical realities and specific consequences of privileging any given conception over another is also important. In this way, a multidimensional approach encompasses an informed analysis of the various theoretical components that underlie corporate personhood while also being mindful of the practical effects of corporate personhood that were of main concern to Dewey.

Just as corporations evolve and our views of corporations change, the law develops in a continuously dynamic way.[122] The law is not fixed, nor should it be. As many jurists have noted, the genius of the law is that it "is not simply a deductive exercise" or "an inevitable working out of anything,"[123] but rather, it is "a living organism, ever growing and expanding to meet the problems and needs of changing social and economic conditions."[124] As we formulate laws that regulate corporate activity, we should remain flexible and adaptable as various theories of corporations bring different issues to light. The law should not cater to any static conception of the corporation. Instead, it should reflect the dynamic nature of the theories that describe the corporate person, and should avoid any narrow or fixed framework for analyzing corporate activity.

Broad consideration of the different disciplinary theories of corporate personhood will not be without contention and conflict. There will be, as there always has been, discord among the contrasting normative implications of the various theories. Nonetheless, it is worth the effort because it gives us a more in-depth view of a complicated reality. The more complete a picture we have of the subject of debate, the more informed the debate will be. An expansive view of the corporation that incorporates interdisciplinary input does not promise to end the enduring disputes over corporate rights and duties. As corporations change and societal ideas advance, each generation must struggle to find acceptable answers to the difficult questions regarding the legal and moral status of corporations. A multidimensional approach provides a starting point for tackling such questions with the understanding that the answers may be workable for only a period and then require reformulation at a later time. The corporate person is malleable, not fixed, and its role in our society is, in part, a product of our own continually changing moral, legal, philosophical, and political imagination.

BENEFITS OF INDETERMINACY

The indeterminacy of the various theories of the corporation is a perennial concern among scholars who echo Dewey's complaints about the inconsistent

[122] *See* Ripken, *supra* note 119, at 171–72.

[123] William T. Allen, *Our Schizophrenic Conception of the Business Corporation*, 14 CARDOZO L. REV. 261, 278 (1992); *see also* Samuels, *supra* note 102, at 126 (arguing that law does not deduce or discover legal concepts, but rather, makes the rules that then help shape economic reality).

[124] Russick v. Hicks, 85 F. Supp. 281, 285 (W.D. Mich. 1949).

application of theoretical concepts to legal problems. They bemoan the fact that the body of law with respect to corporate legal personhood often seems incoherent and contradictory as different theories are selectively invoked to justify chosen outcomes. There is a sense that judicial use of the personhood theories results in post-hoc rationalizations and in legal reasoning that is purely results-oriented. That the competing theories contribute to the indeterminacy of the law is considered a problem that warrants correction.

The objection to indeterminacy reflects an underlying dissatisfaction with inconsistency in general. Legal scholars naturally seek paradigms that are systematically coherent and produce consistent results. The problem with this preference, however, is that legal issues involving people and groups are complex, and sometimes the preoccupation with consistency can detract from considering the full picture. The fact that various legal theories may not be consistently applied in practice does not mean they should be discarded altogether. Indeterminacy is not a damning charge against legal theories and principles. A general claim of legal indeterminacy simply means that the social construction of law refers to other values and goals that are external to the legal system.[125] These other values and norms may derive from pertinent social, ethical, political, and philosophical considerations, all of which are constantly evolving. Indeterminacy is then "a simple recognition of the inevitable reality of social change and evolution in the law."[126]

From this standpoint, indeterminacy should not be regarded as a bad thing. In fact, we should appreciate the value of indeterminacy in the law and the advantage of having diverse views of corporate personhood. The law retains efficacy and legitimacy precisely because it does not emphatically state that the corporation is *x*. The conflicting themes that underlie the theories of the corporations – aggregate v. real entity, contract v. concession, individualism v. collectivism, person v. property, public v. private, shareholder primacy v. common good – all exist in constant tension. They produce contradictory and complementary visions of corporate life. However, the contradictions should be acknowledged and accommodated, not avoided and spurned. The inconsistencies and conflicts are constructive. They reflect the richness of society's diverse values and norms. Appreciating their interplay in the law enhances our positive and normative view of corporations and their role in society.[127] As a complex entity in which all of these contradictory concepts coalesce, the corporation should not be reduced to a single simple theoretical framework that would necessarily be incomplete. Complex entities require complex rules. Although a multidimensional approach to corporations may result in inconsistent outcomes, it recognizes the reality of the multifaceted

[125] Orts, *supra* note 8, at 118.

[126] *Id.*

[127] *See* Bratton, *supra* note 86, at 465.

nature of the corporate person. The "flaws of inconsistency are far less serious than those of unreality."[128]

Indeterminacy in the law allows for selective application of different theories of the corporate person, depending on the situation and the issues to be decided. Because the corporation is a bundle of contrasting and coinciding concepts, the law must mediate between the various conceptual viewpoints. When a problem occurs that raises two valid but inconsistent normative demands, mediation is required, and choosing between the two is ultimately a matter of judgment.[129] By considering the descriptive and normative components of different theories of the corporate person, the law adopts a thicker, more informed conception of the corporation. Equipped with this broader perspective, the legal decision-maker can make a judgment of better quality, rather than a judgment that reflects only a narrow set of concerns. This may lead to favoring different concepts at different times, but this is the nature of mediation. To aim to adopt a clear-cut, unitary theory of the corporation is to close off the advantage of drawing on the insights of different theories even as they compete. The indeterminacy of the law should not be regarded as theoretical failure, but as the beneficial application of a more nuanced approach to corporate personhood.[130] An expansive, more complete view of the corporation can help us determine how best to resolve corporate issues as they arise. To that end, the following chapters explore other dimensions of the corporation and provide a wide-angle view of its personhood.

128 Alan Wolfe, *The Modern Corporation: Private Agent or Public Actor?*, 50 WASH. & LEE L. REV. 1673, 1676 (1993).

129 *See* Bratton, *supra* note 92, at 214.

130 *See* Ripken, *supra* note 119, at 173–74.

2

Philosophical Dimensions of the Corporate Person

Philosophical theories of what it means to be a person identify those aspects of our existence that are considered to be the most important and that define what it is we essentially are. Philosophers have long theorized over the necessary and sufficient conditions of personhood, but there is no consensus regarding the properties, abilities, and characteristics that are required for one to be a person.[1] Some theoretical conceptions emphasize that only intentional, rational agents can be persons. Others require free will and the capacity to form first and second order desires. Still others focus on consciousness, self-awareness, emotional capacity, autonomy of mind and body, or the capacity for language and inter-personal relations. These elements are viewed as qualities that define what a person is and does. Entities and individuals who do not possess or exhibit these qualities do not fit within the category of persons.

These philosophical views deal with personhood as a moral matter, a category that is broader than what the law defines as legal personhood. To be classified as a moral person is to be deserving of certain moral rights and to be obliged to carry certain moral responsibilities that may differ from, or go beyond, the legal rights and liabilities of legal persons. While legal and moral rights and responsibilities are distinct, they are linked by our philosophical beliefs about the value we place on personhood. Our conception of what rises to the level of being a moral person influences our decisions about the types of legal rights and duties such a person must and should have. Philosophical theories identify the essential features of personhood in order to distinguish between persons and non-persons for purposes of moral and legal recognition. These concepts are invoked when philosophers wrestle with issues involving the personhood of beings that may not have full rationality or autonomy,

[1] The philosophical literature on what it means to be a person is extensive. *See, e.g.*, Peter Carruthers, INTRODUCING PERSONS: THEORIES AND ARGUMENTS IN THE PHILOSOPHY OF MIND (1986); Daniel C. Dennett, BRAINSTORMS: PHILOSOPHICAL ESSAYS ON MIND AND PSYCHOLOGY (MIT Press 1981) (1978); THE PERSON AND THE HUMAN MIND: ISSUES IN ANCIENT AND MODERN PHILOSOPHY (Christopher Gill ed., 1990); WHAT IS A PERSON? (Michael F. Goodman ed., 1988); Catherine McCall, CONCEPTS OF PERSON (1990); THE IDENTITIES OF PERSONS (Amélie Oksenberg Rorty ed., 1976).

such as fetuses, infants, the mentally impaired, comatose individuals, animals, or artificially intelligent forms. The analysis of these issues suggests that personhood, as categorical as it is, may not always be an all-or-nothing proposition.

Whether collective entities like corporations can be classified as moral persons raises difficult questions about the exclusive nature of personhood. Corporate entities might possess some but not necessarily all the features of personhood. Which features are necessary and which are sufficient for groups to qualify as persons? Can philosophical theories of individual personhood be usefully applied to group entities like corporations? Must the criteria for individual personhood be identical to the criteria for a non-human entity to be classified as a person? If the requirements for individual and group personhood differ, could personhood then be regarded as existing along a spectrum, with certain individuals and entities qualifying as persons in different degrees?

The philosophical inquiry into the personhood of corporations involves a certain level of attention to the morality of groups and group behavior. As individuals, we are capable of thoughts and actions that can be characterized as morally and ethically right and wrong. Having moral responsibilities as persons means that our motives and actions are worthy of praise or blame for their consequences, aside from any legal accountability that may arise from them. If I deliberately poison my neighbor, my act is subject to moral condemnation. If a corporation deliberately poisons a neighborhood by leaking toxic chemicals into the air, is the corporate act likewise subject to moral condemnation? Are we justified in saying that the corporation has acted immorally and atrociously? The focus is on the moral blameworthiness of the corporation itself, not the blameworthiness of its individual members. Those individuals whose decisions and actions contributed to the harm may be subject to moral judgment, but does the corporate entity itself bear moral responsibility above and beyond that of its individual human participants? On the one hand, we might argue that the corporation is not a person with moral responsibilities because it has no real conscience or soul. It is simply an instrument that cannot itself be morally responsible for how it is used by intentional agents. On the other hand, it may be plausible to place moral blame on the corporation for some magnified collective acts and intentions that cannot sensibly be attributed to any particular human member.

If it is correct to categorize the corporation as its own person, capable of making moral choices and distinguishing between what is morally right and wrong, then it is reasonable to hold a corporation to certain moral standards and expect it to abide by its moral duties to other persons. To extend this further, if the corporation owes moral responsibilities as a moral person, then is it also owed certain moral rights that must be honored by other persons? While some observers like to say that corporations owe moral duties and can be morally accountable for their harmful acts, the same observers feel uncomfortable with the idea that corporations would also in turn have moral rights to be treated and respected as full-fledged moral persons. They worry that acknowledging the moral personhood of corporations will diminish the status of human persons and eclipse individual rights in the shadow of larger-than-human corporate persons. Thus, there are conflicting normative implications of the corporate moral personhood query. As this chapter explains, the range of philosophical theories both for and against corporate personhood underscores the difficulty with differentiating between individual versus collective activity, identity, and intention.

Before continuing with this analysis, one might be tempted to argue that the issues surrounding individual and corporate moral personhood have little practical significance, and that our main concern should be limited to how the law attributes legal liability for individual and corporate actions. In other words, so long as we make effective practical decisions to structure the law to hold corporations sufficiently accountable, why does it matter whether corporations can be categorized as moral persons who are subject to moral blame or praise?

It matters because the manner in which we construct law is always dependent (whether we are conscious of it or not) on our non-legal, philosophical, moral understandings of the world and its inhabitants. Law is a construct that we create based on who we believe we are, what we believe is just, and how we view our relations with others. In crafting legal rules, we are unavoidably guided by our broader system of beliefs. "[L]aw is based on philosophical principles of justice, fairness, rights, impartiality, and … relies on concepts of identity, responsibility, autonomy, consent, and causal transitivity, which are informed by philosophical debate."[2] The debate over whether corporations are moral persons reflects the non-legal theories and beliefs that influence our political judgments about how laws should be designed to govern corporate activity. Our philosophical understanding of corporate moral personhood and responsibility is then of considerable significance because it is this understanding that contributes to the way in which we ultimately shape the rules of corporate legal liability.

INDIVIDUAL MORAL PERSONHOOD

Philosophers have never settled on one accepted theory of personhood. There are several distinct conceptions of personhood that emphasize different requirements for being a person. One classic view is that rationality and the capacity to reason are the essential characteristics of persons. Persons can make intelligent decisions and act rationally. For Immanuel Kant, reason itself is what gives persons their intrinsic value: "rational beings are designated 'persons' because their nature indicates that

[2] Kevin Gibson, *Toward an Intermediate Position on Corporate Moral Personhood*, 101 J. Bus. Ethics (Supp. 1) 71, 75 (2011). Our understanding of who or what we take to be capable of moral reasoning influences how we shape the laws affecting them. For example, we do not extend full legal rights and duties to children in part because we do not deem them to be full moral persons who are morally responsible for their actions.

they are ends in themselves."[3] The emphasis on abstract reasoning and rationality suggests that only rational human adults qualify as moral persons and bearers of rights. Those who do not have sufficient rationality to reason about moral laws and consequently adjust their behavior in light of them are not persons in the fullest sense.[4]

Another model of personhood focuses on the continuity of self-consciousness and memory. To be a person is to be aware of oneself over time, to be able to say that the past self is the same as the current and future self. To have a memory that allows one to identify with one's past statements and actions is an important feature of personhood. A person feels bound to fulfill commitments he or she made at an earlier time because the person has a certain psychological connectedness with the past and present. This emphasis on memory and consciousness is tied to the concept of one's personal identity.[5] Keeping one's identity over time through a continuance of self-awareness and memory is what makes persons unique.

An alternative theory suggests that personhood depends on having freedom of will, and one has freedom of will only when one can have the will one wants to have. This means that persons have the ability not only to possess certain desires (first-order desires), but also to reflect on those desires and to judge whether those desires are worth having. To want a certain desire to be one's will is a second-order volition, and it is the capacity for second-order volitions that is essential to being a person. Persons "are capable of wanting to be different, in their preferences and purposes, from what they are."[6] This ability to engage in reflective self-evaluation and to have one's second-order desires determine or override one's first-order desires is a distinguishing characteristic of persons.

Under another conception of personhood, only those who are capable of verbal communication can be persons. Verbal communication is not simply transmitting information through sounds, but having the ability to represent oneself to others through speech and to convey one's intentions to others by means of language.[7] Persons have the capacity to reason through language. It is "language that makes possible the general, active form of thinking that we human beings display."[8] To be a moral person who is accountable for actions, one must have the capacity for verbal communication because "only those capable of participating in reason-giving can be argued into, or argued out of, courses of action or attitudes, and if one is incapable of

3 Immanuel Kant, Foundations of the Metaphysics of Morals 53 (Robert Paul Wolff ed., Lewis White Beck trans., Bobbs-Merrill Co. 1969) (1785).

4 *See* Rachel Haliburton, Autonomy and the Situated Self 62–66 (2014) (discussing Kantian conception of the self).

5 *See* McCall, *supra* note 1, at 109–24 (discussing John Locke's views of personal identity).

6 Harry G. Frankfurt, *Freedom of the Will and the Concept of a Person*, 68 J. Phil. 5, 7 (1971).

7 *See* Dennett, *supra* note 1, at 270; McCall, *supra* note 1, at 74–75.

8 Philip Pettit, Made with Words: Hobbes on Language, Mind, and Politics 25 (2008). In the philosophical views of Thomas Hobbes, speech is the source of the capacity to think, not a sign of such capacity. *Id.* at 29–30.

'listening to reason' in some matter, one cannot be held responsible for it."[9] Functioning as a person consists in "giving one's word to others, claiming the ability to represent to others what one thinks and wants, and living up to the expectations this representation supports."[10] Utilizing language, "persons are essentially spokespersons who can give their word to others and thereby 'personate' themselves."[11] The ability to intelligibly articulate one's values, interests, and intentions in language is considered an essential feature of personhood.

There are many other conceptions of personhood that focus on other aspects of being a person, including the presence of a conscience, the capacity for feeling emotions (like shame, guilt, courage, or sympathy),[12] the autonomy to control one's own thoughts and bodily actions,[13] or even the necessity of others outside oneself to recognize and treat one as a person.[14] That there are so many important ways in which a person's essence can be described is an indication of the complexity of personhood and the challenge in determining exactly what being a person entails. Theorists recognize that the scope of many of these philosophical models would allow non-human entities to fall within the category of persons but exclude certain classes of human beings. If rationality, intentionality, memory, and communicative capacity, for example, are essential characteristics of persons, then a thinking android or advanced computer with those capabilities might qualify as a person, while a newborn child or an elderly individual with dementia would not.

Some conceptions of personhood, however, insist that personhood is tied uniquely to the human condition. It may be fine to assume that there are certain criteria, such as rationality, self-consciousness, or emotional capacity, that can be used to identify the category of beings called persons. "But this does not justify the assumption that [these] chosen [criteria] can be understood in abstraction from the quite specific form of life on which they arose; that is, quite independently of the fact that they belong to human beings, and that they have developed out of human life."[15] Personhood has a "thoroughly humanist flavor" because it is "part of the culturally embedded lives we share with others," and our individual and communal lives "are most directly impacted by other members of our species."[16] From this

9 Dennett, *supra* note 1, at 283.

10 Christian List & Philip Pettit, Group Agency: The Possibility, Design, and Status of Corporate Agents 172 (2011).

11 Pettit, *supra* note 8, at 2.

12 *See* Richard T. De George, *Corporations and Morality*, *in* Shame, Responsibility and the Corporation 57, 62 (Hugh Curtler ed., 1986).

13 *See* Elizabeth Wolgast, Ethics of an Artificial Person 64–65 (1992).

14 "It is not my awareness of myself but society's awareness of me that constitutes me as a person." Ross Poole, *On Being a Person*, 74 Australasian J. Phil. 38, 51 (1996); *see also* Dennett, *supra* note 1, at 270 (arguing that whether something counts as a person depends in some way on an attitude taken towards it, that our treating it in a certain way is in some respects constitutive of its being a person). From this viewpoint, we become persons by participating in certain forms of social life.

15 Poole, *supra* note 14, at 47.

16 Adam Kadlac, *Humanizing Personhood*, 13 Ethical Theory & Moral Prac. 421, 435 (2010).

perspective, personhood is very much a feature of human identity, and for all its abstractions, it is a mistake to think that we can understand personhood in isolation from the particular form of organic and social life that is human existence. Under this view, human beings are the paradigmatic persons.[17]

The various modes of understanding the term *person* reveal that there are many ways of conceiving of personhood, and these conceptions are not universal or static. They have evolved over time in changing social and cultural environments. Marcel Mauss has shown how the concept of the person has slowly developed over many centuries (from ancient to modern times), through different cultures and civilizations (both eastern and western), to take on different legal, moral, psychological, and metaphysical meanings.[18] Different societies have formed their own views of personhood "according to their systems of law, religion, customs, social structures and mentality,"[19] and these views are modified as societies move forward in knowledge and beliefs. Even models of personhood that limit personhood strictly to human beings have undergone transformation with advances in biological knowledge and accepted cultural notions of when human life begins and ends. As new knowledge, perceptions, and judgments adjust our thinking, the concept of personhood expands and contracts, "so that even today it is still imprecise, delicate and fragile, one requiring further elaboration."[20] Personhood is not a fixed term or category. "[B]oth the meaning of *person* and the class of individuals who are conceived of as persons can [and do] change."[21]

GROUP ONTOLOGY

Given the many different conceptions of personhood, could modern corporations sensibly be classified as persons? Perhaps we could map the theories of personhood

17 *But see* Dennett, *supra* note 1, at 285 (arguing that the concept of a person is itself normative and even human beings may not fully meet the ideal concept).

18 Marcel Mauss, *A Category of the Human Mind: The Notion of Person; the Notion of Self* (W. D. Halls trans.), *in* The Category of the Person: Anthropology, Philosophy, History 1 (Michael Carrithers et al. eds., 1985). For another account of the historical development and transformation of the person concept in the contexts of law, morality, theology, medicine, and psychology, see Kurt Danziger, *Historical Psychology of Persons: Categories and Practice, in* The Psychology of Personhood: Philosophical, Historical, Social-Developmental, and Narrative Perspectives 59 (Jack Martin & Mark H. Bickhard eds., 2013).

19 Mauss, *supra* note 18, at 3. For a good comparative discussion of various notions of person and self among different European, African, and Asian cultures, see generally The Category of the Person, *supra* note 18.

20 Mauss, *supra* note 18, at 1.

21 McCall, *supra* note 1, at 178. This suggests that "entities are not found to be persons, but rather denied or granted the status of 'person,' . . . according to what 'we,' in our particular societies, decide to be the criteria of personhood" at any one time. *Id.* at 70. From this standpoint, personhood is "a matter of decision rather than knowledge, an acceptance of another being into fellowship rather than a recognition of a common essence." Richard Rorty, Philosophy and the Mirror of Nature 38 (1979).

for individuals onto corporate entities and find sufficient common ground to say that corporations meet the conditions of personhood. To analyze the personhood of corporations in this manner raises questions about the ontology of groups and the nature of group agency. Some might argue that the corporation is only a shorthand reference for its human members, and standing alone, it has no independent existence that can intelligibly be the subject of philosophical attention. An analysis of the potential moral personhood of the corporation presupposes that it exists as a real entity in the world, not just a fiction or a term of art to refer to the underlying individuals. Reminiscent of the debate between the aggregate and real entity legal theories discussed in Chapter 1, the philosophical debate over the personhood of collective entities like corporations involves an inquiry into whether corporations themselves have a real existence that is separate from their individual human participants. If the individual human beings who group together to participate in a corporation are persons, does the act of their collective grouping form a different and separate (corporate) person that stands above and apart from them?

This dichotomy between the "aggregate-ness" and the "separate-ness" of the corporation appears in all situations involving organized collective associations. When individuals formally combine as a group, they maintain their status as individual persons, and yet their combined total also seems to produce something that is distinct from themselves. When we refer to "China," we are not necessarily referring to the sum total of all individual Chinese citizens. Rather, there is a sense in which we mean to refer to the national entity itself that has its own identity as a nation in a global community. We say, for example, that China as a nation must take responsibility for its actions and policies, but we recognize that those actions and policies are formed, approved, and implemented by individual human beings. Without the human members who make up the collective, the collective cannot exist and function. Yet, if we do not recognize the group as an independent agent, then moral rights and responsibilities must attach only to the individual human members themselves, and there is no place for group claims or accountability. All group entities, from churches to universities to corporate conglomerates, present this same quandary. Philosophers have pondered whether such groups are nothing more than aggregates of their individual members who alone can be considered persons, or whether the group becomes something different from the individuals within it, having a distinct group personhood of its own.

Some philosophical theories deny the reality of group agents altogether and instead acknowledge only the existence of individuals. Under an eliminativist view, the group is an eliminable subject because all its so-called actions and intentions are merely the actions and intentions of its human constituents. Anything ascribed to a group, must always be redescribed in terms of the individuals within the group.[22] "[W]hen such individuals cooperate in groups, they do not bring

[22] List & Pettit, *supra* note 10, at 3 (describing but rejecting the eliminativist view).

novel agents into existence."[23] The collective organization has no independent ontological status or metaphysical reality of its own. It is entirely dependent on human individuals to act and think and make decisions on behalf of all the members. References to the group entity are merely metaphorical.

This eliminativist philosophy is implicit in most of the legal and economic theories of the corporation. The corporate person is considered a fiction. It is a concept, a metaphor, created to facilitate legal and economic relationships between real people. There is no group person, but only a collection of human individuals who are linked together by an extensive web of contracts and law. "Corporations have no reality over and above their constituents, because they are created by and function only because of them. Thus, corporations cannot exist independently of their constituency in any ontologically independent way."[24] It makes no sense to speak of the personhood or the moral rights and responsibilities of a non-existent object. Moral rights cannot be conferred nor can moral obligations be imposed upon a metaphor. Without a real and separate corporate entity, there is nothing to serve as the bearer of group moral rights or duties.[25]

The eliminativist position holds that individuals are all that really exist and matter. It is rooted in methodological individualism, which focuses on individuals as the foundation for all social phenomena. Human individuals are always the primary unit of analysis, and groups cannot be understood or explained without reference to their individual members.

But certain individual roles and identities make sense only when they are tied to the larger group. The individual senator, the juror, the quarterback each has an identity that is dependent upon the group of which each is a part. Without the identifiable group – the Senate, the jury, or the football team – the individual's role

[23] *Id.*

[24] Patricia H. Werhane, Persons, Rights, and Corporations 51 (1985) (citing Anthony Quinton, *Social Objects*, 76 Proc. Aristotelian Soc'y 1–27 (1976)); *see also* David Millon, *Personifying the Corporate Body*, 2 Graven Images 116, 123 (1995) ("The description of the corporation as a nexus of contracts not only de-personalizes the corporation, it denies that there is any body there at all.").

[25] *See* Jeffrey Nesteruk, Bellotti *and the Question of Corporate Moral Agency*, 1988 Colum. Bus. L. Rev. 683, 688 n.26 (noting that a philosophy that refuses to grant any ontological status to the corporation renders corporate moral agency impossible). Legal realists disagree with this viewpoint. Favoring a pragmatic approach to corporate moral and legal rights, they argue that philosophical discussions of group ontology are indeterminate and pointless. In their view, certain moral and legal rights and duties can be affirmed or denied no matter which ontological position we take. Emphasizing consequences rather than ontology, they argue that we should not be asking the question "what is a corporation?" but instead ask "why should the corporation have a duty to you?" Richard Schragger & Micah Schwartzman, *Some Realism About Corporate Rights*, *in* The Rise of Corporate Religious Liberty 345, 358–61 (Micah Schwartzman et al. eds., 2016); Steven Walt & Micah Schwartzman, *Morality, Ontology, and Corporate Rights*, 11 Law & Ethics Hum. Rts. 1 (2017). The answer to the latter question, however, may be unavoidably wrapped up in the ontological considerations of the former, i.e., the reason why the corporation has a duty is because it is the kind of person that carries a set of abilities enabling it to make intentional and harmful choices, and therefore it is not unjust to hold it to certain moral standards. That is not an unreasonable answer. It is based on moral rather than instrumental reasoning.

does not have meaning. The individual's identity in that role is defined by the group association.

Without denying the importance of individuals, some philosophical theories argue that groups do have a separate social and institutional reality. This is not to say that they have a mysterious life force, or that they have their own organic existence. Rather, they have a presence and identity that is over and above that of their individual members. Groups are not mere fictions or metaphors. China as a nation is not a fiction. The Catholic Church is not a metaphor. They exist as social realities in perceptible and functional ways in our everyday lives. Groups have a continuing identity through time, even if some individual members leave or die and others take their place. In this regard, the group as a whole is independent of the varying membership and identities of specific individuals. It is the relationships and properties linking the individuals together that give groups a reality of their own and provide a basis for differentiating groups from their larger environment.

There is a sense in which group actions and intentions cannot be equated with or reduced to individual actions and intentions. Utilizing developments in rational and social choice theory, contemporary philosophers show that while groups rely or supervene on the contributions of their members, they can also adopt their own group intentions and pursue group goals in complex ways that do not necessarily match the will and goals of specific human members.[26] The intent and attitudes of the group can be qualitatively different from those of its individual constituents. The group has its own agency and autonomy.

This realist philosophy is implicit in the real entity legal theory of the corporation. Under this view, the corporation is not merely a legal fiction, but a social reality that is reinforced through "experience and settled cultural expectations" with "social consequences that are real, practical, and large."[27] While the corporation does not exist in nature in the same way that material life forms do (such as human beings, plants, or animals), it nonetheless exists as a social institution. "It is constructed, defined, and instantiated through social practice ... [I]t is an artificially created fictional institution that nevertheless has 'real' social effects and consequences."[28] To deny the reality and presence of corporations as group agents is "to miss out on a significant aspect of the social world."[29]

[26] *See* List & Pettit, *supra* note 10, at 59–78. A group can establish and develop "a mind of its own" that is "not just a majoritarian or similar reflection of its members' minds." *Id.* at 8. In fact, in some situations, the group "may even have to form an attitude on some issue that all its members individually reject." *Id.* at 5.

[27] Eric W. Orts, Business Persons: A Legal Theory of the Firm 29–30 (2013); *see also* Richard T. De George, *Social Reality and Social Relations*, 37 Rev. Metaphysics, 3, 10 (1983).

[28] Eric W. Orts, *Theorizing the Firm: Organizational Ontology in the Supreme Court*, 65 DePaul L. Rev. 559, 566 (2016) (discussing contemporary philosopher John Searle's theory of the ontology of social facts and social institutions).

[29] List & Pettit, *supra* note 10, at 4. Some philosophical theories prioritize groups over individuals as an ontological matter, arguing that individuals actually derive their personhood and identity from the institutions of which they are members, starting from the family and progressing to other forms of

It is one thing to say that the corporation is a real entity with an identity that is different from its individual participants. To then decide that this real entity has its own moral status, i.e., it can be characterized as a moral person with potential moral rights and responsibilities, is another. Corporations may exist as real objects in the social world, but that does not necessarily mean they can or should be classified as persons capable of moral evaluation. As the following sections explain, there is strong philosophical disagreement over the moral status of corporations and their capacity to be bearers of moral rights and duties.

CORPORATE MORAL STATUS

Popular sentiment about corporations suggests we have a strong intuition toward ascribing moral responsibility to corporations. People feel justified in directing praise, blame, even moral outrage toward corporate entities for their good or bad actions. Interestingly, cognitive neuroscience studies have shown that our brains understand and analyze the actions of corporations and human beings very similarly. Our minds seem wired to view corporations as social beings, not inanimate objects, and we apply similar mechanisms of moral reasoning and perspective taking when evaluating the actions of corporations and individuals. Moral judgments about both individuals and corporations reflect remarkably similar neural reactions within the brain, with a negative emotional bias against corporations when they are involved in anti-social actions.[30] In recent years, corporate actions have been implicated in cases involving catastrophic financial frauds, devastating environmental disasters, hazardous and defective products, patterns of pervasive employee mistreatment, and sometimes tragic loss of life. Society often condemns these actions as being immoral and inexcusable. There is frustration and anger when it appears that corporations are not held accountable in sufficient measure for these harms. Some commentators view the corporation as a "pathological institution" with psychopathic traits reflecting a greedy single-minded interest in profits and a lack of moral concern for others.[31] Others believe it is senseless to direct our indignation at corporations; instead, we should blame the human individuals within the corporation who alone can bear responsibility for bad corporate acts.

Beyond popular sentiment, the debate over whether collective groups like corporations can be morally responsible agents has divided the field of philosophy for decades. The last ten years in particular have seen a resurgence of interest in the

group fellowship and community. *See* Roger Scruton, *Corporate Persons, in* 63 PROC. ARISTOTELIAN SOC'Y, SUPP. VOL. 239, 239–57 (1989).

30 *See* Mark Plitt, Ricky R. Savjani, & David M. Eagleman, *Are Corporations People Too? The Neural Correlates of Moral Judgments About Companies and Individuals*, 10 SOC. NEUROSCIENCE 113 (2015).

31 Joel Bakan, THE CORPORATION: THE PATHOLOGICAL PURSUIT OF PROFIT AND POWER 1–2, 56–57 (2005); Wade Rowland, GREED, INC.: WHY CORPORATIONS RULE THE WORLD AND HOW WE LET IT HAPPEN 241 (Arcade Publ'g 2012) (2005) (describing the corporation as "sociopathic" in its disregard for human values).

issue. Philosophers and business ethicists have devoted much thought to whether corporations should be held morally responsible for their actions, especially considering the ability of today's large multinational corporations to inflict harm on individuals and the environment on an unprecedented scale. There are two diametrically opposed positions on corporate moral personhood: One holds fast to methodological individualism and its emphasis on individual responsibility, while the other embraces methodological holism and the capacity of groups to carry their own moral responsibilities.

Although the two sides have clearly opposed views, their discourse can be muddled at times with differing ways of framing the debate. The issues are frequently presented in terms of whether the corporation can be categorized as a moral actor, moral agent, moral person, moral subject, or morally responsible being, with some scholars viewing some of these terms as interchangeable and others arguing that these terms each have specific distinct meanings. Depending on how they decide to define each term, some view moral agency as a necessary but insufficient condition for moral personhood, while others view moral personhood as a necessary but insufficient condition for morally responsible agency. One way to make some sense of the jumbled terminology is to focus more specifically on whether the issue involves moral responsibilities on the one hand, or moral rights on the other. The conditions required to hold a person morally responsible are not necessarily the same as those needed to entitle that person to moral rights. For example, very young children have certain moral rights, but we do not place full moral responsibilities on them until they are older and more capable. The first task is to identify the necessary conditions for being a morally responsible person and then identify those that are required to be the bearer of moral rights. Whether corporations can fill these conditions is hotly contested.

In the sections that follow, we will tackle first the possibility of assigning moral responsibilities to the corporation and then discuss the possibility of extending moral rights to the corporation. In each setting, the discussion will begin with an analysis of the arguments against assigning the relevant moral status to corporations, and then proceed with an examination of the arguments in favor of treating corporations as moral beings. As we shall see, the moral status of corporate persons is complex and malleable, continually entwined with, yet conceivably separate from, that of its individual members.

CORPORATE MORAL RESPONSIBILITY

To be morally responsible for an action is to be deserving of praise or blame for the action. It is the kind of causal responsibility that we attribute to agents who act intentionally. An earthquake may be causally responsible for injuring many people, but we do not blame it or say that it acted immorally in causing those injuries. However, a man who purposely drives his car into a group of people and injures them is justly to blame and morally responsible for his act; his car is not. Moral responsibility is reserved for moral agents whose intentional acts merit moral judgment.

Those who argue that corporations are not moral agents view the corporation as being much like the car driven by the man into the crowd. Attributing moral blame to a corporation is "no wiser than attributing intention and blame to a dagger, a fountain pen, a Chevrolet, or any other instrumentality of crime."[32] It is not the corporation that has blameworthy intentions and commits blameworthy acts, but the individuals in the corporation who engage in the wrongdoing. The corporation is a vehicle created and utilized by human beings for their own ends. They alone have the qualities necessary to be moral agents who are morally responsible for their deliberately chosen actions. When they act collectively as a group, they may be individually responsible for their collectively produced outcome, but the collective entity itself does not bear additional responsibility.

One of the central arguments against corporate moral responsibility is that autonomy is a crucial condition for moral agency and that corporations lack the requisite autonomy to be genuine moral agents.[33] Corporations cannot perform actions autonomously because every corporate act is dependent upon the actions of its human members who are themselves autonomous beings. Control is always in the hands of individual members who ultimately are the ones to decide whether to act in ways that constitute the corporate action.[34]

Moral responsibility for an act can be attributed only to the person who originated the act in his own body, a body over which he has direct autonomous control. Since corporate action never originates in a body belonging to the corporation, but in the bodies of human beings who directly control their own actions, corporations do not originate acts in the manner required for moral responsibility to apply. Therefore, it is inappropriate to blame a corporation for acts brought about wholly by bodily movements that are under the autonomous control of agents other than itself. Collective agents like corporations lack the kind of control over their actions that is required for moral responsibility.[35]

Indeed, the fact that the corporation does not have a corporeal body ties into a related argument concerning the corporation's inability to think, reason, and form intentions in an autonomous manner. Moral responsibility requires a person's

32 Albert W. Alschuler, *Ancient Law and the Punishment of Corporations: Of Frankpledge and Deodand*, 71 B.U. L. Rev. 307, 313 (1991).

33 *See* David Rönnegard, *How Autonomy Alone Debunks Corporate Moral Agency*, 32 Bus. & Prof. Ethics J. 77 (2013).

34 Pekka Mäkelä, *Collective Agents & Moral Responsibility*, 38 J. Soc. Phil. 456, 465 (2007).

35 Manuel G. Velasquez, *Why Corporations Are Not Morally Responsible for Anything They Do*, 2 Bus. & Prof. Ethics J., no. 3, Spring 1983, at 1, 7. This has been called a state of "fractured autonomy" in which it is theoretically impossible for one person to take responsibility for actions done by another. One who is fully autonomous acts as a self-legislating individual, commanding oneself to act and acting under one's own direction. Wolgast, *supra* note 13, at 64–67.

actions be intentional, but corporations are incapable of having their own intentions because they do not have minds. Findings in cognitive science suggest the mind is inherently embodied: "[r]eason . . . arises from the nature of our brains, bodies, and bodily experience. This is not just the innocuous and obvious claim that we need a body to reason; rather, it is the striking claim that the very structure of reason itself comes from the details of our embodiment."[36] If this is true, then rationality, intentionality, and the ability to reason are beyond the capacity of the corporation.

Even if it could be conceded that the corporation has certain decision-making procedures and structures that allow it to form abstract group intentions and reasons for acting, those intentions are really just the intentions of its human members.[37] The very act of setting up a system that collectivizes the inputs of individual members to form group judgments reflecting group beliefs is a manifestation of the purposes and desires of the individual members. They have agreed to forego their personal preferences and submit to a corporate decision-making procedure that they have licensed. All of the morally relevant choices are made by the individuals who devise the procedure and agree to abide by its results.[38] Once a corporate procedural decision is made, the organization still depends on its individual members to carry it out.

Moral responsibility requires an agent to be the author or "ultimate originator" of an event, i.e., the agent must "act on springs of action" that are "authentically" its own.[39] The corporation is not the ultimate originator of its derived intentions and actions, and it does not engage in autonomous moral reasoning. It is simply inappropriate to speak *of* the goals and intentions of an organization; rather, we should speak of the goals and intentions *for* the organization of various individual human constituents.[40]

Another obstacle to categorizing corporations as morally responsible agents is that corporate organizations appear to lack the essential component of free will. A person with free will has the capacity for second-order volitions, the ability to reflect upon one's desires and decide which desires are worthwhile, or moral, or better to have than others. One can prioritize one's desires and independently choose to act in accordance with one's preferred desires. Some argue that the corporation does not have such freedom; rather, it is structurally constrained to pursue one set of desires, i.e., to make profits. It is compelled and expected by its members to focus on

36 George Lakoff & Mark Johnson, PHILOSOPHY IN THE FLESH: THE EMBODIED MIND AND ITS CHALLENGE TO WESTERN THOUGHT 4 (1999). The importance of the body exists in many philosophical conceptions of personhood. *See, e.g.*, THE PHILOSOPHY OF THE BODY: REJECTIONS OF CARTESIAN DUALISM (Stuart F. Spicker ed., 1970).

37 Larry May, *Vicarious Agency and Corporate Responsibility*, 43 PHIL. STUD. 69, 71 (1983); Velasquez, *supra* note 35, at 8–9.

38 David Rönnegard, THE FALLACY OF CORPORATE MORAL AGENCY 54 (2015); Mäkelä, *supra* note 34, at 462.

39 Ish Haji, *On the Ultimate Responsibility of Collectives*, 30 MIDWEST STUD. PHIL. 292, 293 (2006).

40 Michael Keeley, *Organizations as Non-Persons*, 15 J. VALUE INQUIRY 149, 153 (1981).

achieving their economic goals. It does not have free will to prioritize other types of desires over those of profit maximization. This is arguably true at least for the for-profit corporation.

In this respect, the corporation appears to be more like a machine than a person. It is unreasonable to expect a machine to comply with the principles of morality. "We cannot and must not expect formal organizations . . . to be honest, courageous, considerate, sympathetic, or to have any kind of moral integrity. Such concepts are not in the vocabulary, so to speak, of the organizational language-game."[41] Corporations could conceivably incorporate moral considerations into their goal set, but these would simply be limiting conditions on corporate action, not an authentic use of moral language or the genuine exercise of free will. These constraints prevent corporations from being classified as morally responsible agents.

Corporations also lack the capacity to feel emotions the way that human beings do. Under some philosophical theories, it is our emotional capacity that lies at the heart of what it means to be a person. It is argued that moral agency stems from an ability to have certain reactive attitudes.[42] Moral agents have a conscience and can feel shame, guilt, anguish, and remorse when they commit bad acts. They can feel sad for, empathize with, and care about others who have been harmed. They can also feel indignant, resentful, and angry when they themselves have been wronged. When their actions are praiseworthy, they can experience joy and pride. Morally responsible people act in moral ways knowing that these emotions will accompany their actions. The capacity for all of these affective responses is an important feature of being a morally responsible agent. Corporations do not appear to have the ability to feel emotions in this way. The corporation's individual members certainly can feel burning shame, searing guilt, or deep sadness if the corporation is causally responsible for a severely harmful act, but the corporate entity itself does not possess those feelings. Even if corporations could be said to be intentional agents with their own purposes, goals, and beliefs, they lack the capacity for phenomenal consciousness and self-awareness that is characteristic of moral agents.[43] Chess-playing computers are intentional and programmed to have certain purposes and goals, but they are not moral agents. They have no real feelings or phenomenal character. If the corporation is viewed in the same way, it has no capacity for the types of felt experience, inner emotional life, and subjective viewpoint that are necessary for

[41] John Ladd, *Morality and the Ideal of Rationality in Formal Organizations*, 54 MONIST 488, 499 (1970).

[42] Thomas Szanto, *Do Group Persons Have Emotions – Or Should They?*, *in* ANALYTIC AND CONTINENTAL PHILOSOPHY: METHODS AND PERSPECTIVES: PROCEEDINGS OF THE 37TH INTERNATIONAL WITTGENSTEIN SYMPOSIUM 261, 266–69 (Sonja Rinofner-Kreidl & Harald Wiltsche eds., 2016).

[43] Matthew Baddorf, *Phenomenal Consciousness, Collective Mentality, and Collective Moral Responsibility*, PHIL. STUD., doi: 10.1007/s11098-016-0809-x (2016); *see also* Amy J. Sepinwall, *Blame, Emotion, and the Corporation*, *in* THE MORAL RESPONSIBILITY OF FIRMS 143, 144 (Eric W. Orts & N. Craig Smith eds., 2017) ("[I]t makes sense to blame only those who can experience guilt, affect is required to experience guilt, corporations have no capacity for affect, and so it makes no sense to blame corporations.").

moral competence. As a result, it would be inappropriate to place moral responsibility on the corporation for its actions.

Those who reject the moral agency of corporations argue that any talk of corporate intentions, actions, or autonomy is always metaphorical and not literal. We can speak *as if* corporations have their own goals and beliefs, or commit intentional actions, or make deliberate decisions, but these are merely metaphorical statements based on analogies to the way human beings think and act.[44] We can say that a corporation is *like* a moral agent, that it performs actions in ways that resemble autonomous intentional behavior. But we cannot say that corporations *are* moral agents, that their intentions are real in an intrinsic, literal sense. The bottom line is that corporations are not conscious, sentient beings, and any attempts to classify them as moral agents are always too much of a stretch because they must rely too heavily on analogies to human behavior.

The underlying theme in many of the objections to corporate moral agency is that because the corporation does not think, act, or feel in *exactly* the same way human beings do, it cannot be held to the same moral standards that we place on human beings. If we cannot prove that corporate intentions are literally the same as human intentions, and that corporations are causally responsible for their own actions in precisely the same way humans are, then we cannot conclude that corporations are moral agents, and we cannot fairly attribute moral responsibility to them. As some philosophers argue, we can never successfully prove that corporate intentions and actions are like those of human beings because, quite simply, corporations are not human beings. They do not have unified conscious minds like humans, and they never will.[45] If the standard for moral responsibility is to have the capacity to think, act, and feel just like human beings do, then nothing other than a human being can ever be a moral agent.

What are the consequences of concluding that corporations are not moral agents and are incapable of bearing moral responsibilities? In situations where the corporation is involved in a harmful act, we must identify the individuals within the corporation who are to blame for their participation in the wrongdoing and hold them morally responsible. The proper subjects of responsibility are the individual members whose decisions and actions caused the corporation to be engaged in the harmful behavior. They will not be able to escape blame by shifting the responsibility onto the corporate entity. Those who espouse an individualist philosophy favor this approach because they worry that if we place moral responsibility on the

44 Manuel Velasquez, *Debunking Corporate Moral Responsibility*, 13 Bus. Ethics Q. 531, 545–47 (2003); *see also* Michael McKenna, *Collective Responsibility and an Agent Meaning Theory*, 30 Midwest Stud. Phil. 16, 31 (2006) (There may be "good moral reasons to treat corporations . . . *as if* they were competent moral agents *even if there is no good metaphysical reason to think that they really are*.").

45 Velasquez, *supra* note 44, at 549–50. "Moral responsibility can be attributed to agents only if they have certain mental states in the same literal sense that humans have mental states." David Rönnegard & Manuel Velasquez, *On (Not) Attributing Moral Responsibility to Organizations*, *in* The Moral Responsibility of Firms, *supra* note 43, at 123, 130.

organization, individual members within the corporation will be let off the hook. Increased attention on corporate moral responsibility threatens to dilute or overshadow individual responsibility.[46] If individual responsibility is minimized, the individuals who escape blame and punishment may have little incentive to correct their behavior and the corporate wrongdoing might recur as a result.

Another worry is that treating corporations as moral agents, and blaming and punishing them for moral violations, results in causing some individuals to suffer for the wrongful acts of others. Any form of corporate punishment necessarily penalizes innocent individuals. The costs of corporate fines and penalties will ultimately be borne by shareholders, employees, and consumers who had nothing to do with the decisions made by the guilty individuals who caused the corporation to engage in wrongful acts. Corporate punishment is inherently vicarious collective punishment that is itself unjust. To avoid punishing the innocent, it is argued that corporations should not be treated as morally responsible agents.[47]

There will be situations, however, when corporate acts cause harm but we cannot fairly identify and hold any one individual in the corporation morally responsible for the harmful action. Many members may have contributed a small part to the decision-making procedure that resulted in the corporate wrongdoing, but they themselves did not understand the larger context, nor did they realize their contribution would be incorporated into a broader process that would result in a wrongful corporate act. If we say in such cases that corporations are not moral agents and cannot be held morally responsible, and no particular individuals are responsible either, who will bear the moral blame for the harm? The answer is no one, according to those who deny the moral agency of corporations. In these situations, the concept of accident applies, not the concept of moral responsibility.[48] To place moral blame on an entity that lacks the kind of autonomy, intentionality, and causal powers required for moral agency is to improperly make a scapegoat of the corporation.

All of these arguments rejecting the moral agency of corporations are vigorously countered by those who believe corporations meet the necessary conditions for being morally responsible agents. They disagree with the individualist position that all group activity is reducible to and must be explained by individual action.

46 *See* Ian Maitland, *How Insiders Abuse the Idea of Corporate Personality*, *in* The Moral Responsibility of Firms, *supra* note 43, at 106, 106–12 (arguing that the idea of corporate responsibility has been exploited to divert responsibility from the human members who have committed wrongful acts, thereby shielding the true wrongdoers from liability and improperly directing the blame and punishment on the corporate entity).

47 *See* John Hasnas, *The Phantom Menace of the Responsibility Deficit*, *in* The Moral Responsibility of Firms, *supra* note 43, at 89, 99–102. Hasnas also argues that there is no practical gain to be derived from attributing moral responsibility to corporations because they are already subject to civil, administrative, and metaphorical liability for their wrongful acts. *See id.* at 94–97.

48 Velasquez, *supra* note 44, at 550; *see also* Rönnegard, *supra* note 33, at 97 ("No one needs to be *morally* responsible for events. There may only be *causal* responsibility where the corporate structure might play an important role.").

Instead, it is argued collective groups have the capacity for certain forms of autonomy, intentionality, and deliberate action that are consistent with moral agency.

Peter French was one of the earliest philosophers to claim that corporations could form intentions that were separate from the intentions of individual members. French argued that corporate intentionality could be traced to what he called the corporation's internal decision (CID) structure. CID structures have two elements: (1) an organizational flowchart delineating the levels of authority within the corporate hierarchy and (2) corporate rules that are usually manifested in corporate policies. To make corporate decisions, the CID structure receives input from various individuals within the corporate hierarchy, evaluates the information in light of basic corporate policies, and engages in a decision-making and ratification process. "When operative and properly activated, the CID structure accomplishes a subordination and synthesis of the intentions and acts of various biological persons into a corporate decision."[49] The CID structure transforms individual intentions and decisions into corporate decisions that reflect corporate beliefs and desires. The collective decision-making procedure can unify the different intentions of corporate members and produce corporate intentions that are distinct from those of the individuals. The corporation might intentionally pursue a course of action that is not precisely the same action that any one member intended that the corporation pursue. It is on the basis of this corporate intention that a genuinely collective action could be attributed to the organization. To the extent intentionality is necessary to be morally responsible, corporations meet this condition because they operate as intentional actors.

These arguments have been bolstered by contemporary philosophical work that asserts corporations are capable of having their own rational point of view (RPV) from which practical deliberation proceeds. The RPV is a logically coherent set of commitments about fact and value, i.e., a logically integrated complex of beliefs and desires that generates corporate actions that are instrumentally rational.[50] When the corporation makes decisions to act in a certain way based on this set of commitments, it does not act randomly or arbitrarily. Instead, it acts in a rational, intentional, and predictable manner, pursuing identified goals for logical reasons in light of a coherent understanding of the empirical situation. Corporations, like other organized purposive collective groups, have an interest in making decisions and acting in ways that are consistent with their stated goals. At times, they inevitably face discursive dilemmas that require them to decide whether to make judgments based on the preferences of the current individuals within the group, or to collectivize reason and make judgments that are consistent with the pattern of judgments and

49 Peter A. French, Collective and Corporate Responsibility 41 (1984).

50 Kendy M. Hess, *"If You Tickle Us . . .": How Corporations Can Be Moral Agents Without Being Persons*, 47 J. Value Inquiry 319, 323 (2013). The concept of the "rational point of view" is drawn from Carol Rovane's analysis of personal identity. Carol Rovane, The Bounds of Agency: An Essay in Revisionary Metaphysics 23 (1998).

commitments the group has previously made.[51] These collectivized judgments may be discontinuous with the attitudes of the individual members, but the group must make the hard choice to act in an organizationally consistent way, even when individual members disagree, so that the group can be a credible and reliable promoter of its interests. If the corporation were to make decisions and act in ways that mirror the desires of its individual members, it would run the risk of being perceived as irrational and inconsistent as it sought to reflect the desires of a continually shifting membership of individuals. "All this means is that corporations have rational reasons for behaving in certain ways because they have interests in pursuing their established corporate goals despite the temporary, conflicting self-interests of managers and directors."[52] Acting in accordance with its organizational commitments leads to a rational unity in the judgments, intentions, beliefs, and desires displayed by the corporation, and this rational unity contributes to the corporation's capacity to be morally responsible for its actions.

If the corporation can have beliefs, desires, and intentions that are not identical to those of its individual members, proponents of corporate moral agency argue that it can be viewed as an autonomous entity with a mind of its own.[53] Corporations adopt certain positions and goals, and they develop strategies and plans for achieving those goals. They are highly structured entities that place individual members in positions to consistently produce corporate actions in line with those articulated corporate goals and plans, regardless of whether the individual members share them. The members may in fact personally disagree with the corporate commitments that are made.[54] "By various means, corporations can and do adopt goals and plans that do not align with – or that conflict with – the preferences of their members, and they establish mechanisms which ensure that the members implement those plans in pursuit of those goals regardless of member indifference or contrary preferences."[55]

In some cases, individual members may be unaware that their attitudes are being incorporated into the corporate RPV, establishing a corporate commitment or mind-set that does not reflect the particular desire of any individuals. For example, in the corporate decision-making process, certain members may be asked for their input on discrete, isolated issues without understanding how their input will be integrated into the big picture. As a result, none of them fully appreciate the larger implications of their singular contributions. The complex decision-making procedure may require

51 *See* List & Pettit, *supra* note 10, at 42–58; Philip Pettit, *Responsibility Incorporated*, 117 Ethics 171, 181–84 (2007). List and Pettit show that in many cases it is not possible for the group decision to be a straightforward majoritarian or non-majoritarian function of the attitudes of the individual members.

52 C. Soares, *Corporate versus Individual Moral Responsibility*, 46 J. Bus. Ethics 143, 145 (2003).

53 List & Pettit, *supra* note 10, at 75–78.

54 *See* Virginia Held, *Corporations, Persons, and Responsibility*, *in* Shame, Responsibility and the Corporation, *supra* note 12, at 159, 171–72; David Troup Risser, *Power and Collective Responsibility*, 9 Kinesis 23, 29–30 (1978).

55 Gunnar Björnsson & Kendy Hess, *Corporate Crocodile Tears? On the Reactive Attitudes of Corporate Agents*, 94 Phil. & Phenomenological Res. 273, 276 (2017).

input from hundreds of members from dozens of different sectors within the corporation over a period of several months or years. It is inappropriate in such cases to say that the final intent of the corporation is really just a reflection of the attitudes of the specific individuals who each played a small role in forming the broader intentionality of the corporation. No individual member deliberately chose or aimed for the final outcome. The collective nature of the corporation's decision-making system transformed the individual inputs, making the individual intentions and attitudes unrecognizable when the final corporate intention was formulated. Looking at any particular collective position or decision does not allow us to confidently deduce the underlying individual preferences or motivations that generated it.[56] In this way, the corporation can be said to have a certain autonomy in developing and holding its *own* beliefs, desires, and intentions.[57]

Similarly, theorists argue the corporation is capable of producing actions that are its own, distinguishable from the specific actions of individual members. When individuals perform actions in their appropriate roles in the corporation, authorized by the proper procedures and consistent with the corporate commitments that result from the corporate RPV, their collective actions become genuinely corporate actions. The larger, global actions ascribed to the corporation cannot be directly ascribed to the individual members. For example, in saying that the corporation "released a new product in the market," we do not mean that any particular individual in the corporation did so. There were numerous actions within the corporation that brought about the creation of the new product and its approval and release for sale to consumers. The combined effect of these individual actions produced the distinctly corporate action of releasing the product into the market in line with the corporation's goals and plans.

The actions of individual constituents themselves are affected and changed by the corporate culture, climate, and actions of other individuals in other divisions of the corporation, and by the ways in which goals are interpreted at each stage of activity. "[E]ach individual input becomes transformed as it mixes with other constituent and agent input and as corporate 'directives' are interpreted."[58] The final result is a collective action that can be attributed to the corporate entity itself.

Moreover, the corporation can be said to have a level of control over these collective actions. If an essential condition of moral responsibility is that one must have autonomous control over one's actions, we might question how a corporation can have the requisite control when its individual members are themselves autonomous agents who are in control of everything they do. One response is that

[56] Meir Dan-Cohen, Rights, Persons, and Organizations: A Legal Theory for Bureaucratic Society 29 (2d ed. 2016).

[57] Kendy M. Hess, *Because They Can: The Basis for the Moral Obligations of (Certain) Collectives*, 38 Midwest Stud. Phil. 203, 208–15 (2014).

[58] Patricia H. Werhane & R. Edward Freeman, *Corporate Responsibility*, *in* The Oxford Handbook of Practical Ethics 514, 523 (Hugh LaFollette ed., 2003).

corporations through their rules, policies, and structural procedures create systems in which individual members must perform certain tasks designed to realize the corporation's goals. The corporation programs the required tasks to be implemented by some individuals, and it does not matter who those individuals are. If certain individuals cannot or will not perform the actions, they can be replaced by others who can or will. The corporation controls for the performance of those actions by acting as the planner or the "programming cause," while the individuals play the immediate productive role of enacting the plan and thereby serving as the "implementing cause" of the corporate action.[59] In this regard, the corporation is the relevant controlling factor in the final corporate action, and this supports the attribution of moral responsibility to the corporation. It is the formal organizational structuring mechanisms, as well as the informal corporate culture and norms, that together form the context in which individual actions take place. These formal and informal corporate practices may persist even as different individual members come and go. Corporations are able to control and change these corporate practices, and as such, may be considered responsible for the outcome of actions that are prescribed by these practices.[60]

This is not to say that individual members are dispensable or superfluous. On the contrary, we know that corporations can act only through their human constituents. The corporation would not have the capacity for beliefs, desires, intentions, and actions without the appropriate contributions from the individual members who form its physical base. The corporation is profoundly dependent on this physical base for the existence, development, and effectiveness of its RPV and for implementing the corporate actions that the RPV generates.[61] Like all collective groups, the corporation must supervene on the contributions of its members for all its activities.

However, proponents of corporate moral agency argue that this is not demonstrably different from ordinary human individuals, since human beings must also rely on contributions from their physical base to form and carry out their intentions and actions. In order to think and act in morally significant ways, individuals must rely on their constituent parts, e.g., their brain, emotions, limbs, organs, neurons, and cells. This does not undermine the individual's control and responsibility for the individual's motives and actions. When a person deliberates over a choice of action, the person's brain is active; neurons fire in the brain as the person engages in deliberate thought. Yet we do not say that the person's neurons are deliberating. We say that the person is deliberating. One's deliberating consists in one's neurons performing their distinctive activities. In the same way, a corporation's deliberating

59 List & Pettit, *supra* note 10, at 162. List & Pettit utilize the concept of "multi-level causality" to demonstrate how the corporation can cause its individual members to act in ways that, in turn, cause relevant actions to occur. *See id.* at 159–63.

60 Mihaela Constantinescu & Muel Kaptein, *Mutually Enhancing Responsibility: A Theoretical Exploration of the Interaction Mechanisms Between Individual and Corporate Moral Responsibility*, 129 J. Bus. Ethics 325, 326–27 (2015).

61 Hess, *supra* note 50, at 326.

consists in its members performing their distinct functions in their appropriate roles within the corporate hierarchy. From this perspective, corporate responsibility is no more reducible to individual responsibility than individual responsibility is reducible to responsible neurons.[62] While we can concede that the corporation is reliant on the actions of its human members, the "agency of the group relates in such a complex way to the agency of individuals that we have little chance of tracking the dispositions of the group agent ... if we keep our gaze fixed at the level of individuals. We will fail to see the wood for the trees."[63]

In line with this reasoning, supporters of corporate moral agency argue that corporations can possess and exercise their own free will. If the corporation is viewed as moving via strings pulled by others, as acting not from its own springs of action but from external sources, then it is not the author or ultimate originator of its own intentions and actions, and it lacks the free will necessary to be a morally responsible agent. However, those who view corporations as moral agents believe that the actions of the corporation are by definition grounded in the corporation's beliefs and desires, which are themselves internal to the corporation through its RPV. As long as the corporation's beliefs and desires come about through the processes that are channeled by the commitments of the corporate RPV, those beliefs and desires can be viewed as the corporation's own; they "originate" in the corporate structure. Since individual members' contributions are limited and shaped by the formal and informal rules and roles that guide members' actions, the corporation is plausibly the ultimate originator of its beliefs and desires, thereby displaying the type of free will necessary for moral agency.[64]

As mentioned previously, opponents of this reasoning argue that corporations are constrained by the profit maximization norm and do not have the free will to prioritize other desires or goals, nor do they have the freedom to choose to act in ways that limit profit making. This observation is valid to a degree, but a corporation does not act only to maximize profits; it acts to maximize profits *in a certain way*. It does have freedom to make choices as to how to make those profits in a moral way if it desires. It has "leeway to act in ways that are better or worse from a moral perspective. In practice, the legal duties of a company will rarely, if ever, *require* directors to take one particular course of action from a range of available options each subject to competing considerations."[65]

To the extent free will requires the capacity for second-order volitions and the ability to reflect upon and weigh the relative worth of one's various desires,

62 Kendy M. Hess, *The Free Will of Corporations (and Other Collectives)*, 168 PHIL. STUD. 241, 249, 257 (2014). One potential objection to this line of reasoning is that an individual's internal body parts are not themselves independent autonomous agents. They are owned entirely by the individual. The corporation, however, does not own its individual members. They are autonomous agents in their own right.

63 List & Pettit, *supra* note 10, at 76.

64 Hess, *supra* note 62, at 249–59.

65 Chris Chapple, THE MORAL RESPONSIBILITIES OF COMPANIES 56 (2014).

philosophers argue that corporations seem capable of engaging in such judgments. Moral agents with free will are able to choose their desires and goals, after careful deliberation and reflection, and revise them in light of moral reasons. Through their decision-making structures and in connection with their RPV, corporations have the ability to consider their values, goals, and actions, and then assess whether they are good or bad, right or wrong, beneficial or harmful. Corporations can have critical or evaluative beliefs that certain values, goals, and actions ought to be desired from a rational, prudential, or moral standpoint.[66] The corporation is capable of having an understanding of the moral quality of what it is doing. It can bring about changes in its beliefs, desires, intentions, and actions in response to normative demands. In light of morally relevant new information or criticism, a corporation can alter its behavior if, in its judgment, the corporation's behavior is determined to be inappropriate based on the corporation's appreciation of the moral aspects of a given situation. In this respect, a corporation is capable of being responsive to reasons and choosing freely to act in accordance with its preferred desires and goals.[67]

Of course, this deliberative process and reason-responsiveness is reliant on the cognition and actions of the corporation's individual members. Some members will propose certain actions, other members will evaluate them in light of the morally relevant information at hand, some members may offer possible amendments or alternatives, others may then provide critical reflection on all the options, still others may assess costs and benefits, and a final group may then draw conclusions and adopt formal plans or actions. The group's deliberation is distributed cognition.[68] The complex nature of the organization with its authority structures and established roles is able to richly employ human cognition and turn individual contributions into the group's reflective judgments. In some sense, corporations can be said to learn and to bring about changes in their behavior in light of moral reasons. "When certain organizational arrangements are in place, an organization will foster the learning of its members [including the learning of morally relevant information] and take the follow-up steps that convert that learning into standard practice. Then it is functioning as a learning system, generating innovations."[69]

Although corporations might be viewed as meeting many of the important conditions for moral agency, there is still the argument that they lack the capacity to feel emotions. Corporations themselves do not experience the reactive attitudes of guilt, sadness, and regret when they have committed a wrong, or the feelings of indignation, anger, and resentment when they have been wronged by someone else.

66 Pettit, *supra* note 51, at 185.

67 Hess, *supra* note 62, at 255. Reason-responsiveness means that an agent is "sensitive to an appropriate *pattern* of reasons" and would "respond in importantly different ways were different reasons present." McKenna, *supra* note 44, at 25. The "range of reasons to which an agent is responsive must exhibit a rich and stable pattern. This pattern must reveal an appreciation for a broad range of sane reasons, including moral ones." *Id.*

68 Deborah Perron Tollefsen, Groups as Agents 129 (2015).

69 Paul R. Lawrence & Davis Dyer, Renewing American Industry 262–63 (1st paperback ed. 1984).

However, supporters of corporate moral agency argue that even if such emotions cannot be felt firsthand, morality is about how we *respond* to each other, not about how we *feel*, and that corporations can respond in ways that manifest the appropriate reactive attitudes in the face of moral wrongs.[70] For example, a corporation can express remorse over a blameworthy act by taking actions and making statements that reflect acknowledgment of the wrong it has committed. It can publicly admit it is to be blamed, take steps to remedy the situation, apologize to victims who may have been harmed, and compensate them for their damages. These would be the same reactions we would expect to be displayed by a human individual who feels guilty for committing a blameworthy act. From this account, the sensation of feelings is not necessarily constitutive of emotions. The fact that corporations themselves cannot experience feelings per se, does not mean that they lack the capacity for reactive attitudes.[71] They are capable of states that are sufficiently similar to guilt and indignation as evidenced by their reactive stances. These states are arguably the "moral equivalents" of emotions and provide support for the moral agency of corporations.[72]

Putting these arguments all together, proponents of corporate moral agency believe that corporations can and should be treated as morally responsible agents even though they do not have the phenomenal consciousness of human beings.[73] We know corporations are inanimate, lack consciousness, and must supervene on the actions of their individual members, but we still have a natural inclination to ascribe responsibility to the corporation for its intentions and actions. In some ways, "acceptance of corporate moral agency seems to be a better reflection of 'reality' in the sense of how most people interpret the world around them."[74] To deny that collective groups like corporations can be morally responsible is akin to arguing that "no state has ever wrongly bombed a city and that no state has ever deserved blame for imprisoning an innocent person. These claims are implausible."[75] There is a sense in which certain actions can occur only through the collectively organized operation of a group, and the group must then bear responsibility for the consequences of those actions. Theorists maintain that complex, sophisticated collective

70 *See* Chapple, *supra* note 65, at 133.

71 Tollefsen, *supra* note 68, at 131 (describing the views of Margaret Gilbert, one of the few theorists who argue that collective groups have the capacity for collective remorse).

72 Björnsson & Hess, *supra* note 55, at 274, 283. That a corporation cannot experience real affect or feelings does not necessarily undermine its moral agency. Indeed, some commentators argue that the emphasis on emotion and feelings is misguided and that moral action is possible in the absence of feelings: "collective guilt feelings are not required for an adequate collective acknowledgment of collective guilt, and the language of feelings is a poor choice." Tracy Isaacs, Moral Responsibility in Collective Contexts 92 (2011).

73 *See* Kendy M. Hess, *The Modern Corporation as Moral Agent: The Capacity for "Thought" and a "First-Person Perspective,"* 26 Sw. Phil. Rev., no. 1, Jan. 2010, at 61; Christian List, *What Is It Like to Be a Group Agent?*, Noûs 1, doi: 10.1111/nous.12162 (2016).

74 Geoff Moore, *Corporate Moral Agency: Review and Implications*, 21 J. Bus. Ethics 329, 339 (1999).

75 David Copp, *The Collective Moral Autonomy Thesis*, 38 J. Soc. Phil. 369, 383 (2007).

groups can transcend their individual members in morally relevant respects and that individualist philosophies lose sight of the real force of collective activity.

Supporters of corporate moral agency reject the argument that ascriptions of moral responsibility to corporations will result in letting blameworthy individuals off the hook or increase the probability that harmful actions will recur as those individuals escape punishment. Corporate moral responsibility does not *replace* individual responsibility, but *adds* to it. Placing responsibility on corporations for their actions "means there is more responsibility in the world, not less."[76] That corporations can be deemed morally responsible does not mean that individuals who can be identified as blameworthy no longer bear moral responsibility for their contributions. There is nothing in the philosophical account of corporate moral responsibility that dilutes individual moral responsibility. Corporate moral responsibility does not free up individuals to dodge responsibility, nor does it increase the risk of recidivism by individual members. Indeed, were we to place blame only on identifiable individual offenders and not hold the corporation responsible, there is every chance that the offending activity might recur because the corporate structure has had no need of change, and it remains poised to repeat the activity with a new set of individuals in place. Something of moral significance is lost when we focus exclusively on placing blame on individuals. We fail to understand and address the larger culture and context in which those individuals are embedded and in which they are pressed to behave in furtherance of collective goals.

There will undoubtedly be times when it will be impossible to inculpate any individuals because blameworthy corporate actions resulted from a series or combination of blameless primary individual actions. No one individual is at fault for the harm caused by the collective corporate act. A large corporation's organizational design may not allow members in different sections of the corporation to communicate effectively with one another, making it difficult for them to foresee the potentially harmful impact of their combined individual actions. It may not be possible to pinpoint individual wrongdoers when numerous individuals are involved in the entire decision-making process, all contributing only a finite amount to the final corporate action. It is a structural feature of the corporation that allows for a nexus of actions by its members to ultimately produce harm, a result that arguably can only properly be attributed to the corporation, not the individuals themselves.[77] In such situations, the corporation should be morally responsible for the policies and practices that provide the environment in which individual actions are likely to combine to cause harm.[78]

[76] Tollefsen, *supra* note 68, at 132; *see also* Isaacs, *supra* note 72, at 65.

[77] Larry May, The Morality of Groups: Collective Responsibility, Group-Based Harm, and Corporate Rights 87 (1987); Michael B. Metzger, *Corporate Criminal Liability for Defective Products: Policies, Problems, and Prospects*, 73 Geo. L.J. 1, 57 (1984).

[78] Paul B. Thompson, *Why Do We Need a Theory of Corporate Responsibility?*, *in* Shame, Responsibility and the Corporation, *supra* note 12, at 113, 123; Patricia H. Werhane, *Corporate and Individual Moral Responsibility: A Reply to Jan Garrett*, 8 J. Bus. Ethics 821, 822 (1989). Failure to hold the corporation

If the corporation is held responsible and punished for its harmful acts, there inevitably will be innocent individuals who will suffer and bear certain costs. Innocent employees, shareholders, and even consumers who had no connection to the blameworthy corporate acts will ultimately feel the consequences of any punishment of the corporation, whether it be fines, penalties, negative publicity, or changes in corporate structure. While this is regrettable, commentators contend that it is not sufficiently compelling to discard corporate moral responsibility attributions altogether. Those who support corporate moral agency argue that innocent members may suffer, but that does not mean they are being unjustly punished for the corporation's wrongdoing. The children whose father is convicted and sentenced to jail for a crime are made to suffer in a way, but it would be wrong to say that they are being punished for someone else's crime or that it is unjust to punish their father. The reality is that whenever there is collective responsibility, "the costs are *always* going to be borne by innocent members," and the collective entity itself, which has no phenomenal consciousness, "will feel nothing."[79] There is no getting around that fact. Yet, this is not a reason to deny the moral responsibility of corporations. That "some members of a group may suffer the consequences of group sanctions is an unfortunate consequence but not something that should question the legitimacy of our practice of sanctioning groups."[80]

Advocates of corporate moral agency also suggest that there are practical reasons for attributing moral responsibility to corporations. They argue that holding corporations responsible serves an important deterrent effect, discouraging future wrongful acts by the corporation or others. It also has an expressive function, sending a message to the community that certain harmful corporate acts cannot be tolerated. Corporations have come to play such a dominant role in modern society, and our dependence on them for our most basic goods and services has become so pervasive, that we seem to be constrained to turn over increasingly greater levels of control and responsibility to corporations. Some commentators believe that corporations with all of their resources, power, and reach should be held to even higher standards of responsibility than human beings.[81] Large modern corporations are capable of committing harms on a scale that is far greater than what individuals alone presumably could do. If responsibility is usually tied with capacity, then corporations ought to carry more responsibility as they have tremendous capacity to do things beyond what individuals are capable of doing alone. Corporations may be better able than human individuals to act in a purposeful, rational, and calculating

morally responsible is said to lead to an overall "deficit of responsibility." List & Pettit, *supra* note 10, at 165.

79 Isaacs, *supra* note 72, at 63.

80 Tollefsen, *supra* note 68, at 133. *But see* Hasnas, *supra* note 47, at 101–02 (Punishing innocent stakeholders of the corporation "is not some unfortunate side effect," but an unjust form of "vicarious collective punishment" because "the harm [intentionally] falls on innocent stakeholders as principals, not as third parties.").

81 Soares, *supra* note 52, at 146.

manner, incorporating vast amounts of information in their sophisticated decision-making processes. Because corporations "have access to practical and theoretical knowledge which dwarfs that of individuals," they arguably "must have, in addition to good intentions, superhuman intelligence."[82] Under this view, corporations should bear even greater moral responsibility than human beings when corporations fail to utilize such intelligence in morally appropriate ways.

While some philosophers agree that corporations should be held morally responsible for their actions, they remain unconvinced by all of these arguments in favor of corporate moral agency. They acknowledge that corporations possess many of the properties of intentionality, rationality, and control that allow us to make moral judgments about corporate actions, but they nonetheless believe that corporations' dependence on the contributions of their individual members bars corporations from rising to the level of full-fledged moral beings. So, for example, various theorists have referred to corporations as, at best, "secondary moral agents,"[83] or "morally significant systems,"[84] or "administrators of duty,"[85] or "restricted persons,"[86] all of which mean that corporations meet the conditions for being morally responsible but they do not enjoy equal moral status with human beings. The point of making this distinction is that it allows corporations to be held to certain moral standards and justifiably blamed if those standards are not met, but it prevents corporations from holding moral rights in equal measure with individuals. It is one thing to say that corporations must carry moral responsibilities for their actions, but it is another to claim that corporations have moral rights and can demand to be treated with the same respect and dignity that are afforded to human persons. As the following discussion explains, philosophers are just as divided on the question whether corporations are capable of possessing their own moral rights as they are on the issue of corporate moral responsibilities.

CORPORATE MORAL RIGHTS

Corporations may meet many of the criteria for moral responsibility, but there is often resistance to the notion that corporations then hold the same moral status as human beings for purposes of claiming moral rights. This is frequently where the terminology of moral personhood enters the discussion. Many scholars distinguish between one who is a moral agent subject to moral responsibilities, and one who is

82 Thomas Donaldson, CORPORATIONS AND MORALITY 125 (1982); *see also* Michael McDonald, *The Personless Paradigm*, 37 U. TORONTO L.J. 212, 219–20 (1987).

83 Werhane, *supra* note 24, at 52–59.

84 James Dempsey, *Corporations and Non-Agential Moral Responsibility*, 30 J. APPLIED PHIL. 334, 344 (2013).

85 Wim Dubbink & Jeffery Smith, *A Political Account of Corporate Moral Responsibility*, 14 ETHICAL THEORY & MORAL PRAC. 223, 233, 237 (2011).

86 Jeffrey Nesteruk & David T. Risser, *Conceptions of the Corporation and Ethical Decision Making in Business*, 12 BUS. & PROF. ETHICS J., no. 1, Spring 1993, at 73, 86–88.

a moral person entitled to moral rights.[87] Some argue that the conditions necessary to establish moral agency and the assignment of moral responsibilities are more stringent than those required to establish moral personhood and the entitlement of various rights. Others argue the direct opposite, i.e., the conditions required to be a moral person with moral rights are stricter than those required to be a morally responsible agent. From these respective positions, corporations are viewed as being either full-fledged moral persons entitled to moral rights, or merely moral agents with no claim to any moral rights at all.

Different theories of rights can be utilized to analyze whether corporations should be considered right-holders. The two dominant theories are the interest theory and the choice theory. According to the interest theory, the function of rights is to further the interests of the right-holder. Rights are viewed as a means of protecting someone's important interests or well-being. A necessary and sufficient condition of being a right-holder is having an interest of sufficient weight.[88] One can be a right-holder even if one does not satisfy the criteria for moral agency and the attribution of moral responsibilities. Thus, young children and the mentally impaired would have moral rights to protect their interests, such as the right to life or to be treated with dignity and fairness, even though their youth or impairments would prevent them from bearing moral responsibilities.

Under the interest theory, corporations arguably could have interests of their own that make them legitimate right-holders. A corporation could conceivably have an interest in being treated fairly, or in preserving its property, or in pursuing its goals without coercive intervention. These interests would be candidates for protection under an interest theory of rights. Critics of this view argue that corporations do not have their own interests. The familiar individualist stance insists that corporate interests are really just the individual members' interests and that groups do not have independent interests of their own. Because any interests that the corporation can be said to have are derivative and reflective of those of its constituents, the corporation itself does not qualify to be a right-holder under the interest theory of rights.

According to the choice theory of rights, one possesses a right only if one has control over the performance of a corresponding duty by someone else. Rights confer control over others' duties to act in specific ways. The right-holder has the choice to enforce or waive the performance of the duty that is correlative with the right.[89] In this regard, rights are fundamentally about choice and control. To qualify

87 *See* De George, *supra* note 12, at 63; Amy J. Sepinwall, *Denying Corporate Rights and Punishing Corporate Wrongs*, 25 Bus. Ethics Q. 517, 518 (2015). In direct contrast, some scholars use the term moral person to refer not to one who has moral rights, but to one who is subject to moral obligations and blame. *See, e.g.*, Michael J. Phillips, *Corporate Moral Personhood and Three Conceptions of the Corporation*, 2 Bus. Ethics Q. 435, 436 (1992). Still others use the terms moral agent and moral person interchangeably to mean any entity that has moral rights and/or responsibilities.

88 Adina Preda, *Group Rights and Group Agency*, 9 J. Moral Phil. 229, 231 (2012).

89 *Id.* at 232.

as a right-holder, one must have the capacity to choose and to exercise the requisite control. Moral agents who are capable of making reasoned choices and controlling their actions are qualified to be holders of rights. Because young children and the mentally impaired are generally not viewed as moral agents who are capable of choice and control, they would be excluded from holding rights under this theory.

Corporations arguably may qualify as right-holders. As discussed previously, many theorists believe that corporations are moral agents with the ability to reason, reflect, deliberate, and make rational choices. Corporations are said to have control over their intentions and actions through their organized internal decision-making systems and structural procedures. If this is true, then corporations meet the conditions not only for bearing moral responsibilities, but also for claiming moral rights. To the extent that proponents of corporate moral agency have established that corporations are autonomous agents who can make morally relevant judgments and exercise control, they also have grounds for arguing that corporations qualify as moral persons with rights.

Opponents of corporate moral agency clearly disagree. They maintain that we speak of corporations as if they have the capacity for choice and control, but in reality it is always the individuals within the corporate entity who are doing the choosing and controlling. Groups do not exist or act as distinct entities separate from their members. From this perspective, corporations cannot be classified as holders of moral rights under any theory.

Many theorists reject the idea of granting corporations moral standing to claim rights. While it may be acceptable to refer to corporations as moral actors or moral agents who must be morally accountable for their actions, it does not then follow that they are moral persons with all the rights that flow from the elevated status of personhood.[90] Corporations may meet all the demanding requirements of moral agency, but even the highly sophisticated moral agency of corporations does not entail moral personhood. It is argued that personhood, with its attendant rights and protections, does not automatically flow from being a moral agent. Something more is required to be a person who is eligible to hold rights.

According to one view, what corporations lack is the real vulnerability that comes with being a person. Persons are physically, emotionally, and mentally vulnerable to certain kinds of painful experiences. They know what it is to feel hurt, to suffer, to fear, and to depend. These vulnerabilities are at the core of our need for rights and protections from the actions of others who would exploit our fragility.

> It is our vulnerabilities, as much or more than our powers, that are both distinctive and constitutive of our personhood. It is only because we persons have the specific vulnerabilities that we do – to physical and emotional suffering, to worry and weariness, to humiliation and despair – that we are entitled to or even in need of the specific protections typically granted to us.[91]

[90] *See* List & Pettit, *supra* note 10, at 158–69, 178–85; Hess, *supra* note 50, at 321.

[91] Hess, *supra* note 50, at 335.

From this perspective, there is no justification for assigning certain rights to corporations for they do not share the same vulnerabilities. Corporations can suffer reverses, or have their interests affected negatively, but they are not subject to physical pain and emotional distress as individuals are. Without the capacity for these types of vulnerable states, corporations are not appropriate bearers of moral rights.

This point ties into a related argument about the intrinsic value of persons. It has been suggested that corporations' lack of capacity for phenomenal consciousness disqualifies them from having their own intrinsic moral significance.[92] Formal organizations such as corporations function like intelligent machines without phenomenal consciousness and the ability to have felt experiences. They are instrumentalities and exist only as means, not as ends in themselves. "As such they are not equal members in the Kantian kingdom of ends, and they do not deserve or admit of the special kind of respect that gives rise to the individual's [rights]."[93] Human persons are ends in themselves, have inherent moral worth, and are therefore deserving of rights. Corporations, however, do not have the same fundamental value, dignity, and worth, and there is no comparable justification for affording the same moral rights to corporations.

We can treat the corporation *as if* it has rights in order to *protect the members* of the corporation. The human individuals who utilize the corporation for their benefit should not lose their rights when they join together and act in the name of the collective group. To mistreat the corporation or to harm its interests is really to mistreat and harm the underlying human beings who are behind the corporate name. We can use the corporation as a placeholder for the individuals and assign it certain rights to represent their interests. Any rights the corporation possesses are entailments of the corporate members' rights. The corporation can be the bearer of derivative rights, or rights that are derived from the human beings within the corporation and that are granted in virtue of realizing their rights.[94]

A similar approach is to say that corporations have secondary moral rights, or rights that stem from their capacity to perform secondary actions, i.e., actions that are constituted by the primary actions of rational autonomous individuals.[95] The contributions of these individuals are what bring about corporate actions, and it is their individual rights that serve as the basis for the corporation's secondary rights. The corporation's derivative or secondary rights will always be weaker and less comprehensive than individual rights. The corporation, as sophisticated as it is, is not itself a moral person in the same way that human beings are, and thus the rights

92 List, *supra* note 73, at 21–22.

93 Dan-Cohen, *supra* note 56, at 55.

94 Lucia M. Rafanelli, *A Defense of Individualism in the Age of Corporate Rights*, 25 J. Pol. Phil. 281, 282 (2017).

95 Werhane, *supra* note 24, at 61.

of the corporation can never supersede or be greater in scope than those of human persons.

There is an asymmetry here in the treatment of corporate moral responsibilities versus moral rights. One might think that rights and responsibilities come and go together, that they function as counterparts of each other. However, many proponents of corporate moral agency assert that corporations can have moral responsibilities but they have no independent or equal claim to moral rights. The justification for this disparate treatment centers around the consequences of extending rights to corporations. The worry is that if corporations are deemed moral persons with their own moral worth, then their claim to moral rights will overpower that of individuals. Corporations would be able to exercise their rights in a way that could challenge, undermine, or trump fundamental individual rights. If corporations themselves are moral persons, then the individual members comprising the corporation would have to be viewed as "lesser moral persons" because they are merely constituent parts of the larger whole.[96] In situations where corporate interests compete or conflict with members' interests, the corporation's rights could possibly override the rights of individual members. This may lead to a dangerous kind of organizational totalitarianism wherein "the corporation, as a larger-than-human person whose ends and well-being are more important than those of its members," becomes so dominant that "the interests of the corporation's members may legitimately be sacrificed to the corporation's interest and the good of the individual may be subordinated to the corporation's good."[97] With full personhood status, corporations will obtain too much in the way of rights and power, effectively diminishing the status of human persons and hindering individual rights.

Those who embrace a form of normative individualism argue that group concerns should never take priority over the needs and interests of individuals. Under a normative individualist framework, a policy is good only if it is good for individual human beings.[98] Because individuals are taken to be the primary units of moral significance, it is argued that the design of our social, political, legal, and economic institutions should uphold first and foremost the interests of human beings and be sensitive to their concerns. In the corporate context, corporations have the potential to dominate individuals and threaten their interests. We must think carefully about affording rights to corporations because of the negative impact they may have on the lives of human beings. Under this view, any allowance of corporate rights must be justified in terms of its effect on the preservation of individual rights and the furtherance of individual interests.

96 *Id.* at 40.

97 Velasquez, *supra* note 35, at 15–16; *see also* Roger F. Gibson, Jr., *Corporations, Persons, and Moral Responsibility*, 21 J. THOUGHT, no. 2, Summer 1986, at 17, 24 ("So what do we moral persons have to gain by admitting corporations into the moral community? Nothing. And what do we have to lose? A lot.").

98 List & Pettit, *supra* note 10, at 182.

Opponents of corporate moral personhood contend that many moral rights simply would not make sense in the corporate context. For example, if the corporation, like a human person, had the right to life, then the involuntary dissolution of a corporation would be a form of murder and a violation of the corporation's moral rights.[99] A hostile corporate takeover would violate the acquired company's moral right to be free and autonomous, negating its right not to be enslaved. How would the corporation's moral right to pursue happiness be defined, or its right to good health? It is one thing to say a corporation should not be dissolved because jobs would be lost or consumers will suffer, but it is quite another to advocate the sanctity of the corporation's so-called moral right to life and the pursuit of happiness. It is argued that these rights, among others, have no logical application in the corporate context and that moral personhood is appropriately tied only to human individuals.

However, the fact that certain rights do not apply in the exact same way to corporate groups as they do to individuals does not necessarily mean that corporate groups cannot have *any* moral rights. It may very well be that corporations are moral persons for purposes of *some* moral rights and that these rights apply to the corporation in ways that are analogous, although not identical, to those of individual moral persons. That some rights may not operate in the same way in the corporate context is not automatic grounds for concluding that corporations cannot be moral persons. Proponents of corporate moral personhood maintain that corporations do have the necessary qualifications for being right-holders and that their capacity for moral rights is very much tied to their capacity for moral responsibilities.

Under one point of view, if we establish that corporations are moral agents who are morally responsible for their actions, then we can also conclude that corporations are moral persons who possess moral rights. This is because moral agency entails personhood, i.e., moral agents are necessarily moral persons. Some theorists argue that the requirements to be a moral agent are higher than those for a moral person, such that if one fulfills the necessary conditions for moral responsibility, one has already met the conditions required for moral personhood.[100] The necessary conditions for holding rights are not as stringent as those for having moral responsibilities. One might be a moral person with rights and entitlements but not have the qualifications needed to be held morally responsible for one's actions. Thus, for example, very young children or mentally impaired individuals by virtue of their

[99] John Ladd, *Persons and Responsibility: Ethical Concepts and Impertinent Analogies*, *in* Shame, Responsibility and the Corporation, *supra* note 12, at 77, 86; *see also* De George, *supra* note 12, at 61 ("If we recognize corporations as moral persons, and if moral persons have the right to life, will we next be told that society has the same obligation to keep corporations alive as to keep human beings alive?"). If a corporation entered into a negotiated agreement to merge itself into another company, would that be a type of suicide?

[100] *See* McKenna, *supra* note 44, at 21 ("[P]ersonhood is a necessary but not a sufficient condition for morally responsible agency."). "[A]n irreducible collective agent must pass an *extremely* high bar in order to be regarded as a morally responsible agent, one that surpasses the already high bar for personhood." *Id.* at 24.

immaturity or incapacities are not morally responsible agents, but that does not undermine their status as persons with moral rights to life, to be treated with dignity, and so forth. Any individual or entity then that can meet the high bar of being a moral agent with moral responsibilities is also necessarily a holder of rights. To the extent corporations have the capacity to carry moral responsibilities, corporations also have a claim to moral rights. In other words, "if corporations are moral agents, . . . then corporations are necessarily moral persons."[101]

From this perspective, moral rights are linked to moral duties; they go hand in hand. Any analysis of corporate moral responsibilities without reference to corresponding corporate moral rights is incomplete. It seems incongruous to argue that corporate groups should be morally liable to others without having any right to make demands of their own. Once we recognize that corporations can have "corporate interests, decision-making capacities, and moral responsibility, . . . consistency requires us to take seriously the rights that companies may have in these regards."[102] If we expect corporations to bear increasingly greater responsibilities and to be held accountable when they fail to fulfill them, then we should be willing to extend to them greater rights and protections as they endeavor to carry out their duties. Likewise, with greater rights, power, and control come greater responsibilities, duties, and accountability. If corporations have moral rights, then they have the obligations connected with them as well. One scholar has argued that although the "precise calibration of rights to responsibilities" is difficult to articulate, there should be some parity with the corporate "basket of rights" and the "basket of responsibilities," i.e., they "should generally be filled or emptied together; their weight should be directly proportionate to one another."[103]

Advocates of corporate moral personhood believe that corporations are "full-fledged moral persons and have whatever privileges, rights and duties as are, in the normal course of affairs, accorded to moral persons."[104] The corporation's rights are not limited to those that are derived from or represent only the rights of their individual members. Rather, the corporation as a moral person with its own intentions, choices, interests, and goals, can possess its own independent, non-derivative, original rights. These rights protect the group itself. The normative individualism that systematically prioritizes the good of individuals over any collective group

101 Sepinwall, *supra* note 87, at 523–24. Some theorists would prefer to deny altogether the status of corporations as morally responsible agents than to acknowledge corporate moral agency and be obliged to accept that corporations can have moral rights. *See, e.g.*, Ladd, *supra* note 41, at 508.

102 Chapple, *supra* note 65, at 187; *see also* Frank Hindriks, *How Autonomous Are Collective Agents? Corporate Rights and Normative Individualism*, 79 ERKENNTNIS 1565, 1566 (2014) ("As obligations and rights go together, responsibility also presupposes rights."); Patricia H. Werhane, *Corporate Moral Agency and the Responsibility to Respect Human Rights in the UN Guiding Principles: Do Corporations Have Moral Rights?*, 1 BUS. & HUM. RTS J. 5, 5 (2016) (If corporations "have responsibilities to respect human rights, then those whose rights are to be respected by corporations have reciprocal obligations to respect corporate rights.").

103 Ronald J. Colombo, THE FIRST AMENDMENT AND THE BUSINESS CORPORATION 98 (2015).

104 Peter A. French, *The Corporation as a Moral Person*, 16 AM. PHIL. Q. 207, 207 (1979).

produces an unjustified regime of unequal standing. Critics of normative individualism argue that to assume something is good only if it is good for individuals is simply to assume one's conclusion, not to present an argument for it. It always and automatically prejudices the answers against collective groups.[105] We could just as easily adopt a competing principle of normative collectivism that assumes policies are good only if they promote the welfare of collective groups and communities rather than individuals. If corporations are the right sort of entities to qualify for moral personhood, then there is little justification for systematically depriving them of the rights that accompany that status.

The moral rights of the corporation do not need to mirror those of individuals. The scope and application of corporate rights may differ from that of individual rights without diminishing the personhood of corporations. Rights that seem uniquely suited to individuals may not be applicable in the corporate context. For example, the individual moral right to bodily integrity (the right not to be physically assaulted) would not be applicable in the same way to a corporation since it has no physical body. Likewise, the individual right to marry a partner of one's choosing or to have children cannot literally be exercised by a corporation. Even the staunchest supporters of corporate moral personhood recognize that collective groups cannot possess and exercise in the same ways all the same rights that individuals have. No one disputes the fact that there are some rights that simply do not logically apply to corporations.

Nonetheless, corporations may have analogous rights or counterparts to individual rights that make sense for the corporation to exercise. For example, the corporation may have claims to the moral right to be treated fairly with equal consideration, to have freedom of choice and action, to enjoy private ownership, or to be free from undue outside interference. Some scholars argue that if corporations truly have the capacities required to be moral agents with moral responsibilities in society, then they possess all the qualities needed to entitle them to rights to engage in the broader social and political processes in which they operate, including the right to vote and the right to political expression.[106] Thus, this discourse into which types of moral rights can be appropriately extended to corporations begins to spill over into the legal realm and engenders arguments about the ultimate legal rights of corporations.

While the philosophical arguments for corporate moral personhood have their own literature, and are distinct from debates about corporate legal rights, the philosophical and legal inquiries have important links to each other because legal rights and responsibilities are often grounded in philosophical understandings of moral rights and responsibilities. Philosophers explain that legal rights are constructed to protect moral rights and that the underlying basis for a legal right is

105 *See* Chapple, *supra* note 65, at 149–50.

106 *See, e.g.*, John Hasnas, *Should Corporations Have the Right to Vote? A Paradox in the Theory of Corporate Moral Agency*, J. Bus. Ethics, doi:10.1007/s10551-016-3172-0 (2016).

a more general moral principle or moral right.[107] Thus, philosophical ideas about moral rights generate justifications for certain legal rights. Although legal and moral rights may not parallel each other exactly, a legal right is often thought to enforce the most important aspects of the corresponding moral right. In this regard, legal rights tend to flow from and follow moral rights. The philosophical dialogue regarding the moral personhood of corporations and their capacity to be moral right-holders suggests that corporations should be entitled to various legal rights that are consistent with their moral status as persons. As we will see in Chapters 4 and 5, various constitutional and legal rights have been extended to corporations to protect certain basic freedoms that are rooted in moral rights. As will be discussed, these are controversial legal issues, and just as philosophers have sharply disagreed over the capacity of corporations to be moral persons with moral rights, so have legal jurists disagreed over the scope of constitutional rights that are appropriate for corporations.

UNIQUE CORPORATE PERSONHOOD

In striving to identify the essential qualities and features that characterize persons, philosophers take human individuals to be the consummate exemplars of personhood. In doing so, some theorists deny that anything other than human beings can be persons. From their perspective, collective groups like corporations can never be persons with their own moral rights and responsibilities because they do not have mental states that are identical to those present in individual human minds.[108] Yet such heavy reliance on standards of individual personhood may not necessarily be warranted. It may be possible to have both human and corporate moral persons without requiring identical sets of elements for each. Although groups do not form intentions, or have conscious minds, or perform actions *exactly* the way humans do, they arguably have rationally equivalent processes that allow us to understand them as making purposeful decisions and performing deliberate actions. This is not an unreasonable understanding. To refuse to consider it seems little more than to reassert that only human individuals can be persons.

Rather than applying the criteria for individual personhood to groups (which will always result in groups coming up short), we could consider the possibility that different criteria exist for groups to possess a form of personhood that is not identical to that of individuals, but still meaningful in its own sense. Notions of personhood are not necessarily universal. If we acknowledge that the standards used for judging individuals need not be the same as those we use for judging collectives, we can view collectives as having a capacity to bear responsibility in their own way. It may be

[107] Werhane, *supra* note 24, at 60, 63; *see also* Dan-Cohen, *supra* note 56, at 49 ("[L]egal rights are, at bottom, moral rights (broadly understood). According to this view, the articulation, the elaboration, the elucidation, and the application of legal rights all require an understanding of and an appeal to some underlying moral considerations.").

[108] *See* Velasquez, *supra* note 44, at 549–50.

better "to treat the moral responsibility of corporations in its own terms, without trying to simply *transfer* the criteria or conditions for individual moral responsibility to the collective level."[109] The fact that corporations lack the phenomenal consciousness of human individuals, for example, would not bar corporations from having moral status. They are still capable of a certain "form of consequentialist cognition about moral questions that . . . in the opinion of many philosophers [is] all the moral competence one needs."[110] In the end, it may not be possible for corporations to be morally responsible in the same way that individuals can be, but they nonetheless can be responsible in a way that is appropriate for corporations.[111] The manner in which moral duties and obligations are incurred, fulfilled, and enforced may be different for corporate entities than for individuals, but those duties and obligations are significant nonetheless.

Perhaps the same might be said for moral rights. Corporate entities may have sufficient autonomy for some moral rights, but not for all the ones that accrue to human beings. Corporate moral personhood does not have to attribute to the corporation the identical set of rights attributed to human individuals. Indeed, certain human rights that apply to human beings by virtue of their biology could not even be logically utilized by corporate entities. While the content and scope of moral rights, and the way in which they are exercised and enforced, may be very different for corporations than for individuals, philosophers suggest that corporations are nonetheless capable of being holders of their own rights. They may not be as extensive or enduring as individual rights, but they are uniquely suited and appropriate for corporations to exercise for limited purposes.

The arguments discussed in this chapter show that we often have an initial tendency to view personhood in all-or-nothing terms. Either one is a person, or one is not. Either one has the full panoply of rights and responsibilities that come with being a person, or one bears none of them. Viewed in this manner, personhood appears to be a fairly straightforward concept, invariably associated with fully rational, autonomous, adult human beings. But the more we explore the nature and contours of personhood, the more we realize it is not that simple. Rather than an either/or, all-or-nothing proposition, personhood might possibly be better described as existing along a continuum. Toward one end of the spectrum, we find merely metaphysical beings or very simple agents who are capable of the most minimal sense of acting intentionally. At the other end, there are highly complex agents who

109 Mihaela Constantinescu, *Attributions of Moral Responsibility: From Aristotle to Corporations*, 62 ANNALS U. BUCHAREST PHIL. SERIES, no. 1, 2013, at 19, 32; *see also* Held, *supra* note 54, at 168 ("[W]e need to recognize two different kinds of responsibility: corporate and personal. Instead of applying the criteria of personal responsibility to corporations, we need to devise criteria appropriate for corporations as distinct kinds of entities."); Kendy Hess, *The Unrecognized Consensus About Firm Moral Responsibility*, *in* THE MORAL RESPONSIBILITY OF FIRMS, *supra* note 43, at 169, 179 (criticizing "the habit of assuming that all moral agency must be like human moral agency in every respect").

110 Chapple, *supra* note 65, at 135.

111 *See* Soares, *supra* note 52, at 143.

in the most robust sense have all of the capacities of full-fledged moral beings.[112] In between, there are a wide range of possibilities for various degrees or categories of personhood. Certain individuals, creatures, or groups, including corporations, may possess some of the qualities that constitute personhood and fall at various points along the spectrum. This may create the possibility for corporations to have certain moral responsibilities that impact how we can expect them to act, along with certain moral rights that affect how they can expect to be treated. The moral life of the corporation may not be as rich or as extensive as that of individuals, but it may be sufficiently meaningful to view corporations as persons to a degree.

To take into account these philosophical and moral components of the personhood of corporations enhances our understanding of the complex nature of the corporation. It is a multidimensional entity with unique capacities and properties that come to light when viewed through the lens of moral philosophy. The theories of corporate personhood that emerge from philosophical inquiry into the nature of persons reveal the complicated philosophical and moral dimensions of the corporation. The theories inform our beliefs about what corporations are and what they are capable of doing. Corporations seem to be more than simple legal constructs or mere collections of people, yet they do not fit within the realm of full moral human personhood. They are in a category of their own, persons to a degree and in a particular sense. As such, perhaps we can hold them to certain expectations that we have of persons, even limited ones. In turn, perhaps they can expect to be held in the regard that persons, even limited ones, are due.

112 *See* Tollefsen, *supra* note 68, at 53; Preda, *supra* note 88, at 233, 241 (discussing the different levels of agency).

3

Social Science Dimensions of the Corporate Person

Several different social science disciplines shed their own unique light on corporate personhood. For example, the fields of organizational behavior, psychology, sociology, economics, anthropology, linguistics, and political science all highlight different facets of the corporate person. They speak to the complexity of the corporation, its role in society, and its powerful influence on human thought and behavior. The large, formally organized corporation in particular is viewed as an independent and active agent that develops a distinct identity and position in the world. It is capable of profoundly affecting and interacting not only internally with the human individuals who are its members, but also externally with the world of people who stand outside of its operations. This chapter will explore both these internal and external sociological dimensions of the corporation to illuminate the nature of the corporation as a person from various social science perspectives.

ORGANIZATIONAL STRUCTURE AND BEHAVIOR

Those who study the structure and processes of large, complex organizations have identified several characteristics that make the organization a unified and distinctive phenomenon. First is the presence of a *hierarchical structure*. The organization has defined levels of authority and activity. They are ordered in a hierarchical pattern designed to coordinate and tie together the various parts into an integrated whole. The organization also displays *permanence*. It has an enduring existence as a distinct entity, even when individual members come and go. The identity of its human participants may change over time, but the organization retains its own identity and functions. Its current decisions are shaped by actions and events occurring in the past (reflecting a sense of memory) as well as those anticipated in the future (reflecting a sense of planning). In this regard, it has a persistence and stability as an independent entity through time. Another feature of the organization is its capacity for intelligent *decision-making*. It is able to collect, analyze, and synthesize information to make deliberate and rational choices to act in line with its preferences. These choices and preferences will not simply mirror those of the individual members but rather reflect the organization's own collective goals and judgments. The organization has a system of processes for bringing individual input together to form independent organizational decisions.

The *large size* of the organization is an implicit characteristic, referring to the large scale of its operations as well as the large number of individuals who are involved in the enterprise. The organization's size contributes to its need for *formalization*. Guidelines become necessary to direct the different kinds of interactions and activities that are to be conducted by the individual members. Formal procedures and policies are put into place as stable directives so that individuals in various positions know exactly what role they are to play and what tasks they are expected to perform. Any individual can then step into a specified position within the organization and understand the formal requirements for carrying out the duties of that position. The *complexity* of the organization is also a function of its large size and structure. The numerous interdependent levels and units within the organization relate to each other in intricate ways and are coordinated to work together effectively as a whole. When the organization ultimately acts or makes a decision, it is the end product of a long and sophisticated set of interactions and processes that involve participants at many levels. The complex nature of the organization's structure and operations makes it difficult to trace the collectively formed intentions and actions of the organization directly to those of any particular individuals.

Overall, the organization is formed to achieve certain objectives, and in this manner, it serves an instrumental purpose. In other words, the organization is *goal-oriented*, and its activities are directed toward attaining specified organizational goals. These goals may have been defined early on by the organization's founders, or they may have developed over time with input from subsequent participants and interest groups. The organization's goals are dynamic, subject to change or displacement. They may not always reflect the individualized goals of any particular members of the organization, but rather may be an outgrowth of systemic functions of the collective nature of the organization itself. All together, these organizational characteristics describe a highly structured, complex entity that is capable of making rational decisions and acting in extraordinarily efficient and effective ways to achieve organizational objectives.[1]

These observations from organizational theory conceptualize the corporation as an independent decision-making entity. It is purposeful and intelligent, capable of learning and applying new knowledge to accomplish its goals more effectively.[2] From this modern, functionalist perspective, there is no need to invoke

[1] These organizational characteristics are discussed by Meir Dan-Cohen and Henry Tosi in their excellent explanations of the distinctiveness of organizations. *See* Meir Dan-Cohen, RIGHTS, PERSONS, AND ORGANIZATIONS: A LEGAL THEORY FOR BUREAUCRATIC SOCIETY 27–33 (2d ed. 2016); Henry L. Tosi, THEORIES OF ORGANIZATION 2–3 (2d ed. 1984).

[2] *See* Mary Jo Hatch with Ann L. Cunliffe, ORGANIZATION THEORY: MODERN, SYMBOLIC, AND POSTMODERN PERSPECTIVES 303–06 (3d ed. 2013) (discussing organizations as self-organizing systems that can learn to learn).

metaphysical or ontological theories to accept that the corporation is a real and functional organizational system.

The corporation as an organizational reality stands on its own as an object of study and evaluation. Researchers in organizational behavior examine individual and group behavior within the corporation from a psychological and sociological standpoint. They have an understanding of the corporation as a separate and distinct agent that has the capacity to affect the thoughts, attitudes, and behavior of individuals within the organization. The corporation is viewed as having characteristics of its own, and these characteristics directly and indirectly influence the actions of its members. In this regard, the corporation takes on subtle elements of personhood, appearing and acting as its own person, having its own identity and presence, moving intentionally and purposefully toward its goals, engaging and interacting with individual members, and affecting their behavior in significant ways.

The manifestations of personhood that are often associated with organizations mirror those of human persons, including such concepts as life cycles, identity, personality, character, conscience, image, reputation, citizenship, and social influence. These dimensions of the organizational person reflect the complicated nature of organizations as macro-versions of ourselves as individuals – "human beings writ large."[3]

ORGANIZATIONAL LIFE CYCLES

Life cycle theorists suggest that stages of growth and development are observed not only in human beings, but also in human organizations like corporations.[4] The concept of a life cycle implies that there is a relationship between one's age and one's development, both physically and psychologically. Maturity in thought and action comes about as a result of the experiential process of moving through various life stages. For example, human individuals experience the stages of infancy, childhood, adolescence, adulthood, and old age. Each stage is accompanied by a particular set of physical and psychological characteristics. Development of the mind and body typically occurs through a sequential cycle and proceeds in an orderly and predictable fashion.

Organizations may also be said to evolve over time and to experience certain life cycles of their own. They move in and out of various stages of growth. As they mature and expand, they learn and develop more sophisticated ways of thinking and operating. They undergo changes in their structure, goals, processes, leadership practices, and so on.

[3] Kenneth E. Goodpaster, CONSCIENCE AND CORPORATE CULTURE 19 (2007).

[4] Eric G. Flamholtz & Yvonne Randle, *Implications of Organizational Life Cycles for Corporate Culture and Climate*, *in* THE OXFORD HANDBOOK OF ORGANIZATIONAL CLIMATE AND CULTURE 235, 237 (Benjamin Schneider & Karen M. Barbera eds., 2014).

Researchers suggest that there are five basic stages in the organizational life cycle: birth, growth, maturity, diversification, and decline.[5] In each phase, the organization assumes a new and different form. The new forms involve changes in the formalization of organizational structures and systems, as well as changes in management focus or strategy. Some life cycle models tie the stages to the age of the organization, e.g., the birth stage may be defined as the period spanning the first ten years of the organization's operations. Other models define the stages in terms of the size of the organization, e.g., the growth stage may be defined as the period in which the organization earns up to $100 million in annual revenues, or employs more than a certain number of people. Alternatively, the stages can be identified in terms of a combination of the organization's age and size.

However the stages are explicitly defined, it is clear that each stage is associated with a particular set of characteristics that describes what the organization is experiencing as it moves through the life cycle. For instance, in the birth stage, the emphasis is on identifying a market need and creating products or services that fulfill that need. The organization's atmosphere is described as creative and innovative. In the growth stage, the organization experiences intense demand for its products or services, rapid increases in sales and expansions of staff, increased financing, and greater formalization of its planning and control systems. The atmosphere often seems intense and frenzied. As the organization enters the stage of maturity, growth may be at a slower pace, the organization becomes more professionalized, and the focus is on increasing efficiency and developing stability. The atmosphere is calmer and more focused. In the diversification stage, the organization must diversify, find new market niches, or innovate in various ways in order to continue to survive and grow. Without such changes, the organization can begin to enter a stage of decline, in which demand for its products and services decreases, product innovation is minimal, and profitability begins to fall. If the organization is unable to define or create new markets for its products, the decline can lead to the ultimate failure of the organization. Unlike human beings, organizations do not inevitably enter stages of decline and death. They can continue to exist indefinitely as long as they are able to maintain healthy patterns and adapt strategically to their changing environments. Transitions from one stage to the next often involve crisis or a mismatch between the organization's current form and the expectations of the stage at which it should be operating, given its size and/or age. In this sense, the organization experiences "organizational growing pains"[6] that signal the need for changes if the organization is to preserve its health and well-being and continue to operate effectively.

Thus, organizational persons can be said to experience life cycles in ways that bear resemblance to those of human persons. Growing up is not easy for humans

[5] *Id.* at 238.
[6] *Id.* at 242.

and organizations alike. Various challenges must be overcome along the way. With age and maturity, a person's values and sense of self change over time. This can also be true for organizations. Just as human persons experience growth and change in their identity, character, and personality as they progress through their life cycle stages, so too do corporate organizations experience transformations in their identity, character, and personality as time passes. As we will see, these aspects of the corporation also reflect the sociological dimensions of its personhood.

CORPORATE IDENTITY

In the psychological and sociological literature, the concept of individual identity involves the sense that a person has about him or herself. It addresses the issue of "who am I?" To claim a certain identity is to focus on aspects of oneself that make one unique or that distinguish oneself from another person. Identity deals with self-referential meaning, or one's attempt to understand oneself.[7] Our past and present experiences, circumstances, and interactions with others help to form our sense of identity, and we can project that sense into the future.

Organizational scholars suggest that corporate organizations can also form and maintain their own identity as persons. The concept of corporate identity refers to how an organization defines itself, i.e., how it expresses and distinguishes itself in relation to others. It is grounded in how the organization's internal members collectively perceive, understand, and respond to the question, "who, or what, are we?" as an organization. A corporation's identity can be viewed fundamentally as that which is "central, enduring, and distinctive" about the corporation.[8] This means that identity involves those features of the corporation that are at its core rather than peripheral, that these core elements persist over time, and that these characteristics delineate how the corporation is similar to and different from others. By invoking a classification scheme and locating themselves within it, organizational members define their organizational identity in a relational and comparative manner, e.g., "we are a pharmaceutical company, similar to, but distinguished from, other pharmaceutical companies in the following ways."

7 Michael G. Pratt, *Disentangling Collective Identities*, *in* 5 Research on Managing Groups and Teams: Identity Issues in Groups 161, 164 (Jeffrey T. Polzer ed., 2003).

8 Stuart Albert and David Whetten are credited with introducing the concept of organizational identity as that which is "*central*, *enduring*, and *distinctive*" about the organization, establishing the widely known CED definition of organizational identity. *See* Dennis A. Gioia & Aimee L. Hamilton, *Great Debates in Organizational Identity Study*, *in* The Oxford Handbook of Organizational Identity 21, 23 (Michael G. Pratt et al. eds., 2016) (citing Stuart Albert & David A. Whetten's seminal article, *Organizational Identity*, *in* 7 Research in Organizational Behavior 263 (L. L. Cummings & Barry M. Staw eds., 1985)).

This view of corporate identity is tied to a "social actor" perspective of organizations.[9] Under this approach, corporations are viewed as persons in society with a status similar to that of individuals. To facilitate this social standing, organizations, like individuals, must be identifiable and distinguishable from others. They become known through their important, enduring, and distinctive features that are then recognized by other social actors around them. Organizations develop their own separate identity as persons who are capable of interacting with other organizational persons and individuals in society. From this perspective, corporate identity is literal, not a metaphor; it is a property of the organization that can be observed, molded, and maintained. It is relatively stable and facilitates the view of the corporation as the same single unitary actor from one day to the next. The corporate identity becomes a critical and essential part of the organization's continued existence. "As an organization acquires a self, a distinctive identity, it becomes an institution. This involves [adopting] values, ways of acting and believing that are deemed important for their own sake. From then on self-maintenance becomes more than bare organizational survival; it becomes a struggle to preserve the uniqueness of the group."[10]

An alternative approach to corporate identity is found in the "social construction" perspective. It focuses on how organizational members interpret and attach meaning to their experience with the organization.[11] Corporate identity is viewed as a socially constructed phenomenon that is constantly being forged as the corporation's internal members interact with each other and with outsiders. Just as human individuals develop their identities over time through social interactions and relationships, corporate identities are formed through the joint communications and experiences of corporate participants. Internal corporate members engage in an ongoing conversation with outside stakeholders who provide feedback as to how they perceive the corporation from their external standpoint. In response to this feedback, the corporate members continually renegotiate their collective interpretation of the organization based on their shared experience.[12] Under this view, corporate identity is not a fixed property of the organization, but a fluid and dynamic concept that is always in the process of being made. This process-oriented approach to corporate identity emphasizes the perpetual work that is needed for corporations to form, maintain, and sometimes attempt to change conceptualizations of who they are.

9 *See* Glen E. Kreiner, *Organizational Identity: Culture's Conceptual Cousin*, *in* THE HANDBOOK OF ORGANIZATIONAL CULTURE AND CLIMATE 463, 464–65 (Neal M. Ashkanasy et al. eds., 2d ed. 2011); David A. Whetten & Peter Foreman, *An Organizational Identity Lens for Organizational Climate Scholarship*, *in* OXFORD HANDBOOK OF ORGANIZATIONAL CLIMATE AND CULTURE, *supra* note 4, at 443, 445.

10 Philip Selznick, LEADERSHIP IN ADMINISTRATION: A SOCIOLOGICAL INTERPRETATION 21 (1957).

11 *See* Gioia & Hamilton, *supra* note 8, at 24–25, 27–29.

12 Hatch, *supra* note 2, at 313–15; Mary Jo Hatch, *Material and Meaning in the Dynamics of Organizational Culture and Identity with Implications for the Leadership of Organizational Change*, *in* HANDBOOK OF ORGANIZATIONAL CULTURE AND CLIMATE, *supra* note 9, at 341, 345–47.

Corporate identity is constantly under social construction. The "enduring" nature of corporate identity is better described as "evolving" or "continuous."

Some scholars believe that both the social actor and social construction perspectives together contribute to a better understanding of corporate identity. Identity formation involves a dynamic and ongoing process in organizations, just as it does in individuals. For people, certain aspects of individual identity stabilize over time and become distinctive identifying features of a person. This happens in organizations as well: "an initial socially constructed framing of an inter-subjective group or social identity may eventually scale up to become a property of the organization as a whole."[13] Under this view, corporate identity emerges through a process of movement from "I think this is who we are," to "we think this is who we are," to "this is who we are."[14] Certain features of corporate identity begin from this interpretative, subjective starting point, but then solidify into objective manifestations of the corporation's institutionalized status as a real and independent actor. Thus, the social construction and social actor models are complementary and work in tandem to explain the ways in which corporations can take on their own identity.

Like individuals, corporations at times can experience identity threats.[15] Organizational crises, competition, and environmental changes can trigger threats to the corporation's identity. These events and occurrences can cause members to question their beliefs about what is central, enduring, and distinctive about the organization. In the face of challenges, corporations at times must change or redefine their identities. Identity scholars note that various life-changing events, such as marriages, births, or divorces can trigger the need for reevaluation of a person's self-definition. Likewise, in the life cycle of organizations, certain marker events such as mergers, acquisitions, takeovers, divestitures, and even periods of rapid growth or decline, can pose the need for reformulations of corporate identity.[16] In this regard, corporate identities are established and reestablished over the course of time in ways that are analogous to that of individuals.

In human beings, identity is linked to one's personality and character. Distinctive personality and character traits are part of what make up one's identity as a person. An organization has something that is functionally similar to a personality or character. It is the organizational culture. The corporation's identity is displayed through its culture, and the culture of the corporation has a significant role in helping to define the corporate identity.

13 Joep P. Cornelissen et al., *Bridging and Integrating Theories on Organizational Identity*, *in* Oxford Handbook of Organizational Identity, *supra* note 8, at 200, 208.

14 Blake E. Ashforth, *Organizational, Subunit, and Individual Identities*, *in* Oxford Handbook of Organizational Identity, *supra* note 8, at 79, 81–84.

15 Jennifer L. Petriglieri & Beth A. Devine, *Mobilizing Organizational Action Against Identity Threats*, *in* Oxford Handbook of Organizational Identity, *supra* note 8, at 239, 239–41.

16 Stuart Albert & David Whetten, *Organizational Identity*, *in* Revealing the Corporation: Perspectives on Identity, Image, Reputation, Corporate Branding, and Corporate-Level Marketing 77, 87–88 (John M. T. Balmer & Stephen A. Greyser eds., 2003).

CORPORATE CULTURE

Corporate culture is the total body of shared beliefs, knowledge, values, goals, norms, and assumptions that make up the way of life within an organization.[17] Anthropologists have long studied culture as a means of understanding how people in a particular group come to interpret the world and each other. Culture embodies the customary and traditional ways of thinking and acting that are widely shared among the members. To describe corporate culture as the character of the organization implies something deep, fundamental, and pervasive about the mindset and the internal workings of the organization. The culture of the corporation has been compared to an iceberg. Only the tip is visible and accessible. The larger and deeper substance is hidden beneath the surface.

The visible part represents those aspects of culture that can be seen, heard, and felt – the artifacts of culture. They include the architecture of the company's physical environment, the office layout, the way members dress and talk, the use of language and technology, the company's products and logos, its rituals, traditions, and ceremonies, and the myths and stories that are told among members to display and reinforce the way of life within the organization. The feel and the atmosphere of the work environment, along with the way that members treat and interact with each other, are part of the culture that develops in the organization. All of these artifacts constitute the first or outer layer of the organization's culture.

Just below the surface lies the second layer consisting of the core values and beliefs of the organization. The outwardly visible artifacts of culture reflect the invisible values of the company. All organizations have a choice as to which sorts of values they will collectively espouse. The values represent those goals and principles that members believe have intrinsic worth. They define what the organization cares about most, and they help to establish how organizational priorities are ordered. The cultural values set forth certain norms and expectations for behavior among the members of the corporation. Norms provide unwritten standards of behavior that express how members should act in order to produce outcomes that are valued by the organization. The norms establish patterns of behavior by ensuring members understand what sorts of actions are considered normal and appropriate, and they create pressures on members to act in organizationally acceptable ways.

The third or deepest layer of corporate culture consists of the organization's basic underlying assumptions. These are the tacit, unconscious, ingrained ideas that reflect what organizational members perceive, think, and feel about their reality. They are considered the taken-for-granted shared assumptions about the world that guide the way members reason and behave in the organizational setting. These

[17] *See* Hatch, *supra* note 2, at 158–61.

underlying assumptions are deeply embedded and sometimes difficult to articulate because they are not always recognized on a conscious level.[18]

Corporate culture is thus multilayered. It is a relatively stable set of elements that helps define the essential character of the corporation. Because the culture permeates and is reflected in so many layers of the organization, it persists even as individual members come and go. A corporation's culture can endure over successive generations, and in some cases, can be difficult to change. While the surface level artifacts might change over time, the core values and deep-seated assumptions of the organization's culture are slower to change. Corporate culture is often perpetuated in part because the members who are attracted to, selected by, and remain with the corporation tend to share the corporation's values and assumptions. These members tend to fit well in the cultural environment. They are likely to agree with and continue the various cultural forms that exist in the organization, thereby reinforcing the culture of the organization as time passes.[19]

This is not to say that cultures remain static or permanently fixed. In fact, cultures are always evolving as corporations encounter changes and challenges in their environment. As the organization's products, markets, technologies, strategies, ideas, and goals change, its mindset and culture can change too. Some organizational theorists argue that culture never stops changing but is in continuous flux as the organization constantly interacts with its environment and its members. Cultures can evolve as organizations move through various stages of the organizational life cycle. Corporate culture might stay fairly steady while the corporation is in a particular stage, but then change incrementally as the corporation enters another life cycle stage. In this sense, culture is both stable and dynamic.[20]

Organizational scholars have identified and observed many different types of organizational cultures. Researchers have developed mechanisms such as the "Organizational Culture Inventory" and the "Organizational Culture Assessment Instrument" to measure, identify, and classify cultural orientations within organizations.[21] Several typologies of corporate culture have been created to categorize and label different types of cultures. For example, a clan culture is characterized by teamwork, a commitment to employees, and a family-like atmosphere; a hierarchy culture embraces formalization, structure, stability, and smooth functionality; an adhocracy culture is focused more intently on being dynamic,

[18] Edgar Schein is credited with developing this three-tiered framework for understanding organizational culture. *See* Edgar H. Schein with Peter Schein, Organizational Culture and Leadership 17–25 (5th ed. 2017). For helpful discussions of the multileveled structure of corporate culture, see Mark G. Ehrhart et al., Organizational Climate and Culture: An Introduction to Theory, Research, and Practice 135–37 (2014); Hatch, *supra* note 2, at 168–71.

[19] Ehrhart et al., *supra* note 18, at 152–53.

[20] *See id.* at 180–83; Schein, *supra* note 18, at 10.

[21] *See* Robert A. Cooke & Janet L. Szumal, *Using the Organizational Culture Inventory to Understand the Operating Cultures of Organizations, in* Handbook of Organizational Culture & Climate 147 (Neal M. Ashkanasy et al. eds., 2000); Benjamin Schneider & Karen M. Barbera, *Introduction, in* Oxford Handbook of Organizational Climate and Culture, *supra* note 4, at 3, 7.

entrepreneurial, innovative, and cutting-edge; and a market culture emphasizes competition, productivity, and efforts to increase market share. Other ways of categorizing and labeling corporate cultures reveal yet a different set of cultures, including a mission culture that emphasizes a shared vision for the future; a consistency culture that has strong values for tradition, conformity, and coordination; an adaptability culture that values flexibility, change, and organizational learning; and an involvement culture that emphasizes team orientation, empowerment, participation, and high levels of organizational commitment. An organization can also be described as having a constructive culture, as distinguished by achievement, self-actualizing, humanistic-encouraging, and affiliative norms; or a passive-defensive culture, as characterized by avoidance, approval, dependent, and conventional norms; or an aggressive-defensive culture that is supported by power, oppositional, competitive, and perfectionistic norms.[22] It is not surprising that there are so many different types of organizational cultures. Just as there is an enormous range of personalities and mindsets among human individuals, organizational cultures vary widely among different corporations. Each corporation has its own unique history, founders, values, goals, and challenges, and its culture will be the unique product of all those elements.

In some ways, the dominant culture or character of the corporation is functionally similar to the concept of personality in human individuals. People have an outer layer, an outward appearance and demeanor that reflect their own personal style and way of interacting with others. People also possess underlying values, beliefs, and assumptions that form the deeper core of their personality and explain why they think and act the way they do. One's personality tends to be fairly stable and constitutes an important part of one's identity. A corporation's unique and enduring culture likewise contributes to its distinct identity. Individual personalities can change over time as people move through different life stages. Similarly, corporate cultures undergo change in different periods of the organizational life cycle. Some personalities are more "likable" than others; some produce more favorable interactions and relationships than others. Different corporate cultures contribute to positive and negative outcomes for corporations as well. Just as psychologists have developed personality tests to assess personality traits and types among individuals, organizational scholars have devised assessment tools to identify the cultural orientations of organizations. From these measures, researchers confirm what corporate managers know very well: Different corporate cultures can play a significant role in affecting the financial and nonfinancial performance of organizations.[23]

22 For discussions of these and other typologies of organizational culture, see Schein, *supra* note 18, at 281–88; Hatch, *supra* note 2, at 172, 186.

23 Sonja A. Sackman, *Culture and Performance*, *in* HANDBOOK OF ORGANIZATIONAL CULTURE AND CLIMATE, *supra* note 9, at 188, 217. Much attention has been devoted in the popular business management literature to the topic of corporate culture. Authors identify the specific traits that are associated with excellent corporate cultures, highlight the competitive advantages of having a strong and healthy culture, and specify the ways in which successful corporate cultures can be created,

The culture of the corporation is not the sum of the aggregated varied personalities of its individual participants who come and go. It is a group level phenomenon that is an integral part of the collective as a whole. In this regard, the corporation stands as an organizational person with a character of its own.

CORPORATE CLIMATE

A related concept in the organizational literature involves the climate of the corporation. While corporate culture and climate seem similar, many organizational scholars make a clear distinction between the two. Corporate climate is not the equivalent of culture, but is a product or manifestation of culture. The climate represents the atmosphere that is experienced by members in the organizational setting. To speak of the climate of the corporation is to refer to how it feels to be in the environment of the organization. Climate is defined as the shared perceptions organizational members have about the corporation and their work environment, about the formal and informal policies, practices, and procedures they see in operation, and about the behavior they see being openly rewarded, supported, and expected.[24] The climate within the corporation is an observable, perceptible artifact of the underlying culture. Culture is broader, deeper, and more encompassing. Culture explains the *why* of organizational behavior, and climate reveals the *what* of organizational culture.[25] Researchers focus on different climates for specific domains of organizational functioning. Numerous dimensions of climate have been analyzed, including climates for service, safety, innovation, justice, leadership, emotion, support, communication, and control.

Corporate climates can have a large impact on what members feel and how they behave in their organizational roles. Positive work environments that are characterized by positive emotional climates, social support, and human flourishing have been linked to higher levels of organizational involvement and commitment, productivity, job satisfaction, and performance. Group efficacy and group creativity is fostered in settings with a positive affective tone. In contrast, climates that are characterized by fear, insecurity, silence, or conflict have been associated with various negative outcomes, including bullying, aggression, absenteeism, and theft.

maintained, and fostered. *See, e.g.*, S. Chris Edmonds, The Culture Engine: A Framework for Driving Results, Inspiring Your Employees, and Transforming Your Workplace (2014); Eric G. Flamholtz & Yvonne Randle, Corporate Culture: The Ultimate Strategic Asset (2011); Edgar H. Schein, The Corporate Culture Survival Guide (new & rev. ed. 2009).

24 *See* Ehrhart et al., *supra* note 18, at 69.

25 *See* Neal M. Ashkanasy & Charmine E. J. Härtel, *Positive and Negative Affective Climate and Culture*, *in* Oxford Handbook of Organizational Climate and Culture, *supra* note 4, at 136. The concept of culture arose from the disciplines of anthropology and sociology, while the concept of climate emerged from the field of gestalt psychology. Until fairly recently, the respective academic studies of organizational culture and climate have long existed on parallel tracks with little overlap. Schneider & Barbera, *supra* note 21, at 3–4.

Negative or unhealthy organizational climates produce worse outcomes for individuals and organizations.[26]

One particular climate that has been the object of significant attention is the ethical climate of organizations. Ethical climate is defined as the shared perceptions of what constitutes ethically correct behavior and how ethical issues should be handled in the organization.[27] The ethical climate of the corporation arises out of its underlying moral and ethical culture. Corporations can have very different cultures with respect to moral thought and action in business. Organizational scholars have identified varying types of organizational moral cultures. For example, in a culture of defiance, members are encouraged to try to skirt around the law, cut ethical corners, and take whatever means necessary to achieve organizational goals, even if it involves bending the rules at times. In a culture of compliance, the organization strives to meet minimally all legal and ethical obligations, not with a sense of enthusiasm, but with a grudging sort of acceptance of law and ethics as a burdensome cost that must be borne. A culture of neglect is characterized by a failure to know or understand the relevant laws and ethical rules binding the business, a failure to detect and deter wrongful conduct within the corporation, or a sheer lack of interest in making the effort to diligently follow the law. In contrast, a culture of character is marked by an express commitment to ethical conduct, a prioritizing of ethical values, and an affirmative desire to do the right thing even in difficult circumstances.[28] The corporation's ethical climate will stem from and reflect its moral and ethical culture.

Researchers have studied various ethical climates and developed models to index them into specific categories that range from prioritizing external laws and standards (law and code climate), internal corporate rules and procedures (rules climate), individual members' personal moral and ethical codes (independence climate), organizational self-interest and company profits (instrumental climate), and the interests of all stakeholders in the business (caring

[26] *See* Ashkanasy & Härtel, *supra* note 25, at 138–42; Charmine E. J. Härtel & Neal M. Ashkanasy, *Healthy Human Cultures as Positive Work Environments*, *in* HANDBOOK OF ORGANIZATIONAL CULTURE AND CLIMATE, *supra* note 9, at 85, 85–87; Tanya Vacharkulksemsuk et al., *Establishing a Positive Emotional Climate to Create 21st-Century Organizational Change*, *in* HANDBOOK OF ORGANIZATIONAL CULTURE AND CLIMATE, *supra* note 9, at 101, 104; Gerben A. van Kleef & Agneta H. Fischer, *Emotional Collectives: How Groups Shape Emotions and Emotions Shape Groups*, 30 COGNITION & EMOTION 3, 12 (2016).

[27] Patricia H. Werhane & R. Edward Freeman, *Corporate Responsibility*, *in* THE OXFORD HANDBOOK OF PRACTICAL ETHICS 514, 523 (Hugh LaFollette ed., 2003). Bart Victor and John Cullen were the first to introduce the concept of ethical climate in organizations. *See* Bart Victor & John B. Cullen, *The Organizational Bases of Ethical Work Climates*, 33 ADMIN. SCI. Q. 101 (1988); Bart Victor & John B. Cullen, *A Theory and Measure of Ethical Climate in Organizations*, 9 RES. CORP. SOC. PERFORMANCE & POL'Y 51, 51–52 (1987).

[28] Ronald R. Sims & William I. Sauser, Jr., *Received Wisdom, Groupthink, and Organizational Ethical Culture*, *in* RECEIVED WISDOM, KERNELS OF TRUTH, AND BOUNDARY CONDITIONS IN ORGANIZATIONAL STUDIES 373, 394–96 (Daniel J. Svyantek & Kevin T. Mahoney eds., 2013).

climate).[29] In some companies, the climates may overlap, or one particular climate may dominate, depending on the type and strength of the underlying overall moral and ethical culture of the organization.

The ethical climate in the organization shapes the ethical decision-making of the members. It influences the way individual members believe they should behave in the face of ethical issues. In general, climates that condone or encourage unethical behavior are related to detrimental ethical outcomes, while climates that support and expect ethical conduct tend to have more favorable correlates.[30] In particular, climates that emphasize integrity, social responsibility, compliance with external and internal rules, and ethical treatment of others are less likely to produce unethical judgments and outcomes. Such climates lead to greater work engagement and dedication, job satisfaction, moral decision-making, organizational citizenship behavior, and success in handling ethical issues. In contrast, instrumental ethical climates that stem from cultures of defiance or neglect are associated with unethical choices, deviant workplace behavior, misconduct, and negative ethical outcomes.

In fact, sociologists have identified certain criminogenic or crime-facilitative corporate systems in which cultural and climatic factors generate or encourage criminal activity within the organization. Corporate cultures with heavy demands to achieve certain profit goals or to meet strict sales quotas can cause employees to resort to deviant practices. The corporate environment presents constant pressures or extremely tempting conditions that facilitate and encourage the commission of crime by corporate members. A recent example involves Wells Fargo, which was required to pay heavy fines and settlement fees when regulators uncovered a system-wide scheme of unlawful sales practices involving the creation of millions of fake customer accounts that were never authorized by customers.[31] An independent board investigation found that the corporation's aggressive sales culture, highly competitive climate, and unrelenting managerial pressures created enormous burdens on employees to meet unrealistic sales goals by selling unwanted and unneeded

[29] David M. Mayer, *A Review of the Literature on Ethical Climate and Culture*, *in* Oxford Handbook of Organizational Climate and Culture, *supra* note 4, at 415, 416. Measurement devices such as the Ethical Climate Questionnaire and the Ethical Climate Index have been used to identify and measure ethical climates in organizations. *See id.* at 416–17; *see also* Stephen P. Robbins & Timothy A. Judge, Organizational Behavior 531–32 (17th ed. 2017).

[30] *See* Jennifer J. Kish-Gephart et al., *Bad Apples, Bad Cases, and Bad Barrels: Meta-Analytic Evidence About Sources of Unethical Decisions at Work*, 95 J. Applied Psychol. 1, 21 (2010); Mayer, *supra* note 29, at 429–30; Dane K. Peterson, *Deviant Workplace Behavior and the Organization's Ethical Climate*, 17 J. Bus. & Psychol. 47 (2002); Müjdelen Yener et al., *The Effect of Ethical Climate on Work Engagement*, 58 Procedia Soc. & Behav. Sci. 724 (2012).

[31] *See* Matt Egan, *Wells Fargo Ups Its Customer Settlement to $142 Million over Fake Accounts*, CNN Money (Apr. 21, 2017), http://money.cnn.com/2017/04/21/investing/wells-fargo-expands-customer-settlement/index.html [https://perma.cc/Q3LV-ZZ2E]; Matt Egan, *Wells Fargo Uncovers up to 1.4 Million More Fake Accounts*, CNN Money (Aug. 31, 2017), http://money.cnn.com/2017/08/31/investing/wells-fargo-fake-accounts/index.html [https://perma.cc/Y24F-Q5KT].

products to customers and opening accounts without their consent.[32] The unlawful activity occurred for over a decade as supervisors and managers continued to place increasingly greater demands on employee performance. The scandal at Wells Fargo illustrates how flawed moral cultures and unethical climates can generate improper conduct. Of course not all individuals will respond in the same manner to organizational pressures, and some people will resist any demands to commit unethical acts. Nonetheless, it is important to recognize the capacity of corporate culture and climate to shape and direct individual behavior in the corporation. In certain cases, "at least some criminal behavior usefully may be viewed not as personal deviance, but rather as a predictable product of the individual's membership in or contact with certain organizational systems."[33]

These findings have normative implications for the morality of group behavior. If moral individual behavior requires the support of the right sort of organization, then corporations should create cultures and climates that do not require people to be heroes of self-sacrifice to do the right thing.[34] It is unrealistic for organizations to rely entirely on individual integrity to guide behavior. People in organizations need ethical guidance, and organizations should provide a context that supports ethical behavior and discourages unethical behavior. The way to develop a more moral organization may not necessarily be by ensuring that all individual members are moral people, but by forming an environment in which ordinary people have reason to act morally.

The ethical climate of the organization could be considered the functional analogue of the moral disposition of an individual. A person's personal ethics and morals help to guide what the person will do when faced with moral dilemmas. Corporate ethical climates likewise guide and influence how the organization and its members will act when confronted with ethical conflicts. In certain respects, the ethical climate serves as a form of group conscience within the organization. Individual human beings have a conscience that moves and constrains their thoughts and actions. One's conscience provides an inner awareness of right and wrong and an ability to evaluate contemplated actions from a moral point of view. Similarly, if an ethical climate provides a sense of ethical awareness of right and wrong actions, the climate acts as the conscience of the organizational person. Corporations that exhibit little or no ethical awareness have been compared to individuals who lack a fully developed conscience, perhaps due to immaturity, disability, or even psychopathy.[35] Because climate can be the result of an organization's culture at a given stage of growth, it is possible for ethical climates to

32 Indep. Dirs. of the Bd. of Wells Fargo & Co., Sales Practices Investigation Report (2017), https://assets.documentcloud.org/documents/3549238/Wells-Fargo-Sales-Practice-Investigation-Board.pdf [https://perma.cc/4JKQ-P382].

33 Martin L. Needleman & Carolyn Needleman, *Organizational Crime: Two Models of Criminogenesis*, 20 Soc. Q. 517, 517 (1979); *see also* Ralph Estes, Tyranny of the Bottom Line: Why Corporations Make Good People Do Bad Things (1996).

34 Edwin Hartman, Organizational Ethics and the Good Life 68, 72 (1996).

35 *See* Joel Bakan, The Corporation: The Pathological Pursuit of Profit and Power 56–57, 60, 134–35 (2005) (referring to the corporation as a psychopath without a conscience).

mature or change over time. As organizational cultures and climates vary with the life cycle of a corporation, research suggests that ethical climates can change as the organization moves through various life cycle stages.[36]

GROUP IDENTIFICATION AND SOCIALIZATION

Corporate culture and climate are not traceable to any one individual alone; they are a property of the group. They are not the aggregate of members' personalities or moods. They are group level phenomena that arise out of the corporation's group history, structure, goals, and values. Social psychology's long tradition of research on groups has consistently emphasized that groups are different from and more than the sum of their individual members. The group takes on an *esprit de corps*, or force of its own. People are highly influenced by organizational cultures and climates because of the power of the group. They are changed and affected by group membership, whether they are conscious of it or not. Corporate cultures and climates shape the thoughts and actions of members as they come to understand what is expected of them, what they must do to fit in, and "how things work around here." There are psychological and sociological dimensions to this that involve group identification, socialization, and integration.

Individuals who become members of groups can come to identify with the group. Organizational identification refers to members' perceptions of oneness with the organization. It involves the extent to which they feel a strong social and psychological connection with the organization. When individuals identify with the group, the group becomes an important part of their self-concept, and they define themselves in part by the same attributes that they believe define the organization. Group identification can be particularly high in certain types of organizations, e.g., nonprofit associations or corporate groups that are formed by individuals who share similar values.

One's self-image can be wrapped up in one's identification with the group. Social identity theory suggests that people can have emotional reactions to the failures and successes of their group because their self-esteem is tied to the accomplishments of the group.[37] Studies show that when members believe that their organization has a positive and desirable reputation among outsiders, members' own self-esteem is enhanced because they have a sense of pride in the organization and their affiliation with it. Conversely, when the organization has a negative or undesirable identity, members' self-concept can be eroded as they experience feelings of shame, embarrassment, and even disgrace.[38] These feelings arise because people form their own

[36] Mayer, *supra* note 29, at 428.

[37] Robbins & Judge, *supra* note 29, at 278.

[38] Kimberly D. Elsbach & Janet M. Dukerich, *Organizational Identity and the Undesired Self*, *in* Oxford Handbook of Organizational Identity, *supra* note 8, at 257, 260; Petriglieri & Devine, *supra* note 15, at 245.

identity in part by membership in groups. "With a societal culture that valorizes a focus on work, the identity derived from organizational membership is increasingly salient and important to people."[39]

Group identification is often the natural result of a process of socialization whereby new members are transformed from outsiders to insiders.[40] Through formal and informal practices, members begin to internalize cultural values, norms, goals, and expectations. The desires and interests of the organization become commingled and integrated with those of the individual. An affinity with the group builds until the individual gains satisfaction not just when his or her personal interests are fulfilled, but when the interests of the group are too. Organizational identification has been shown to lead to greater cooperation and work effort, organizational citizenship behaviors, job satisfaction, lower turnover, and a commitment to advancing the company's goals and purposes.[41]

Human beings are social creatures. Feelings of belonging and acceptance in a group can contribute enormously to a person's sense of well-being and self-worth. However, group dynamics can also exert significant pressures on an individual to conform to group standards even when the individual initially may not be inclined to agree. Evidence reveals that social pressures can lead people to silence themselves to avoid the disapproval of others, or to avoid looking foolish or disagreeable, especially when leaders in the group exhibit confidence in their beliefs and decisions. People generally do not like to be the sole dissenters. They prefer to reach consensus rather than engage in conflict. In certain cases, these pressures to conform can lead individuals to engage in behaviors they otherwise would not. They can also produce group decisions that are not as good as they could have been had individual members disclosed their true concerns and opposing viewpoints.

In fact, group dynamics can produce groupthink, group polarization, and the amplification of errors in decision-making. Instances of groupthink occur when the group's desire for consensus in decision-making is so strong that it overrides the motivation to realistically assess alternative courses of action. As group members begin to think more and more alike, the tendency toward unanimity triggers a process of rationalization, self-censorship, and suppression of dissent. Groupthink can contribute to tunnel vision and group decisions that ultimately produce negative outcomes.[42] Group polarization is also a frequent pattern among

39 Petriglieri & Devine, *supra* note 15, at 244.

40 Daniel C. Feldman & Olivia Amanda O'Neill, *The Role of Socialization, Orientation, and Training Programs in Transmitting Culture and Climate and Enhancing Performance*, *in* OXFORD HANDBOOK OF ORGANIZATIONAL CLIMATE AND CULTURE, *supra* note 4, at 44, 47.

41 Elsbach & Dukerich, *supra* note 38, at 258; Ayla Zehra Öncer & Müge Leyla Yildiz, *The Impact of Ethical Climate on Relationship Between Corporate Reputation and Organizational Identification*, 58 PROCEDIA SOC. & BEHAV. SCI. 714, 717 (2012); Whetten & Foreman, *supra* note 9, at 447.

42 *See* Irving L. Janis, GROUPTHINK: PSYCHOLOGICAL STUDIES OF POLICY DECISIONS AND FIASCOES (2d ed. 1982). Groupthink has been observed more often in case studies than in experimental settings. Social psychologists suggest that groupthink is ubiquitous and occurs not only in highly cohesive groups, but also in everyday ordinary group situations. *See* Robert S. Baron, *So Right It's Wrong: Groupthink and*

groups. Groups tend to adopt more intense or extreme versions of the positions held by individual members before group discussions began.[43] For example, if individual members are optimistic about a contemplated course of action, the group is likely to become even more optimistic as a result of group discussions. If the individual members are tolerant of a high level of risk, the group becomes comfortable with even higher levels of risk. The behavioral research literature has firmly established that groups have a tendency to amplify the errors and biases of their members.

*****

All of these group level phenomena show that groups have a way of taking on their own ethos and dynamics, and they can have significant effects on the way people think and act. The group can be a powerful force that nudges the attitudes and behavior of its members in certain directions, both good and bad. In the corporate setting, individual members can face cultural pressures to conform to organizational norms and expectations. In fact, when corporate cultures are strong and group identification is high, the corporation can affect what members believe will make them happy, in part, by defining what counts as personal success and well-being. In this regard, cultures can shape a person's second-order desires, causing one not only to want certain things, but also to want to want them, i.e., to desire to be the type of person who values these things.[44] For example, in a corporate culture that values competitiveness, members may not only want to win, but also want to be the sort of persons who genuinely value winning. To the extent individuals' values and principles are shaped by their corporate environment, the individuals are in some sense creatures of the corporation, rather than the other way around.

It is true that corporations would not exist without individuals, but it is equally true that phenomena such as corporate culture or group polarization would not exist without collective organizations. Altogether, the social and psychological dimensions of organizational behavior suggest that the corporation itself is something greater than the aggregation of its individual members. It seems to be its own person with an independent identity and character. It can form a corporate personality, ethos, and belief system that influence its individual members in real and palpable ways. If corporate culture can be viewed as the character of the corporate person, it not only affects individuals within the organization, but it also affects how the corporation is perceived by people who are external to its operations. As the next sections explain, there are external sociological dimensions to the corporation that are also an important part of its personhood.

the Ubiquitous Nature of Polarized Group Decision Making, in 37 Advances Experimental Soc. Psychol. 219, 228 (Mark P. Zanna ed., 2005).

43 Donelson R. Forsyth, Group Dynamics 382–85 (6th ed. 2014); Cass R. Sunstein & Reid Hastie, Wiser: Getting Beyond Groupthink to Make Groups Smarter 77–88 (2015).

44 *See* Hartman, *supra* note 34, at 152–53; Edwin M. Hartman, *The Commons and the Moral Organization*, 4 Bus. Ethics Q. 253, 255 (1994).

BRAND IDENTITY IN SOCIETY

As social institutions, corporations have a strong presence in society. They are ubiquitous. Places of public enjoyment like sports stadiums, parks, and concert venues all bear corporate names today. Popular culture is filled with images of specific corporate personalities. Colonel Sanders and the GEICO Gecko are easily identifiable corporate symbols. Corporate slogans such as "Just Do It" for Nike, and "The Happiest Place on Earth" for Disneyland, help to form corporations' external personality. These symbols and slogans have a way of personifying and linking the corporation to the public. They do so by creating intellectual and emotional bonds with people.[45] Corporations as social beings seek to project a particular image and have an enduring relationship with other members of society. In this way, they display elements of personhood that involve heightened self-awareness as well as inter-personal relations.

The brand identity of the corporation is a significant part of its persona. Corporations recognize the importance and influence of their brand as an element of who they are and how their image is perceived by others. A corporation's image and reputation are enormously valuable to the company. The total value of the top ten global brands in 2017 was estimated to be close to $790 billion.[46]

The significance of the corporation's brand identity lies in its ability to present the corporation as a social person to whom others can relate. Corporations use branding techniques to create unique and attractive identities for themselves. With a distinct and identifiable brand, a corporation distinguishes itself from others and builds its own community of followers or loyal friends. Corporate brands allow corporations to form strong personal ties with those who like and embrace the brands. People use brands to help define who they are, to express themselves, and to form their own self-identity.[47] To drive a certain type of car, wear a certain type of watch, or carry a certain type of handbag, is to say something to the world about who one is or wishes to be. Corporate brands simultaneously allow one to feel a sense of belonging with similar others and a sense of differentiation from people with dissimilar status or interests.[48]

In some sense, the corporation acts like a person in a friendship group. It tries to form relationships with people who can or want to identify with it. Through its brand

45 *See* Giep Franzen & Margot Bouwman, The Mental World of Brands: Mind, Memory and Brand Success (2001); Marc Gobé, Emotional Branding: The New Paradigm for Connecting Brands to People (2001).

46 *See* Interbrand, *Best Global Brands 2017 Rankings*, www.interbrand.com/best-brands/best-global-brands/2017/ranking/ [https://perma.cc/QD6E-CDNT].

47 *See* John M. T. Balmer, *Corporate Brand Cultures and Communities*, *in* Brand Culture 34, 36–37 (Jonathan E. Schroeder & Miriam Salzer-Mörling eds., 2006); Wally Olins, *How Brands Are Taking over the Corporation*, *in* The Expressive Organization: Linking Identity, Reputation, and the Corporate Brand 51, 62–63 (Majken Schultz et al. eds., 2000).

48 *See* Mary Jo Hatch & Majken Schultz, Taking Brand Initiative: How Companies Can Align Strategy, Culture, and Identity Through Corporate Branding 22 (2008).

identity, the corporation seeks to be a popular, likeable person with whom others may want to associate. The corporation's brand identity not only creates a bond between the corporation and its customers, but also fosters social bonds among customers who share enthusiasm for the brand. They feel an affinity for people who are similar to them in tastes and style. Thus, the corporation's identity can be very influential in shaping the personal and social identities of its individual stakeholders. Corporations recognize the importance and power of their brands as an integral feature of their identity and influence in society.

People also view corporations as having certain personalities that are part of their corporate identity. Corporations are perceived as having various personality traits that can be described in the same sorts of terms that are used to describe individuals: "Apple is innovative," "LEGO is fun," and "Disney is creative." The corporation projects a particular image as a person with human-like characteristics.

We generally have anthropomorphic tendencies to assign human qualities to non-human organisms and objects. For example, we attribute human characteristics to animals, machines, and even simple geometric figures moving on a screen.[49] Yet with collective groups like corporations, there seems to be something more than mere anthropomorphic inclinations when we speak of corporations as having their own identity, culture, and personality. The language that is used to talk about corporate entities reflects a conception of corporations as persons with capacities for intentionality, moral responsibility, and character. In fact, as the next section explains, analysis of the way we linguistically refer to corporate activity reveals a lot about how our minds and language are constituted to perceive and describe corporations as independent persons.

LINGUISTIC TREATMENT OF CORPORATIONS

Our regular interactions with corporations and the way we personify them in our ordinary discourse reflects and reinforces our tendency to regard them as persons. Linguistics scholars maintain that our everyday language and speech patterns affirm our view of corporations as real persons.[50] Our normal linguistic usage places corporations in the position of having dispositions and displaying behaviors that we typically associate with individuals. We regard corporations as being able to "act," "decide," "think," and "desire." We say, for example, that Walmart *denied* that

49 *See* Kristin Andrews, *Beyond Anthropomorphism: Attributing Psychological Properties to Animals*, *in* The Oxford Handbook of Animal Ethics 469 (Tom L. Beauchamp & R. G. Frey eds., 2011); Fritz Heider & Marianne Simmel, *An Experimental Study of Apparent Behavior*, 57 Am. J. Psychol. 243 (1944); Paul Morris et al., *Beyond Anecdotes: An Empirical Study of "Anthropomorphism,"* 8 Soc'y & Animals 151 (2000); Paola Riva et al., *Humanizing Machines: Anthropomorphization of Slot Machines Increases Gambling*, 21 J. Experimental Psychol. Applied 313 (2015).

50 *See, e.g.*, Sanford A. Schane, *The Corporation Is a Person: The Language of a Legal Fiction*, 61 Tul. L. Rev. 563 (1987).

it *knew* about the wrongdoing, Amazon *believes* it *treats* its employees fairly, Microsoft *was thrilled* about its victory in court, and Facebook *loves* the millennial generation. We readily use these sorts of cognitive verbs, which depict mental states, to describe corporations. We also employ various activity verbs to explain what corporations do. When we say the company *discriminated*, or *covered up* the mistake, or *undermined* its competitor, the words themselves show how we understand corporations to be their own persons with the capacity to act and bear responsibility for their actions. When these cognitive and activity verbs are used with corporations as nouns, the verbs have essentially the same meaning that they have with human persons as nouns.[51] Our vernacular implies that corporations have human-like capacities and qualities. "So far as language is concerned, institutions do not have bodies . . . but they certainly do have minds. They think and they feel and they say . . . [T]here are many activity verbs that are compatible with, and literally applicable to, institutional nouns, so that, linguistically, the institutions are viewed as competent to perform the designated acts."[52]

Grammatical analysis also indicates that a corporation is regarded as being its own person, not an aggregate of the individuals who are its members. The corporation, as a noun, is treated as singular and incompatible with plural verbs and pronouns. For instance, one says "the corporation *has* filed *its* quarterly report," not "the corporation *have* filed *their* quarterly report." We typically use singular verbs and pronouns when referring to corporations, suggesting that the singular corporate noun refers to the corporate person alone, not its constituent members.[53] Linguistically treating the corporation as a single unit is consistent with the way we generally view institutions that are made up of a number of individuals. Philosophers have noted that we describe many collective associations in terms that do not refer to their individual members. When we say the United States invaded Normandy, we do not mean to say that all individual Americans invaded Normandy. While Germany is said to be densely populated, no individual German can be said to be so; similarly, when we speak of a large multinational corporation, we are not referring to the physical size and nationality of its individual members.[54]

To be sure, our language does not equate organizations with human beings in all their capacities. Physiological verbs have no literal application to corporations.[55] We do not say the corporation cried, or ate lunch, or stared at the moon. However, our word choices do impute many human capacities to corporations, including mental states and the ability to engage in social interactions. "As a consequence, language treats the ensuing thoughts and actions as belonging to the institutions

51 *See id.* at 603–04.

52 *Id.* at 607.

53 *See id.* at 601.

54 *See* Richard T. De George, *Social Reality and Social Relations*, 37 Rev. Metaphysics 3, 9–10 (1983); Anthony Quinton, *Social Objects*, 76 Proc. Aristotelian Soc'y 1, 8 (1976).

55 Physiological verbs could have metaphorical applications to institutional nouns in some cases. *See* Schane, *supra* note 50, at 602–03.

themselves – and not to the hidden [embedded] members."[56] In this regard, there is a natural propensity within our dialogue to see the corporation as an independent person. The corporation's personhood status is woven into the fabric of our language.

If language naturally flows as an expression of the meaning we perceive in our minds, then perhaps it is unsurprising that our language would reflect a perception of corporations as persons. Proponents of the real entity view of corporations argued a century ago that our minds are naturally inclined to understand corporations as separate persons: "We do not need to be instructed to regard a corporation as an entity and to regard that entity as a person: our minds are so constituted that we cannot help taking that view."[57] "Clearly there is compulsion in our personalising [the corporation]. We do it because we must. We do it because we feel in these things the red blood of a living personality."[58] Our ordinary speech affirms our mental perception that corporations can bear many of the qualities associated with personhood.

Grammatical investigation of language is a form of psychological investigation.[59] The words we use to describe what we perceive in the world not only reflect our thinking, but they also shape our thoughts and guide our perceptions. As discussed in Chapter 1, language as a system of discourse conditions the way we think about things and interpret the world around us. Language contributes to the formation of prevailing judgments and understandings. From this perspective, the vocabulary we use to characterize corporations influences how we see and relate to them. Naming and classifying individuals and corporations as persons is significant. "The kinds of persons we understand ourselves and others to be are tied up with practices of naming."[60] Utilizing the language of personhood for corporations can play a role in reinforcing and solidifying a view of them as persons.

Postmodern philosophies view language as much more than a descriptive tool. Rather than merely describing reality, language is the medium through which our reality is constructed. The world around us is made by, rather than mirrored in, language.[61] Things take shape and have their meaning as a result of the way we talk about them. "Meaning becomes intimately tied to, indeed driven by, language use."[62] Discourse analysis "examines how language constructs phenomena, not

56 *Id.* at 607.

57 Arthur W. Machen, Jr., *Corporate Personality*, 24 HARV. L. REV. 253, 347, 363 (1911).

58 Harold J. Laski, *The Personality of Associations*, 29 HARV. L. REV. 404, 405 (1916).

59 Michael A. Tissaw, *The Person Concept and the Ontology of Persons*, *in* THE PSYCHOLOGY OF PERSONHOOD: PHILOSOPHICAL, HISTORICAL, SOCIAL-DEVELOPMENTAL, AND NARRATIVE PERSPECTIVES 19, 20 (Jack Martin & Mark H. Bickhard eds., 2013).

60 Jeff Sugarman, *Persons and Historical Ontology*, *in* PSYCHOLOGY OF PERSONHOOD, *supra* note 59, at 81, 84.

61 Hatch, *supra* note 2, at 13; Andreas Georg Scherer, *Modes of Explanation in Organization Theory*, *in* THE OXFORD HANDBOOK OF ORGANIZATION THEORY 310, 325 (Haridimos Tsoukas & Christian Knudsen eds., 2003).

62 Mats Alvesson, *Organizational Culture: Meaning, Discourse, and Identity*, *in* HANDBOOK OF ORGANIZATIONAL CULTURE AND CLIMATE, *supra* note 9, at 11, 20.

how it reflects and reveals it."[63] It is through the "process of differentiating, fixing, naming, labelling, classifying and relating – all intrinsic processes of discursive organization – that social reality is systematically constructed."[64] The discourses we engage in create the institutions and relations that make up our social world. To name or label something, to speak of it in a certain way, and to verbalize a set of ideas around it, have powerful effects on what it becomes, how it is regarded, and how it is treated. In this regard, language can be viewed as "generative," "transformative," and "constitutive."[65] Through its ability to influence thought and discussion, language helps to shape reality. Referring to corporations as persons can have meaningful constitutive effects. "Language is, in short, our most powerful technology of personification,"[66] bringing about new possibilities for thinking and new forms of personhood. Thus, the language we use to speak about corporations can contribute to what sorts of persons they can become and what role we allow them to play in our social world.

SOCIAL ROLE OF CORPORATE PERSONS

If corporations are viewed as persons in society, they, like other members of society, are obliged to meet certain societal expectations and fulfill certain prescribed roles. Sociologists maintain that society not only places economic and physical demands on corporations to produce and exchange goods and services in a market, but it also makes social, cultural, legal, and political demands on corporations to perform particular functions and maintain appropriate outward appearances.[67] Society rewards organizations that satisfactorily supply the environment with goods and services and that reasonably conform to the values, norms, rules, and beliefs that are integral to societal structure. The reward for meeting these demands is social legitimacy, which is just as critical for organizational survival as any other essential resource.[68]

The corporation's membership in society as a person is challenging. We expect the corporation to fill multiple social roles simultaneously. It should be an efficient supplier of desirable products, a skilled innovator, a source of profitable investment, a law-abiding citizen, an ethical employer, a responsible steward of environmental resources, an honest taxpayer, a charitable neighbor, and a fair competitor. That corporations are tasked with serving all these multiple functions simultaneously

63 Nelson Phillips & Cynthia Hardy, Discourse Analysis: Investigating Processes of Social Construction 6 (2002).

64 Robert Chia, *Discourse Analysis as Organizational Analysis*, 7 Organization 513, 513 (2000).

65 Sugarman, *supra* note 60, at 83–84; *see also* John R. Searle, Making the Social World: The Structure of Human Civilization 84–86 (2010) (explaining how language enables us to create social institutions).

66 Sheryl N. Hamilton, Impersonations: Troubling the Person in Law and Culture 9 (2009).

67 *See* Hatch, *supra* note 2, at 74.

68 *See id.*

speaks to the complexity of our society and the interdependence of corporations and individuals.

The role and prevalence of corporations in our daily lives cannot be overstated. Corporations construct our homes, they light our streets and buildings, they produce the foods we eat, they carry water into our neighborhoods, they manufacture our clothes, they establish banks for our savings, they insure against accidents that may befall us, they operate hospitals for our care, they publish the books we read, they channel the news of current events to us, they provide the means of our transportation; the list could continue. Through the production and distribution of countless goods and services, corporations supply the material needs of modern society. We have come to accept that corporations play an essential part in providing for the health, welfare, and security of the population.

Acknowledging the roles that corporations play in our lives always tends to engender normative arguments about the roles that corporations can and should play. Questions abound as to what the primary functions and purposes of the corporation ought to be. As the corporation meets the demands of an increasingly complex society, should it operate predominantly to maximize shareholder profits or should it carry broader social responsibilities to other societal sectors? Is the main purpose of the corporation to create wealth for its owners or must it also provide for the conditions necessary to promote the common good? How should the corporation balance or prioritize its many constituent interests? To whom should the corporation owe its greatest loyalty? Is it reasonable to demand that the corporate person simultaneously fulfill the expectations of all its stakeholders? These questions are all but impossible to resolve to the satisfaction of everyone who poses them because they are grounded in a debate within a liberal regime that is at odds with itself.

More specifically, those who argue corporations exist to enhance the economic well-being of their shareholder investors emphasize the importance of upholding private property rights. The shareholders are viewed as the residual owners of the corporation, and because it is their property, they have the right to expect that it will be operated to further their own interests. Under this shareholder primacy principle, the corporation's dominant purpose should be to maximize profits and create wealth.[69] In pursuing this goal, the corporation is able to accomplish what it has always been prized for doing so well: producing the best possible goods and services to meet the increasing demands of society in the most cost-efficient way. In this

69 A famous judicial articulation of the profit maximization principle is found in Dodge v. Ford Motor Co., 170 N.W. 668, 684 (Mich. 1919): "A business corporation is organized and carried on primarily for the profit of the stockholders." For discussions and critical analysis of the shareholder primacy norm, see David Millon, *The Single Constituency Argument in the Economic Analysis of Business Law, in* Law & Economics: Toward Social Justice 43, 45–47 (Dana L. Gold ed., 2009); Jill E. Fisch, *Measuring Efficiency in Corporate Law: The Role of Shareholder Primacy*, 31 J. Corp. L. 637, 646–50 (2006).

regard, the focus on maximizing shareholder profit is viewed as producing benefits for everyone in society.[70]

Alternatively, a stakeholder approach sees a much broader role for the corporation. Beyond shareholders, there are numerous stakeholders, including employees, suppliers, creditors, and the community, who contribute to the corporation; without them, the corporation would not function, let alone thrive. They have a right to expect that their unique investments in the corporation will be rewarded as well.[71] Under this view, the corporation's purpose in society is to serve not only the shareholders' interests, but also the interests of all of the corporation's constituent members.[72] Often tied to this perspective is an underlying concern for greater corporate social responsibility. The corporation must be careful not to affirmatively harm others in pursuit of its economic goals.[73] It should understand and utilize the privileged position it has to influence and contribute to the community for the larger common good.

This debate between those who argue that the primary role and purpose of corporations is to create and maximize shareholder wealth and those who believe the corporation's role must be to serve the broader public interest is perennial because the moral principles underlying both arguments are so fundamental and enduring. The shareholder approach and the stakeholder approach both faithfully reflect deeply held values of liberal society. Stakeholder theory invokes distributive justice and public citizenship; shareholder theory invokes liberty and private property interests. All are important and cherished values of civil society and are legitimate expressions of liberalism. We hold strongly to our rights to freedom and to seek our own self-interest, but we also value the importance of community and social responsibility. The goals of self-interest are always constrained by fundamental social, legal, moral, and ethical rules and norms. These differences in opinion over the role and purpose of corporations reflect differences in normative priorities that are not resolvable through practical rationality. Because both the shareholder and stakeholder positions are valid expressions of important moral principles, "the decision between them is a normative toss-up."[74] We must continually strive to find an acceptable equilibrium between them as the position of the corporate person in modern society becomes ever more complex.

70 *See* Christopher D. Stone, WHERE THE LAW ENDS: THE SOCIAL CONTROL OF CORPORATE BEHAVIOR 85 (1975); Ronald Chen & Jon Hanson, *The Illusion of Law: The Legitimating Schemas of Modern Policy and Corporate Law*, 103 MICH. L. REV. 1, 44, 46–48 (2004); Michael E. DeBow & Dwight R. Lee, *Shareholders, Nonshareholders and Corporate Law: Communitarianism and Resource Allocation*, 18 DEL. J. CORP. L. 393, 416–19 (1993).

71 *See* R. Edward Freeman, *A Stakeholder Theory of the Modern Corporation*, *in* ETHICAL THEORY AND BUSINESS 56 (Tom L. Beauchamp & Norman E. Bowie eds., 6th ed. 2001).

72 *See* Charles Handy, *What's a Business For?*, HARV. BUS. REV., Dec. 2002, at 49, 51–55.

73 Patricia H. Werhane, PERSONS, RIGHTS, AND CORPORATIONS 70 (1985).

74 S. A. Cortright & Ernest S. Pierucci, *Clearing Ground: Toward a Social Ethic of Corporate Management*, *in* RETHINKING THE PURPOSE OF BUSINESS 136, 161 (S. A. Cortright & Michael J. Naughton eds., 2002).

Perhaps it is somewhat odd to argue over what should be the primary purpose of the corporation. Like human persons, corporations can have competing values, goals, purposes, and roles. Nothing prevents individuals from pursuing multiple objectives, wearing several hats, or performing different duties as situations vary. If we were to ask what is the primary purpose or role of human beings, the answers would be varied, contested, and rooted in numerous alternative values. In some ways, it can be similarly difficult to identify the single chief purpose of the corporate person and expect it to fulfill no more than that role alone. Moreover, there are many different types of corporations ranging from large, publicly held entities, to small, family owned businesses; some are for-profit firms, others are nonprofit; some are formed to advance certain long-term political, educational, religious, or social objectives; others are formed to engage in a single, short-term economic venture. The roles and purposes of these various entities will be different. We have to balance different values as we consider the varied roles that corporations can play. We want for-profit corporations to create wealth and maximize gain, but within appropriate legal and moral constraints and keeping in mind the welfare of the community in which we all live.

There may be a false opposition between "making money" on the one hand, and "doing good" on the other.[75] Corporations can serve multiple aims, and indeed, like human persons, they must find effective ways to pursue different objectives and fulfill varied roles. Corporations can make money *and* do good simultaneously. They can also make money *by* doing good, as well as do a lot of good *by* making money. Like any member of society, they can have economic and non-economic objectives, and we expect them to ably maintain both. If corporations are viewed to some extent as persons in society, some suggest that it may be helpful to talk about them normatively as "citizens" of the community, with "both the responsibilities and the benefits of that status."[76] Citizenship involves a "relationship of shared identity and mutual concern with the larger society."[77] Citizens are entitled to certain benefits and privileges, but they have duties and obligations as well. Citizens are free to pursue their own self-interest, but they must also remain aware of how that pursuit may damage innocent others. Responsible citizens care about their community. They have a sense of loyalty toward it, a commitment to its betterment. If the corporation's role in society is as a citizen, we would expect it to have a shared commitment to the welfare of the larger community. The corporate citizen would be sensitive to the impact it has on others who are affected by its activities and would take steps to avoid harming others in society. To focus exclusively on self-interest without regard for the social costs would be improper for the good corporate citizen, just as it would for the good human citizen. Thus, as

75 James Boyd White, *How Should We Talk About Corporations? The Languages of Economics and of Citizenship*, 94 Yale L.J. 1416, 1418 (1985).

76 *Id.*

77 Robert C. Solomon, Ethics and Excellence: Cooperation and Integrity in Business 84 (1992).

a normative matter, the corporation should continually seek to balance its interests against those of the broader community in order to participate properly as a citizen in society.

MEDIATING ROLE IN A POLITICALLY PLURALIST SOCIETY

Political theory and philosophy also envision an important role for corporate persons in a liberal democracy. Theories of political pluralism emphasize the distinctiveness and significance of organizations in society.[78] Groups and organizations form naturally as individuals associate together to promote their shared interests and goals. People form collective associations of all kinds for various reasons. They may coalesce around shared political causes, financial endeavors, leisure activities, religious beliefs, or social projects, to name a few. Associations may be large or small; they may be commercial or nonprofit entities; they may be highly formalized or less structured. Groups provide venues for individuals to experience a sense of community and to feel a level of connection and identification with others who share similar objectives, values, concerns, or interests.

In his widely read book, *Democracy in America*, nineteenth-century political scientist Alexis de Tocqueville noted the ubiquity and importance of groups and associations in America.[79] He argued that the development of the human mind occurs only through the "reciprocal action of men upon one another," and that membership in groups is what enables individuals to learn, grow, and thrive.[80] He viewed organizations as critical to a healthy democratic society because not only do they contribute to human flourishing, but they also help to preserve freedom by standing as an effective counterweight to potentially coercive state power. Strong state authority always poses the risk of crowding out individual rights and liberty. Individuals who alone may not be able to combat government power can band together in associations to protect themselves against the threat of state oppression or majoritarian tyranny.[81] In this regard, associations become central and constitutive elements in a thriving democracy.

In a pluralist society, organizations carry their own special status as centers of representation for individuals. German political theorist Otto Gierke similarly hailed the importance of associations and community groups as representative institutions. He argued that the government had a much weaker claim as a representative body than "the authentic, spontaneously formed, and essentially

78 *See* Dalia Tsuk, *From Pluralism to Individualism: Berle and Means and 20th-Century American Legal Thought*, 30 Law & Soc. Inquiry 179, 189–91 (2005) (book review).

79 Alexis de Tocqueville, Democracy in America (Harvey C. Mansfield & Delba Winthrop eds. & trans., Univ. of Chi. Press 2000) (1840).

80 *Id.* at 491.

81 *See* Ronald J. Colombo, The First Amendment and the Business Corporation 9, 20 (2015) (discussing Tocqueville's views).

timeless communities" that constituted associations.[82] This conception of associations drew on the image of the medieval institutions of guilds, townships, and free cities that had powers of autonomous self-direction and served as centers for collective and participatory self-government.[83] These groups empowered individuals to determine the course of their own lives, rather than submitting to the direction of a centralized state that was perceived as anti-democratic and unwilling to afford citizens meaningful political participation and power. From this standpoint, associations were crucial entities that served as a challenge to and a freedom from centralizing, dominating state authority.

In this sense, associations and organizations are viewed as intermediate institutions that act as important buffers between individuals and the state. They compose an intermediate organizational level in society that mediates between large political nation-states and individual citizens.[84] In modern political discourse, mediating institutions are typically associated with the family, religious organizations, neighborhoods, and voluntary associations.[85] In these groups, individuals interact closely with other members. It is in the context of these settings that people form their identities and their sense of self. Individuals' membership in social groups affects how they define and identify who they are.[86] Within these mediating institutions, individuals learn important social norms and values that foster cooperation and fellowship. They also cultivate the habits of character that are necessary to live with and among other groups in a pluralist society.

Business ethicists suggest that corporations can have a role as mediating institutions in society today.[87] They can "act as a vital countervailing force against the state."[88] In fact, they may be the only effective modern counterweight to the state because they are one of the few private forces that have the capacity, resources, power, and incentive to check government power.[89] Corporations serve as groups in which members can coalesce around a common goal and form their social identities as they interact with other members. To the extent that so many people

82 Joshua Barkan, Corporate Sovereignty: Law and Government under Capitalism 81 (2013).

83 *See* Mark M. Hager, *Bodies Politic: The Progressive History of Organizational "Real Entity" Theory*, 50 U. Pitt. L. Rev. 575, 611–15 (1989).

84 *See* Dan-Cohen, *supra* note 1, at 161; Eric W. Orts, Business Persons: A Legal Theory of the Firm 49 (2013).

85 *See* Peter L. Berger & Richard John Neuhaus, To Empower People: The Role of Mediating Structures in Public Policy 3 (1977).

86 *See* Christian List & Philip Pettit, Group Agency: The Possibility, Design, and Status of Corporate Agents 195–97 (2011); *see also* Henry Meyer Magid, English Political Pluralism: The Problem of Freedom and Organization 12 (AMS Press, Inc. 1966) (1941) (discussing the view of pluralist John Figgis who believed groups play a vital role in the self-development of individuals).

87 *See* Timothy L. Fort, *Business as Mediating Institution*, 6 Bus. Ethics Q. 149, 151, 155–57 (1996). "The most prominent form of community in the contemporary business world is that of the corporation." Jeffrey Nesteruk, *Law, Virtue, and the Corporation*, 33 Am. Bus. L.J. 473, 480 (1996).

88 Stephen M. Bainbridge, *Community and Statism: A Conservative Contractarian Critique of Progressive Corporate Law Scholarship*, 82 Cornell L. Rev. 856, 897 (1997) (book review).

89 *See* Colombo, *supra* note 81, at xv, 72.

spend most of their day working in or interacting with corporate organizations, "the corporation represents a value-laden institution that outranks the local community as a focus of loyalty and a medium for self-realization."[90] Indeed, it has been suggested that the traditional sources of social support and identity formation such as the family, church, and small town, have declined in our mobile and entrepreneurial society, and corporate organizations have taken their place.[91] "As globalization marches forward, the corporation rivals race, ethnicity, class, gender, and nationality as a site of individual identity construction."[92] If corporations have become an important form of community, they may be seen as performing a mediating function for individuals in society.

Viewing corporations as mediating institutions places them in a very positive light: They are critical instruments of freedom, democracy, and individual flourishing. Under this view, the corporation plays a significant part in helping people live more fulfilling lives. Aristotle argued that human beings are not intended merely to live, or to survive, but they are intended to "live well," or to flourish.[93] Corporations can provide individuals with the means to flourish by giving them the time and resources to focus on endeavors beyond merely surviving. "[I]f everyone were required to feed, clothe, and otherwise provide for himself and his family ... with the sole use of his own means and enterprise, ... each person would spend all of his time merely surviving," rather than having the freedom to seek a more enriching existence.[94] Corporations serve society by providing essential goods and services that meet the real material needs of consumers. By doing so, they free people to engage themselves in additional pursuits that allow them to grow and develop in other ways. Corporations that function properly contribute to the common good. The common good of the community is the sum of all those social conditions

90 Norton E. Long, *The Corporation, Its Satellites, and the Local Community*, *in* THE CORPORATION IN MODERN SOCIETY 202 (Edward S. Mason ed., 1959). "[P]eople may be more citizens of the corporations for whom they work than of the local communities in which they reside." *Id.*

91 *See* Daniel Bell, THE COMING OF POST-INDUSTRIAL SOCIETY: A VENTURE IN SOCIAL FORECASTING 289 (1973); Solomon, *supra* note 77, at 146–47. Many corporations now provide fitness centers, daycare facilities, free eateries, and rest areas for the convenience of employees, allowing them to spend more time physically at the workplace and forming closer bonds with fellow members. In many companies, employees are also allowed to bring their pets to work daily. In a sense, the corporation becomes an extended home and the members form an extended family. Nancy Messieh, *12 Tech Companies That Offer Their Employees the Coolest Perks*, NEXT WEB (Apr. 9, 2012), https://thenextweb.com/insider/2012/04/09/12-startups-that-offer-their-employees-the-coolest-perks/ [https://perma.cc/H2U7-X4DY].

92 Kenneth Lipartito & David B. Sicilia, *Afterword: Toward New Renderings*, *in* CONSTRUCTING CORPORATE AMERICA: HISTORY, POLITICS, CULTURE 343, 347 (Kenneth Lipartito & David B. Sicilia eds., 2004).

93 *See* James V. Schall, *The Corporation: What Is It?*, 4 AVE MARIA L. REV. 105, 112 (2006). "Aristotle's central ethical concept is a unified, all-embracing notion of 'happiness' (or, more accurately, *eudaimonia*, perhaps better translated as 'flourishing' or 'doing well')." Solomon, *supra* note 77, at 105.

94 Schall, *supra* note 93, at 110.

that support the full development of human personality and facilitate the fulfillment of each person's life.[95]

In all practicality, the advantages we enjoy in modern society would not be ours without the coordinated actions of numerous corporations. Our "normal progress through the day would be unsustainable without these creatures that routinely deliver unimaginable prodigies of organization and performance."[96] Corporations undertake and accomplish extraordinary tasks through concerted action that no human being could achieve by individual effort alone. They are "a tool for complex and coordinated action of a scale, consistency, and perseverance vastly beyond the range of biological individuals or informal groupings."[97] In developed economies, we expect to have options to purchase a broad array of products. Many of the goods we buy are too complicated for individual producers to manufacture and bring to the marketplace by themselves. It is the corporation that has the capacity to produce the vast supply of things we need and desire, to do so more cheaply and efficiently, to consistently satisfy the increasingly complex demands of the modern community, and to thereby contribute to social stability.[98] Without corporations, "our quality of life could simply not be what it is . . . [O]ur diets would lose much of their variety, our health care would be much more primitive, we would travel less, know less, and generally live poorer lives."[99] Described in the most positive terms, the goods and services provided by corporations ultimately have the ability to improve life, prolong its duration, help the needy, increase human welfare, and enrich humanity. "Misery and poverty, we know now, can invade liberty as deeply as an oppressive State, and the corporate system obviously can provide, and even distribute, goods and services in volume sufficient to combat both."[100] Viewed in this light, corporations play an extremely important and beneficial role in society as organizational persons that support and enhance the welfare of human persons.

CORPORATE POWER IN SOCIETY

There is an opposing political pluralist vision of the corporation that views it in an entirely different light, one that is highly critical of the immense power of corporations in modern society. This viewpoint acknowledges that corporations produce much that is worthwhile, but it argues that it is at too high a cost to individuals. From this alternative view, corporations are persons with unmatched weight and influence

95 Robert G. Kennedy, *Corporations, Common Goods, and Human Persons*, 4 Ave Maria L. Rev. 1, 18 n.58 (2006).

96 Marc Galanter, *Planet of the APs: Reflections on the Scale of Law and Its Users*, 53 Buff. L. Rev. 1369, 1370 (2006).

97 *Id.*

98 *See* Peter F. Drucker, Concept of the Corporation 225–29 (rev. ed. 1972).

99 Kennedy, *supra* note 95, at 19.

100 Adolf A. Berle, Jr., *Foreword*, *in* Corporation in Modern Society, *supra* note 90, at ix, xi.

in society, and corporate power is a force that is all but impossible to channel in appropriate directions.

While corporations can provide society with many benefits, the prevalence and power of large corporations can also cause grave harms. Many people believe that corporate power is not benign and beneficial, but a dangerous threat to individual welfare and democratic ideals. As the biggest centers of non-governmental power in society, corporate persons have the potential to overpower individuals. The wealth, size, and geographic reach of corporations can be immense. Large public corporations can grow to a massive size, accumulating staggering amounts of assets, collecting billions of dollars in revenues, employing vast numbers of people, and operating factories, branches, and facilities in locations all over the world. The annual revenues of the largest corporations far surpass the revenues of most countries in the world combined.[101] The economic power of corporations is indisputably enormous. Their economic resources breed increasingly greater economic advantage and position. Larger corporations have the ability to squeeze out smaller individual competitors and reinforce their own market dominance. Indeed, a corporation does not need to be a giant multinational conglomerate to exercise tremendous economic control over others. For example, corporations of much smaller scale can still be vitally important to small communities that rely on the corporations for jobs and revenues. In deciding whether to maintain its operations in a particular community or move to another location, a single corporation can be "the decisive factor in the life or death of a small community."[102]

The financial wealth of the corporation is not exclusively an economic resource; it is also a source of substantial political power. Corporations transform their massive economic power into significant political influence in the legislative and political realm. It is common knowledge that corporations spend millions of dollars annually in lobbying efforts to impact government policies. Corporate money is used to make campaign contributions, to support or defeat specific political proposals, to curry favor with public officials, and to lobby on behalf of industry interests. These practices are not new. Corporations have always used their economic power to insert themselves into the political arena. Even in the early history of the modern corporation, economists in the late-nineteenth century acknowledged "the power of corporations to make the political machine their instrument and the legislator their servant."[103] Critics noted how "[v]ery insidious is the power that massed capital

101 Zlata Rodionova, *World's Largest Corporations Make More Money than Most Countries on Earth Combined*, INDEPENDENT (Sep. 13, 2016), www.independent.co.uk/news/business/news/worlds-largest-corporations-more-money-countries-world-combined-apple-walmart-shell-global-justice-a7245991.html [https://perma.cc/QBU5-RUYC].

102 Thomas Donaldson, CORPORATIONS AND MORALITY 8 (1982).

103 Warren J. Samuels, *The Idea of the Corporation as a Person: On the Normative Significance of Judicial Language*, *in* CORPORATIONS AND SOCIETY: POWER AND RESPONSIBILITY 113, 120 (Warren J. Samuels & Arthur S. Miller eds., 1987) (referring to remarks made in 1899 by conservative economist John Bates Clark).

knows how to use in controlling the so-called representatives of the people."[104] Today, it is no secret that corporations give substantial sums of money to both major political parties and to competing candidates with the expectation that, in return, corporations will gain access to the officials who are ultimately elected, and with that access, "a disproportionate influence on those in power ... At a critical level, [corporate] contributions that underwrite elections are leverage for enormous political influence."[105]

The thrust of much of the political activity of corporations is to avoid or soften legal regulation of corporate business. Through their relationships with legislators and their influence on proposed legislation, corporations help to shape the laws by which they are governed.[106] Corporations often fund the research that is ultimately used by government agencies to support the regulations that they adopt. More directly, corporations in certain industries typically provide input to government agencies as they formulate rules to regulate corporate activity, resulting in "the government effectively adopt[ing] the standards worked out with the industry."[107] Commentators have noted the almost exclusive role corporations and their attorneys have had in creating and controlling the direction of important state corporation statutes.[108] Critics argue that the extensive investment of corporate money in the political and legislative regime threatens the integrity of democratic politics and undermines public confidence in democratic ideals.

The influence of corporations goes beyond the economic and political systems to reach the core of our culture itself. Through corporate products, services, marketing, and advertising, corporations permeate our lives daily and shape the culture in which we live. Corporate decisions on what foods to produce, what products to manufacture, what research to fund, what natural resources to use, what news to transmit, along with countless other fundamental corporate choices, have a direct impact on our health, our thoughts, our activities, and the overall quality of our lives. Corporations' sophisticated advertising campaigns play a role in structuring people's desires and aspirations. Perhaps without always being completely conscious of it, people take their cues from corporate advertising to formulate who they want to be, what they believe will make them happy, and how they must go about achieving the good life. Corporate messages help to frame the way individuals look at themselves and judge others. This form of corporate power is particularly significant because it influences the very nature of a person's desires and preferences.

Those who worry about corporate power warn that corporations have the capacity to inflict irreparable harm on individuals. The corporation can cause death, disease,

104 *Id.*

105 FEC v. Wis. Right to Life, Inc., 551 U.S. 449, 506–07 (2007) (Souter, J., dissenting).

106 *See* Stone, *supra* note 70, at 94; Jill E. Fisch, *The "Bad Man" Goes to Washington: The Effect of Political Influence on Corporate Duty*, 75 Fordham L. Rev. 1593, 1604–08 (2006).

107 Stone, *supra* note 70, at 95.

108 *See* Comment, *Law for Sale: A Study of the Delaware Corporation Law of 1967*, 117 U. Pa. L. Rev. 861 (1969).

and severe injury due to any number of its decisions resulting in environmental hazards, unsafe products, inadequate quality control, and dangerous working conditions.[109] Through their employment practices, corporations can subject employees to workplace alienation, discrimination, or serious deprivations of income, well-being, and personal freedom. Overall, corporations can exert various forms of direct and indirect influence, control, and even coercion over individuals within the corporation, over politicians and regulators, over members of the consuming public, and over whole communities whose welfare is tied to corporate activities.

Many believe that individuals are no match for corporate persons and that great care must be taken to protect individuals from the potentially coercive effects of corporate control. Individuals stand in a vulnerable position vis-à-vis large corporations because "the moment a powerful [corporate] group begins to act toward a common end it produces a capacity for aggression that individuals can only in the rarest cases combat."[110] The dangers associated with concentrated corporate power fuel the concern that the state is not the only source of control to threaten individuals in society. Rather, "the corporation's economic, social, and cultural impact has become so pervasive in modern society so as to make corporate power, in effect, comparable to the coercive power of the state."[111] Giant corporations possess functions and powers that are traditionally associated with the government, making corporations tantamount to sovereign government-like bodies that "rival the sovereignty of the state itself."[112] From this political pluralist perspective, corporations are not only constitutive elements of modern society, but also centers of political and economic power that are equivalent to state power. Corporations have thus come to be systems of private government. "Their power and influence, both externally in the national political order and internally in the so-called corporate community, make them a true form of governance."[113]

Under this view, the "rights of the citizenry need protection from invasion by the 'private governments' of corporations as much as they need protection from invasion by Congress or by state or local governments."[114] Individuals arguably can be victims of corporate oppression as easily as they can be victims of oppression by the state. Indeed, corporations potentially "could be even more oppressive than the state, because they [are] not subject to the restraints of formal procedure, judicial review,

109 *See* Abraham J. Briloff, *LBOs and MBOs in the Takeover Alphabet Soup: Some Questions for Lawyers, Answers from an Accountant*, 15 J. CORP. L. 171, 195 (1990).

110 George F. Deiser, *The Juristic Person*, 57 U. PA. L. REV. 300, 302 (1909).

111 Tsuk, *supra* note 78, at 180 n.2.

112 Earl Latham, *The Body Politic of the Corporation*, *in* CORPORATION IN MODERN SOCIETY, *supra* note 90, at 218, 218.

113 Arthur S. Miller, *Corporations and Our Two Constitutions*, *in* CORPORATIONS AND SOCIETY, *supra* note 103, at 241, 242.

114 Russell B. Stevenson, Jr., *Corporations and Social Responsibility: In Search of the Corporate Soul*, 42 GEO. WASH. L. REV. 709, 731–32 (1974).

and public scrutiny."[115] Some commentators suggest that the dominance of corporate persons in society results in a diminution in status of natural persons who can no longer bargain as equals.[116] Because individuals are vulnerable in the face of corporate power, the democratic state must assume the role of a countervailing power to protect individual rights and liberties from increasing encroachment by corporate bureaucracies.[117] This has led to the idea that certain guarantees of the Bill of Rights should be extended to shield individuals not just from overreaching by the state, but also from that of corporations.[118] Seen in this light, corporations are more than mediating institutions that serve to protect individuals from the overwhelming power of the state. Corporations themselves are private forms of government that can dominate and overpower individuals. The state must regulate and restrain corporate persons to the greatest extent possible to protect individuals from the formidable effects of corporate power.

Overall, the role and purposes of corporations in society are deeply contested. The large corporation, like the state, indisputably is a source of tremendous political and social power. The powers of the corporation and the state must be balanced in ways that do not inhibit the productive activities of both. As we shall see in the next chapter, the law has been used as a mediating force to attempt to direct and articulate that balancing process.

*****

The discussion in this chapter suggests that the corporation can be viewed as a special kind of person in society, occupying that important space between individuals and the government. The corporation bears characteristics that are similar to those of individual persons. It can have its own life cycle, identity, character, and personality. We speak of the corporation in linguistic terms that reflect and reinforce its apparent personhood. The corporation has the power to profoundly affect the lives of its internal members, as well as the lives of those in the broader society in which it operates. The corporation's role in society is not unidimensional, but rich and complex. It is a member of the larger community, but it is a community in itself as well. The corporation produces enormous benefits, but also poses significant dangers to individuals and the political system. That so many social science disciplines each have distinct and significant insights into the corporation reveals the many dimensions of the corporation as a person. These various academic perspectives suggest that the corporate person is more than merely a legal fiction or an

115 Sanford A. Lakoff, *Private Government in the Managed Society*, *in* PRIVATE GOVERNMENT 218, 225 (Sanford A. Lakoff with Daniel Rich eds., 1973).

116 Warren J. Samuels & Arthur S. Miller, *Introduction: Corporate America*, *in* CORPORATIONS AND SOCIETY, *supra* note 103, at 1, 7.

117 Dan-Cohen, *supra* note 1, at 159.

118 *See* A. A. Berle, Jr., *The Developing Law of Corporate Concentration*, 19 U. CHI. L. REV. 639, 643 (1952); Adolf A. Berle, Jr., *Constitutional Limitations on Corporate Activity – Protection of Personal Rights from Invasion Through Economic Power*, 100 U. PA. L. REV. 933, 942–43 (1952).

economic device. It has substance as a real and active agent whose presence in society carries considerable social, political, and cultural significance.

As we have seen, the role of the corporate person in society is open to different interpretations depending on one's normative vision of the ideal political state. One may view corporations as sources of oppressive power that must be curbed by the government. Alternatively, one may see the corporation as a protector of individual autonomy and a bulwark against coercive state power. The common thread is a recognition that corporations are socially, economically, and politically important and have the power to affect society in dramatic ways. As Adolf Berle and Gardiner Means observed almost a century ago, the "giant corporation is a tremendous force which can harm or benefit a multitude of individuals, affect whole districts, shift the currents of trade, bring ruin to one community and prosperity to another. The[se] organizations ... have passed far beyond the realm of private enterprise – they have become more nearly social institutions."[119]

To acknowledge that corporations are powerful social institutions complicates our understanding of the role of the corporate person in relation to the state and individuals in society. Some commentators maintain that the struggle over corporate personhood is no less than a part of the larger struggle over the future of American democracy.[120] Because we can so vigorously disagree on our prescriptions for achieving the ideal democratic society, our views of the corporation's role in that endeavor will always be contentious and controversial. One's ultimate opinion depends very much on one's definition of the nature and purpose of the corporate person in society, and that definition can be extraordinarily complex.

The opposing views of the corporation's function in society reflect the obvious duality of corporate life. The corporation provides society with enormous advantages and benefits but simultaneously subjects society to profound dangers and risks. Like natural persons, corporate persons have both the capacity to inflict immense harm and the capacity to do tremendous good. They are two sides of the same corporate personhood coin. Corporations have been called the "angels and devils" of our economy and politics.[121] We fear their bigness, their power, and complexity. "Yet we also plainly want bigness. We feel that we need it; above all, we irresistibly patronize it."[122] "We thus appear to want things both ways: we know, at least intuitively, about the power of business and fear it; at the same time, few wish to forgo the bounty that corporate enterprise provides."[123] Perhaps it is this deep and intractable dissonance

119 Adolf A. Berle, Jr. & Gardiner C. Means, The Modern Corporation and Private Property 46 (1932).
120 *See* Hager, *supra* note 83, at 639.
121 Howard Jay Graham, *An Innocent Abroad: The Constitutional Corporate "Person,"* 2 UCLA L. Rev. 155, 155 (1955).
122 *Id.* at 157.
123 Samuels & Miller, *supra* note 116, at 4.

that explains why our law and our society have been conflicted about the corporation's role, rights, and responsibilities for a long time.[124] As the next chapter discusses, this dissonance and inconsistency is especially evident in the treatment of corporations as constitutional persons for purposes of constitutional rights.

[124] *See* William T. Allen, *Our Schizophrenic Conception of the Business Corporation*, 14 Cardozo L. Rev. 261, 264 (1992).

4

Constitutional Dimensions of the Corporate Person: Corporate Free Speech

The term "corporation" does not appear anywhere in the United States Constitution, yet the United States Supreme Court has held that corporations are entitled to claim an extensive array of constitutional rights. The justifications for these rights have developed from the many different conceptions of the corporation as a legal, moral, economic, social, and political actor. In particular, the constitutional dimension of the corporation's personhood is an extension of its legal personhood. Therefore, the fundamental legal theories of the corporate person, i.e., the artificial person, aggregate, and real entity theories, have had a role in supporting the extension of constitutional rights to corporations. The moral and sociological dimensions of the corporate person have also been important. In determining the scope of corporate constitutional rights, the Supreme Court has considered the actual and normative roles and purposes of corporations in our pluralistic and democratic society. Considerations of corporate power, both economic and political, have contributed as well to the debate over which constitutional rights appropriately apply to corporations. Thus, the many different aspects of the corporate person we have analyzed in the prior chapters of this book are played out in the context of conceptualizing the corporation as a constitutional person capable of claiming rights that are guaranteed under the United States Constitution.

The development of corporate constitutional rights over the years has not followed a consistent pattern or relied on a single coherent theory. The Supreme Court has drawn on many contrasting views of the corporation at different times to support the selective extension of some, but not all, constitutional rights to corporations. Sometimes the Court refers to the corporation as simply a collection of individuals whose individual constitutional rights should continue to be protected when they choose to come together and act in corporate form. At other times, the Court seems to view the corporation as a separate entity that has its own beliefs and goals and is entitled to constitutional protection in pursuing its interests. The result is a patchwork of constitutional jurisprudence that upholds the constitutional status of corporations in some contexts and not others, a jurisprudence that renders itself open to criticism for being inconsistent, ad hoc, and results-oriented.

This chapter will provide some historical background for the development of corporate constitutional rights. It will reveal how the various theories of the corporate person have been utilized to include the corporation in the community of constitutional claimants. In this chapter and the next, we will explore three of the most controversial arenas today for battles on corporate constitutional personhood: corporate free speech rights, corporate religious rights, and corporate racial equality rights.

Whether corporations should be granted the same rights that are afforded to human persons under the Constitution has become the topic of intense public debate. The Supreme Court's decisions in the last decade to expand First Amendment corporate political free speech rights as well as religious exercise rights have been very controversial. Should corporations be considered persons whose political speech deserves protection under the First Amendment? Does it make sense to say that corporate persons, like natural persons, have the right to voice their opinions and contribute to the marketplace of ideas? What about religious beliefs? Can corporations be regarded as having a religion, the exercise of which is entitled to legal protection? Is the corporate person capable of having a faith, a guiding spiritual principle, or a set of beliefs that typically represent what it means to be religious? While it may seem sensible to say a church or religious organization possesses certain religious rights, is it equally plausible for a large business company to claim a right to exercise its religious freedoms? If corporate persons can identify with a particular religion, can they also identify with a particular race? If the corporation can indeed claim a certain racial identity (perhaps based on the predominant racial identity of its owners and/or employees), then is the corporation entitled to protection against racial discrimination or unequal treatment based on the corporation's race? There is strong disagreement over the best way to answer these questions. The Supreme Court has held that corporations are capable of engaging in speech and religious practices that are entitled to protection, and some courts have held that the corporation may acquire a racial identity for purposes of bringing race discrimination claims. These holdings are based on competing views of the corporation that implicate different aspects of its personhood.

Discussion of these issues often invokes the aggregate theory of the corporate person, which emphasizes that the corporation is merely the collection, or aggregate, of the human individuals who make up the corporation. The aggregate theory directs us to look through the corporate entity and see the real people behind it. When we uphold the rights of the corporation, what we are really doing is protecting the rights of its human members. It is their speech, religion, and race that we respect and want to protect from infringement or discrimination.

This aggregate approach may work when we are dealing with small, private, closely held companies that have a few shareholders or employees. As they exercise their rights through the vehicle of their small businesses, we tend to see the corporation as just an extension of their individual personhood. However, we are inclined to think a bit differently when we talk about a large, multinational, publicly held corporation. The thrust of the aggregate theory seems to lose some of its force as the number of shareholders and employees increases in the corporation. It becomes harder to comfortably argue that the speech, religion, or race of the corporation merely reflects that of the human individuals within the company who are numerous and diverse.

Moreover, the evident purpose of the corporate entity influences our perception of its rights. Some tend to look more skeptically at for-profit corporations than nonprofit entities. For example, many people are inclined to support the free speech rights of a nonprofit corporation, or an organization formed to serve specific political, educational, community, or religious purposes. The nature of those entities is to express and promote their particular perspective presumably for the greater public interest, and we are reluctant to impede the exercise of their right to do so. People are less likely to feel the same way about corporations whose purpose is to generate profits. People assume that a business corporation's sole objective in exercising a right to speak or to claim a religious or racial identity is to advantage itself financially in the market and that this is somehow less deserving of protection.

Thus, both the size and purpose of the corporation affect how society views the corporate person and its constitutional rights. Certain constitutional protections seem appropriate for some entities but not all. The Supreme Court itself has struggled with making these distinctions and determinations. This is partly why our corporate constitutional jurisprudence seems to lack consistency and coherency. This is also what concerns so many average citizens who are suspicious of the entire concept of corporate personhood. While they do not take issue with the protection of constitutional rights for human persons (even as they exercise those rights through their small businesses or nonprofit associations), they lament the law's extension of constitutional rights for large, for-profit corporations that claim rights that are arguably meant for individuals. The extent to which corporate persons should have constitutional rights has never been an easy issue to resolve, and it becomes increasingly more difficult as different types of corporations proliferate in our modern pluralistic society.

The intent of this chapter is not to argue in favor of or against corporate constitutional rights, or to propose a singular, overarching theory for deciding corporate rights cases. It is doubtful that such a unifying theory could even be constructed or applied in a useful way to all corporate entities, given the many different types of organizations that utilize the corporate form. Rather, this discussion draws on the various elements of corporate personhood to help inform the analysis of why we would (or would not) want to extend rights to corporations in any given set of circumstances. Looking at the multidimensional nature of the corporation as a person gives us a broader understanding of the complex role and purposes of corporations in our legal, political, and social systems.

EARLY DEVELOPMENT OF CORPORATE CONSTITUTIONAL PERSONHOOD AND RIGHTS

Although the United States Constitution does not mention corporations, the Framers were well aware of the corporate form. The original American colonies were corporations chartered by the English Crown. In colonial America, charters were granted by special acts of state legislatures for corporate enterprises that served public purposes and met specific social needs, such as building a canal or providing for banking services. States strictly regulated corporations in the public interest. Corporations were viewed as artificial persons, or concessions of the government, dependent on the state for their existence and obliged to fulfill a public purpose.[1]

One of the earliest constitutional issues involving corporations was whether they could be considered "citizens" for purposes of federal court diversity jurisdiction under Article III of the Constitution.[2] In *Bank of the United States v. Deveaux*, the Supreme Court held that a corporation itself is not a citizen for the purpose of establishing federal court jurisdiction over cases involving citizens of different states.[3] Only the citizenship of the corporation's individual members could be utilized to determine whether the corporation could sue or be sued in federal court. Chief Justice John Marshall stated: "That invisible, intangible, and artificial being, that mere legal entity, a corporation aggregate, is certainly not a citizen; and, consequently, cannot sue or be sued in the courts of the United States, unless the rights of the members, in this respect, can be exercised in their corporate name."[4] Under this view, the corporation is not a separate person; the corporation is simply its human members. Looking through the artificial corporate form, the Court saw the real natural persons who came together to act in the corporate name. Thus, the Court relied on an aggregate conception of the corporate person in denying the corporation any independent citizenship status, thereby restricting corporate access to federal court through diversity jurisdiction.

The result in *Deveaux* was later overturned in *Louisville, Cincinnati, & Charleston Railroad Co. v. Letson*, when the Court found that corporations are citizens of the state of their incorporation for jurisdictional purposes.[5] The Supreme Court held that a corporation that is "created by a state to perform its functions under the authority of that state . . . [is] a person, though an artificial one, inhabiting

[1] See discussion of the earliest American corporations and the artificial person theory of the corporate person in Chapter 1 of this book. Chapter 1 also describes the growth in size and number of corporations during the nineteenth and twentieth centuries and the corresponding development of the aggregate and the real entity theories of the corporation.

[2] U.S. CONST. art. III, §2 ("The judicial Power shall extend . . . to Controversies . . . between Citizens of different States.").

[3] Bank of the U.S. v. Deveaux, 9 U.S. (5 Cranch) 61 (1809). For an excellent discussion of the case, see Adam Winkler, WE THE CORPORATIONS: HOW AMERICAN BUSINESSES WON THEIR CIVIL RIGHTS 35–70 (2018).

[4] *Deveaux*, 9 U.S. at 86.

[5] Louisville, Cincinnati, & Charleston R.R. Co. v. Letson, 43 U.S. (2 How.) 497 (1844).

and belonging to that state, and therefore entitled, for the purpose of suing and being sued, to be deemed a citizen of that state."[6] Thus, the Court reversed course and adopted a view of the corporation as its own separate person with its own citizenship, independent of the citizenship of its individual members.[7] One of the consequences of this decision was to afford greater access for corporations to sue and be sued in federal court.

Another important constitutional issue that arose in the early-nineteenth century involved the corporation's rights under the Contracts Clause of Article I of the Constitution. In *Trustees of Dartmouth College v. Woodward*, the Supreme Court was asked to decide whether the state of New Hampshire had the authority to modify the corporate charter of Dartmouth College, which had previously been granted by the King of England.[8] The Court held that the state had no power to change the university's charter because the Constitution bars states from impairing contracts, and Dartmouth's charter constituted a contract between the government and the original donors and founders of the university.[9] In the opinion, Chief Justice Marshall issued his widely quoted description of the corporation as "an artificial being, invisible, intangible, and existing only in contemplation of law. Being the mere creature of law, it possesses only those properties which the charter of its creation confers upon it."[10] This certainly sounds like an affirmation of the artificial person or concession theory of the corporation. Yet, a close reading of the case reveals that the Court based its decision on the recognition that the corporation is ultimately the individuals who compose it, and those individuals have constitutional rights that must be preserved.[11] The state's obligation to uphold the original charter of the corporation protects the constitutional rights of the individuals behind the corporation who received the charter. In this regard, the Court utilized the aggregate theory of the corporation to establish corporate constitutional rights with the true aim of protecting the contract and property interests of the individual members.

Two decades later, the Supreme Court declined to draw again on this aggregate theory to decide whether corporations have the constitutional status of "citizens" under the Privileges and Immunities Clause of Article IV of the Constitution. In *Bank of Augusta v. Earle*, the Supreme Court held that corporations are not citizens for purposes of the constitutional guarantee that citizens of one state shall be

6 *Id.* at 555.

7 Congress later established by statute that, for diversity jurisdiction, a corporation is a citizen of the state of its incorporation and the state where it has its principal place of business. *See* 28 U.S.C. §1332(c) (2016).

8 Trs. of Dartmouth Coll. v. Woodward, 17 U.S. (4 Wheat.) 518 (1819).

9 *Id.* at 625–27.

10 *Id.* at 636. One commentator notes that while Justice Marshall's famous description of the corporation has been utilized even by Supreme Court justices to justify limiting corporate rights, Justice Marshall's actual views in support of corporations would not entail a restrictive interpretation of their rights. *See* Christopher J. Wolfe, *"An Artificial Being": John Marshall and Corporate Personhood*, 40 Harv. J.L. & Pub. Pol'y 201, 202, 230–35 (2017).

11 17 U.S. at 643–44.

entitled to all the same privileges and immunities of citizens in other states.[12] The Court described the corporation not as an aggregate of its individual members, but as an artificial person created by the charter of its home state. Refusing to look through the corporation's artificial form to the natural persons behind it, the Court declined to focus on the citizenship or contract interests of the human members. Instead, the Court preferred the artificial person or government concession view of the corporation: "Whenever a corporation makes a contract, it is the contract of the legal entity; of the artificial being created by the charter; and not the contract of the individual members. The only rights it can claim are the rights which are given to it in that character, and not the rights which belong to its members as citizens of a state."[13] While human individuals were citizens who had the privilege of making contracts and conducting business in any state, corporations did not have that status. Thus, the Court preserved the right of each state to regulate within its borders the business of foreign corporations incorporated in other states.

By the mid-nineteenth century, special legislative chartering of corporations gave way to general incorporation statutes. As discussed in Chapter 1, once individuals could freely form corporations without the need for a specific act of the state legislature to grant a corporate charter, the focus shifted from the state as the authority and originator of the corporation to the human individuals who incorporated the business for their benefit. The corporation looked less like an artificial person created as a concession of the government for public purposes, and more like a vehicle through which private parties could arrange to pursue their own mutual economic interests. As will be seen, in an important shift again toward the aggregate view of the corporation, the Supreme Court held through a progression of cases that corporations have constitutional rights to equal protection and due process of law.

The corporation's right to equal protection as a person under the Fourteenth Amendment began in part in a somewhat unusual way with the important case of *Santa Clara County v. Southern Pacific Railroad Co.*[14] The defendant railroad company had argued that the state taxed its property differently than the property of individuals, and that this unequal treatment was a violation of the equal protection clause of the Fourteenth Amendment. The attorney for the railroad company

[12] Bank of Augusta v. Earle, 38 U.S. (13 Pet.) 519 (1839). The specific issue was whether a bank incorporated in Georgia could conduct ordinary banking business transactions in Alabama in competition with Alabama banks.

[13] *Id.* at 587. Using similar language, the Court later reaffirmed that corporations are not citizens under the meaning of the Privileges and Immunities Clause: "The term citizens . . . applies only to natural persons, members of the body politic, . . . not to artificial persons created by the legislature, and possessing only the attributes which the legislature has prescribed." Paul v. Virginia, 75 U.S. (8 Wall.) 168, 177 (1868). However, in a series of later cases, the Supreme Court gradually recognized the right of corporations to work in multistate markets free of discrimination and arbitrary expulsion. *See* Herbert Hovenkamp, *The Classical Corporation in American Legal Thought*, 76 Geo. L.J. 1593, 1650 (1988).

[14] Santa Clara v. S. Pac. R.R. Co., 118 U.S. 394 (1886).

urged the court to view the corporation in realistic terms, as a collection of real people who compose the business, and to recognize that the property of the corporation is actually the property of the individual members.[15] From this point of view, the corporation is not an abstract artificial entity or a concession of the state, but an aggregate of the natural persons who make up the corporation and who are united in a shared business purpose. To deprive the corporation of its business property ultimately is to deprive the individual owners of their private property. The corporation thus maintained that it was entitled to equal protection as a person under the Fourteenth Amendment.

This argument had been persuasive in a companion case, *San Mateo v. Southern Pacific Railroad Company*, in the lower court a few years prior to *Santa Clara*.[16] Justice Stephen Field, who was on the Supreme Court at the time of the *Santa Clara* case, had actually served as one of the judges in the companion *San Mateo* case in the lower court and had written a lengthy opinion supporting the railroad company's position. He agreed that the corporation was a person within the meaning of the Fourteenth Amendment and that the taxes imposed on the company violated its right to equal protection. Drawing upon a view of the corporation as an aggregate of its members, he stated that the court must always "look beyond the name of the artificial being to the individuals whom it represents" and protect their interests.[17] He reasoned that the property rights of the individual members must not suddenly lose their constitutional protection when the members join a corporation.[18]

When the *Santa Clara* case came before the Supreme Court, the railroad company likewise argued that it was entitled to the same constitutional safeguards as individuals under the Fourteenth Amendment. The Supreme Court agreed, but the opinion curiously contained no substantive analysis or explanation of the constitutional issue. Rather, in the introductory portion of the case, the Reporter's Note states that prior to oral argument, the Chief Justice declared from the bench:

> The court does not wish to hear argument on the question whether the provision in the Fourteenth Amendment to the Constitution, which forbids a State to deny to any person within its jurisdiction the equal protection of the laws, applies to these corporations. We are all of opinion that it does.[19]

15 *See* Morton J. Horwitz, Santa Clara *Revisited: The Development of Corporate Theory*, 88 W. VA. L. REV. 173, 177–78 (1985) (citing the arguments of John Norton Pomeroy, attorney for the railroad company).

16 San Mateo v. S. Pac. R.R. Co., 13 F. 722 (C.C.D. Cal. 1882).

17 *Id.* at 744; *see also id.* at 747–48.

18 Justice Field wrote: "It would be a most singular result if a constitutional provision intended for the protection of every person against partial and discriminating legislation by the states, should cease to exert such protection the moment the person becomes a member of a corporation." *Id.* at 744.

19 Santa Clara v. S. Pac. R.R. Co., 118 U.S. 394, 396 (1886). For a fascinating explanation of the circumstances leading to the Reporter's Note, see Winkler, *supra* note at 3, 144–53.

This brief and conclusory statement has been widely criticized for lacking logic, history, and reason to support it.[20] It casually established that corporations are persons under the Fourteenth Amendment and became the precedent for future extensions of constitutional rights based on the corporation's personhood. The text of the Fourteenth Amendment does not contain a reference to corporations, and there was nothing explicit in the legislative history of the Amendment to suggest that corporations were intended to be included in its protections.[21] It was accepted that the purpose of the Fourteenth Amendment was to provide procedural and substantive rights to newly freed slaves.[22] Positioned between the Thirteenth Amendment, which abolished slavery, and the Fifteenth Amendment, which prohibited racial discrimination in voting, the Fourteenth Amendment was intended to guarantee due process and equal protection rights for all persons, regardless of race.

The pronouncement in favor of the constitutional personhood of corporations in *Santa Clara* shifted the focus of subsequent Fourteenth Amendment cases toward corporations. For the first fifty years after the adoption of the Fourteenth Amendment, more than fifty percent of the Supreme Court cases applying the Fourteenth Amendment involved corporations, and less than one half of one percent involved race discrimination claims.[23] Although subsequent Supreme Court justices individually denounced the *Santa Clara* result,[24] the Court repeatedly confirmed that

20 *See, e.g.*, John J. Flynn, *The Jurisprudence of Corporate Personhood: The Misuse of a Legal Concept, in* CORPORATIONS AND SOCIETY: POWER AND RESPONSIBILITY 131, 133, 136 (Warren J. Samuels & Arthur S. Miller eds., 1987); David H. Gans & Douglas T. Kendall, A *Capitalist Joker: The Strange Origins, Disturbing Past, and Uncertain Future of Corporate Personhood in American Law*, 44 J. MARSHALL L. REV. 643, 658–61 (2011); Dale Rubin, *Corporate Personhood: How the Courts Have Employed Bogus Jurisprudence to Grant Corporations Constitutional Rights Intended for Individuals*, 28 QUINNIPIAC L. REV. 523, 551–59 (2010).

21 One of the attorneys for the Southern Pacific Railroad Company, who was also a member of the Congressional committee that drafted the Fourteenth Amendment, suggested that a group of the drafters used the word "person" rather than "citizen" with the intent to include corporations within the Amendment's protections, suggesting a "conspiracy theory" behind the Fourteenth Amendment. Various commentators have rejected this conspiracy theory, however, arguing that no independent corroborating evidence supports the railroad attorney's claim and that he was not entirely forthright in describing the legislative history of the Fourteenth Amendment. *See* discussions in Louis B. Boudin, *Truth and Fiction About the Fourteenth Amendment*, 16 N.Y.U. L.Q. REV. 19 (1938); Howard Jay Graham, *The "Conspiracy Theory" of the Fourteenth Amendment*, 47 YALE L.J. 371 (1938); Howard Jay Graham, *The "Conspiracy Theory" of the Fourteenth Amendment: 2*, 48 YALE L.J. 171 (1938); Gregory A. Mark, Comment, *The Personification of the Business Corporation in American Law*, 54 U. CHI. L. REV. 1441, 1462–63 (1987).

22 Earl M. Maltz, CIVIL RIGHTS, THE CONSTITUTION, AND CONGRESS, 1863–1869, at 93–120 (1990).

23 Conn. Gen. Life Ins. Co. v. Johnson, 303 U.S. 77, 90 (1938) (Black, J., dissenting); *see also* Jack M. Balkin, *How Social Movements Change (or Fail to Change) the Constitution: The Case of the New Departure*, 39 SUFFOLK U. L. REV. 27, 53 (2005) ("[T]here is something deeply distressing about the fact that an amendment designed to protect the rights of black citizens was soon interpreted to given [sic] them virtually no protection whatsoever and instead gave constitutional protection to corporations.").

24 *See, e.g.*, Wheeling Steel Corp. v. Glander, 337 U.S. 562, 579–80 (1949) (Douglas, J., dissenting) ("'Persons' in the first sentence plainly includes only human beings, for corporations are not 'born or naturalized.' . . . I can only conclude that the *Santa Clara* case was wrong and should be overruled.");

corporations were persons within the meaning of the equal protection clause of the Fourteenth Amendment.[25] Shortly after *Santa Clara*, the Supreme Court built upon this foundation and held that corporations were also persons for purposes of the due process clause of the Fourteenth Amendment and the Fifth Amendment.[26] The status of the corporation as a constitutional person became firmly entrenched in constitutional doctrine and set the stage for corporations to gain additional constitutional rights.

TWENTIETH-CENTURY EXPANSION OF CORPORATE CONSTITUTIONAL PERSONHOOD AND RIGHTS

As corporations grew in size and number near the end of the nineteenth century, corporate rights and liabilities expanded along with them. As explained in Chapter 1, many scholars and jurists began to embrace the idea that corporations have a real and separate existence apart from their shareholders, and the real entity theory of the corporation emerged as another way of viewing the corporation. The real entity theory supported the idea that the corporation was its own person and could initiate and bear responsibility for its own actions and intentions. The corporation's separate personhood coincided with an increased interest in corporate criminal liability for wrongful corporate acts.[27] The corporation itself could be convicted of a crime, due to its organizational acts and culpable intent, independent of the criminal liability of specific individuals within the corporation. As legislatures and courts saw a growing need to hold corporations responsible for criminal acts, corporate attorneys began to argue that corporations were entitled to many of the same constitutional rights intended to protect individuals in criminal proceedings. In light of the Supreme Court's prior holdings granting equal protection and due process rights to corporations, the Court gradually and selectively extended additional rights to corporations under several provisions of the Constitution. In doing so, the Court did not adopt a single, coherent theory of the corporation to guide its reasoning, but utilized different conceptions of the corporation and public policy concerns to support its conclusions.

Conn. Gen. Life Ins. Co., 303 U.S. at 85–87 (Black, J., dissenting) ("Neither the history nor the language of the Fourteenth Amendment justifies the belief that corporations are included within its protection … [I]ts purpose was to protect weak and helpless human beings … not … to remove corporations in any fashion from the control of state governments.").

25 *See, e.g.*, Gulf, Colorado & Santa Fe Ry. Co. v. Ellis, 165 U.S. 150, 154 (1897); Covington & Lexington Tpk. Rd. Co. v. Sandford, 164 U.S. 578, 592 (1896); Pembina Consol. Silver Mining & Milling Co. v. Pennsylvania, 125 U.S. 181, 188–89 (1888).

26 *See* Chicago, Burlington & Quincy R.R. v. Chicago, 166 U.S. 226, 241 (1897); Noble v. Union River Logging R.R. Co., 147 U.S. 165, 176 (1893); Chicago, Milwaukee, & St. Paul Ry. Co. v. Minnesota, 134 U.S. 418, 440–41, 456–57 (1890) Minneapolis & St. Louis Ry. Co. v. Beckwith, 129 U.S. 26, 28 (1889).

27 *See* William S. Laufer, Corporate Bodies and Guilty Minds: The Failure of Corporate Criminal Liability 9–15 (2006).

In *Hale v. Henkel*, the Court held that corporations are entitled to Fourth Amendment protection against unreasonable searches and seizures by the government. The Court stated that a corporation is "an association of individuals under an assumed name and with a distinct legal entity. In organizing itself as a collective body, it waives no constitutional immunities appropriate to such body."[28] Although describing the corporation as "an association of individuals" implied an aggregate view of the corporate person, the references to the corporation as "a distinct legal entity" and "collective body" also suggested that the corporation is a separate, real entity that is entitled to claim constitutional protection in its own right. The corporation thus has an independent claim to be free of unreasonable searches and seizures of corporate property.

In the same case, however, the Court held that the corporation is not a person for purposes of the self-incrimination clause of the Fifth Amendment. While the Fifth Amendment prevents individuals from being compelled to incriminate themselves in criminal cases, the Court held that this right does not apply to corporations. The court described the corporation as "a creature of the State ... incorporated for the benefit of the public ... Its rights to act as a corporation are only preserved to it so long as it obeys the laws of its creation."[29] This language reflected the artificial person or concession theory of the corporation. Having received the concession of the state to exist, the corporation could not then use the Fifth Amendment to avoid providing the state with essential information about acts it committed in violation of the state's laws. Thus, in *Hale v. Henkel*, the Supreme Court utilized different conceptions of the corporation simultaneously to grant one constitutional right and deny another.

The Court relied on the artificial person theory again in *United States v. Morton Salt Co.* to deny the corporation's claim to Fourth Amendment privacy rights. The Court reasoned that the government allows corporations the privilege of engaging in commerce, and with that privilege come enhanced measures of regulation that the corporation is obliged to accept. As an artificial person, the corporation cannot be treated in the exact same way as natural persons. Corporations "can claim no equality with individuals in the enjoyment of a right to privacy."[30]

Corporations later gained the Fifth Amendment right against double jeopardy[31] and the Seventh Amendment right to trial by jury.[32] In extending double jeopardy rights to corporations, the Court reasoned that a corporate person has the same

28 Hale v. Henkel, 201 U.S. 43, 76 (1906).

29 *Id.* at 74–75.

30 Unites States v. Morton Salt Co., 338 U.S. 632, 652 (1950). More recently, the Supreme Court has held that the corporation does not have a statutory right to privacy under the "personal privacy" exemption of the Freedom of Information Act. *See* FCC v. AT&T, Inc., 562 U.S. 397 (2011). "'Personal' in the phrase 'personal privacy' conveys more than just 'of a person.' It suggests a type of privacy evocative of human concerns—not the sort usually associated with an entity like, say, AT&T." *Id.* at 406.

31 United States v. Martin Linen Supply Co., 430 U.S. 564 (1977).

32 Ross v. Bernhard, 396 U.S. 531 (1970).

interests of a natural person in avoiding "embarrassment, expense and ordeal and . . . liv[ing] in a continuing state of anxiety and insecurity."[33] This language appears to reflect a real entity view of the corporation as a person that can experience real hardship from repeated conviction attempts. Interestingly, the Court did not try to reconcile its differing positions with regard to its previous denial of the Fifth Amendment privilege against self-incrimination and its grant of the Fifth Amendment double jeopardy right to corporations. The uses of the term "person" in both clauses of the Fifth Amendment are analytically indistinguishable. The self-incrimination clause follows immediately after and is grammatically part of the double jeopardy clause, but the corporation is treated very differently under each one. This is indicative of the Supreme Court's selective approach to corporate constitutional rights and the seeming incoherence of its corporate personhood jurisprudence. The Court has explained its reasoning not by way of explicitly invoking the various legal theories of the corporation, but by classifying rights like the privilege against self-incrimination as purely "personal" ones, and therefore applicable only to human individuals.[34]

A steady expansion of the constitutional rights of the corporate person occurred in the latter half of the twentieth century to further protect the corporation's contract and property interests, its rights to fair criminal trials and procedures, and even its rights to free speech.[35] Through this process, the Supreme Court did not always justify its decisions with consistent and explicit references to particular legal theories of the corporation. Rather, in somewhat ad hoc fashion, the Court chose at times to look to the history or underlying purpose of the constitutional right at issue, or to articulate certain important public policies that it sought to uphold. As corporations grew and changed in structure and size, as their role and presence in society intensified, and as societal needs raised new and different public policy concerns, the Court found it increasingly difficult to maintain a unified and consistent theoretical view of the corporation for purposes of extending corporate constitutional rights. In the last several decades, the Court seems to be explicitly theorizing about the personhood of corporations less and less and focusing instead on the nature and purpose of the right at issue to determine its applicability to corporations. Over time, the corporation has been granted many, but not all, of the same constitutional protections of natural persons. The expansion of rights for the corporate person has continued in recent years particularly with regard to rights to political speech and religious freedom.

Opponents of corporate constitutional rights find all of this deeply troubling. The concern is that allowing corporations to be the holders of constitutional rights empowers them to such a degree that it ultimately diminishes the rights and well-

33 430 U.S. at 569.

34 United States v. White, 322 U.S. 694, 698 (1944) (describing the constitutional privilege against self-incrimination as "essentially a personal one").

35 *See* Elizabeth Pollman, *Reconceiving Corporate Personhood*, 2011 UTAH L. REV. 1629, 1655–58.

being of individuals. Critics of corporate rights often assert that the root of corporate power can be traced to the doctrine of corporate personhood, that this dangerous doctrine began when the Supreme Court in the *Santa Clara* case casually declared that corporations are persons for purposes of the Fourteenth Amendment, and that thereafter the Court has utilized the concept of corporate personhood to treat corporations like natural persons with the same rights and privileges. These assertions are not entirely accurate.

Corporations do not have rights that are identical to those of individuals. For example, corporations cannot vote; they have no privilege against self-incrimination; they cannot claim protections against excessive bail because corporations cannot be jailed; and they have speech rights that are more limited than those of individuals. The Supreme Court has never equated corporate persons with individual persons for purposes of all constitutional rights. Nor was the *Santa Clara* case itself the origin of the personhood and rights of corporations. As previously discussed, corporations were held to have certain contract rights and citizenship status even prior to *Santa Clara*. The legal and sociological personhood of corporations had already been established well before the late-nineteenth century.[36] Thus, the idea that *Santa Clara* began a jurisprudence that granted all subsequent extensions of constitutional rights to corporations based on their personhood is somewhat misplaced.

It may seem slightly odd that a corporation can be a constitutional person for certain rights and not others. How does the corporation act as a person for one constitutional right, but then stop being a person for another? Once the corporation has been granted the coveted status of a constitutional person, should it not then have the capacity to claim all the rights and privileges that come with that designation? It turns out "constitutional personhood is not a universal binary switch; a person is not a constitutional person across all constitutional rights by virtue of a successful claim for one specific right. Instead, constitutional personhood is switched on – or not – for each individual right claimed by the claimant."[37] The Supreme Court apparently has extended to corporations certain rights under the Constitution when pragmatic concerns and policy interests make it wise or convenient to do so. The effect is a constitutional personhood jurisprudence that often seems somewhat results-oriented.[38] The Court has arguably utilized

36 One scholar suggests that the deference to corporations and their autonomy stretches back to feudal doctrines treating medieval corporations such as guilds, universities, and cities, as quasi-sovereign bodies and limiting the state's authority to regulate them. *See* Daniel J. H. Greenwood, *Neofeudalism: The Surprising Foundations of Corporate Constitutional Rights*, 2017 U. ILL. L. REV. 163, 165–71.

37 Zoë Robinson, *Constitutional Personhood*, 84 GEO. WASH. L. REV. 605, 654–55 (2016). The constitutional rights of aliens and felons, for example, may be different from those afforded to other individuals. *See id.* at 632–46.

38 Jess M. Krannich, *The Corporate "Person": A New Analytical Approach to a Flawed Method of Constitutional Interpretation*, 37 LOY. U. CHI. L.J. 61, 64 (2005); Note, *What We Talk About When We Talk About Persons: The Language of a Legal Fiction*, 114 HARV. L. REV. 1745, 1754 (2001).

alternative theories of corporate personhood to support particular results, rather than as guiding principles to help reach them.[39]

To be fair, perhaps the Court at various points has implicitly utilized broader philosophical, moral, and social conceptions of corporate personhood to drive some of its decision-making in constitutional cases. Nonetheless, given the complex, multidimensional, dynamic nature of personhood, it is no wonder that the cases present a patchwork of seemingly contradictory positions. Because corporate personhood itself is complicated and can be analyzed from varying angles in different contexts, the jurisprudence surrounding it is infected by that complexity. Depending on which angle one takes, one will see the corporation in very different lights. That the Court has never developed a single coherent set of theoretical justifications for its corporate constitutional jurisprudence is not surprising given the difficulty of formulating a unified view of corporate personhood across all situations.[40]

Some scholars have argued that, despite the seeming inconsistencies, there may be a unifying theme underlying the corporate constitutional cases: a concern for protecting the rights and interests of the individuals involved. The corporate person ultimately represents the shared interests of the human participants in the corporate enterprise. In giving effect to the status of the corporation as a constitutional person in any given case, the Supreme Court "reinforce[s] the underlying rights, duties, and expectations of the multiple human beings who constitute the corporate universe and who are the true holders of the rights in question."[41] Under this view, corporations hold rights in order to protect the individuals behind them. Corporate constitutional rights are "derivative" rights intended to protect the rights of the natural persons who are either represented by the corporation or who interact with the corporation in some way.[42] This perspective draws partially on an aggregate conception of the corporate person wherein the corporation is viewed as an association of individuals whose interests must be preserved. From this viewpoint, whenever the Court upholds the

39 Phillip I. Blumberg, *The Corporate Entity in an Era of Multinational Corporations*, 15 Del. J. Corp. L. 283, 318 (1990); *see also* Greenwood, *supra* note 36, at 168 ("If the Court invokes whichever metaphors or theories support its conclusion without regard to consistency or plausibility, the theories and metaphors are doing only rhetorical work; they are rationalizations rather than rationales.").

40 To be sure, even the constitutional personhood of human individuals arguably lacks a unified theoretical framework as evidenced by the fact that the Court has vested different natural persons with different constitutional rights; felons, aliens, and minors have different or diluted constitutional rights. *See* Robinson, *supra* note 37, at 607–09. The "question of who or what holds any given constitutional right has been assessed on an ad hoc basis, right-by-right and claimant-by-claimant." *Id.* at 608.

41 Burt Neuborne, *Of "Singles" Without Baseball: Corporations as Frozen Relational Moments*, 64 Rutgers L. Rev. 769, 784 (2012). For an alternative argument that the Court's corporate rights jurisprudence can be explained by a unifying preference for "organizational neutrality," i.e., a selective ascription of corporate rights "such that entrepreneurs are neither rewarded nor punished for selecting the corporate form" to do business, see Vincent S.J. Buccola, *Corporate Rights and Organizational Neutrality*, 101 Iowa L. Rev. 499, 502–03 (2016).

42 Margaret M. Blair & Elizabeth Pollman, *The Derivative Nature of Corporate Constitutional Rights*, 56 Wm. & Mary L. Rev. 1673, 1678, 1695, 1731 (2015).

rights of the corporation, the Court is trying to shield the rights of the relevant human beings who are tied to the corporation or impacted by its activities. However, other competing conceptions of corporate personhood have also served as justifications for the Court's decisions to extend or contract corporate rights.

The assertion that the Court's jurisprudence ultimately focuses on the rights of the corporation's human participants is a descriptive claim, i.e., it attempts to describe or explain the way corporations have been treated for purposes of constitutional analysis. But it is also a normative claim, i.e., it argues that issues involving corporate constitutional rights should be driven by a concern for enforcing the individual rights and duties shared by the human participants of the corporate community. In other words, corporate rights should be upheld to enforce the rights of real people. The normative argument requires that, in any given case, if we are going to recognize a corporate right, we must be able to identify the specific, relatively stable group of natural persons from whom the corporate right is derived.[43] However, this begs the question: Which of the many human beings who participate in the corporation or are affected by its activities should we choose to be the source of the original right? The shareholders? The employees? The consumers or members of the larger community? In situations where interests may strongly conflict among the various groups of individuals, the analysis becomes formidably complicated. Never has this been more evident than in the context of establishing corporate rights to free speech under the First Amendment.

FIRST AMENDMENT FREEDOM OF SPEECH

The First Amendment contains no explicit reference to "persons" as holders of free speech rights. "The Constitution says very little about who and what the First Amendment protects."[44] The language simply prohibits Congress from making laws "abridging the freedom of speech."[45]

The First Amendment is supported by several important rationales. Freedom of speech in particular serves many essential functions in a free and democratic society. One of the most important functions is to promote the marketplace of ideas. Justice Holmes famously stated that "the best test of truth is the power of the thought to get itself accepted in the competition of the market."[46] Limits on the free and open

43 *Id.* at 1735, 1739.

44 Richard L. Hasen, PLUTOCRATS UNITED: CAMPAIGN MONEY, THE SUPREME COURT, AND THE DISTORTION OF AMERICAN ELECTIONS 21 (2016).

45 U.S. CONST. amend. I. The use of the definite article "the" in the clause "the freedom of speech" invokes the existing common law understanding of free speech. *See* Anthony Lewis, FREEDOM FOR THE THOUGHT THAT WE HATE: A BIOGRAPHY OF THE FIRST AMENDMENT 40 (2007) (One interpretation of the Free Speech Clause is that the "word 'the' can be read to mean what was understood at the time to be included in the concept of free speech."). I thank John Eastman for informing me of this point.

46 Abrams v. United States, 250 U.S. 616, 630 (1919) (Holmes, J., dissenting). For a critical analysis of the marketplace of ideas approach, see Stanley Ingber, *The Marketplace of Ideas: A Legitimizing Myth*, 1984 DUKE L.J. 1.

exchange of communicated ideas inhibit the ability of individuals to widen their perspective, to evaluate the merits of their beliefs in light of what others have said, and to make well-informed decisions.

Political speech in particular must be vigorously safeguarded to allow citizens to engage in robust debate and to continually strive to form a more perfect union based on a diversity of political thoughts and opinions. Societies that are marked by suppression of certain viewpoints reflect totalitarian systems that are incompatible with democratic ideals. Free speech rights serve as a check on government power, allowing people to voice their concerns and criticisms without fear of reprisal. This in turn enables strong democratic self-government.

Freedom of speech is also imperative to uphold the autonomy and dignity of the speaker. The use of speech as a means of self-expression, self-determination, and self-fulfillment is inherently valuable because "expression is an integral part of the development of ideas, of mental exploration and of the affirmation of self."[47] Expressing oneself is a critical component of affirming one's sense of identity and personhood. To silence individuals or inhibit their ability to speak freely diminishes their status as persons and undermines their autonomy. From this point of view, the value of free speech is tied to the interests of the speaker.[48]

Beyond the autonomy of the speaker, freedom of speech also promotes the autonomy of the listener.[49] Any paternalistic interference from the state in filtering out unwanted political speech is an affront to the listening audience. Listeners should be able to hear all messages and decide for themselves which ones have validity. It is critical for listeners to receive information and gain exposure to differing viewpoints in order to make informed and intelligent judgments on matters of public concern. Suppressing certain types of statements, or preventing people from having access to the full range of communicated ideas, fails to afford individuals the respect and dignity they are due. The First Amendment is intended to protect the interests of listeners just as much as those of speakers.

It is not entirely clear whether the values underlying the protection of individual free speech under the First Amendment apply equally to corporate speech. The Supreme Court has had to consider these values and the purposes of the First Amendment in deciding several key cases involving corporate speech rights. Over the years, the Court has held that corporate persons do have significant rights under the First Amendment, although the rights are not entirely identical to those of individuals.

47 Thomas I. Emerson, *Toward a General Theory of the First Amendment*, 72 YALE L.J. 877, 879 (1963).

48 *See* C. Edwin Baker, *Scope of the First Amendment Freedom of Speech*, 25 UCLA L. REV. 964, 990–96 (1978).

49 *See* Ronald J. Colombo, THE FIRST AMENDMENT AND THE BUSINESS CORPORATION 129–31 (2015). One way of categorizing these interests is to say that the interests of the speaker involve the "active" aspect of free speech, and the interests of the listener involve the "passive" aspect, both of which are critical to support individual autonomy. *See* Meir Dan-Cohen, RIGHTS, PERSONS, AND ORGANIZATIONS: A LEGAL THEORY FOR BUREAUCRATIC SOCIETY 92–93 (2d ed. 2016).

DEVELOPMENT OF CORPORATE SPEECH RIGHTS

There are different types of corporate speech rights, and the Supreme Court has adopted different parameters for corporations to exercise them.[50] Corporations have the right to engage in commercial speech, which allows corporations to propose commercial transactions and engage in advertising. In *Virginia State Board of Pharmacy v. Virginia Citizens Consumer Council*,[51] the Supreme Court held that the First Amendment prohibits laws that unduly abridge the commercial speech of corporations. At issue was a state law banning drug price advertising by pharmacy companies. In upholding corporate commercial speech rights, the Court focused on the interest of listeners, i.e., the consuming public, to receive the advertising information from the corporation. The case established that any non-deceptive commercial expression made by a business is a form of speech that is entitled to First Amendment protection because "the free flow of commercial information is indispensable" to the functioning of a free market economy.[52] Even so, commercial speech can be regulated and limited in the public interest. Laws that regulate commercial speech are subject to an intermediate level of judicial scrutiny. They must serve substantial government interests, they must do so directly, and they must restrict no more speech than is necessary. States may regulate the content of commercial speech to ensure that it does not contain false or misleading information.[53]

Corporations also have political speech rights. Political speech has much stronger First Amendment protection than commercial speech. Speech of a political nature is exactly the type of speech the First Amendment at its core was intended to safeguard. Verbal utterances and written communications are not the only forms of political speech. In *Buckley v. Valeo*, the Supreme Court found that the expenditure of money for political purposes can also amount to a form of protected speech. The Court recognized that "virtually every means of communicating ideas in today's mass society requires the expenditure of money."[54] When people must spend their money to finance the creation and dissemination of their message, their use of money becomes an integral part of their act of speaking. In this sense, political spending is equated with political speech. Restrictions on election-related spending inhibit political speech and diminish the amount of information available in the public marketplace of ideas. The Court reasoned that a "restriction on the amount of money a person or a group can spend on political communication during a campaign necessarily reduces the quantity of expression by restricting the number of issues discussed, the depth of their exploration, and the size of the audience

50 Adam Winkler, *Corporate Personhood and the Rights of Corporate Speech*, 30 Seattle U. L. Rev. 863 (2007).

51 Va. State Bd. of Pharmacy v. Va. Citizens Consumer Council, Inc. 425 U.S. 748 (1976).

52 *See id.* at 765.

53 *See* Cent. Hudson Gas & Elec. v. Pub. Servs. Comm'n of N.Y., 447 U.S. 557, 563–66 (1980).

54 Buckley v. Valeo, 424 U.S. 1, 19 (1976).

reached."[55] While recognizing that those with more money may be able to engage in more political speech than those with lesser means, the Court nonetheless maintained that the government has no compelling interest in "equalizing the relative ability of individuals and groups to influence the outcome of elections."[56] Indeed, "the concept that government may restrict the speech of some elements of our society in order to enhance the relative voice of others is wholly foreign to the First Amendment."[57]

The Supreme Court has made clear that political speech, regardless of who utters it, is entitled to the highest level of protection under the First Amendment. In *First National Bank of Boston v. Bellotti*,[58] a Massachusetts law prohibited corporations from spending money to influence public referenda campaigns that were not directly related to their business interests. It appeared in this case that the state wanted to suppress corporate opposition to a state income tax proposal.[59] The Court invalidated the law on the grounds that it unconstitutionally infringed on corporate political speech. The Court held that the corporation is a person possessing the right to free expression under the First Amendment.[60]

Rather than invoking theories of corporate personhood to hold that corporate persons have the same status as individual persons under the First Amendment, the Court in *Bellotti* focused instead on the value of the speech, regardless of its source, in the public marketplace of ideas. Affirming the right of listeners to hear the speech and the voters' need to be informed, the Court framed the issue in terms of whether the speech itself is the kind that should be protected. If it is, the identity of the speaker, whether corporate or individual, should make no difference. "The proper question therefore is not whether corporations 'have' First Amendment rights and, if so, whether they are coextensive with those of natural persons. Instead, the question must be whether [the statute] abridges expression that the First Amendment was meant to protect. We hold that it does."[61] Because laws burdening such political speech restrict the dissemination of important political information, they are subject to strict scrutiny. They must be supported by a compelling government interest, and they must be narrowly tailored to achieve that interest. The state argued it had

55 *Id.*
56 *Id.* at 48.
57 *Id.* at 48–49.
58 First Nat'l Bank of Boston v. Bellotti, 435 U.S. 765 (1978).
59 *See* Flynn, *supra* note 20, at 147; William Patton & Randall Bartlett, *Corporate "Persons" and Freedom of Speech: The Political Impact of Legal Mythology*, 1981 Wis. L. Rev. 494, 497 (1981).
60 435 U.S. at 780–81.
61 *Id.* at 776; *see* Mark M. Hager, *Bodies Politic: The Progressive History of Organizational "Real Entity" Theory*, 50 U. Pitt. L. Rev. 575, 640–45 (1989) (discussing *Bellotti*). Scholars have argued that this reasoning reflects a utilitarian view of the First Amendment as a means to an end: "the freedom of speech exists primarily to facilitate the greater good that arises through informed decision making, and only secondarily to secure rights. Free speech protections create space for a free market of conflicting views." Timothy K. Kuhner, Capitalism v. Democracy: Money in Politics and the Free Market Constitution 70 (2014).

a compelling interest in preventing the use of corporate funds to further political views with which some shareholders might disagree. The Court was unpersuaded by the state's argument. To the extent there may be shareholders who disagree with the use of corporate money to fund political speech and to advance political causes they do not support, the Court stated that such dissenting shareholders can protect their own interests through the "procedures of corporate democracy" and by filing derivative suits against corporate managers.[62]

Two years after *Bellotti*, the Court extended corporate speech rights to include non-election related corporate speech about political issues of public concern. In *Consolidated Edison Co. v. Public Service Commission*,[63] the Court ruled unconstitutional a state regulation prohibiting a utility company from inserting literature in its monthly customer bills that discussed certain controversial public policy issues. Applying strict scrutiny to the law, the Court struck it down because it unduly restricted the political speech of the utility. The Court concluded that whenever the state "restricts the speech of a private person, the state action may be sustained only if the government can show that the regulation is a precisely drawn means of serving a compelling state interest."[64] The utility company could be construed as a private person whose speech was being impaired by the government without compelling reason.

The speech rights of corporations were further broadened in another case involving a utility company, *Pacific Gas & Electric Co. v. Public Utilities Commission*,[65] but this time the utility company (PG&E) was being forced by the state to include a third party's speech in the company's own billing statements to consumers. PG&E objected to the state's order that a public interest group representing the interests of the utility's customers could use extra space in PG&E's company newsletter to communicate the group's views to customers. The Supreme Court declared the state's order to be unconstitutional because it infringed on PG&E's free speech rights. The Court held that PG&E had the *negative* speech right not to be associated with, or feel compelled to respond to, the speech of the public interest group in PG&E's newsletter. "For corporations as for individuals, the choice to speak includes within it the choice of what not to say."[66] The Court found that the state's order improperly "forces speakers to alter their speech" in a manner that violates the First Amendment.[67] While not explicitly drawing on legal theories of corporate personhood, the language the Court uses seems to liken corporations to natural persons with capacities for choice in what they wish to say, as well as having human-

62 435 U.S. at 794–95.
63 Consol. Edison Co. v. Pub. Serv. Comm'n, 447 U.S. 530 (1980).
64 *Id.* at 540.
65 Pac. Gas & Elec. Co. v. Pub. Utils. Comm'n, 475 U.S. 1 (1986).
66 *Id.* at 16.
67 *Id.* at 9.

like interests in not being compelled to speak or to change what they were going to say.

One strand of corporate political speech that has merited special analysis involves the use of corporate funds to engage in advocacy of specific political candidates. This type of speech has been treated differently than corporate speech that involves the use of corporate funds to address political issues or ballot measures. For over a hundred years, federal laws have prohibited corporations from making monetary contributions to candidates for political office.[68] Corporations are permitted to raise funds through voluntary contributions from corporate managers, shareholders, and employees, and deposit them in separate, segregated accounts (commonly known as political action committees, or PACs) that can then be used to finance candidate-related speech.[69] In a number of campaign finance cases, the Supreme Court upheld these campaign finance restrictions in order to protect the interests of dissenting members of the corporation who may not personally agree with the corporation's political positions.[70] The reasoning is that money belonging to shareholders should not be utilized by corporate executives to directly aid political candidates who are not supported by all the shareholders. The Court has noted that "the special characteristics of the corporate structure require particularly careful regulation," and it is appropriate to treat "unions, corporations, and similar organizations differently from individuals."[71]

For example, in *Austin v. Michigan State Chamber of Commerce*, the Court upheld a state law barring corporations from using general corporate treasury funds to finance advocacy in favor of political candidates.[72] To make such expenditures, corporations were required by the law to use PACs funded by the voluntary contributions of their members in segregated accounts. The state deemed these corporate spending restrictions necessary to prevent corporations from "obtain[ing] an unfair advantage in the political marketplace," resulting in a corrosion of politics.[73] The Supreme Court agreed and held that it would be improper for corporations to utilize the state-conferred benefits of the corporate form, which allow corporations to enjoy limited liability, perpetual life, and the accumulation of vast amounts of money for economic purposes, and then turn around and use that money for political purposes.[74] The Court expressed concern over the potential for corporate wealth and power to distort the public debate and dilute other voices in

68 The first such federal campaign finance statute was the Tillman Act of 1907. *See* Thomas W. Joo, *The Modern Corporation and Campaign Finance: Incorporating Corporate Governance Analysis into First Amendment Jurisprudence*, 79 Wash. U. L.Q. 1, 8 (2001); Adam Winkler, *"Other People's Money": Corporations, Agency Costs, and Campaign Finance Law*, 92 Geo. L.J. 871, 918–26 (2004).

69 *See* Joo, *supra* note 68, at 13–15; Winkler, *supra* note 68, at 928.

70 *See* Winkler, *supra* note 50, at 869.

71 FEC v. Nat'l Right to Work Comm., 459 U.S. 197, 209–11 (1982).

72 Austin v. Mich. State Chamber of Commerce, 494 U.S. 652 (1990), *overruled by* Citizens United v. FEC, 558 U.S. 310 (2010).

73 *Id.* at 659–60.

74 *Id.* at 658–59.

the political marketplace. Relying on this anti-distortion rationale, the Court decided that corporations must be subject to more restrictive standards than individuals under the First Amendment.

In order to address concerns regarding the use of corporate money in elections, Congress enacted the Bipartisan Campaign Reform Act (BCRA) in 2002, which imposed substantial restrictions on the ability of corporations to use corporate funds to influence elections of candidates for federal office. Soon thereafter, the Supreme Court was presented with the case of *McConnell v. Federal Election Commission*, which challenged the constitutionality of the BCRA.[75] Following the reasoning of *Austin*, the Court refused to strike down the statute. The Court reaffirmed the importance of preventing the distortion of political public discourse by the insertion of large amounts of corporate money, and it also expressed concern about possible corruption of the political process. The Court acknowledged the government's interest in preventing "both the actual corruption threatened by large financial contributions and the eroding of public confidence in the electoral process through the appearance of corruption."[76] Thus, both the *Austin* and *McConnell* cases made clear that the government could place substantial restrictions on corporate political speech to protect the overall integrity of the political marketplace.

The holdings in *Austin* and *McConnell* did not survive, however, because the controversial case of *Citizens United v. Federal Election Commission* took a very different approach. Rejecting the anti-distortion and anti-corruption interests that were central to the outcomes in *Austin* and *McConnell*, the Court in *Citizens United* strengthened the free speech rights of corporations to use corporate funds to support or oppose candidates for political office. In doing so, the *Citizens United* case caused a firestorm of debate over the nature, role, and purposes of corporations. It also brought a renewed urgency to the question whether corporations really are persons deserving of the same constitutional rights that are accorded to natural persons.

CITIZENS UNITED V. FEDERAL ELECTION COMMISSION

In a sharply divided 5–4 decision, the Supreme Court in *Citizens United v. Federal Election Commission* invalidated strict federal campaign finance laws and upheld the First Amendment rights of corporations to spend general corporate funds to support or oppose candidates in political elections.[77] Finding that political speech is constitutionally protected whether it is uttered by an individual or a corporation, the Court expressly overruled *Austin* and *McConnell*, which had upheld prohibitions on corporate expenditures in political elections.

75 McConnell v. FEC, 540 U.S. 93 (2003), *overruled by* Citizens United v. FEC, 558 U.S. 310 (2010).

76 *Id.* at 136. The Court held that the "ability to form and administer separate segregated funds … has provided corporations and unions with a constitutionally sufficient opportunity to engage in express advocacy" of political candidates. *Id.* at 203.

77 Citizens United v. FEC, 558 U.S. 310 (2010).

The *Citizens United* case drew widespread negative reaction and criticism as soon as it was decided. Then President Obama lamented, "[t]his ruling strikes at our democracy itself ... I can't think of anything more devastating to the public interest."[78] Politicians made public statements "strongly disagree[ing] with the Supreme Court's conclusion that money is speech, and that corporations should be treated the same as individual Americans when it comes to protected, fundamental speech rights."[79] Legal scholars attacked the reasoning of the decision. The Court was accused of partisanship and judicial activism, and polls showed that the vast majority of Americans opposed the ruling. Many people were angry that the Court had decided that corporations are "persons" for purposes of the First Amendment and entitled to the same rights as human persons in the expression of political speech. The case brought renewed fervor to a popular movement aimed at abolishing the constitutional personhood of corporations to strip corporations of all constitutional rights.[80]

The Supreme Court, however, never expressly stated in *Citizens United* that corporations are "persons" entitled to the same treatment as individuals under the First Amendment. Instead, the Court chose, as it did in *Bellotti*, to frame the issue in terms of whether the *speech* is the type of speech the First Amendment protects, not whether the *speaker* is the type of person who can claim First Amendment rights. It did not matter whether the speaker was a corporation or a human being because the political speech at issue in the case was covered by the First Amendment. The personhood of corporations was not the explicit basis of the Court's decision; the majority did not focus on corporate personhood anywhere in its opinion. However, critics argue that the unstated premise of the case is that corporations are persons that enjoy the same free speech rights as human persons. Commentators contend that the Court may have "avoid[ed] saying 'corporate personhood' out loud," but the "'personification' of corporate entities pervades the case," and any recognition of corporate First Amendment rights "results in recognition ... of a corporate Constitutional person."[81] Thus, one of the lingering effects of *Citizens United* has been to make the personhood of corporations an important part of the public conversation about the role and rights of corporations in society.

78 Sheryl Gay Stolberg, *Obama Turns Up Heat Over Ruling on Campaign Spending*, N.Y. Times, Jan. 24, 2010, at A18.

79 *See, e.g.*, Senator Christopher S. Dodd, Press Release, *Sen. Dodd Introduces Constitutional Amendment to Reverse Supreme Court Campaign Finance Ruling*, U.S. Fed. News, Feb. 25, 2010, 2010 WLNR 3913103.

80 *See* Susanna Kim Ripken, *Corporate First Amendment Rights After* Citizens United: *An Analysis of the Popular Movement to End the Constitutional Personhood of Corporations*, 14 U. Pa. J. Bus. L. 209, 224–44 (2011); Susanna Kim Ripken, Citizens United, *Corporate Personhood, and Corporate Power: The Tension Between Constitutional Law and Corporate Law*, 6 U. St. Thomas J. L. & Pub. Pol'y 285, 291–99 (2012).

81 Jeff Clements, Citizens United *and Corporate Personhood: Jeff Clements Responds to Kent Greenfield's Washington Post Op-ed*, Free Speech for People (Jan. 23, 2012), http://freespeechforpeople.org/node/315 [https://perma.cc/9HKD-SLNX].

The facts of the case revolved around the campaign finance restrictions contained in the BCRA, the same federal campaign finance statute that the Supreme Court had upheld in the *McConnell* case in 2003. Citizens United was a nonprofit corporation that released a film entitled, *Hillary: The Movie*, during Hillary Clinton's candidacy for the Democratic presidential nomination in 2008. The movie was "a feature-length negative advertisement that urge[d] viewers to vote against [Hillary] Clinton for President ... [T]he thesis of the film is that she is unfit for the Presidency."[82] The corporation wanted to increase the movie's public distribution by making it available through video-on-demand in the days leading up to the primary election, but it feared that doing so would violate the provisions of the BCRA. Those provisions prohibited corporations from using general treasury funds to make independent expenditures for an "electioneering communication," which was defined as "any broadcast, cable, or satellite communication" that refers to a political candidate for federal office and is made within thirty days of a primary election.[83] The initial question presented to the Supreme Court was whether the BCRA provision applied to the video-on-demand movie. However, after oral argument, the Court asked the parties for new briefing to address the much broader question of whether the BCRA provisions limiting corporations' independent spending in federal elections should be declared unconstitutional.

By a narrow majority, the Court held in a 5–4 decision that the BCRA's ban on corporate campaign expenditures violated the corporation's right to free speech and must be invalidated. The Court reaffirmed that the First Amendment protects corporate political speech. In the majority opinion written by Justice Kennedy, the Court stated that "political speech does not lose First Amendment protection 'simply because its source is a corporation.'"[84] A corporation, just like an individual, can contribute to the marketplace of ideas by expressing opinions and spending money to support or oppose political candidates. In this regard, the majority focused on the rights of listeners to hear the information. "Political speech is 'indispensable to decisionmaking in a democracy, and this is no less true because the speech comes from a corporation rather than an individual.'"[85] The Court rejected the idea that political speech of corporations should be treated differently under the First Amendment merely because corporations are not natural persons. Instead, the First Amendment protects all political speech and does not allow restrictions based on a speaker's corporate identity.

The Court found the corporate source of the speech to be irrelevant. In this regard, the majority's approach was firmly opposed to that taken previously by the Court in the *Austin* and *McConnell* cases. In *Austin* and *McConnell*, the Court

82 558 U.S. at 325.

83 2 U.S.C. §§ 441b(b)(2), 434(f)(3)(A) (2005) (transferred to 52 U.S.C. §§ 30118(b)(2), 30104(f)(3)(A) (2016)).

84 558 U.S. at 342 (quoting First Nat'l Bank of Boston v. Bellotti, 435 U.S. 765, 784 (1978)).

85 *Id.* at 349 (quoting *Bellotti*, 435 U.S. at 777).

focused directly on the identity of the speaker as a corporation and upheld restrictions on its speech precisely because corporations have abilities to amass wealth in ways that are different from that of individuals. The Court in *Austin* and *McConnell* was persuaded by fears that large aggregations of corporate funds might have distorting effects in the political marketplace when they are deployed to influence elections. In contrast, the majority in *Citizens United* rejected this anti-distortion rationale. The majority felt it was improper to focus on the economic wealth of corporate speakers and the potential unfair advantage that wealth might afford to corporations in the political domain. "The First Amendment's protections do not depend on the speaker's 'financial ability to engage in public discussion.'"[86] The Court reasoned that because the First Amendment prohibits the suppression of political speech based on the speaker's identity, it necessarily also forbids limitations on political speech based on a speaker's wealth. It is not the job of the First Amendment to equalize all voices in the public square by stifling some that are perceived to be more powerful in order to enhance others that are perceived to be relatively weaker.[87]

Moreover, the Court reasoned that under the anti-distortion rationale, even the political speech of media corporations could be banned. While the corporate form of giant media companies allows them to accumulate wealth that could also distort the public debate when they engage in political commentary, the law does not permit the suppression of their political speech. Media corporations are exempt from bans on corporate expenditures, but with today's technology and avenues for immediate and worldwide dissemination of information, it is difficult to distinguish between media companies and others who use such technologies to comment on political and social issues. According to *Citizens United*, the anti-distortion approach taken in *Austin* is untenable because it requires every organization that is perceived as being too wealthy to be subject to speech restrictions. That type of censorship is impermissibly unbounded; such censorship "is vast in its reach," "suppressing the speech of manifold corporations, both for-profit and nonprofit," both small and large.[88]

In addition to dismissing the anti-distortion concerns, the Court also rejected the argument that corporate political speech must be strictly limited to prevent corruption, or the appearance of corruption, of political officials.[89] The *McConnell* case had addressed the potential for money to buy political favors from elected officials and the need for strict spending rules to combat the corruption of the political system. The Court in *Citizens United* viewed corruption narrowly as interactions that involve *quid pro quo* treatment, i.e., dollars that directly result in political favors. Political spending that results in mere influence over or access to elected officials

86 *Id.* at 350 (quoting Buckley v. Valeo, 424 U.S. 1, 49 (1976)).
87 *Id.* (citing *Buckley*, 424 U.S. at 48).
88 *Id.* at 354–55.
89 *Id.* at 356–61.

does not mean the officials and the political system are corrupt. The Court acknowledged that some amount of favoritism and influence are unavoidable in representative politics as officials are expected to respond to the voices, and support the interests, of the voters who put them into office. The type of independent expenditure that the Citizens United organization utilized in the form of the *Hillary* movie did not involve direct contributions to any elected official or a *quid pro quo* expectation of any kind. In the Court's opinion, political speech of this type does "not lead to, or create the appearance of, *quid pro quo* corruption," nor does it "cause the electorate to lose faith in our democracy. By definition, an independent expenditure is political speech presented to the electorate that is not coordinated with a candidate."[90] Thus, the Court dismissed the anti-distortion and anti-corruption rationales discussed in its prior opinions. The Court expressly overruled *Austin* and *McConnell* in striking down the BCRA's ban on corporate independent expenditures.

The Court also contested the familiar argument that corporate political speech must be limited to protect the interests of dissenting shareholders who may disagree with the political positions expressed by the corporation.[91] In the majority's view, this concern for nonconsenting shareholders would allow the government to ban the political speech of media corporations as well, it being unreasonable to assume that all shareholders of large media companies unanimously agree with all political viewpoints expressed by the companies. If corporations' free speech rights must be limited out of concern for dissenting shareholders, then the BCRA provisions should have banned corporate speech at all times, not just in the thirty days prior to a primary election. In this regard, the Court found the statutory restrictions to be underinclusive at achieving the purported governmental purpose. They were also deemed to be overinclusive because the restrictions applied to the speech of all corporations, even those with only a single shareholder where no potential for dissenting shareholder views realistically existed. In the final analysis, the Court maintained that shareholders who disagree with the corporation's decisions to use corporate money to fund certain political views can protect themselves through the standard "procedures of corporate democracy."[92]

In arriving at its decision to invalidate the corporate speech restrictions in the BCRA and to solidify the First Amendment free speech rights of corporations, the Court did not directly discuss the issue of corporate personhood. The majority never stated that because corporations are persons, they must be treated just like individuals under the First Amendment. Rather than emphasizing the separate

90 *Id.* at 359–60.

91 *Id.* at 361–62.

92 *Id.* at 362. In referring to the procedures of corporate democracy, the Court presumably meant the various avenues provided by corporate and securities laws for shareholders to protect their interests, including bringing shareholder derivative suits against corporate managers for alleged breaches of fiduciary duties, electing new directors, making shareholder proposals in annual proxy statements, or selling their investments in the company.

personhood of corporations, the majority opinion referred to corporations as "associations of citizens." This terminology focused more on the aggregate nature of the corporation as a collection of individuals whose rights should not be diminished when they organize themselves into a corporation. For example, in the Court's discussion of its misgivings with the anti-distortion rationale, it noted that wealthy individuals and unincorporated associations are permitted to spend unlimited amounts on independent expenditures, "[y]et certain disfavored associations of citizens – those that have taken on the corporate form – are penalized for engaging in the same political speech."[93] The Court viewed the corporation as a group of individuals who should be entitled to the same First Amendment protection when they speak individually and when they speak in concert.

Justice Scalia in his concurring opinion similarly referred to the associational root of the corporation's constitutional rights. He insisted that "the individual person's right to speak includes the right to speak *in association with other individual persons*."[94] He pointed out that the speech of the Republican Party or the Democratic Party is not the speech of an individual person, but it is still protected because it is "the speech of many individual Americans, who have associated in a common cause ... The association of individuals in a business corporation is no different – or at least it cannot be denied the right to speak on the simplistic ground that it is not 'an individual American.'"[95] That corporations are not human beings and cannot speak in a literal sense is a fallacious argument, in Justice Scalia's opinion. "The authorized spokesman of a corporation is a human being, who speaks on behalf of the human beings who have formed that association – just as the spokesman of an unincorporated association speaks on behalf of its members."[96]

By focusing on the nature of the *speech*, Justice Scalia and the majority of the Court found no need to address the nature, or the personhood, or the identity of the *speaker*. Justice Scalia stated that the First Amendment prohibits "excluding any category of speaker, from single individuals to partnerships of individuals, to unincorporated associations of individuals, to incorporated associations of individuals."[97] This implies that *what* is said is far more important than *who* says it. Yet, a few sentences later in the very same paragraph, Justice Scalia highlighted the importance of the corporate identity of the speaker: "[T]o exclude or impede corporate speech is to muzzle the principal agents of the modern free economy. We should celebrate rather than condemn the addition of this speech to the public debate."[98] These statements suggest that the value of the speech is intimately tied to who is speaking – in this case, "the principal agents of the modern free economy," i.e.,

93 *Id.* at 356.
94 *Id.* at 392 (Scalia, J., concurring).
95 *Id.*
96 *Id.* at 392 n.7.
97 *Id.* at 393.
98 *Id.*

corporations. Such an interpretation is surely contrary to the message Justice Scalia intended to convey with his statements, but this seems to demonstrate the difficulty with analyzing speech in isolation, entirely separate from its source.

While the majority and concurring opinions in *Citizens United* did not refer explicitly to the personhood of corporations, the dissenting opinion, written by Justice Stevens, touched on the topic. The dissent insisted that "corporations have no consciences, no beliefs, no feelings, no thoughts, no desires. Corporations help structure and facilitate the activities of human beings . . . and their 'personhood' often serves as a useful legal fiction. But they are not themselves members of 'We the People' by whom and for whom our Constitution was established."[99] Corporations are not real persons with interests in self-expression, dignity, and autonomy, which are among the cherished values that the First Amendment is intended to protect. According to the dissent, it is critical to distinguish between corporate persons and human persons, only the latter of which can be rightfully regarded as actual members of society: Corporate "'speakers' are not natural persons, much less members of our political community."[100] Any speech interests corporations may have are derived largely from the rights of the individual members of the corporation and the rights of listeners to hear the information. Faulting the majority for focusing so heavily on the speech at issue and refusing to account for the nature of the speaker, the dissent argues that the majority's denunciation of identity-based distinctions has rhetorical appeal but obscures the reality of how speech rights have been differentially accorded to different classes of speakers. For example, it is constitutionally permissible to regulate speech based on the speaker's identity in many other contexts, as evidenced by the contrasting speech rights of students, prisoners, military personnel, foreigners, and government employees.[101]

The dissent maintained that it is wrong and harmful to treat corporations like natural persons in the political sphere. With their wealth and power, corporations have the ability to drown out individual voices and gain special advantages from the politicians they support. According to the dissent, the majority's rejection of the anti-distortion and anti-corruption rationales for campaign finance laws reflects a failure to acknowledge the realities of political dynamics. Corruption does not manifest in only *quid pro quo* arrangements; it can take many forms. "Corruption operates along a spectrum," and "the difference between selling a vote and selling access is a matter of degree, not kind."[102] The dissent

99 *Id.* at 466 (Stevens, J., dissenting).

100 *Id.* at 424.

101 *Id.* at 420–21. Rather than identifying only categories of natural persons whose speech is restricted based on their identity, Justice Stevens in his dissent might have more persuasively argued that certain organizational persons, such as municipal corporations, the Army, and government-owned corporations, are subject to restrictions on their political speech precisely because of their identity. *See* Eric W. Orts, *Theorizing the Firm: Organizational Ontology in the Supreme Court*, 65 DePaul L. Rev. 559, 577–78 (2016).

102 *Citizens United*, 558 U.S. at 447–48.

characterizes the majority's opinion as "a rejection of the common sense of the American people, who have recognized a need to prevent corporations from undermining self-government ... and who have fought against the distinctive corrupting potential of corporate electioneering."[103]

Criticizing "the majority's 'crabbed view of corruption,'"[104] the dissent emphasizes that the campaign finance laws, stretching back to the Tillman Act in 1907, were intended to combat actual and perceived corruption and to protect the interests of shareholders in preventing the use of their money to support candidates they oppose.[105] The ability to form and administer separate segregated funds in PACs with money given voluntarily by corporate members is a viable alternative for express corporate advocacy that does not entail the use of other people's money by corporate managers. The Citizens United group had every right to utilize funds from its PAC to engage in electioneering communications; doing so would have ensured that the rights of objecting shareholders would have been protected. From the dissent's point of view, the majority's belief that the "procedures of corporate democracy" are available to protect the interests of dissenting shareholders is unrealistic, for the odds of shareholders successfully suing corporate managers for breaches of fiduciary duty, or electing new directors and officers, or even recognizing that corporate money has been spent on objectionable electioneering, are exceedingly low.[106] Shareholders do not have sufficient methods for ensuring that corporate speech reflects their own opinions and values. Considering all of the problems associated with corporate speech, the dissent maintained that corporations should not be treated like individuals for purposes of First Amendment political speech rights.

CORPORATE SPEECH AND NOTIONS OF CORPORATE PERSONHOOD

Unlike various prior constitutional law cases that have extended constitutional rights to corporations, the *Citizens United* case notably lacks references to the nature of corporations as persons. The majority never explicitly relied on the concept of corporate personhood in its opinion, and the dissent never accused the majority of justifying its decision on the grounds that corporations are persons worthy of holding constitutional rights.

Yet critics of the case believe the Court's holding is driven by a view of the corporation as a person who is entitled to the same constitutional rights as individuals: "A crucial basis for this decision is that corporations, as 'persons,'

[103] *Id.* at 479.

[104] *Id.* at 452 (citing McConnell v. FEC, 540 U.S. 93, 152 (2003)). For strong critiques of the majority's narrow view of corruption, see Steven H. Shiffrin, What's Wrong with the First Amendment? 109–11 (2016); Zephyr Teachout, Corruption in America 227–45 (2014).

[105] 558 U.S. at 433, 475–76.

[106] *Id.* at 476–78.

enjoy free-speech rights."[107] Some of the wording in the opinion suggests that the important First Amendment values supporting a person's self-expression and dignity apply equally to corporations. For example, the Court stated: "By taking the right to speak from some and giving it to others, the Government deprives the disadvantaged person or class of the right to use speech to strive to establish worth, standing, and respect for the speaker's voice."[108] Similarly, the Court asserted: "The Government has 'muffle[d] the voices that best represent the most significant segments of the economy' ... And 'the electorate [has been] deprived of information, knowledge and opinion vital to its function.'"[109] This language implies that corporate persons, like natural persons, have their own voice and are entitled to be heard, especially because their role in society places them in the position of providing unique and helpful information to the listening public. They also apparently have aspirations to gain regard and respect in society. Critics argue that the personification of corporations pervades the case as the Court uses words like "speaker," "voice," "disadvantaged person or class," "worth," and "respect" when discussing corporations and corporate speech. This linguistic treatment "tacitly assume[s] equivalency in this case between people and corporations."[110] The case seems to affirm corporate personhood and further entrench the idea of corporations as social, legal, and political persons in society. Some of the strongest opponents of the holding argue that the Court not only acknowledged the personhood of corporations, but enhanced its meaning to such a level that it gives corporations greater power and status than individuals.[111]

Citizens United is undoubtedly a deeply divisive case. Reactions to it were intense on both sides of the issue. Those who opposed the decision called it "a dramatic assault on American democracy that overturned more than a century of campaign finance precedent."[112] Others disagreed entirely, arguing that the decision was "not a departure from long-standing precedent," but merely "a relatively minimal final straw" that "only removed an artificial barrier" to corporate

107 Nancy Price & David E. Delk, *Corporations Are Not People*, ALLIANCE FOR DEMOCRACY, www.theallianceFordemocracy.org/brochure.pdf [https://perma.cc/3WH3-HKXM]; *see also* Erwin Chemerinsky, *The Most Important Decision of the Term*, TRIAL, May 2010, at 54, 56 (arguing that the case rested on the "key premise" that "corporations have the same free speech rights as citizens").

108 *Citizens United*, 558 U.S. at 340–41.

109 *Id.* at 354 (citations omitted).

110 Clements, *supra* note 81.

111 "The controversial 'corporate personhood' legal doctrine was affirmed as the law of the land." Price & Delk, *supra* note 107. "What this court did in this case was make [corporations] a master race. They amplified their voice. And supercharged their power. To us, [the court] gave second class citizenship." *Manski-McCabe-Graves: 'Overrule the Court' Rally in Madison*, DEMOCRACY SQUARE (Feb. 16, 2010), http://ds.liberalart.space/news/manski-mccabe-graves-overrule-court-rally-madison [https://perma.cc/TJ4C-JB8G].

112 Katrina vanden Heuvel, *Stanching the Flow of Corporate Dollars into Campaigns*, WASH. POST: OPINIONS (Nov. 8, 2011), www.washingtonpost.com/opinions/stanching-the-flow-of-corporate-dollars-into-campaigns/2011/11/04/gIQAy2cR1M_story.html [https://perma.cc/G2LQ-QKU2].

speech.[113] Both sides were probably correct: "*Citizens United* was at once both revolutionary and conventional."[114] It is clear that the case heightened rather than resolved the tension over the free speech rights of corporations.

The primary reason for the conflict is that opposing groups hold competing conceptions of the corporation. The same is true for the Justices who composed the Court's majority and those who formed its dissent. Though neither side openly elaborated on it, each side focused on different dimensions of the personhood of corporations in its reasoning. Indeed, it has been argued that the Justices have followed a long-standing pattern of silently utilizing diverging theories of the corporate person to support their conclusions.[115] As the following discussion demonstrates, these diverging theories reflect the multidimensional nature of the corporation, and they provide a framework for understanding the debate over corporate claims to free speech rights.

AGGREGATE ELEMENTS OF CORPORATE PERSONHOOD AND SPEECH

One aspect of the corporation's personhood is its aggregate nature. Corporations are collections of people who join together to pursue their mutual interests. As discussed in Chapter 1, the aggregate theory of the corporation looks through the corporate form to see the human members who compose the organization. The individual corporate participants are considered the true creators and sustainers of the corporate entity, rather than the state. The *Citizens United* majority focused on this aspect of corporations when it described corporations as "associations of citizens." From this viewpoint, corporate speech rights are necessary to uphold the speech rights of the individuals who make up the corporation. They do not lose their rights to express their views, desires, and interests when they choose to combine and act in corporate form.

These ideas reflect an image of corporations as essentially the equivalent of their human members. Companies with only a single shareholder, or a small group of shareholders and employees, seem to fit this model well. In small closely held corporations, or family owned and operated businesses, we perceive the members as closely aligned in their interests and beliefs. When such a corporation spends

113 Roger Coffin, A *Responsibility to Speak:* Citizens United, *Corporate Governance and Managing Risks*, 8 HASTINGS BUS. L.J. 103, 118 (2012); Justin Levitt, *Confronting the Impact of* Citizens United, 29 YALE L. & POL'Y REV. 217, 220 (2010).

114 Adam Winkler, Citizens United, *Personhood, and the Corporation in Politics, in* CORPORATIONS AND AMERICAN DEMOCRACY 359, 387 (Naomi R. Lamoreaux & William J. Novak eds., 2017).

115 Stefan J. Padfield, *The Silent Role of Corporate Theory in the Supreme Court's Campaign Finance Cases*, 15 U. PA. J. CONST. L. 831, 833–34 (2013). In arguing that corporate theory matters, Padfield suggests that "while it may not be possible to tie a particular corporate theory to a particular result in a particular case, corporate theory may nonetheless make a particular outcome more or less likely." *Id.* at 861.

money on political speech, we see it as representing the views of the individual participants whose interests in self-realization, autonomy, and dignity deserve protection under the First Amendment.

The same approach is applied to nonprofit associations that are organized to promote the shared interests of their members. Those interests might involve political, religious, cultural, educational, or other social views. Individuals are drawn together by their common beliefs, and the associations they form often advocate for their interests. For example, political parties, religious organizations, universities, and social associations engage in speech that is viewed as representing the ideas of their members, and we support their right to speak under the First Amendment. The aggregate nature of such associations, whether they be the Democratic Party, the Mormon Church, the ACLU, the NRA, the Sierra Club, or the Citizens United organization, influences our perception that their organizational speech right flows from the right of their human participants to express their beliefs and opinions. The concept of the organization as a Tocquevillian association and a mediating institution, as discussed in Chapter 3, reappears in this context. Such associations serve as critical instruments of freedom, democracy, and individual flourishing. They provide an avenue for individuals to form their own identities and express themselves.

Corporate speech rights that stem from the aggregate view of corporations need not be limited to small businesses or nonprofit organizations. There is also support for upholding the political speech of certain for-profit corporations under the aggregate approach. In "postmodern corporations," as described by Ronald Colombo, corporate members that include investors, owners, officers, employees, customers, and other participants come together around a shared set of values, beliefs, and goals that are in addition to profit-making.[116] While making money is an important objective, the members of postmodern corporations are also committed to a wide range of other values, such as principles of social responsibility, environmental sustainability, or religious tenets. The rise of "B corporations" and "benefit corporations," which are designed to promote a general or specific public benefit as well as to make profits, illustrates the desire of many investors to participate in companies with a shared commitment to certain social or moral values.[117] These companies enable mission-driven businesses to pursue a material, positive impact on society and the environment in addition to making profits. Such corporations may also represent Tocquevillian associations that serve as a vehicle for individual

[116] Colombo, *supra* note 49, at 55–58. Chick-fil-A, a fast food company that has previously donated money to groups advocating a traditional definition of marriage, is cited as an example of a postmodern corporation whose expressive acts reflect a set of values that may not revolve solely around making profits. *Id.* at 124.

[117] *See id.* at 62–63; Eric W. Orts, Business Persons: A Legal Theory of the Firm 210–12 (2013); Michael Vargas, *The Next Stage of Social Entrepreneurship: Benefit Corporations and the Companies Using This Innovative Corporate Form*, Bus. L. Today, July 2016, www.americanbar.org/publications/blt/2016/07/01_vargas.html [http://perma.cc/JW2L-MP5S].

expression of values, beliefs, and priorities. When they engage in acts of expression or political advocacy, they represent the views of their members whose speech is entitled to First Amendment protection.[118]

In the context of the large, public corporation, it seems more difficult to say that the political speech of the corporation represents the beliefs of its members. Yet even here, arguments can be made that corporate speech furthers the ends of the individual participants who collectively join the corporation with common interests in financial gain. When corporations engage in political speech, they presumably do so with the goal of furthering their financial interests that, according to the aggregate view, are ultimately the financial interests of the individual members. There is some evidence to suggest that political speech can increase the economic value of corporations that engage in it, which benefits the members themselves.[119] Accordingly, the speech of the for-profit corporation arguably does represent the values and interests of the human members, at least to the extent they have joined the corporation because they have common financial interests that they seek to further. "Far from a distortion of the political views of their shareholders, then, corporate speech would seem to be a reliable expression of it."[120]

The aggregate theory's emphasis on the human members of the corporation sees the corporation as existing for the benefit of those members, not for the broader benefit of the state. It involves a private, rather than public, orientation toward the corporate person. It seeks to enforce the rights and interests of the private parties who participate in the enterprise, rather than place burdens on the corporation to serve the public interest. The main priority is to ensure the freedom of individuals to exercise the fullest range of their rights through the corporate form, whether they involve private property rights, contract rights, or speech rights.

However, a focus on the aggregate aspects of the corporate person can also cut the other way when it comes to corporate speech. If corporations are viewed merely as the sum of their human participants, then corporations themselves do not possess the self-expression, autonomy, or dignity interests that support First Amendment

118 Colombo, *supra* note 49, at 70–75, 136.

119 *See* Robert J. Shapiro & Douglas Dowson, Manhattan Inst., Corporate Political Spending: Why the New Critics Are Wrong (2012), www.manhattan-institute.org/pdf/lpr_15.pdf [https://perma.cc/L3ZM-UKQM]; Thomas Stratman & J. W. Verret, *How Does Corporate Political Activity Allowed by* Citizens United v. Federal Election Commission *Affect Shareholder Wealth?*, 58 J.L. & Econ. 545, 545 (2015) ("Our findings show that corporate political activity enhances shareholder wealth, particularly in firms that are small to medium sized, firms that spend relatively less on lobbying, and firms operating in more heavily regulated industries."). *But see* John C. Coates IV, *Corporate Politics, Governance, and Value Before and After* Citizens United, 9 J. Empirical Legal Stud. 657 (2012). *But cf.* Michael Hadani, Jean-Philippe Bonardi & Nicolas M. Dahan, *Corporate Political Activity, Public Policy Uncertainty, and Firm Outcomes: A Meta-Analysis*, 15 Strategic Org. 338, 357 (2016) ("We find only weak evidence to support the view that CPA [corporate political activity], either indirectly (or even directly), impacts firms' bottom line. This by no means indicates that CPA is ineffective.").

120 David G. Yosifon, *The Public Choice Problem in Corporate Law: Corporate Social Responsibility After* Citizens United, 89 N C. L. Rev. 1197, 1223 (2011).

protection. Corporations should have no independent claim to free speech rights because they do not possess their own interests in self-realization and self-determination.

Moreover, in the case of large, for-profit corporations, it is not realistic to think that the shareholders have joined together primarily to promote their shared convictions and to engage in self-expression. The large multinational corporation does not look like an expressive association of individuals who seek to promote their deeply held beliefs and opinions. There seems to be no self-determination value either at the corporate level or at the individual constituent level that can be invoked to justify corporate free speech rights in large public companies.

Even if we did focus on the individuals within the entity, to say that the corporation is really just its human members begs the question as to which members are the relevant ones for purposes of forming corporate speech. The answer need not necessarily be only the original or current shareholders. It could conceivably include employees, suppliers, creditors, and others who are also essential contributors to the corporate enterprise. The question becomes particularly difficult to resolve as the size of the corporation grows. Opponents of corporate speech rights argue that the speech of large, public companies cannot possibly reflect the unanimous views of all of its myriad constituents. Shareholders and employees change constantly; it is impossible to identify the individuals for whom the corporation is speaking. The most that can be said is that corporate speech most likely represents the opinions of the select group of corporate executives who manage the corporation.

From this perspective, there really is no such thing as corporate speech. Commentators argue that speech is not a legal concept, but a physical act; it is a distinctly human act that is the product of human thought.[121] They contend that corporations are not real persons who think and reason and speak. Because expression can be made only by natural persons, it is a category mistake to think an entity like a large corporation is capable of the physical act of speech.[122] Any speech issued by the corporation is simply the expression of the natural persons who control the corporation and its resources, i.e., the corporate managers who use corporate funds to disseminate their views.[123] Critics contend that constitutional protection for corporate political speech simply further entrenches the power of these members of the corporate elite.

[121] Charles R. O'Kelley, Jr., *The Constitutional Rights of Corporations Revisited: Social and Political Expression and the Corporation After* First National Bank v. Bellotti, 67 GEO. L.J. 1347, 1351 (1979).

[122] *Id.* at 1368. The argument that corporations are incapable of any physical acts can be taken too far, since all physical acts of the corporation whether buying a piece of property, or moving into a new warehouse, or hiring a new employee, are accomplished through its human agents. If it is a category mistake to talk of large corporations as being capable of speech, then "the same category-mistake is made in speaking about the corporation's doing anything." Note, *Constitutional Rights of the Corporate Person*, 91 YALE L.J. 1641, 1655 n.55 (1982).

[123] *See* Patton & Bartlett, *supra* note 59, at 509.

Many shareholders, employees, and other corporate constituents may disagree with the views expressed on behalf of the corporation. Thus, the so-called speech of the company is not an expression of the views of all its individual members. Rather than supporting the free speech rights of corporations, the aggregate view can actually weigh against them. If all the corporation's members cannot agree on what to say, then the corporation really should not say anything at all. The dissent in *Citizens United* raised this concern, arguing that it is unfair to effectively force dissenting shareholders to finance the dissemination of corporate political views with which they disagree.[124] The shareholders do not have the ability to disapprove of the corporate speech beforehand. They have a right not to have their investments associated with beliefs they do not hold. Because nonconsenting shareholders realistically have little substantive practical control over the use of their money to fund such corporate speech, and because such shareholders cannot always easily exercise their option to exit the corporation, great caution must be taken in allowing corporate managers to exercise any political speech rights on behalf of the corporation.[125] Even unions are prohibited from using union members' dues to support political causes that members personally oppose.[126] Likewise, corporate shareholders' funds should not be utilized to contribute to political agendas they do not set.

We could counter these arguments with the observation that dissenting members can exist in all types of organizations. The presence of such members does not negate the ability of the organization's representatives to express coherent organizational views to further the interests and goals of the members as a whole. It is not reasonable to think that statements issued by the NAACP or the Catholic Church are unanimously endorsed by all of their diverse members. That some of the members may not agree with various positions publicly held by the association has never been a justification for restricting the speech of the organization altogether. The members voluntarily contribute their resources to the association so that its

124 Citizens United v. FEC, 558 U.S. 310, 475–78 (2010) (Stevens, J., dissenting).

125 Commentators note that the "procedures of corporate democracy" cited by the *Citizens United* majority as a means of protecting dissenting shareholders are fairly ineffective. For example, it is not easy for shareholders to unseat incumbent directors and elect new ones; shareholder proposals at annual meetings rarely succeed; derivative suits challenging corporate spending decisions typically fail because the business judgment rule protects such decisions; shareholders often are never informed of the nature or extent of the political expenditures made by the corporation; and shareholders who own their shares through mutual funds or retirement plans cannot directly sell their stock as a method of protesting the corporation's political speech. Indeed, for many dissenting corporate members, including shareholders, employees, creditors, and significant customers, the burden and cost of severing their relationship with the company may be too high to utilize exit as a viable means of expressing disagreement with the company's political expenditures. *See* Neuborne, *supra* note 41, at 793; Elizabeth Pollman, *Constitutionalizing Corporate Law*, 69 VAND. L. REV. 639, 667, 677 (2016); Elizabeth Pollman, *Citizens Not United: The Lack of Stockholder Voluntariness in Corporate Political Speech*, 119 YALE L.J. ONLINE 53, 56–58 (2009).

126 *See* Reza Dibadj, *Expressive Rights for Shareholders after* Citizens United?, 46 U.S.F. L. REV. 459, 467–48 (2011).

decision-makers can decide how to use them to promote the association's overall objectives. There will invariably be individuals in organizations who disagree with some of the views expressed by the organization, but the members defer to the organization's leaders to speak on the organization's behalf. This is the nature of group activity and speech. The aggregate aspects of the association do not undercut that. "Members surely anticipate that this will be the case when they decide to become members of the group but figure that the gains they realize from positions they share with the group will more than offset losses associated with the group's advance of positions they oppose."[127] The same may be said of shareholders who are members of corporations.

Some shareholders of corporations may not personally support the views expressed on behalf of the corporation, but the corporate group structure requires that they defer to the actions and decisions of the group leaders to represent the group's best interests. If the shareholders wish to obtain the gains that come with investing in the corporation, they understand that corporate funds may be used at times in ways with which they may not agree. The shareholders have nonetheless decided to pool their resources and give them to the group's decision-makers so they can decide how to spend the resources. From this point of view, the managerial decision to spend corporate money on political speech is like any other business decision that corporate leaders must make. Shareholders may disagree with the corporate managers' decision to use corporate resources to increase employee salaries, or make corporate charitable contributions, or launch a risky product line, or engage in political advocacy, but these are all leadership decisions that managers are obliged to make on behalf of the group, even if the decisions are not uniformly endorsed by the individuals who make up the corporate entity. Shareholders share the universal corporate goal of increasing their financial welfare, and they accept that their ideas on the best methods to attain that result may differ from those of the corporation's leaders.

From a broader perspective, critics of corporate speech rights may be assuming that shareholders have fundamental objections to political engagement by corporations when in fact shareholders may benefit from corporate political speech and activity. Some research has suggested that corporate political spending increases firm value and benefits shareholders. For publicly traded companies, the effects of political lobbying have been reported in stronger financial performance and greater stock market returns. Over the long term, politically connected firms can outperform their peers by two to three percent per year.[128] These findings, however, are

127 Yosifon, *supra* note 120, at 1223.

128 *See* Shapiro & Dowson, *supra* note 119, at 17. One study found that the economic value of a $1 business campaign contribution in terms of lower state corporate taxes is approximately $6.65. Robert S. Chirinko & Daniel J. Wilson, *Can Lower Tax Rates Be Bought? Business Rent-Seeking and Tax Competition Among U.S. States* 20 (Fed. Reserve Bank of S.F. Working Paper Series, Paper 2009–29, 2010), www.frbsf.org/economic-research/files/wp09-29bk.pdf [https://perma.cc/AM84-8WHP].

contrasted with other empirical work indicating that corporate political spending can correlate with lower shareholder value.[129] While the shareholders of a particular corporation may not necessarily agree with all of the political causes or candidates supported by that corporation, if the corporation is providing the shareholders with a hefty return on their investment, they may not care where the corporation's political expenditures go.[130] That we do not see shareholders rising up in overwhelming numbers to object to corporate political speech, or to demand prohibitions of such speech in articles of incorporation, or to pressure state legislatures to adopt incorporation statutes that make such speech *ultra vires*, suggests that corporate political speech may benefit shareholders by increasing their share value, and this financial gain is in part what they hope to achieve by their membership in the corporation. The significant percentage of people who invest in corporations and become shareholders indicates that this ownership system, in which they place their money in the hands of managers who will make decisions on how to utilize the funds to garner a healthy return, remains an attractive option for reaching individuals' financial goals.

The fear that corporations will spend far too much of the shareholders' money on political speech is tempered by the reality that corporations cannot afford to spend too much money on political speech alone. The idea that *Citizens United* opened the door for corporations to spend "unlimited" sums of money on advocating for or against political candidates is somewhat misleading. "Unlimited" does not mean "infinite;" it means "not limited by the government." Corporations have only so much money that can be spent on any number of things, including research and development, marketing, employee salaries, or dividends. The corporation cannot deplete its resources to engage in political speech. Only a finite amount can be spent on things like charitable donations or political expenditures before the corporation will feel the pressure to pay out its many other constituents first.

The discussion over the interests of dissenting shareholders has been especially complicated in the context of media corporations. If the speech of large corporations must be restricted to ensure that dissenting shareholders will not be compelled to fund corporate political views they do not support, the restrictions would have to be applied to the political speech of large media corporations as well, since it is unreasonable to assume that all media corporation shareholders unanimously

129 *See* Michael Hadani & Douglas A. Schuler, *In Search of El Dorado: The Elusive Financial Returns on Corporate Political Investment*, 34 Strategic Mgmt. J. 165 (2013); John C. Coates & Taylor Lincoln, *Fulfilling the Promise of* 'Citizens United', Wash. Post: Opinions (Sep. 6, 2011), www.washingtonpost.com/opinions/fulfilling-the-promise-of-citizens-united/2011/09/02/gIQAa4np7J_story.html [https://perma.cc/2Q8M-TEBM]; *see also* Shapiro & Dowson, *supra* note 119, at 17–22 (describing and refuting three studies that argue corporate political activity harms shareholders).

130 "Given the choice between a successful growing company supporting a candidate with whom the shareholder has a disagreement and a company whose stock is sinking but one who may back the same candidate, the rational investor would choose the company whose stock is on the rise." Coffin, *supra* note 113, at 158.

share the same political views that are expressed by the company. However, supporters of an exception for the unfettered free speech rights of media corporations contend that there really are no dissenting shareholders in media corporations for whom we need be concerned. We can presume that all shareholders of media corporations expect the company to be involved in political commentary and they have basically authorized the use of corporate funds for political speech with the knowledge that such speech is the business of the media.[131] Therefore, media corporations are entitled to wider latitude under the First Amendment than other large for-profit corporations.

However, this approach to sweeping away the dissenting shareholder problem by essentially inferring the consent of all media corporation shareholders to the company's political speech can be utilized with virtually any type of corporation. Shareholders can effectively be put on notice that all corporations can engage in political speech, and the voluntary choice to invest in the company indicates implied consent to the use of corporate funds for that purpose. Shareholders can be presumed to expect that the corporation will make various business expenditures, including political ones. In this manner, all large corporations, whether they are media corporations or not, can be treated consistently under the First Amendment.

In reply, those who contend that media corporations deserve differential and more deferential First Amendment treatment argue that the freedom of the press is a special right that protects the political speech of media corporations. Because the text of the First Amendment expressly mentions the press, media corporations have a claim to greater speech protections that are not available to anyone else. The dissent in *Citizens United* emphasized that the press plays a unique role in facilitating public discourse: "media corporations differ significantly from other corporations in that their resources are devoted to the collection of information and its dissemination to the public."[132] From this point of view, the institutional press merits special constitutional protection.

In his concurring opinion, Justice Scalia refuted the dissent's view that the freedom of the press applies only to formal media corporations and does not apply to individuals or other corporate entities. The press clause was intended to protect *publishing activities*, whether conducted by individual editors, printers, or formal media institutions.[133] In support of this view, commentators argue that freedom of the press refers to a certain type of protected activity, not a specific category of protected persons. Freedom of the press is "not a constitutional right for a particular group of people or organizations. Rather it is a right to engage in a certain class of

[131] *See* Joo, *supra* note 68, at 6 n.16.

[132] Citizens United v. FEC, 558 U.S. 310, 473–74 (2010) (Stevens, J., dissenting) (quoting Austin v. Mich. State Chamber of Commerce, 494 U.S. 652, 667 (1990)).

[133] *Id.* at 390 (Scalia, J., concurring).

activities (such as publishing newspapers and pamphlets), whether the person doing so is a professional member of the media or not."[134]

Defining press activities in this manner complicates the question of who counts as the media in the modern age of blogs and social media, "since anyone can gather and report news on Twitter, or provide commentary about a candidate or campaign on Facebook, or post a campaign-oriented video on a blog."[135] If "anyone with a platform to speak or reach a wide audience [can] be considered a member of the press," must a "wide audience" be defined as "a threshold number of Facebook friends or Twitter followers?"[136] Once the First Amendment is interpreted to include protection for all presslike activities, justification for the specialized treatment of media corporations tends to weaken. This pattern of focusing on the nature of the speech or the press activity, rather than the identity of the speaker or issuer of the public commentary, is what the Supreme Court increasingly relies upon to expand political speech rights for corporate persons of all types under the First Amendment.

REAL ENTITY ELEMENTS OF CORPORATE PERSONHOOD AND SPEECH

A more holistic conception of the corporate person as a real and separate entity adds another set of considerations to the analysis of corporate speech. The real entity approach, as discussed in Chapter 1, views the corporation as more than its individual members. When people come together to form an association for some shared purpose, the group becomes something larger than and different in kind from the individuals themselves. Group entities like an army, a university, or a church are distinct units that have an identity that is separate from the various individuals who are part of their membership. Different individuals may join or leave, but the entity retains its singularity. A corporation, particularly a large one, can similarly be viewed as an independent entity whose existence and identity remain the same even if its membership of individual participants changes over time.

Under this view, the corporation can form a collective will and perform collective actions that cannot be traced directly or entirely to any one individual; they result from the combined contributions of many different members. This concept of group agency and autonomy is related to philosophical theories of corporate personhood that attribute moral status to corporations. As discussed in Chapter 2, certain

134 Ilya Somin, *People Organized as Corporations Are People Too*, VOLOKH CONSPIRACY (Jan. 21, 2010, 5:12 PM), http://volokh.com/2010/01/21/people-organized-as-corporations-are-people-too/ [https://perma.cc/6GXF-P25L]; *see also* Michael W. McConnell, *Reconsidering* Citizens United *as a Press Clause Case*, 123 YALE L.J. 412, 418, 432–46 (2013).

135 Hasen, *supra* note 44, at 139. "[T]here is a broad division between those who believe the First Amendment protects journalism as an industry and those who believe the protection applies to all presslike activities." *Id.* at 168.

136 Ilya Shapiro & Caitlyn W. McCarthy, *So What If Corporations Aren't People?*, 44 J. MARSHALL L. REV. 701, 714–15 (2011).

philosophical conceptions of the corporate person suggest that corporations are moral persons with the capacity to hold their own beliefs, desires, values, and intentions, and they are able to exercise control over their own actions. In this regard, it is possible to attribute moral responsibility to the corporation itself, above and beyond that attributed to any individual member, for corporate wrongdoing. By the same token, corporations as moral persons might also be entitled to certain moral rights that would then support the extension of various legal rights.[137]

The real entity dimension of the corporate person is also tied to the sociological, organizational behavior, and political pluralist models of the corporation discussed in Chapter 3. These social science disciplines show that organizations can have their own character, brand identity, personality, and presence in society. They have the ability to project certain images of themselves, to communicate particular messages, and to interact with people, influencing the thoughts and behavior of their individual members as well as those in the larger community. Organizations of all kinds form naturally as people join together to pursue shared interests and to accomplish tasks they cannot do alone. A political pluralist vision regards organizations as important buffers between individuals and the state. Intermediate institutions like the corporation can play a role in acting as a counterweight to protect individuals from potentially overbearing government power. The corporation may be one of the few private forces with the capacity, resources, and incentive to check the power of the state. This viewpoint affirms a private, not public, conception of the corporation, with an emphasis on enabling, rather than restricting, the corporation's ability to pursue its interests.

If these various social science perspectives of the corporate person are applied to the concept of corporate speech, the corporation can be viewed as a real and separate agent, capable of having its own beliefs, desires, and goals, as well as its own speech that reflects and expresses its values. The speech of the corporation is formed as a result of the individual inputs of its human members. Their contributions are necessary to form the corporate speech, but the ultimate combined speech act, like other corporate acts, cannot be characterized as the direct equivalent of the speech or the view of any one particular individual. The corporate decision-making processes turn individual actions and preferences into corporate ones. The resulting corporate acts are generated from the corporation's rational point of view. In this regard, the corporation's speech does and does not represent the views of its contributing members at the same time. The corporate speech incorporates the input of individual participants, but it

137 As discussed in Chapter 2, philosophical theories that reject the full moral agency of the corporate person argue that corporations should not be entitled to any legal rights that exceed their justified moral rights claims. To hold otherwise would make corporations "super-persons" with "undue power ... that can be misused to the detriment of individuals." Patricia H. Werhane, PERSONS, RIGHTS, AND CORPORATIONS 64 (1985). This is exactly the concern raised by the *Citizens United* dissent with regard to the capacity of the corporation to misuse its power to dilute the voices of individuals if the corporation is given broad First Amendment free speech rights.

cannot necessarily or always be equated one-to-one with the views of particular corporate members. The speech is distinctly the corporation's own, and it can be of value to listeners who may benefit from hearing a distinctly corporate point of view from a source that represents a significant segment of society.[138] On matters that involve substantial corporate knowledge and expertise, the speech of the corporation could make unique contributions to the marketplace of ideas.[139] The majority in *Citizens United* took this approach in upholding the organization's First Amendment rights, focusing on the relevance of the speech itself and the listeners' interests in hearing it. Moreover, if the corporation is viewed as an important intermediate institution that serves as a countervailing force against government power, then protecting its ability to speak promotes the democratic structure of society.

However, the real entity aspects of corporate personhood do not ineluctably lead to the conclusion that corporate political speech must be protected under the First Amendment. While the corporation may have the capacity to form its own distinctly corporate speech, commentators have argued that such corporate political speech is inevitably always commercial speech because it cannot be divorced from the underlying corporate goal of maximizing profits, at least that is arguably the case in for-profit corporations.[140] The overriding purpose of such corporations is to generate profits, so whenever they spend money to voice their opinions in the political arena, they do so ultimately to advance their own economic interests. Their speech is instrumental speech, motivated by the pursuit of a very narrow end. The corporation engages in political spending in order to influence the political environment to make it more business friendly. The intent is to reduce burdensome regulation on the corporation's activities or to promote favorable legislation that affords corporations more freedom to act in ways that maximize profits and shift costs onto others. The corporation tends to be a one-sided participant in the political debate, using its speech consistently to promote the single corporate goal of increasing its financial value.[141] Such speech can be inherently misleading because it masquerades as political speech when it is really intended to further the pecuniary gain of the corporate speaker. Moreover, profit-oriented speech is said to lack the crucial connection with individual liberty, self-expression, and self-realization, all of

[138] *See* Dan-Cohen, *supra* note 49, at 96–98.

[139] *See* Martin H. Redish & Howard M. Wasserman, *What's Good for General Motors: Corporate Speech and the Theory of Free Expression*, 66 GEO. WASH. L. REV. 235, 236 (1998).

[140] *See* Tamara R. Piety, *Against Freedom of Commercial Expression*, 29 CARDOZO L. REV. 2583, 2645 (2008); Anne Tucker, *Flawed Assumptions: A Corporate Law Analysis of Free Speech and Corporate Personhood in* Citizens United, 61 CASE W. RES. L. REV. 497, 524 (2010).

[141] *See* Kuhner, *supra* note 61, at 82–85; Daniel J. H. Greenwood, *Essential Speech: Why Corporate Speech Is Not Free*, 83 IOWA L. REV. 995, 1051–52 (1998). Corporate speech is said to lack the varied, diverse, and conflicting values and goals that individuals have when they speak. Greenwood, *supra*, at 1040–41. "[C]orporate nature is far simpler than human nature:" corporations are oriented toward profit maximization, lacking the unique human qualities of pity and genuine regard for the well-being or the suffering of others. Kuhner, *supra* note 61, at 84.

which are fundamental First Amendment values.[142] As a result, corporate speech should be regulated more rigorously in the public interest and should not be given the same wide latitude that individual speech enjoys under the First Amendment. Contrary to the majority's position in *Citizens United*, it is not just the speech that is important. The identity and the incentives of the speaker are also highly relevant to the listener when assessing the speech.

The difficulty with these arguments, however, is that a large amount of individual speech can be purely economically motivated too, as individuals engage in political advocacy to advance their own financial interests as well. For example, individuals may advocate for certain politicians who support lowering their individual tax burdens and allowing them to keep more of their earned income. The "profit motive is often the 'but-for' cause of [all types] of political speech, in that many authors would not write books or articles, or speakers give keynote addresses at conferences, unless there was money in it."[143] Nothing in the First Amendment restricts the political speech of individuals merely because it may be motivated primarily by the economic concerns of the speaker. Thus, to say that corporations may have economic motivations for speaking does not necessarily mean that their speech should be restricted. Moreover, it may not be completely fair to say that corporate speech is always only profit-driven. Corporate law does not require corporate directors to focus purely on making shareholder profits to the exclusion of all other considerations. In making business decisions, directors are permitted to take into account other factors in good faith, including compliance with the law, the interests of other constituents, ethical concerns, and the health of the community.[144] The political speech of nonprofit corporations, benefit companies, and other civic associations are certainly not always economically motivated. As such, it does not seem entirely appropriate to single out corporate speech for greater restriction due to its presumed economic orientation.

In many instances, the distinction between economic speech and political speech is all but impossible to draw. For example, when a corporation makes a public statement denying that it uses sweatshop labor in its overseas manufacturing facilities, it is not only making a political statement about its views on acceptable labor practices, but also attempting to preserve its public image and goodwill among its customer base to protect its bottom line.[145] Thus, the political speech unavoidably includes economic components. Likewise, any "proposals to enter into economic transactions always have political content," for the promotion of any product or

142 *See* First Nat'l Bank of Boston v. Bellotti, 435 U.S. 765, 804–05 (1978) (White, J., dissenting); C. Edwin Baker, *Commercial Speech: A Problem in the Theory of Freedom*, 62 IOWA L. REV. 1, 3 (1976).

143 Yosifon, *supra* note 120, at 1226.

144 *Id.* at 1226–27.

145 This is what Nike did in the late 1990s in the face of allegations that it mistreated and underpaid workers in foreign facilities. *See* Kasky v. Nike, Inc., 45 P.3d 243 (Cal. 2002). For a discussion of the *Nike* case, see Tamara R. Piety, BRANDISHING THE FIRST AMENDMENT: COMMERCIAL EXPRESSION IN AMERICA 4–9 (2012).

service is inevitably a political claim that it is valuable and other things are worth less.[146] "There is no way to completely eradicate the economic speech elements from political speech or vice versa."[147]

The real entity aspects of the corporate person indicate that the corporation's presence and identity in society are accompanied by real power and influence. The immense wealth and size of large corporations cause grave concern because their massive economic resources can potentially be utilized to overpower and oppress individuals and to exert control over the legislative and political systems of governance. As explained in Chapter 3, this image of the corporate person draws on a political pluralist vision that sees modern corporations as a threat to individual welfare and democratic ideals. In the context of corporate speech, corporate power can be particularly worrisome. Armed with the right to engage freely in political speech, corporations can outspend most individuals and thereby dominate the political marketplace of ideas with their own corporate messages. Critics argue that corporations can crowd out all other speech because "in our country the power of persons to put their messages across loudly and repeatedly [due to] their economic power and influence effectively silences other . . . voices."[148] With First Amendment protection, corporate speech becomes a "state-created amplification system, available only to relatively few, which can effectively drown out the speech of other natural persons."[149]

The concern over corporate domination of the political process was raised by the *Citizens United* dissent. Criticizing the majority's denial of the likelihood that corporate speech will distort the public discussion, the dissent emphasized the importance of "preserving some breathing room around the electoral 'marketplace' of ideas, . . . the marketplace in which the actual people of this Nation determine how they will govern themselves."[150] The majority rejected this argument and focused instead on the relevance of the speech for the listener's ear. Listeners should not be prevented from hearing speech that might be informative and pertinent simply because the source of the speech might be wealthy. The inherent worth of the speech does not depend on the identity or financial capacity of the speaker. It is important to protect the listener's right to have relevant information to make informed decisions.

146 Greenwood, *supra* note 141, at 1001.

147 Tucker, *supra* note 140, at 523.

148 J. M. Balkin, *Some Realism About Pluralism: Legal Realist Approaches to the First Amendment*, 1990 Duke L.J. 375, 379. Senator Sheldon Whitehouse makes this point forcefully in his book, Captured: The Corporate Infiltration of American Democracy (2017). He argues that corporations, with their resources and unlimited life spans, are tireless, relentless, and single-minded in their pursuit of purchasing political influence. *Id.* at 6–7. In his experience, the "corporate agenda" is the "loudest, strongest, and most persistent corporate voice . . . in Congress." *Id.* at 58.

149 Patton & Bartlett, *supra* note 59, at 511.

150 Citizens United v. FEC, 558 U.S. 310, 473 (2010) (Stevens, J., dissenting) (citations omitted).

These are valid points, but the majority's expressed concern for listeners' rights may also cut the other way. If the goal is to ensure that voters hear all different viewpoints in order to make informed and intelligent political choices, that goal can be frustrated if voters are inundated primarily with the views of one side of the debate, the side that can afford to pay for its views to be heard loudly and repeatedly. "Virtually all of the information acquired by voters in the political arena is information which someone else wishes them to have – information for which someone is willing and able to pay the voter's costs of acquisition. The patterns of subsidized information play a significant role in determining the content of political choice."[151]

The human mind is capable of processing only so much speech. The idea that more speech is always better assumes individuals in our society have "infinite free time to listen to and contemplate every last bit of speech uttered by anyone, anywhere."[152] But in the real world, listeners are constrained by their own processing limits and are not capable of taking in boundless measures of speech. They are vulnerable to hearing only those messages that are sufficiently powerful to dominate the political discourse, and no more. Furthering the interests of listeners may require curbing rather than enhancing the speech of the corporate person to ensure the relative ability of numerous viewpoints to be heard. This is the exact opposite of what the *Citizens United* majority believed to be the appropriate outcome: "[T]he concept that government may restrict the speech of some elements of our society in order to enhance the relative voice of others is wholly foreign to the First Amendment."[153]

Nonetheless, the same capacity to dominate the marketplace of ideas applies to wealthy individuals, and the First Amendment does not prohibit their speech. The reality is that, although the wealthiest speakers do have the capacity to fill the marketplace with their messages, the speakers with the most money do not always win. Money does not invariably buy elections. There have been political campaigns in which one candidate or party outspent the other and still lost the election. It is not always the case that the side with the most financing will persuade the electorate to vote in its favor. Like any wealthy individual, corporations may choose to spend large amounts of their money on political speech, and their speech may fill the marketplace, but that speech does not necessarily guarantee the outcome preferred by the corporation. It is not a foregone conclusion that corporate money will always distort the political process and produce the result that is favored by the corporation.

Moreover, in the current technological age of social media and YouTube, whether corporations have the unilateral ability to dominate the public discourse and crowd out individuals from voicing their opinions may be arguable. When individual YouTube videos and social media postings can "go viral" and be viewed by millions of people in a matter of hours, individuals have more power than ever

151 Patton & Bartlett, *supra* note 59, at 504.
152 558 U.S. at 472 (Stevens, J., dissenting).
153 *Id.* at 349–50 (quoting Buckley v. Valeo, 424 U.S. 1, 48–49 (1976)).

before to express themselves and disseminate their views without great cost. The production and distribution costs that once were barriers to entering the political speech marketplace increasingly no longer stand as obstacles to political engagement. Accordingly, the presence of corporate speech in the political marketplace does not necessarily lead to the conclusion that there will be disproportionate exposure to corporate points of view and that individual speech will effectively be muted.

ARTIFICIAL PERSON ELEMENTS OF CORPORATE PERSONHOOD AND SPEECH

As described in Chapter 1, the view that corporations are artificial persons, or concessions of the state, emphasizes that the personhood of corporations is only a fictional legal construct designed to facilitate the law's treatment of corporations. The corporation is a creature of the state and possesses only those features of personhood that the state bestows upon it. The corporation's rights, powers, duties, and obligations are all defined by the law and can easily be expanded or contracted by the law when it is in the public interest to do so. From this perspective, the corporation is not a collection of people (as described by the aggregate conception), nor is it an independent agent (as described by the real entity conception); it is a collection of capital, organized by legal rules to accomplish certain commercial tasks that ultimately benefit the economy and society as a whole.[154]

The dissent in *Citizens United* appeared to share this vision when it asserted that corporations have been "effectively delegated responsibility for ensuring society's economic welfare" and that corporate personhood is a "legal fiction."[155] While the dissent expressly denied that its reasoning was based on the artificial person or concession theory of corporate personhood, the dissent's analysis appeared to embrace this view in arguing that the Framers viewed corporations as "artificial entities," that "the legitimacy of every corporate activity was thought to rest entirely in a concession of the sovereign," and that "the Framers thus took it as a given that corporations could be comprehensively regulated in the service of the public welfare."[156]

Under the artificial person view, there is nothing inherent in the nature of the corporation that entitles it to be the claimant of any constitutional rights. Whatever speech rights the government chooses to bestow on corporations flow from the government's judgment as to what is proper, prudent, and beneficial for the polity. This approach to corporate rights reflects a public, rather than private, oriented

[154] Some have argued that the corporate voting system that allocates one vote per share, rather than one vote per person, reveals that the corporation represents not a unity of citizens, but a unity of capital. *See* Hager, *supra* note 61, at 652–53.

[155] 558 U.S. 310, 465–66 (citations omitted).

[156] *Id.* at 428–29, 428 n.55 (citations omitted).

approach to corporate activity. It provides greater justification for government restrictions on corporate speech. Because the corporation's very existence and license to operate is authorized by the state for the public benefit, the corporation is beholden to the state for whatever speech rights it receives and is obliged to abide by the conditions set forth by the state. Corporations must accept the bitter with the sweet. To receive the benefits bestowed by the state's recognition, they must accept the burdens imposed by the state at the same time.

Opponents of corporate speech rights contend that corporations are and should be treated as creatures of the law, not as speakers whose voices merit protection in the same way as individuals. The state provides the corporate form with advantageous legal features, such as limited liability, perpetual life, and special tax breaks. These benefits enable corporations to accumulate wealth much more efficiently, and this wealth translates into economic and political power. Corporations should not be permitted to use these state-conferred advantages to engage in political speech that overpowers that of individuals. Indeed, in any contexts where "the corporate form magnifies the nature of the right beyond what humans would have," it would be improper to allow the corporation to exercise the right to the detriment of individuals.[157] In enabling corporations to affect political outcomes by spending substantial amounts of their wealth on political speech, the *Citizens United* case has elevated corporations to a height that is not warranted by their status as mere concessions of the state.

If the use of state-conferred benefits to accumulate wealth can serve as the justification for restricting corporate political speech, it would potentially justify restrictions on individual speech as well, for individuals also receive various economic advantages from government legislation. Capital gains tax laws that benefit successful individual investors, and inheritance laws that direct the flow of property to heirs of large estates, allow individuals to accumulate more wealth than they otherwise would have without these state-conferred advantages. But no one believes such individuals should have limited political speech rights as a result of utilizing these beneficial laws to their economic advantage.[158] Even "the use of the roads, the protection of the police, [and] the availability of courts to redress private and public grievances" can be construed as "government-conferred benefits" for individuals, yet "[f]ew would argue that because the state confers these advantages on natural persons the government should be able to regulate individuals' political speech, or that the government could condition these benefits on individuals' willingness to subject their political speech to government regulation."[159]

157 Kent Greenfield & Adam Winkler, *The U.S. Supreme Court's Cultivation of Corporate Personhood*, Atlantic (June 24, 2015), www.theatlantic.com/politics/archive/2015/06/raisins-hotels-corporate-personhood-supreme-court/396773/ [https://perma.cc/FV24-LTS3] ("Rights to spend money in elections should be different for corporations because the benefits they receive from the government give them an improper advantage in influencing government policy.").

158 *See* Redish & Wasserman, *supra* note 139, at 284–85.

159 Yosifon, *supra* note 120, at 1220.

If the political process can be distorted by economic inequalities between speakers, then the wealth of individual speakers could be just as troubling as that of corporations. Commentators note that wealthy individuals spend significant sums engaging in political speech. In fact, "most of the money flooding into the electoral process is not coming from corporations. It's coming from rich individuals . . . ;" corporate money has been "dwarfed by the torrent of individual money."[160] It is difficult to justify restricting the speech of corporations on the basis of their wealth when "the threat to democracy posed by allowing corporations, with their immense aggregations of wealth, to function as political speakers" is present "under the same regime that allows individuals citizens, who may also accumulate tremendous wealth, to spend as much of that wealth as they choose on political speech."[161]

There is a certain dissatisfaction with regulating the speech of corporate persons when individuals and other artificial persons are treated differently despite sharing similar characteristics. This dissatisfaction is common among those who defend corporate speech rights. They raise the "what about so-and-so?" argument. If corporations' speech rights must be restricted based on the dangers of corporate wealth, what about the speech rights of wealthy individuals who choose to spend their personal fortunes on political advocacy? If corporate speech is regulated because corporations are artificial entities with state-conferred benefits, what about the speech of churches, nonprofit organizations, and universities that also receive beneficial treatment from the state? If corporate speech must be restricted because it is motivated by profit concerns, what about the speech of media corporations that are profit-oriented in nature as well? The worry is that once limits are imposed on corporate speech on the basis of certain articulated grounds, the speech of other entities and individuals will also be vulnerable to regulation on the basis of analogous grounds.

The Supreme Court raised this slippery slope argument when upholding the speech rights of corporations in the *Bellotti* case: "If a legislature may direct business corporations to 'stick to business,' it also may limit other corporations – religious, charitable, or civic – to their respective 'business' when addressing the public."[162] Such limitations on speech are deemed unacceptable, so if the speech of other associations is going to be protected, corporate speech must be protected as well. Thus, the Court has rejected the idea that the for-profit nature of the corporation alone is sufficient justification for limiting its speech rights, since the justification can open the door to restricting the speech of others based on judgments about their particular purpose. "[T]o legislate congruence between an organization's formal

160 Kent Greenfield, *In Defense of Corporate Persons*, 30 CONST. COMMENT. 309, 326 (2015); *see also* Kent Greenfield, CORPORATIONS ARE PEOPLE TOO (AND THEY SHOULD ACT LIKE IT) 24–25, 130–31 (2018) (citing figures that show political spending by wealthy individuals far outweighs that of publicly traded companies).

161 Amy J. Sepinwall, Citizens United *and the Ineluctable Question of Corporate Citizenship*, 44 CONN. L. REV. 575, 579 (2012).

162 First Nat'l Bank of Boston v. Bellotti, 435 U.S. 765, 785 (1978).

purpose and its latitude of expression risks sliding into an abyss of legislative repression in which the state could define the permissible limits of religious or charitable activity."[163] The complexity of the corporate person makes it particularly challenging to justify restrictions on the speech of corporations without also jeopardizing the speech rights of entities like the ACLU and the NRA, or wealthy individuals like Warren Buffet, Charles Koch, and Mark Zuckerberg.

The government undoubtedly provides the corporate form with advantageous legal features, such as limited liability, perpetual life, and the ability to accumulate and distribute large sums of money. However, scholars have noted that it is improper to say that because the corporation has been given these state-conferred benefits, the corporate person must forfeit any constitutional rights to which it would otherwise be entitled. The doctrine of unconstitutional conditions prohibits the government from coercing, inducing, or pressuring a party to waive its constitutional rights in exchange for the privilege of engaging in state authorized activities.[164] The Court in *Citizens United* emphasized this point directly: "It is rudimentary that the State cannot exact as the price of those special [corporate] advantages the forfeiture of First Amendment rights."[165] Individuals who choose to adopt the corporate form to take advantage of its limited liability feature should not have to give up their political speech rights in exchange for the privilege of incorporating. This point relies on a combination of both the aggregate and artificial person aspects of the corporate person.

SPECTRUM OF CONSTITUTIONAL CORPORATE PERSONHOOD

All the competing arguments for and against corporate constitutional rights stem from the many different facets of the corporate person as viewed from varying legal, philosophical, moral, sociological, economic, cultural, and political perspectives. Because the roles and purposes of corporations in society are complex and ever evolving, we are continually faced with the challenge of deciding which rights and responsibilities are appropriate for corporations to hold. The Supreme Court has granted corporations certain constitutional rights over time, both reflecting and extending the evolving conception of the corporation as a person whose interests are important and worth protecting.

While the Court has not always explicitly invoked the various theories of corporate personhood in its analysis, those theories continue to influence how the Court views the nature and function of the corporation as a legal, social, and economic institution. In recent cases, the Court has apparently tried to avoid direct discussion

[163] Patton & Bartlett, *supra* note 59, at 500–01.

[164] Richard A. Epstein, Citizens United v. FEC: *The Constitutional Right That Big Corporations Should Have But Do Not Want*, 34 HARV. J.L. & PUB. POL'Y 639, 647 (2011).

[165] Citizens United v. FEC, 558 U.S. 310, 351 (2010) (quoting Austin v. Mich. State Chamber of Commerce, 494 U.S. 652, 680 (1990) (Scalia, J., dissenting)).

of myriad elements of corporate personhood, yet it is evident that those elements persist in informing the Court's analysis, and they ultimately shape the resulting jurisprudence. That the Justices may not wish to go on the record as espousing a particular view of corporate personhood does not make the issue go away. The differing and complementary conceptions of the corporation as a person are woven into constitutional doctrine by implicit reliance, if not by explicit endorsement. All the competing conceptions of the corporate person are operating at once, consciously and subconsciously, to adjust the way the Justices view the positive and normative roles of the corporation in society. As a result, the different aspects of personhood interact and propel judicial wrangling over the acceptable scope of corporate rights.

The corporate speech cases reflect this process. In *Citizens United*, the majority and the dissenting Justices held contrasting theoretical visions of the corporation's personhood, and although neither side engaged in an open defense of its theoretical assumptions, those assumptions seemed to drive the analysis.[166] Both sides appeared "to be animated by markedly different – if not fully articulated – visions of corporate personhood, and its public or private origins and character."[167] In *Citizens United*, the majority focused on the private aspects of the corporation's ontology as an aggregate or association of citizens, while the dissent highlighted the public aspects of the corporation's purpose as a tool for the public good. Both sides were correct, for the complex corporate person encompasses both private and public dimensions, but both were unyielding in their refusal to acknowledge that complexity. Emphasizing certain elements of the corporation's personhood to the exclusion of others has led both sides to conflicting and inconsistent judgments that often seem overly categorical or absolute.

The variations in corporate personhood theories are not entirely to blame for the inconsistencies in corporate speech decisions. The larger body of First Amendment law itself is marred by inconsistent tests and attempts to uphold conflicting principles. The "Court lacks a disciplined and coherent explanation of its own First Amendment jurisprudence."[168] As the Court tries to balance various First Amendment values against the private needs of individuals and the public needs of society, the "upshot has been a series of unstable constitutional compromises that have left the jurisprudence of campaign finance reform [in particular] vulnerable to

166 *See* Padfield, *supra* note 115, at 363 (There is a "disconnect between what the Justices are saying and doing ... Rather than identify, explain, and defend their chosen theory of the corporation, the Justices ignore or deny any role for corporate theory at all."); *see also* Darrell A. H. Miller, *Guns, Inc.:* Citizens United, McDonald, *and the Future of Corporate Constitutional Rights*, 86 N.Y.U. L. Rev. 887, 915 (2011).

167 Lyman Johnson, *Law and Legal Theory in the History of Corporate Responsibility: Corporate Personhood*, 35 Seattle U. L. Rev. 1135, 1142 (2012).

168 Robert C. Post, Citizens Divided: Campaign Finance Reform and the Constitution 4 (2014). The Court's First Amendment opinions have been defined by "overreaching rhetoric and clumsy doctrinal tests." *Id.*

wildly inconsistent holdings."[169] The Court has clearly struggled to articulate unified justifications for extending speech rights in certain contexts and limiting them in others. It turns out that there really is no single set of First Amendment rules, but different rules for different contexts.[170] Not all individuals are treated the same under the First Amendment. We have different levels of rights for different categories of persons; children, students, felons, and foreigners, for example, are treated differently under the First Amendment. Constitutional personhood is not an all-or-nothing proposition. It is tiered and multilayered for individuals, calling for different applications at different times.

The same can be true for different types of corporations in different contexts. The various aspects of corporations' personhood, identity, and purpose can shape the parameters of the rights we choose to extend to corporations. Acknowledging the various dimensions of the corporation's personhood does not necessarily require that corporate persons receive identical treatment under the Constitution as individuals. As discussed in the philosophical treatment of personhood in Chapter 2, personhood may exist along a spectrum and coincide by degrees with certain moral and legal responsibilities and rights. That corporations may be regarded as having a level of personhood that meshes with some level of constitutional protection does not mean that corporations should be treated exactly like individuals for purposes of all constitutional rights. It is appropriate to recognize that corporations are not persons in the natural and fullest sense, and therefore, differential constitutional treatment is warranted. Yet, at the same time, we cannot deny the reality of the complex nature of the corporation's personhood from the numerous interdisciplinary perspectives described in this book. Nor can we ignore the complex implications that flow out of that reality for affording corporate persons some measure of constitutional protection. "To say that 'corporations are persons' and therefore should possess the full complement of constitutional rights afforded to individual citizens is too simplistic and absolute. Yet it is also too simplistic and absolute to say that 'corporations are not people' and therefore deserve no constitutional rights."[171] A more textured understanding is required. "Neither absolutist position of 'no regulation of rights' or 'no boundaries to regulation' seems persuasive."[172]

The wisest approach probably lies somewhere in between the two extremes, with different types of corporations requiring different treatment, just as different categories of individuals are accorded different sets of rights depending on the context. The multidimensional nature of corporations suggests that their personhood can be on a spectrum. It may be appropriate for some, but not all, corporations to have some, but not all, of the same rights as individuals. For example, there may be aspects of the personhood of small, nonprofit, cultural and political associations that

169 *Id.* at 61.
170 Hasen, *supra* note 44, at 100.
171 Orts, *supra* note 117, at 249.
172 *Id.* at 245.

differ from those of large, publicly held, for-profit corporations, necessitating the consideration of different concerns and rights. Not all corporations need be treated the same, and there is no single overarching theory of personhood that can be usefully applied in a uniform manner to all corporations. This book does not purport to have an exhaustive formula for determining categorically which constitutional rights should be afforded to which corporations under which circumstances, although it should be noted that some scholars have thoughtfully attempted to construct a taxonomy of the corporation and a method for facilitating such determinations.[173]

The goal of this discussion is to underscore the deficiency with binary (all-or-nothing) and blanket (one-size-fits-all) approaches to corporate constitutional rights. These absolutist approaches suggesting that corporations should or should not be treated just like natural persons, or arguing that corporations of every type must be treated identically, fail to account for the complexity and layers of personhood among both individuals and corporations. Certain rights may apply to certain types of corporations and not others, just as they do with individuals. Perhaps an increasingly more nuanced approach to corporate constitutional rights is warranted as the types and purposes of corporations become increasingly more diverse and complicated in modern society. In the context of political speech in particular, "the constitutional freedom of speech [today] carries a much more complex and nuanced political identity."[174]

There is the perennial concern for consistency and uniform application of standards. Critics worry that if we extend a certain right to one type of corporation we are obliged to extend that right to all corporate entities. Likewise, denying constitutional protection to some corporations would then lead to the denial of that protection to all others. For example, if we decide to restrict the speech of ordinary commercial corporations, then similar restrictions might need to be made for the speech of media corporations, or religious and political organizations. This deep concern for consistency and uniformity in treatment among corporations tends to obscure the value of recognizing important distinctions among them. There is nothing inherently improper in treating different corporations differently. Corporate persons are multidimensional and varied, and they call for multidimensional and varied treatment. Focusing explicitly on the many different elements of their personhood brings transparency to the determination of corporate rights and

173 *See, e.g.*, Colombo, *supra* note 49, at 189–212. Colombo carefully "divide[s] the universe of corporations into different categories based upon constitutionally salient characteristics [and] explain[s] why corporations falling within a particular category should (or should not) be entitled to assert the freedom of speech, religion, or association." *Id.* at xix; *see also* Greenfield, Corporations Are People Too, *supra* note 160, at 70–170 (discussing which constitutional rights corporations should be able to claim, which they should not, and when).

174 Wayne Batchis, The Right's First Amendment: The Politics of Free Speech & the Return of Conservative Libertarianism, at x (2016).

illuminates why we favor (or disfavor) the extension of such rights in specific circumstances.

These multiple dimensions complicate not only the debate over corporate free speech rights, but also, as we shall see in the next chapter, the heated conflicts over other recent expansions of corporate rights, including rights to religious freedom and racial equality.

5

Constitutional Dimensions of the Corporate Person: Corporate Religion and Race

The idea that the corporation is a person entitled to certain constitutional rights has become the subject of intense debate in the context of religion and race. To what extent can and should corporations be regarded as persons with the status to claim fundamental religious liberty rights and racial equality rights? Can a corporation be associated with a certain religion or race if most or all of its human members identify with one religion or race? Does it make sense to say that the corporation itself can possess and exercise religious beliefs, thereby entitling it to religious liberty rights? Is it possible for a corporation to have a racial identity, thereby affording it standing to claim it has been discriminated against on the basis of its race? Cases involving such questions have generated significant controversy in recent years. The Supreme Court has affirmed the statutory right of corporations to freely exercise religion, and federal courts have developed a body of law to allow corporations to assert racial discrimination claims. The debates over corporate religion and race reflect the tensions that arise out of the competing conceptions of the personhood of corporations.

FIRST AMENDMENT RIGHT TO FREEDOM OF RELIGION

The First Amendment states that "Congress shall make no law respecting an establishment of religion, or prohibiting the free exercise thereof."[1] The Free Exercise Clause protects both the freedom to hold whatever religious beliefs one chooses and the freedom to act in accordance with those religious beliefs. The government is prohibited from dictating what people believe and inhibiting their religiously motivated conduct. To deny individuals the freedom to think, believe, and act in ways that are consistent with their fundamental religious convictions is an affront to their autonomy. At the same time, there are limits on what individuals can and cannot do in the name of religion. Religious liberty is not absolute. Upholding

[1] U.S. Const. amend. I.

free exercise rights requires a balancing of interests to enable people to live in harmony in a diverse and pluralistic society.

To uphold the values underlying the free exercise right, laws that burden a person's religious exercise are subject to a certain level of judicial scrutiny. Prior to 1990, the Supreme Court applied strict scrutiny to any laws that substantially burdened the exercise of one's religion. The government was required to show a compelling interest to justify enforcing any law that substantially affected people's ability to freely practice their religion. The government also had to show that the law was the least restrictive means of achieving the government's interest. Absent a showing of a compelling government interest, the Supreme Court rejected the application of laws to individuals who proved that the laws unduly interfered with the exercise of their religious beliefs.

For example, in *Sherbert v. Verner*, the Court upheld the free exercise claim of a woman who was a member of the Seventh-Day Adventist Church and refused to work on Saturday in accordance with her religious faith.[2] She was fired from her job and was prohibited by the state's unemployment compensation statute from collecting unemployment benefits because her refusal to work for religious reasons was not justified under the statute. Applying strict scrutiny, the Supreme Court held that the state law had placed an unconstitutional burden on the free exercise of her religion without a compelling government interest.

Likewise, in *Wisconsin v. Yoder*, the Court upheld the right of Amish parents to resist the state's compulsory education laws requiring children to attend school until the age of sixteen.[3] In accordance with their Amish faith, the parents stopped sending their children to school after the eighth grade, arguing that the state's interest in forcing their children to attend school for a few additional years was not sufficiently compelling to justify the burden on the exercise of their religious convictions and their centuries-old religious way of life. The Supreme Court agreed and upheld the free exercise rights of the Amish claimants to be exempt from the state's compulsory education law. Together, the holdings of *Sherbert* and *Yoder* were understood to require courts to examine with strict scrutiny any laws that substantially infringed on religious freedom.

That standard changed in 1990 with the Supreme Court's decision in *Employment Division v. Smith*.[4] In *Smith*, the Supreme Court moved away from the strict standards set forth in *Sherbert* and *Yoder* and held that the compelling government interest requirement does not apply to laws that are neutral and generally applicable to the entire population, i.e., laws that do not specifically target the exercise of a particular group's religious beliefs. When two Oregon

2 Sherbert v. Verner, 374 U.S. 398 (1963).

3 Wisconsin v. Yoder, 406 U.S. 205 (1972).

4 Emp't Div. v. Smith, 494 U.S. 872 (1990), *superseded by statute*, Religious Freedom Restoration Act of 1993, Pub. L. No. 103–141, 107 Stat. 1488 (codified as amended at 42 U.S.C. §§ 2000bb to 2000bb-4 (2012)).

residents who worked as counselors at a drug rehabilitation center were fired from their jobs for ingesting the hallucinogenic drug peyote during religious services at their Native American Church, they filed for state unemployment benefits. Given that peyote was a controlled substance prohibited by the state's criminal drug laws and that their use of it constituted a crime, their claim for unemployment benefits was denied on the grounds that they were fired for work-related misconduct. They argued that the law violated their right to freely exercise their religion, but the Supreme Court disagreed, holding that "the right of free exercise does not relieve an individual of the obligation to comply with a 'valid and neutral law of general applicability on the ground that the law proscribes (or prescribes) conduct that his religion prescribes (or proscribes).'"[5] The Court recognized that government regulation of conduct will inevitably infringe from time to time on the religious freedom of certain individuals, but it is not practical to allow every person to follow his or her own particular religious beliefs in violation of neutral laws that apply across the board and that are supported by legitimate government interests. "To permit this would be to make the professed doctrines of religious belief superior to the law of the land, and in effect to permit every citizen to become a law unto himself."[6]

The Court's rejection of the compelling government interest test in *Smith* was widely viewed as a threat to religious freedom and prompted a strong reaction from Congress. Because the *Smith* case seemed to signal a significant reduction in the rights of individuals to act in accordance with their religious beliefs, Congress enacted the Religious Freedom Restoration Act in 1993 to restore the strict scrutiny standard that had existed prior to *Smith*.

RELIGIOUS FREEDOM RESTORATION ACT

Drawing on broad bipartisan support, Congress passed the Religious Freedom Restoration Act (RFRA) to undo the effect of *Smith* on religious free exercise claims.[7] Under RFRA, the government is prohibited from substantially burdening a person's exercise of religion, even if the burden results from a neutral rule of general applicability.[8] As stated in the text of RFRA, the statute's intent was to restore the compelling interest test as set forth in the pre-*Smith* cases of *Sherbert v. Verner* and *Wisconsin v. Yoder*.[9] The government may not "substantially burden a person's exercise of religion" unless the government "demonstrates that application of the burden to the person (1) is in furtherance of a compelling governmental interest; and (2) is the least restrictive means of furthering that compelling governmental

[5] *Id.* at 879 (quoting United States v. Lee, 455 U.S. 252, 263 n.3 (1982) (Stevens, J., concurring)).

[6] *Id.* (quoting Reynolds v. United States, 98 U.S. 145, 167 (1878)).

[7] 42 U.S.C. §§ 2000bb to 2000bb-4 (2012).

[8] *Id.* § 2000bb-1(a).

[9] *Id.* § 2000bb(b)(1).

interest."[10] The statute provides a claim or defense to persons whose religious exercise is substantially burdened by the government. In 2000, Congress amended the federal RFRA to broaden the definition of religious exercise to include "any exercise of religion, whether or not compelled by, or central to, a system of religious belief."[11] The RFRA standards thus provide broad protection for religious liberty.

As enacted, RFRA applied to both federal and state regulation, but the Supreme Court eventually held that Congress did not have the authority to extend RFRA to the states.[12] A few years after its enactment, the Court invalidated RFRA as it applied to state and local governments. In response, many states enacted their own state RFRAs to establish a strict scrutiny standard for state and local laws that substantially burden the free exercise of religion.[13] The federal RFRA remains a valid source for claimants to challenge federal laws that infringe on their rights to freely exercise their religion. It is this statute that became the center of the debate over the religious freedom of corporations in the controversial recent case of *Burwell v. Hobby Lobby Stores, Inc*. The critical question in *Hobby Lobby* was whether corporate claimants are "persons" entitled to the protections of RFRA.

BURWELL V. HOBBY LOBBY STORES, INC.

In a sharply divided 5–4 decision, the Supreme Court in *Burwell v. Hobby Lobby Stores, Inc.* held that for-profit corporations qualify as statutory persons under RFRA with the right to challenge federal laws that infringe on their religious freedom.[14] Finding that the profit-making objective of business corporations is insufficient to distinguish them from other incorporated entities that possess free exercise rights such as churches and religious nonprofit corporations, the Supreme Court held that the government may not force corporations to act in ways that violate the sincerely held religious beliefs of their owners.

In some ways, the *Hobby Lobby* case was quite narrow because it was framed as a matter of statutory interpretation under RFRA, not as an analysis of the broader First Amendment religious rights of corporations. It also involved only closely held, family owned corporations (albeit fairly large in size), not publicly held, multinational corporate giants. Yet the case has been enormously controversial because of its implications for how far the law will go to extend to corporate persons the rights

10 *Id.* § 2000bb-1(b).

11 *Id.* § 2000cc-5(7)(A). This amendment to RFRA was part of the enactment of the Religious Land Use and Institutionalized Persons Act of 2000, another religious freedom statute that subjects state and local land use regulation, as well as state and local prison oversight, to the compelling government interest standard if an affected person's religious exercise is substantially burdened. Pub. L. No. 106–274, 114 Stat. 803 (codified as amended at 42 U.S.C. §§ 2000cc to 2000cc-5 (2012)).

12 *See* City of Boerne v. Flores, 521 U.S. 507 (1997) (declaring RFRA unconstitutional as applied to the states).

13 *See* Christopher C. Lund, *Religious Liberty After* Gonzales: *A Look at State RFRAs*, 55 S.D. L. Rev. 466 (2010) (discussing state RFRAs).

14 Burwell v. Hobby Lobby Stores, Inc., 134 S. Ct. 2751 (2014).

that seem distinctly intended for natural persons. Although the decision rested on statutory grounds, the statute itself was designed to restore constitutional rights. Thus, the case is widely viewed as having important implications for the constitutional scope of religious freedom.

In a diverse and pluralistic society, it is imperative to protect the rights of all individuals to exercise their varying religious beliefs. This is true both when they practice their religious beliefs individually and when they do so in concert with others in a community of believers. Many people are comfortable with the idea of granting free exercise rights to churches and religious organizations because they appear to be associations of like-minded individuals who share similar religious values. But the prospect of giving business corporations the same status, even when their members are likewise unified and committed to the same religious ideals, tends to be much harder to accept. The for-profit nature of the corporation adds a different dimension to the issue and complicates the analysis of individual versus corporate rights. While the majority of the Supreme Court in *Hobby Lobby* attempted to downplay the impact of its holding by framing the issues narrowly, many observers interpret the case as a broader affirmation of the constitutional personhood and rights of corporate entities.

From the viewpoint of both supporters and critics of *Hobby Lobby*, the case can be seen as a natural extension of the Supreme Court's view of corporations in the *Citizens United* decision a few years before. Supporters of corporate constitutional rights argue that if corporations can possess First Amendment rights to engage in political speech to express their political views, as *Citizens United* held, then there is no principled reason why they cannot also possess free exercise rights to engage in conduct that reflects their religious views. *Hobby Lobby* is thus consistent with the direction set by the Court in its prior *Citizens United* holding. Opponents likewise agree that the *Hobby Lobby* result flows naturally from the precedent set by *Citizens United*, but they characterize that precedent as a disaster that solidifies the treatment of corporations as equal persons in society. Once the corporation is viewed as a person entitled to exercise important political speech rights, it is not difficult to extend religious freedom rights to them as well, a result that opponents view as regrettably increasing corporate power at the expense of third parties.

The Supreme Court did not in fact heavily invoke *Citizens United* in reaching its decision in *Hobby Lobby*, nor did the Court expressly rely on theories of corporate personhood to support its conclusion. Yet, as was the case in *Citizens United*, the varying notions of corporate personhood seem to influence both the majority and dissent's discussion of the nature and purposes of corporations, leading to contrary conclusions about the propriety of corporate religious rights.

The facts of the case involved two corporations that objected to the mandates set forth in the controversial Patient Protection and Affordable Care Act (ACA) that was passed by Congress in 2010.[15] The corporations argued that the ACA effectively forced them to be complicit in providing their employees with contraceptives that acted as abortifacients in violation of the corporate owners' sincerely held religious beliefs about the sanctity of human life. Claiming that the ACA provisions substantially burdened the exercise of their religion, the corporations asserted rights under the Free Exercise Clause of the First Amendment and the RFRA.

As explained in the opinion, the ACA requires employers with fifty or more employees to provide group health insurance coverage for their employees. The health insurance must furnish "preventive care and screenings" for women without "any cost-sharing requirements" on the part of employees.[16] Regulations promulgated by the Health and Human Services Department (HHS) required employers to provide coverage for twenty contraceptive methods approved by the Food and Drug Administration, including four methods that could have the effect of preventing an already fertilized egg from developing any further by inhibiting its implantation in the uterus (the "contraceptive mandate").[17] Two of the methods were intrauterine devices and the other two were emergency oral contraceptives commonly known as Plan B and Ella, or the "morning after" pills.[18]

The government established exemptions from the contraceptive mandate for "religious employers" because it recognized that such employers would object to the mandate based on their religious beliefs. In particular, these religious employers believe that human life begins at conception, that these contraceptive methods constitute abortive rather than preventive measures, and that their participation in providing for these contraceptive methods would be wrong, immoral, and violative of their religious convictions. The exempted category of religious employers includes "churches, their integrated auxiliaries, and conventions or associations of churches."[19] Certain religious nonprofit organizations may also obtain an accommodation from the contraceptive mandate if they hold themselves out as religious organizations and have religious objections to providing some or all of the contraceptive services required under the ACA.[20] To implement the religious accommodation, the employer notifies its group health insurer of its objection, and the insurer is then required to exclude contraceptive coverage from the employer's plan and provide separate payments for contraceptive services for plan participants without imposing any cost-sharing requirements on the employer or its employees.[21]

Owners of for-profit businesses with religious objections to the contraceptive mandate did not qualify for any exemptions, and this caused a conflict for corporate

15 Patient Protection and Affordable Care Act, Pub. L. No. 111–48, 124 Stat. 119 (2010) (codified as amended in scattered sections of the U.S. Code).

16 42 U.S.C. § 300gg-13(a)(4) (2012).

17 134 S. Ct. at 2762.

18 *Id.* at 2765; Hobby Lobby Stores, Inc. v. Sebelius, 723 F.3d 1114, 1123 (10th Cir. 2013).

19 134 S. Ct. at 2763 (citing 26 U.S.C. §§ 6033(a)(3)(A)(i), (iii) (2012)).

20 *Id.* at 2763 (citing 45 C.F.R. § 147.131(b) (2013)).

21 *Id.* at 2763 (citing 45 C.F.R. § 147.131(c) (2013)).

entities that opposed the mandate on religious grounds. The penalty for noncompliance with the ACA's requirements required employers to pay $100 per day for each affected individual, and if the employer chose to stop providing health insurance altogether, it would be required to pay $2,000 per year for each of its employees.[22]

The two corporate claimants whose cases were consolidated in the *Hobby Lobby* case challenged the contraceptive mandate on statutory and constitutional grounds based on their sincerely held religious beliefs. One of the corporations, Conestoga Wood Specialties Corp., was a for-profit, closely held Pennsylvania corporation that manufactured wood cabinets and had 950 employees.[23] It was owned exclusively by Norman and Elizabeth Hahn and their three sons who were all devout members of the Mennonite Church, a Christian denomination. They were committed to running their business in accordance with their religious beliefs and moral principles. The company's "Vision and Values Statements" affirmed its endeavor to gain a reasonable profit in a manner that reflected the family's Christian heritage. The board of directors, controlled by the Hahns, had adopted a "Statement on the Sanctity of Human Life" that declared their belief that human life begins at conception. They objected to the ACA contraceptive mandate insofar as it required them to provide health insurance for the four contraceptives that they considered to be abortifacients. In their view, to pay for or facilitate the use of these contraceptive methods would be a wrongful act for which they would be held spiritually accountable. They sued HHS and other federal agencies under RFRA and the First Amendment to enjoin the application of the contraceptive mandate to the corporation.

The district court denied the preliminary injunction, and on appeal the Third Circuit affirmed in a divided opinion, holding that the right to free exercise of religion is a purely personal, inherently human, right that cannot be held by a for-profit corporation.[24] The Third Circuit held that for-profit, secular corporations cannot engage in religious exercise within the meaning of RFRA or the First Amendment because business corporations do not exercise religion in a way that is independent of the actions or belief systems of their individual members. Corporations "do not pray, worship, observe sacraments or take other religiously-motivated actions separate and apart from the intention and direction of their individual actors."[25] The Third Circuit also rejected the claims brought directly by the Hahns themselves, concluding that the ACA affected only the corporation and did not impose any requirements on them personally.

22 *Id.* at 2762 (citing 26 U.S.C. §§ 4980D(a)-(b), 4980H(a), (c)(1) (2012)).

23 *Id.* at 2764.

24 *See* Conestoga Wood Specialties Corp. v. Sec'y of U.S. Dep't of Health & Human Servs., 724 F.3d 377, 384–85 (3d Cir. 2013).

25 *Id.* at 385 (quoting Hobby Lobby Stores, Inc. v. Sebelius, 870 F. Supp. 2d 1278, 1291 (W.D. Okla. 2012)).

The other corporate claimant in the *Hobby Lobby* case was Hobby Lobby Stores, Inc., a nationwide chain of arts and crafts stores, which at the time had 500 locations and over 13,000 employees.[26] David and Barbara Green and their three adult children were devout Christians who owned and operated Hobby Lobby, as well as an affiliated business, Mardel, a Christian bookstore chain with thirty-five bookstores and almost 400 employees. Both Hobby Lobby and Mardel were for-profit, closely held companies incorporated under Oklahoma law. The Greens served as senior executive officers and retained exclusive control over both companies, operating them through a management trust, of which each family member served as a trustee. In accordance with their deep Christian faith, the family provided that the trust and the business would be governed by their religious principles.

Hobby Lobby's statement of purpose expressed the Greens' commitment to "[h]onoring the Lord in all we do by operating the company in a manner consistent with Biblical principles."[27] In accordance with those religious convictions, the Hobby Lobby and Mardel stores closed on Sundays (costing the companies millions in annual sales revenue), played Christian music in the stores, contributed a large portion of their profits to Christian ministries and charities, paid their employees almost twice the minimum wage, and consistently bought hundreds of full-page newspaper ads inviting people to "know Jesus as Lord and Savior."[28] The Greens declined to engage in profitable business transactions that could facilitate alcohol use. For example, they did not sell shot glasses in their stores, they refused to lease building space to a liquor store, and they rejected a lucrative opportunity to transport beer in their company trucks because they felt it would not be in line with their Christian principles.[29] The Green family firmly felt that it would violate their religious convictions to support or facilitate access to contraceptive methods that would function as abortifacients and prevent a fertilized egg from developing after conception.[30] Like the

26 134 S. Ct. at 2765. Today, the company has more than 800 stores and approximately 32,000 employees. *Our Story*, HOBBY LOBBY, www.hobbylobby.com/about-us/our-story [https://perma.cc/A3T5-KAVA].

27 134 S. Ct. at 2766; *Our Story*, HOBBY LOBBY, *supra* note 26.

28 134 S. Ct. at 2766; Lyman Johnson & David Millon, *Corporate Law After* Hobby Lobby, 70 BUS. LAW. 1, 6 (2014/2015); Mark L. Rienzi, *God and the Profits: Is There Religious Liberty for Moneymakers?*, 21 GEO. MASON L. REV. 59, 78–79 (2013).

29 *See* Verified Complaint at 11, Hobby Lobby Stores, Inc. v. Sebelius, 870 F. Supp. 2d 1278 (W.D. Okla. 2012) (No. CIV-12-1000-HE). "[O]ur trucks returning from our Colorado stores could have back-hauled Coors Beer to Oklahoma City on a long-term contract that would have netted us $300,000 a year [at] a time when we really could have used the cash . . . [W]e said no thank you, preferring to let our trucks come back empty until we could find an alternative. Let somebody else haul the beer and take the responsibility for what people do with it." David Green, MORE THAN A HOBBY 144 (2005).

30 There is significant medical debate over whether these contraceptive methods actually prevent implantation or merely fertilization, but the parties conceded that at least some of the methods have the potential to inhibit uterine implantation, which is what the corporate claimants found morally problematic. Hobby Lobby Stores, Inc. v. Sebelius, 723 F.3d 1114, 1123 n.3 (10th Cir. 2013). *See also* Rienzi, *supra* note 28, at 103 n.286; Amy J. Sepinwall, *Conscience and Complicity: Assessing Pleas for Religious Exemptions in* Hobby Lobby's *Wake*, 82 U. CHI. L. REV. 1897, 1899 n.3, 1930–31 n.134 (2015) (citing sources revealing scientific disagreement over whether the four contraceptives at issue lack the potential for abortive effects).

Hahns, the Greens believed that compliance with the contraceptive mandate would connect them to wrongful conduct in a way that would make them complicit and morally responsible for a grave wrong. They objected to the same four contraceptives as the Hahns and likewise sued to challenge the contraceptive mandate under RFRA and the Free Exercise Clause of the First Amendment.

They lost in the district court. But on appeal the Tenth Circuit reversed and held that Hobby Lobby and Mardel were "persons" within the meaning of RFRA and that the contraceptive mandate substantially burdened the exercise of religion by requiring the companies to either compromise their religious beliefs or pay a heavy financial penalty.[31] Unlike the Third Circuit in the Hahns' case, the Tenth Circuit declined to say that the free exercise right is a purely personal guarantee that is categorically unavailable to corporations and other organizations. Thus, the Supreme Court was faced with conflicting circuit court opinions regarding the question whether for-profit corporations like Hobby Lobby and Conestoga are entitled to claim rights to religious freedom.

MAJORITY OPINION IN *HOBBY LOBBY*

The majority opinion written by Justice Alito agreed with the Tenth Circuit's judgment in favor of Hobby Lobby and held that for-profit corporations may claim free exercise rights under RFRA. Interpreting the text of RFRA to reach its conclusion, the Court resolved the case entirely on RFRA statutory grounds and thus declined to reach the constitutional issue under the First Amendment's Free Exercise Clause.

Justice Alito described the corporation in terms familiar under the artificial person and aggregate theories of corporate personhood. He called it a "legal fiction" whose "purpose . . . is to provide protection for human beings."[32] In other words, the corporation serves as a tool for furthering the interests of its individual members. The Court recognized "the rights and obligations of the *people* (including shareholders, officers, and employees) who are associated with a corporation in one way or another. When rights, whether constitutional or statutory, are extended to corporations, the purpose is to protect the rights of these people."[33] With respect to corporate religious rights, the Court found that "protecting the free-exercise rights of corporations like Hobby Lobby, Conestoga, and Mardel protects the religious liberty of the humans who own and control those companies."[34]

31 134 S. Ct. at 2766.

32 *Id.* at 2768.

33 *Id.*

34 *Id.* It is curious that the Court speaks of "shareholders, officers, and employees" as the "people" whose rights are protected through corporate rights, but a few short sentences later, the Court narrows the group of people whose religious rights are at stake to only those "humans who own and control" the corporation. The limiting principle by which employees are excluded from the free exercise protection is left unstated. Gregory A. Mark, Hobby Lobby *and Corporate Personhood: Taking the U.S. Supreme Court's Reasoning at Face Value*, 65 DePaul L. Rev. 535, 545 (2016).

Because RFRA applies to "a person's exercise of religion" but does not define the term "person," the Court utilized the federal Dictionary Act to determine the meaning of the term. Under the Dictionary Act, which defines terms in federal statutes, the word "person" includes "corporations, companies, associations, firms, partnerships, societies, and joint stock companies, as well as individuals."[35] This provided the Court with a "quick, clear, and affirmative answer" to the question whether corporations are entitled to bring RFRA claims.[36] The government conceded that churches and nonprofit religious corporations are persons under RFRA and are entitled to religious exercise rights in order to further the religious freedom of their individual members. The Court found it unreasonable to think that Congress intended the term "person" to mean only natural persons and nonprofit organizations, but not for-profit corporations. The Court found that the profit-making objective alone does not disqualify individuals or their organizations from bringing free exercise claims. Commercial business owners have been permitted in the past to challenge laws that burden the exercise of their religion under the First Amendment even though they operate for-profit enterprises.[37]

The Court further noted that for-profit corporations do not always exist solely to make money. They can be formed for any lawful purpose, and nothing in the law requires them to pursue profits all the time. They can act altruistically and philanthropically, foregoing profits at times to act in socially responsible ways that go beyond what the law requires. Corporations can donate to charities, contribute to environmental causes, and engage in political speech. If they can pursue these varying objectives, it is plausible that they can pursue religious objectives as well. Numerous states now allow companies to operate as "B corporations," "benefit corporations," or "flexible purpose corporations" to enable them to pursue both profits and public benefits.[38] Hobby Lobby and Conestoga had statements of purpose that indicated their desire was not merely to maximize profits, but rather, to honor their religious principles as well. They were closely held companies controlled by family members with sincerely held religious convictions. As such, in the opinion of the Court, the companies could claim the status of persons under RFRA to challenge government action that substantially burdened their exercise of religion.

35 1 U.S.C. § 1 (2012).

36 134 S. Ct. at 2768.

37 The Court cited *Braunfeld v. Brown*, a case involving five Jewish merchants with small retail businesses who challenged a Sunday closing law. Their religious faith required them to close their shops on Saturday. They argued that the law burdened their exercise of religion by placing them at a financial disadvantage since they could not operate six days a week like their non-Jewish competitors. While they lost on the merits, the Supreme Court entertained their claim and did not deny them the ability to challenge the law simply because they were engaged in profit-making enterprises. *See* 366 U.S. 599 (1961).

38 *See* 134 S. Ct. at 2771; *see also* Jane L. Collins & Walker N. Kahn, *The Hijacking of a New Corporate Form? Benefit Corporations and Corporate Personhood*, 45 ECON. & SOC'Y 325 (2016).

To determine whether the contraceptive mandate imposed a substantial burden on their religious exercise, the Court noted the significant economic penalties the companies would incur if they failed to comply with the mandate and the sincerity of the owners' religious beliefs in light of the potentially ruinous fines. For Hobby Lobby, if its health insurance plan did not include all of the mandated contraceptives, the penalty would amount to $1.3 million per day, or about $475 million per year. For Conestoga and Mardel, the penalties would be $33 million and $15 million per year respectively.[39] The Court believed that these fines placed enormous pressure on the owners to modify their behavior and to contradict what their religion told them was the right thing to do. With the power of this financial threat, the contraceptive mandate demanded that they engage in conduct that seriously violated their religious beliefs.

HHS and the dissent argued that the link between the corporations' provision of compliant health insurance and an employee's self-determined choice to utilize one of the objectionable contraceptive methods was too attenuated to draw the dramatic conclusion that the corporations' compliance with the mandate would result directly in abortions. From the government's viewpoint, it was unreasonable for the owners to think that by following the law they would be complicit in and morally responsible for what they believe to be an immoral act by another. The Court disagreed with HHS's assessment, holding that the Court has no business deciding whether a person's religious belief is unreasonable, flawed, or mistaken.[40] Whether it is wrong for a person to perform an innocent act that has the effect of facilitating another person's purported immoral conduct is a deep question of moral philosophy and religion that the Court felt it had no authority to judge. The Court's only job is to determine if the belief constitutes an honest conviction and is sincerely held. Here, there was no dispute regarding the sincerity of the owners' beliefs. Thus, the Court found that the law imposed a substantial burden on the religious exercise of the corporations and their owners.

In applying RFRA's strict scrutiny test, the Court assumed that the government's interest in ensuring that women have cost-free access to the full range of contraceptives was a compelling one, but the majority was not convinced that forcing corporations to supply the mandated insurance was the least restrictive means of meeting that compelling interest. In the majority's view, there were other methods of

39 134 S. Ct. at 2775–76. Some commentators argue that the Court's limited judicial review of the sincerity of the religious claimant's beliefs and the amount of the secular costs of disobeying the law is insufficient to adequately analyze whether the law substantially burdens the claimant's religious exercise. *See, e.g.*, Frederick Mark Gedicks, *"Substantial" Burdens: How Courts May (and Why They Must) Judge Burdens on Religion under RFRA*, 85 GEO. WASH. L. REV. 94 (2017).

40 *See* 134 S. Ct. at 2778–79. While the Court declined to address the merits of this issue, others have argued that there is a reasonable basis for religious employers to believe that their compliance with the contraceptive mandate can have a causal connection with abortive acts, thereby implicating employers' sense of moral responsibility. *See* Douglas Laycock, *Religious Liberty and the Culture Wars*, 2014 U. ILL. L. REV. 839, 852–53, 874–75.

fulfilling the purposes of the contraceptive mandate, and HHS had not shown that those methods were not viable alternatives. For instance, a workable solution was already available in the existing accommodation for religious nonprofit organizations that opposed the contraceptive mandate. Such organizations were permitted to notify the government of their religious objections, and then the health insurer was required to provide the contraceptives separately to the employees without imposing any costs on them. This already implemented framework could easily be afforded to closely held for-profit corporations like Hobby Lobby that carried the same religious convictions. It would be equally effective in accomplishing the government's objective and would be far less burdensome on religious exercise.[41] Thus, the Court held that the contraceptive mandate was not the least restrictive means to support the government's interest, and the Court concluded that the law violated the corporate claimants' free exercise rights under RFRA.

DISSENTING OPINION IN *HOBBY LOBBY*

The dissenting opinion, written by Justice Ginsburg, rejected the proposition that for-profit corporations are "persons" who qualify for religious exemptions under RFRA or the First Amendment.[42] Drawing on language familiar to the artificial person theory of corporate personhood, Justice Ginsburg quoted Chief Justice Marshall's famous phrase in *Trustees of Dartmouth College v. Woodward*: "a corporation is 'an artificial being, invisible, intangible, and existing only in contemplation of law,'" as well as Justice Stevens' dissenting opinion in *Citizens United*: "corporations 'have no consciences, no beliefs, no feelings, no thoughts, no desires.'"[43] While Justice Ginsburg insisted that only natural persons, not artificial legal entities, can exercise religion, she acknowledged that churches and religious nonprofit organizations are entitled to free exercise protections. The reason for the distinction between for-profit and nonprofit entities is because "[r]eligious

41 *See* 134 S. Ct. at 2782–83, 2786. The majority also suggested that another less restrictive alternative would be for the government itself to pay for the four challenged contraceptives for any employees who could not obtain them under their health insurance policies due to their employers' religious objections. *Id.* at 2780. Commentators argued that there were actually several other options for providing the contraceptives to women, including setting up free public clinics, or providing tax credits or subsidies for employees, but instead of pursuing those, the government "adopted the single means that [was] *most* restrictive of the religious liberty of objecting employers." U.S. Comm'n on Civil Rights, Peaceful Coexistence: Reconciling Nondiscrimination Principles with Civil Liberties 269, 276 (2016) (statement of Edward Whelan, President, Ethics and Public Policy Center), www.usccr.gov/pubs/Peaceful-Coexistence-09-07-16.PDF [https://perma.cc/728R-TJX8].

42 *See* 134 S. Ct. at 2794 (Ginsburg, J., dissenting). Only Justice Ginsburg and Justice Sotomayor concluded that for-profit corporations cannot be persons for purposes of claiming free exercise rights under RFRA. The other two dissenting justices, Justice Breyer and Justice Kagan, declined to join this part of the dissenting opinion. They believed the question did not need to be decided since, in their view, the challenge to the contraceptive mandate failed on its merits. *Id.* at 2806 (Breyer J., Kagan J., dissenting).

43 *Id.* (internal citations omitted).

organizations exist to foster the interests of persons subscribing to the same religious faith," but for-profit corporations include workers who are not always "drawn from one religious community."[44] The for-profit corporation does not exist to perpetuate the religious values and goals shared by a community of believers.

Justice Ginsburg emphasized the nature of the corporation as a separate legal entity formed to shield its owners from personal liability. Although it may make sense in the case of a sole proprietorship to view the owner and the business as one and the same, individuals who incorporate their businesses seek to separate themselves from the entity and escape personal responsibility for the entity's obligations. Since their use of the corporate form is to effectuate that legal separation, they should not then be permitted to insist that their individual religious beliefs can flow through or be imputed to the company to protect their individual rights.[45] To allow such identification of the corporation with its owners' religious beliefs is to permit corporate owners to stand behind the corporate veil only when it suits their interests and then to rip it away when it does not. It is not fair to afford corporate owners the benefits of both legal separation and legal unity simultaneously.

While acknowledging that the Green and Hahn families' religious beliefs were sincerely held, the dissent did not agree that the contraceptive mandate substantially burdened the exercise of their beliefs. In the dissent's view, the connection between the corporate owners' religious objections and the contraceptive coverage requirement was too attenuated to be called substantial.[46] A corporation's compliance with the contraceptive mandate does not make the corporation or its owners complicit in any decision by an employee to utilize one of the contested contraceptives. That decision is an autonomous choice made by the employee, rendering the link to the employer's actions so weak that it is not reasonable for the employer to think that providing its employees with a comprehensive health insurance plan that includes the contested contraceptives contributes to the improper termination of a pregnancy.

The dissent also concluded that the contraceptive mandate was the least restrictive means of accomplishing the government's compelling interest in ensuring that contraceptives were available to employees at no cost to them. It is not sufficient to assert, as the majority does, that a less restrictive alternative would be to have the government itself pay for the contraceptives. There is no reasonable stopping point for the use of that alternative in every case where an employer raises a religious objection to compliance with the law.[47]

The dissent criticized the majority for failing to consider the interests of third parties who themselves would be burdened by the religious accommodations given to for-profit corporations whose owners have religious objections to the

44 *Id.* at 2795.
45 *See id.* at 2797.
46 *See id.* at 2799.
47 *See id.* at 2802.

contraceptive mandate. Specifically, the thousands of female employees who work for such corporations, and who do not share their employers' religious beliefs, would be denied direct access to the full range of contraceptive choices that they would have had if their employer were required to comply with the mandate. The dissent argued that accommodations for religious beliefs "must not significantly impinge on the interests of third parties."[48] If the accommodation would be harmful to others or deprive them of rights guaranteed by other laws, the accommodation should not be granted. Although individual free exercise rights are extremely important, they must be balanced against other societal interests, and sometimes certain religious practices will have to yield to the common good.

In response, the majority opinion clarified that nothing in RFRA supports imposing burdens on religious exercise, however onerous or however readily the government interest could be achieved through alternative means, simply because the relevant legal mandate requires the religious believer to confer a benefit on third parties. "By framing any Government regulation as benefiting a third party, the Government could turn all regulations into entitlements to which nobody could object on religious grounds, rendering RFRA meaningless."[49] In this case, the majority emphasized that no women in fact would be negatively impacted by the religious accommodation because HHS already had an existing framework in place to provide contraceptives with no cost to those employees who could not obtain them under their health insurance plans due to their employers' religious objections. The exemption was granted precisely because the government had a feasible alternative to provide the contraceptive benefits without imposing any costs on the employees. No one was denying women access to the contraceptive methods. It was simply a question of who had to pay for them.

Although the majority opinion suggested that its holding was limited to closely held, for-profit corporations where the owners' religious beliefs were more likely to be unified, the dissent maintained that the majority's reasoning extends to corporations large or small, public or private. The dissent pointed out that even closely held corporations that have a relatively small number of owners can in actuality be quite large in size with thousands of employees, all of whom have very different faiths. The dissent argued that *Hobby Lobby* will have extremely detrimental repercussions as for-profit corporations of all sizes will be able to find a haven under RFRA to be exempted from all manner of generally applicable laws, including anti-discrimination laws, based on the corporate owners' religious beliefs.[50]

48 *Id.* at 2790.
49 *Id.* at 2781 n.37.
50 *See id.* at 2797, 2804–05.

RELIGIOUS EXERCISE AND NOTIONS OF CORPORATE PERSONHOOD

In recognizing the religious liberty rights of corporations, the Court in *Hobby Lobby* found that corporations meet the statutory definition of "person" under RFRA, but the Court did not explicitly rely on fundamental theories of corporate personhood to reach its conclusion. The Court did not proclaim that corporations are persons in the broader sense, capable of exercising religion in the same way as individuals and therefore equally entitled to moral and constitutional rights to practice their religion. The majority opinion in *Hobby Lobby* avoided discussion of the moral agency or personhood of the corporation itself and focused instead on the interests of the corporation's individual members.

The *Hobby Lobby* dissent, however, accused the Court of utilizing an "expansive notion of corporate personhood" to justify its reasoning.[51] Commentators agreed that *Hobby Lobby* not only affirmed the personhood of corporations but further expanded it to uphold the religious rights of for-profit corporations for the first time. Critics argued that *Hobby Lobby* "doubles down on corporate personhood and uses it to undercut the rights of living Americans in a way that is very harmful."[52] The concern is that the evolving perception of corporations as persons has bolstered the judgment that corporate persons are worthy of the same rights afforded to individuals.

Public reaction to the *Hobby Lobby* decision was swift and contentious, with strong feelings on both sides of the issue. Opponents claimed it borders on the absurd to say that corporations as inanimate, soulless entities are religious and have a right to freely exercise their religion. Supporters argued that recognition of the corporate right to religious liberty is not an assertion that corporations themselves are religious, but rather a method for protecting the religious freedom of the human members within the corporation. The continuing debate over religion and corporate rights reflects the conflicting beliefs people have about the appropriate role, purpose, and level of power of the corporation in society. Because corporations come in many different forms – public and private, large and small, nonprofit and for-profit – it is difficult to agree on blanket rules that can be applied to the whole range of corporate persons. The multidimensional aspects of corporations raise different arguments for and against allowing corporations of various types to assert the right to free exercise of religion.

AGGREGATE ELEMENTS OF CORPORATE PERSONHOOD AND RELIGIOUS EXERCISE

The aggregate aspect of the corporate person as a collection of its individual participants is central to the assertion that corporations can claim free exercise rights

[51] *Id.* at 2797.

[52] David H. Gans & Ilya Shapiro, Religious Liberties for Corporations?: Hobby Lobby, the Affordable Care Act, and the Constitution 65 (2014) (statements of Gans).

in order to protect the religious freedom of their individual members. The *Hobby Lobby* Court emphasized this view of corporations when it held that the purpose of extending religious rights to corporations is to uphold the rights of the people who own and control the corporation. Rather than focusing on the entity itself, the Court looked through the corporate form and saw the Greens and the Hahns behind it. It is their religious liberty rights that flow through to the corporation such that the corporation's rights are derivative of those of the natural persons who compose it.

Supporters of *Hobby Lobby* argue that denying the corporation religious liberty rights effectively deprives individuals of freely exercising their religious beliefs by means of for-profit corporate enterprise.[53] From this view, it is unfair to tell entrepreneurs who choose to organize their business as a corporation, rather than a sole proprietorship or partnership, that they must forfeit their religious exercise rights.[54] People should not be punished for incorporating their business by losing their rights to religious freedom. Religious individuals would then effectively be denied the advantage of using the for-profit corporate form, while non-religious business owners would not be faced with the same barrier. This relegates the career choices of religious entrepreneurs to the nonprofit world or to only certain types of business organizations, restricting the opportunities they might otherwise have to invest in and work for organizations that operate in ways that are consistent with their deeply held religious principles.[55] In situations involving legal mandates like that in the ACA, owners of for-profit corporations who decide to follow their religious convictions would be required to pay such heavy fines that it could very well put them out of business. To force corporate business owners to choose between violating their religious beliefs or going out of business is an unreasonable demand, and the right to religious freedom forbids applying precisely that type of burden on individuals' religious exercise.[56]

It is the individual human beings within the corporation who feel the weight of the burden placed on them by the government. They are the ones who suffer religious injury when they feel pressured to abandon their religious convictions or abandon their business. One of the Third Circuit judges hearing the appeal of the Hahns noted that "one need not have looked past the first row of the gallery during the oral argument of this appeal, where the Hahns were seated and listening intently, to see the real human suffering occasioned by the government's determination to either make the Hahns bury their religious scruples or watch while their business gets buried."[57] The law protects an individual's freedom of conscience because

53 *See* Ronald J. Colombo, The First Amendment and the Business Corporation 155–56 (2015); Alan J. Meese & Nathan B. Oman, Hobby Lobby, *Corporate Law, and the Theory of the Firm: Why For-Profit Corporations Are RFRA Persons*, 127 Harv. L. Rev. F. 273, 294–95 (2014).

54 *See* Burwell v. Hobby Lobby Stores, Inc., 134 S. Ct. 2751, 2759 (2014).

55 Colombo, *supra* note 53, at 156.

56 *See* Gans & Shapiro, *supra* note 52, at 35–36 (statements of Shapiro); Scott W. Gaylord, *For-Profit Corporations, Free Exercise, and the HHS Mandate*, 91 Wash. U. L. Rev. 589, 638–39 (2014).

57 Conestoga Wood Specialties Corp. v. Sec'y of U.S. Dep't of Health & Human Servs., 724 F.3d 377, 390 (3d Cir. 2013) (Jordan, J., dissenting).

conscience itself is central to a person's sense of self, moral integrity, self-respect, and personhood. Courts refrain from requiring people to do what their conscience tells them is deeply wrong out of respect for their autonomy and dignity as persons.[58] "Protecting religious liberty reduces human suffering; people do not have to choose between incurring legal penalties and surrendering core parts of their identity."[59] The law has long accommodated the claims of conscientious objectors, acknowledging that to compel individuals to act contrary to their conscience inflicts on them a serious moral harm. The *Hobby Lobby* Court was persuaded that the individuals within the corporation were the ones whose moral integrity and personhood were at stake if free exercise rights were not extended to the corporation.

Note that in extending religious liberty rights to corporations, the Court focused on the corporation's individual members as the source of the right much more than the Court did in its analysis of the corporation's political speech rights in *Citizens United*. The Court in *Hobby Lobby* zeroed in on the aggregate nature of the corporation as a collection of individuals, expressing its concerns about burdening the religious exercise of the individual owners within the corporation. In *Citizens United*, however, the majority opinion's predominant worry seemed less about burdening the speech of the corporation's internal members, and more about upholding the corporate speech itself for the benefit of listeners who were external to the corporation. Thus, in the context of analyzing corporate free exercise rights, the aggregate feature of the corporation emerges as a more salient factor to support the right.

Matters of religion and conscience are deeply personal and private. Some commentators contend that individuals' religious liberty is entitled to broad protection in the privacy of their home or at their church, but their religiously motivated conduct merits less deference once they choose to enter the public marketplace or commercial sphere.[60] However, in his concurring opinion in *Hobby Lobby*, Justice Kennedy maintained that individuals should have the right to express their religious beliefs in the many different settings of their life, including "in the political, civic, and economic life of our larger community."[61] Religious faith often permeates all aspects of an individual's life. For many religious adherents, their faith is not an isolated aspect of their existence, nor is it practiced in a compartmentalized way in only limited settings on certain days of the week. Indeed, in many religious communities,

58 *See* Kent Greenawalt, *Religious Toleration and Claims of Conscience*, *in* THE RISE OF CORPORATE RELIGIOUS LIBERTY 3 9 (Micah Schwartzman et al. eds., 2016); Elizabeth Sepper, *Taking Conscience Seriously*, 98 VA. L. REV. 1501, 1526–30 (2012).

59 Laycock, *supra* note 40, at 842.

60 *See* Paul Horwitz, *The* Hobby Lobby *Moment*, 128 HARV. L. REV. 154, 177 (2014) (describing the assumption that "religion should, for the most part, be zoned out of the marketplace and market relations"); *see also* Ronald J. Colombo, *The Naked Private Square*, 51 HOUS. L. REV. 1, 6 (2013) ("The modern business corporation is commonly portrayed as a thoroughly secular institution in which religion plays no role and has no place.").

61 Burwell v. Hobby Lobby Stores, Inc., 134 S. Ct. 2751, 2785 (2014) (Kennedy, J., concurring).

believers are instructed to live out their faith on a daily basis to reflect the same beliefs they proclaim on special days such as the Sabbath.[62] They are encouraged not to live a "divided life,"[63] but to live spiritually integrated lives where their actions, both professional and personal, align with their deepest religious values and beliefs. To the extent believers are exhorted to allow their religious beliefs to influence their decisions and conduct in all the domains of their life, they may feel it is imperative to follow their religious calling in and through their for-profit businesses as well. Religious individuals seek to live out their religious beliefs at home, in their places of worship, and in their work settings, including corporate ones. People have become increasingly more open and assertive about their desire to integrate their spirituality with their business endeavors, creating or choosing to work for companies that pursue both economic and spiritual objectives.[64]

The corporate right to religious freedom recognizes that religion tends to be a communal experience. People practice religion collectively in community with others. They do so in churches, synagogues, and mosques, as well as other religiously affiliated associations such as schools, hospitals, and aid organizations. To fully protect individual religious rights, the free exercise rights of such collective bodies are protected as well.[65] Most people believe that incorporated religious entities like churches and religiously affiliated nonprofit organizations should enjoy the right to free exercise. Their main purpose is to promote the faith of their individual members and advance the religious mission of the organization.

62 *See HHS Proposal Falls Short in Meeting Church Concerns; Bishops Look Forward to Addressing Issues with Administration*, U.S. CONF. OF CATH. BISHOPS (Feb. 7, 2013), http://usccb.org/news/2013/13-037.cfm [https://perma.cc/TN87-EPWS] (statement of Cardinal Timothy Dolan) ("In obedience to our Judeo-Christian heritage, we have consistently taught our people to live their lives during the week to reflect the same beliefs that they proclaim on the Sabbath.").

63 *See* PONTIFICAL COUNCIL FOR JUSTICE AND PEACE, VOCATION OF THE BUSINESS LEADER: A REFLECTION 6 (4th ed. 2014), www.stthomas.edu/media/catholicstudies/center/ryan/publications/publicationpdfs/vocationofthebusinessleaderpdf/PontificalCouncil_4.pdf [https://perma.cc/LEL9-U8A7] ("Dividing the demands of one's faith from one's work in business is a fundamental error" and leads to a "divided life" that "is not unified or integrated" but "fundamentally disordered, and thus fails to live up to God's call."). "The notion that religion is a private thing that can be separated from other aspects of life is inconsistent with the way many people experience religion. For many, religion . . . is at the core of one's being." Frank S. Ravitch, *Be Careful What You Wish for: Why* Hobby Lobby *Weakens Religious Freedom*, 2016 BYU L. REV. 55, 91.

64 *See* Colombo, *supra* note 53, at 64–70; Lake Lambert III, SPIRITUALITY, INC.: RELIGION IN THE AMERICAN WORKPLACE 1–2, 38–39, 54–55 (2009). Somewhat related to this movement toward greater religiosity in the corporate world is the business trend of "workplace spirituality" that has become increasingly more prevalent as companies integrate faith and spiritual values in the corporate setting. *See* Elizabeth A. Clark & W. Cole Durham, Jr., *The Emergence of Corporate Religious Freedom*, *in* THE CHANGING NATURE OF RELIGIOUS RIGHTS UNDER INTERNATIONAL LAW 256, 284 (Malcolm D. Evans et al. eds., 2015).

65 *See* Gilardi v. U.S. Dep't of Health & Human Servs., 733 F.3d 1208, 1212 (D.C. Cir. 2013) (citation omitted), *vacated and remanded*, 134 S. Ct. 2902 (mem.) (2014) ("Because the word religion 'connotes a community of believers,' the prohibition against the impingement on religious free exercise must be understood to cover the activities of both individuals and religious bodies.").

For-profit corporations, however, have a different focus. Their main aim is (or arguably should be) to make money and foster the economic, not the religious, interests of their members. In corporations whose owners are religious, the "corporation's actions may reflect the owners' devotion to religious principles, but the corporation does not exist to facilitate the owners' free exercise of religion."[66] Opponents of *Hobby Lobby* argue that it is troubling to extend religious liberty rights to for-profit corporations because they are not sufficiently akin to churches and religious nonprofit associations to merit the same religious accommodation.

The typical for-profit corporation is not an association of individuals who have joined together for a common religious purpose. The corporation may have many different purposes and objectives, but it is too much of a stretch to say that its *main* purpose is to facilitate its constituents' religious exercise in a way that is similar to a church. It is commonly understood that corporate investors come together in the hopes of generating financial returns on their investment. Other corporate constituents, such as employees, creditors, and suppliers, participate in the organization to further their own financial ends as well. Their membership in the group is not intimately tied to their personal identity or deepest convictions.[67] The large, for-profit corporation in particular is not a cohesive body where members with shared values associate with each other to cultivate their religious faith and perpetuate their religion-centered mission. The only common tie among the aggregate of the for-profit corporation's many individual members seems to be an economic one relating to financial gain.

Supporters of corporate religious liberty rights maintain that this may be true for many for-profit corporations, but it is not necessarily true of all of them. Some for-profit enterprises do have owners who care very deeply about operating a business that reflects their sincerely held religious beliefs, and they do not consider financial gain to be the sole goal of the corporation.[68] Corporations can be formed for any lawful purpose, including purposes that go beyond making money. Corporate charters, bylaws, and shareholder agreements can reflect the shareholders' preferences for the purposes of their business and how they want it to be operated. State statutes authorize business managers to make charitable contributions, and the business judgment rule protects corporate decisions to utilize profits in support of any number of philanthropic endeavors including educational, environmental, or religious ones. Statutes authorizing the formation of "B corporations" and "benefit corporations" enable mission-driven businesses to pursue general and specific

66 Henry L. Chambers, Jr., *Telescoping and Collectivizing Religious Free Exercise Rights*, 75 MD. L. REV. 392, 405 (2015).

67 *See* James D. Nelson, *Conscience, Incorporated*, 2013 MICH. ST. L. REV. 1565, 1582, 1609 (arguing that corporations are not "constitutive communities" in which members view their affiliation with the group as a central aspect of their own identities).

68 *See, e.g.*, Meese & Oman, *supra* note 53, at 278–79 (listing several companies that prioritize religious principles over profits in their corporate activities, including Jewish kosher supermarkets, Muslim grocery stores, and Christian fast-food chains).

public benefits, in addition to making profits, and to serve as vehicles for the communal expression of religious values and priorities.[69] Employees and even customers may choose to associate with certain for-profit corporations that integrate religious values in their business precisely because they share the same values and are attracted to the companies' religious orientation. "Religiously expressive corporations" may not be commonplace, but they do exist, and they arguably constitute a genuine community of individuals who coalesce around a common vision or shared set of religious goals, values, and beliefs.[70] In this subset of for-profit businesses, members seek to integrate their work and faith, and associate with like-minded individuals who have a similar commitment to the same religious principles.[71] This is not unlike religious nonprofit corporations that are formed to pursue similar goals. "There is nothing in the nature of a for-profit corporation that prevents the kind of shared purpose that one finds in a membership organization."[72] If these corporations, whether for-profit or nonprofit, are vehicles for people to realize their values and identities, then extending religious liberty rights to both types of organizations is a means of respecting the religious convictions and consciences of the individual members. "Religious rights do not evaporate the moment profit motive is added to the exercise of religious beliefs."[73]

Nonetheless, in spite of the parallels between such religious for-profit corporations and their nonprofit counterparts, for many observers, for-profit entities simply have a tendency to appear more "secular" than religious. Perhaps this is because the idea of pursuing profits does not seem to accord with the virtues we customarily associate with religious pursuits, like philanthropy, charity, and self-sacrifice.

Even so, many religious adherents contend that there is nothing inherently incompatible with profit-seeking and religious exercise. Indeed, in many religious traditions, the tenets of the faith include important instructions for their members' money-making activities. For example, scholars of Christianity, Islam, and Judaism reveal that the teachings of each religion impose numerous requirements on

69 *See* Marc A. Greendorfer, *Blurring Lines Between Churches and Secular Corporations: The Compelling Case of the Benefit Corporation's Right to the Free Exercise of Religion (with a post-*Hobby Lobby *Epilogue)*, 39 Del. J. Corp. L. 819 (2015).

70 Colombo, *supra* note 53, at 56, 64–68. Another term often used to describe such corporations is "faith-based companies." Rex Ahdar, *Companies as Religious Liberty Claimants*, 5 Oxford J. L. & Religion 1, 4 (2016).

71 The constitutional right to association is often invoked as well to justify protection of individuals' interests in forming and joining groups that embody and further the values that are central to their faith. The Supreme Court has recognized the "right to associate for the purpose of engaging in those activities protected by the First Amendment—speech, assembly, . . . and the exercise of religion. The Constitution guarantees freedom of association of this kind as an indispensable means of preserving other individual liberties." Roberts v. U.S. Jaycees, 468 U.S. 609, 618 (1984).

72 Amy J. Sepinwall, *Corporate Piety and Impropriety:* Hobby Lobby's *Extension of RFRA Rights to the For-Profit Corporation*, 5 Harv. Bus. L. Rev. 173, 192 n.96 (2015).

73 Clark & Durham, *supra* note 64, at 257. It has been observed that internationally, courts and legislatures in other countries have recognized the right of for-profit corporations to claim religious rights. *See id.* at 265–73.

believers in the conduct of business.[74] Believers are admonished to act with honesty and integrity, to refrain from corrupt business practices, to refuse to participate in harmful activity including the production or promotion of harmful goods and services, to forego money-making on certain days such as the Sabbath or other holy days, and to look to their religious faith to be the overriding moral compass in their business dealings. Business owners are viewed as being morally and spiritually accountable for the actions of the business. As faithful believers, they must integrate the precepts of their religion into their money-making endeavors. From the standpoint of these religious traditions, profit-making is not viewed as being inherently separate from religious exercise. The local kosher and halal food market owners' adherence to prescribed food preparation practices flows from sincere religious conviction as well as the desire to operate a profitable business. The dichotomy between profit and religion is said to be a false one and foreign to many religious faiths.

As an empirical matter, religion and profit-making go hand-in-hand in large segments of the commercial world. Nationally we have "a $4.6 billion Christian-products industry, a $12.5 billion kosher-food market, and a growing share of an $800 billion global Sharia-compliant finance market."[75] Faith-based investing in mutual funds and companies that follow certain religious principles is a multi-billion dollar industry.[76] Although religiously oriented companies risk losing a portion of the consumer market that disagrees with their views, some corporations have maintained their religious commitments while remaining quite profitable, such as Chick-fil-A, Forever 21, Tyson Foods, In-N-Out Burger, and Hobby Lobby.[77] That many for-profit companies, large and small, combine money-making with their religious commitments suggests that making profits and exercising religion are not mutually exclusive.

While the *Hobby Lobby* dissent placed for-profit corporations in a completely different category than churches and other nonprofit religious groups that are entitled to religious exercise rights, the distinction between for-profit and nonprofit corporations is not always very clear. The two types of organizations can look very alike in structure, operations, and purpose. Many nonprofit associations and churches are actually incorporated, utilizing the same business form as for-profit

74 *See* Rienzi, *supra* note 28, at 66–73.

75 Michael A. Helfand & Barak D. Richman, *The Challenge of Co-Religionist Commerce*, 64 Duke L.J. 769, 771 (2015) (footnotes omitted).

76 *See* David Gibson, *Doing Good and Doing Well: Faith-Based Investing Converts the Skeptics*, USA Today (May 31, 2017), www.usatoday.com/story/news/nation/2017/05/31/faith-based-investing/102351062/ [https://perma.cc/775N-P4RX]; Anne Tergesen, *Financial Advisers Put Faith in Religion-Based Investing*, Wall St. J. (April 5, 2017), www.wsj.com/articles/financial-advisers-put-faith-in-religion-based-investing-1490363559 [https://perma.cc/C7JR-QCXH].

77 Billy Hallowell, *Here Are 5 Christian Companies That Join Chick-fil-A in Publicly-Proclaiming Their Bible-Based Views*, Blaze (Aug 2, 2012), www.theblaze.com/news/2012/08/02/here-are-5-christian-companies-that-join-chick-fil-a-in-publicly-proclaiming-their-bible-based-faith/ [https://perma.cc/9R7S-4XQN].

corporations.[78] In their day to day operations, both nonprofit and for-profit corporations function with business models that on balance strive to increase revenues and reduce costs. Many churches and nonprofits engage in commercial activity and are in fact extremely profitable. Nonprofit organizations in general have become increasingly more commercialized, often producing goods and services of their own, and generating profits that exceed those of their for-profit counterparts.[79] They have become much more entrepreneurial in nature. Thus, the line between for-profit and nonprofit corporations is not as distinct as one might think and has become increasingly blurred "as nonprofit organizations are adopting more profit-oriented approaches," "for-profit organizations are adopting charitable missions," and "[j]oint ventures between for-profit and nonprofit organizations are becoming more common."[80]

The *Hobby Lobby* dissent nonetheless asserts that a critical distinction does exist in that religious organizations are formed and maintained to foster the interests of people who share the same religious faith, while for-profit corporations can include participants who are not always drawn from one religious community.[81] This raises the same challenge to the aggregate view of the corporate person that appears in the context of corporate speech rights. If the corporation is considered the aggregate of its individual members, and if it is entitled to rights in order to protect the rights of those members, in a corporation with individuals who have differing views and beliefs, which individuals count for purposes of determining the corporation's right? The *Hobby Lobby* Court privileged the religious beliefs of the Green and Hahn families, who were the corporations' owners. It did not consider the beliefs of any other corporate constituents such as the employees. In many for-profit corporations, there may be numerous employees who do not hold the same religious faith as the owners. This is more likely to happen as the size of the corporation gets larger.

Opponents of corporate religious rights argue that allowing corporate owners to live out their religious beliefs through the corporation effectively imposes those beliefs on employees who may have very different or no religious beliefs. These dissenting employees are placed in much the same position that dissenting shareholders hold in the context of corporate political speech when the corporation expresses political views with which they disagree. The corporation's political speech or religious exercise reflects the views of only a segment of the individual

78 *See* Meese & Oman, *supra* note 53, at 285; Elizabeth Pollman, *Line Drawing in Corporate Rights Determinations*, 65 DePaul L. Rev. 597, 617 n.141 (2016).

79 *See* Pollman, *supra* note 78, at 622–23.

80 Eric M. Zolt, *Tax Deductions for Charitable Contributions: Domestic Activities, Foreign Activities, or None of the Above*, 63 Hastings L.J. 361, 396 (2012); *see also* Greendorfer, *supra* note 69, at 839–47. For a discussion of how churches and secular institutions have borrowed from each other and become more alike over time, see D. Scott Cormode, *Does Institutional Isomorphism Imply Secularization?: Churches and Secular Voluntary Associations in the Turn-of-the-Century City*, *in* Sacred Companies: Organizational Aspects of Religion and Religious Aspects of Organizations 116 (N.J. Demerath III et al. eds., 1998).

81 Burwell v. Hobby Lobby Stores, Inc., 134 S. Ct. 2751, 2795 (2014) (Ginsburg, J., dissenting).

participants in the corporation, not all. It seems unfair to effectively force dissenting members to support political or religious beliefs and actions that conflict with their own principles.

But the same predicament occurs in churches and religious organizations. Not all members of religious institutions agree entirely with all of the teachings and views of the institution. Some members of a church may feel that the church's positions on certain matters do not reflect their own individual beliefs. Yet the church does not lose its free exercise rights simply because not all members agree with the stated religious beliefs of the church's hierarchy. Courts defer to the church's leaders to define and articulate the organization's beliefs and to decide how those beliefs are exercised, even though those beliefs may be at odds with the practiced faith of many of its members.

In the typical church setting, however, individuals voluntarily maintain their church membership and can freely leave if they wish. Commentators argue that, unlike voluntary members of a church, most employees of for-profit corporations do not feel the same degree of freedom to leave their source of livelihood.[82] They remain members of the corporation more often because they need a paycheck and they cannot find another job easily, not because they are persuaded by or accept the religious principles of the corporation.

Nevertheless, the Supreme Court in *Hobby Lobby* chose to protect the free exercise rights of the corporation by focusing exclusively on the religious beliefs of the owners, not those of any other constituent group in the corporation. This is in line with other instances when the Court has granted constitutional rights to corporations to protect the interests of the shareholders.[83] *Hobby Lobby* supporters agree that, among all of the different participants in the corporation, the owners really are the appropriate group on which to focus for purposes of establishing the corporation's religious interests, if any. In corporations like Hobby Lobby, where the owners not only have authority over the way the corporation is run but also play a pivotal role in forming the corporation's identity and character, the owners are more likely to bear moral responsibility when the corporation commits a wrong. They are the ones who "set policy, contribute to the corporate vision, [and] articulate or safeguard its mission," so it is right that the "owners should feel more implicated in its acts and, as such, courts have reason to privilege the religious convictions of the owners and to allow the corporation to be run in a way that respects those convictions."[84] The inclination is to look only to those who have the authority to decide whether to continue the business as an incorporated entity at all, to comply with the

82 *See* Caroline Mala Corbin, *Corporate Religious Liberty*, 30 Const. Comment. 277, 300–04 (2015); Leo E. Strine, Jr., *A Job Is Not a Hobby: The Judicial Revival of Corporate Paternalism and Its Problematic Implications*, 41 J. Corp. L. 71, 101–02 (2015).

83 *See, e.g.*, Santa Clara v. S. Pac. R.R. Co., 118 U.S. 394 (1886) (holding that corporations are persons entitled to the right to equal protection under the Fourteenth Amendment because any deprivation of the corporation's property is ultimately a deprivation of the shareholders' private property).

84 Sepinwall, *supra* note 72, at 199–200.

regulation that burdens religious exercise, or to pay the penalty for refusing to comply; the inquiry rules out corporate constituencies who are not burdened by this difficult choice.[85] This usually means it will be the owners' religious values that will be given voice in claiming a corporate religious exemption.

The owners' beliefs, however, will have to be clear and unified to do so. Not all groups of corporate owners will be of the same mind with regard to their religious faith in the way the Greens and Hahns were. The owners may have differing religious beliefs or disagree on how to exercise the religious beliefs they do share. They may subscribe to different levels of observance, generating genuine disputes over religious values and how the corporation is to exercise them. The *Hobby Lobby* Court acknowledged that such disputes may occur, but maintained, just as it did in the *Citizens United* case, that the existing procedures of corporate democracy authorized by state corporate law would provide shareholders with the methods needed to resolve conflicts.[86] While the owners need not be unanimous in their beliefs, they do have to come to some agreement, and courts will need to determine on a case-by-case basis whether a unified religious position exists. In cases where there are warring factions, or a real divide in religious beliefs, the corporate religious exemption may not be appropriate.

In general, the focus on the aggregate aspects of the corporation's religious exercise seems to fit the scenario of the closely held corporation much more easily than the large publicly held company with widely dispersed ownership interests. The religious accommodation appears to make more sense for the small private company, owned and operated by a small number of shareholders, perhaps all close friends or members of the same family, who share the same religious beliefs and are unified in their objectives to run the company in accordance with their stated religious principles. It seems plausible to impute a collective religious identity to the small business such as the Jewish kosher deli or the Muslim grocery store because their identity and objectives boil down to those of their owners. Indeed, this vision of the corporation seems to have motivated the Court's reasoning in *Hobby Lobby*. It is possible for close corporations to be enormous in size, employing thousands of people, as was the case with Hobby Lobby. But it was relevant to the Court that the corporations in that case, although large in size, were closely held and governed exclusively by the Greens and the Hahns. That the corporations were closely held by a small group of family members who were of a single mind with regard to their religious convictions appears to have played a significant role in supporting the Court's decision.

The *Hobby Lobby* Court did not say, however, that its holding was limited exclusively to closely held corporations. It is theoretically possible that a large, publicly held corporation could attempt to bring a free exercise claim to obtain an

85 *See* Thad Eagles, Note, *Free Exercise, Inc.: A New Framework for Adjudicating Corporate Religious Liberty Claims*, 90 N.Y.U. L. Rev. 589, 612 n.109 (2015).

86 134 S. Ct. at 2774–75.

accommodation from a generally applicable law like the ACA. In fact, the *Hobby Lobby* dissent expressed that very concern and predicted that RFRA claims would proliferate as corporations of all sizes would bring claims for accommodations based on religious beliefs.[87] Thus far, however, it has not proven to be the case that large public companies have rushed to file religious free exercise claims to oppose various forms of government regulation. As the majority contended, such claims are unlikely to occur with great frequency given the improbability that numerous diverse shareholders in a publicly traded company would agree to run the corporation in accordance with the same religious beliefs.[88] It would be rare for a large public company to maintain a unified religious mission. Profit maximization is probably a more predominant norm in large publicly held corporations, so there is less likelihood that such corporations could persuasively demonstrate that their business decisions reflect a consistent conformance with specific religious objectives.

The federal government now agrees with this point. After *Hobby Lobby*, the government issued modified regulations on the required coverage for contraceptives under the ACA, extending the religious accommodation to for-profit entities, whether or not they are closely held. Explicitly expressing agreement with *Hobby Lobby*'s reasoning on this point, the federal regulations acknowledge that it is possible, but very unlikely, that a publicly traded company would qualify for a religious exemption given that a public company with numerous unrelated shareholders would rarely if ever choose to operate the company under a singular set of religious principles.[89]

This is not to say that large entities by virtue of their size alone are incapable of demonstrating cohesive beliefs and practices, including religious ones. A large church or a strong army can display great cohesiveness in members' commitment to the group's beliefs, objectives, and practices. This suggests that some corporate entities might be able to take on their own larger religious identity and exercise religious beliefs in their own right, rather than deriving their identity and rights solely from their individual members. As discussed in the next section, the real entity aspects of the corporate person foster this view.

REAL ENTITY ELEMENTS OF CORPORATE PERSONHOOD AND RELIGIOUS EXERCISE

In considering the corporation a real and independent person, rather than an association of individuals, the real entity approach highlights the centrality of the

87 134 S. Ct. at 2797 (2014) (Ginsburg, J., dissenting) ("RFRA claims will proliferate, for the Court's expansive notion of corporate personhood . . . invites for-profit entities to seek religious-based exemptions from regulations they deem offensive to their faith.").

88 *Id.* at 2774.

89 Religious Exemptions and Accommodations for Coverage of Certain Preventive Services Under the Affordable Care Act, 82 Fed. Reg. 47,792, 47,810–11, 47–817 (Oct. 13, 2017) (to be codified at 26 C.F.R. pt. 54, 29 C.F.R. pt. 2590, 45 C.F.R. pt. 147) (citing *Hobby Lobby*, 134 S. Ct. at 2774).

corporate entity as greater than the sum of its parts. In the context of religious liberty rights, this view of the corporation warrants protection for the religious exercise of the group as such, and not only to the extent it enhances individual rights of religious freedom. Although the *Hobby Lobby* Court appeared to utilize an individual-centered conception of corporate free exercise rights, the decision can also be interpreted as endorsing a more entity-centered approach to corporate personhood and corporate rights. Some scholars have argued that the Court "upheld a strong version of corporate personhood distinct from that of its associated constituencies and a strong version of corporate freedom to pursue mixed objectives, not just corporate profits or shareholder financial welfare."[90]

Many of the arguments both for and against the religious liberty rights of corporations track the philosophical debate over corporate moral agency and personhood analyzed in Chapter 2. The discussion of the philosophical theories of moral personhood in Chapter 2 lays out the criteria for attributing moral responsibility and rights to corporations. Those who view corporations as possessing the traits of moral persons, with the accompanying capacity for moral responsibility and moral rights, often accept the possibility for corporations to hold rights of religious freedom as well. In contrast, if corporations are not moral persons and cannot bear moral rights and responsibilities, then it would appear their claim to free exercise rights would be unavailing.

The Free Exercise Clause protects a person's religious *beliefs* and religiously motivated conduct, or *actions*. To the extent corporations are capable of having their own beliefs and performing their own actions in relation to those beliefs, it may be plausible for them to claim their own rights to religious free exercise. Relying on philosophical theories of moral agency and personhood, commentators have argued that corporations are capable of rationality, intentionality, and the formation of corporate beliefs that supervene on, but cannot always be reduced to, those of their individual members. Through their collective information-processing and decision-making systems, corporations can have very sophisticated minds of their own, so to speak. With their capacities for knowledge and volition, corporations are said to be capable of forming subjective intentions and goals. They can possess their own beliefs and desires, and they can commit corporate actions based on their beliefs and desires.

Under this view, corporations as moral agents are capable of knowing the difference between right and wrong and acting in light of this knowledge. They can be the objects of praise or blame for their conduct and bear moral responsibility that is above and beyond that of their individual members. Scholars suggest that a corporation can have an institutional conscience and a desire to strive to do good.[91] It can adopt a set of beliefs that is based on religious principles and then decide to commit

90 Johnson & Millon, *supra* note 28, at 30.

91 *See* Sepper, *supra* note 58, at 1540–43 (explaining and criticizing a "mission-operation" theory of institutional conscience).

acts in accordance with those principles. Under certain philosophical understandings of group agency, corporations can adopt religious beliefs that are not necessarily the same as those of their members. In this manner, the corporation functions as a person in a fundamental way.[92] Corporations are "regularly understood as being capable of acting on a wide range of subjective beliefs and intentions: ethical views, philosophical views, criminal intentions, anti-religious animus, etc. ... There is no basis [for] say[ing] that corporations can form moral views about ethics, philosophy, and the environment, but not about religion."[93]

For those who are not convinced that corporations are capable of possessing religious *beliefs*, one might argue that it is still plausible to say that corporations are capable of *actions* that are explained by reasons rooted in religious tradition. For example, businesses can choose to close on Sabbath days, donate a portion of their profits to missionary groups, provide loans without interest in compliance with Islamic requirements, pay to publish proselytizing ads urging people to accept Jesus Christ as Lord and Savior, or arrange with their health insurance providers to exclude coverage of certain contraceptives that are believed to be abortifacients. These are all actions taken in conformity with religious values, which is a form of exercising religion. The First Amendment and RFRA protect "the *exercise* of religious belief. *Exercise*, belonging in the world of *action*, is within the ambit of corporate capacity."[94] From this perspective, corporate acts that reflect religious concerns can be construed as a form of religious expression. Thus, in focusing on the real entity dimension of the corporate person, the justification for granting free exercise rights to the corporation is not to protect the religious freedom of its individual members, but to acknowledge that the corporation itself is capable of holding religious beliefs and acting on them. As such, it is entitled to protection from substantial burdens on its religious exercise by the government. These "burden[s] can exist without reference to the religious practice of any actual human beings: the corporation itself has religious rights."[95]

If one focuses on the act of religious exercise, rather than the identity of the person engaged in the act, certain parallels can be made with the Supreme Court's treatment of political speech under the First Amendment. In *Citizens United*, the Court emphasized that the relevant issue was whether the *speech* is the type of speech the First Amendment protects, not whether the *speaker* is the type of person who has or can claim First Amendment rights. So long as the speech activity falls within an area the First Amendment is intended to shield, the identity of the speaker, whether human individual, nonprofit association, or for-profit corporation, does not matter.

92 Jason Iuliano, *Do Corporations Have Religious Beliefs?*, 90 IND. L. J. 47, 48–49, 90–93 (2015).

93 Rienzi, *supra* note 28, at 110.

94 Robert K. Vischer, *Do For-Profit Businesses Have Free Exercise Rights?*, 21 J. CONTEMP. LEGAL ISSUES 369, 378 (2013) (emphasis added).

95 David Rosenberg, *The Corporate Paradox of* Citizens United *and* Hobby Lobby, 11 N.Y.U. J. L. & LIBERTY 308, 317 (2017).

The Court held that political speech does not lose First Amendment protection simply because its source is a corporation. Analogously, if the particular act of religious exercise at issue is the type of religious activity the First Amendment or RFRA is designed to protect, then it should not matter whether that religious exercise is conducted by a human individual, a church, a nonprofit religious organization, or a for-profit business. The act is still the same. If the *Citizens United* Court requires us to focus on the speech, not the nature of the speaker, perhaps we are then to focus on the exercise of religion itself, not the one who is exercising it. The relevant inquiry for a claim like Hobby Lobby's would not be to what extent for-profit corporations have free exercise rights, but instead, to what extent does the free exercise right protect religious objections to the contraceptive mandate. Since the RFRA free exercise right would protect churches and nonprofit religious organizations that raised such objections as a form of religious exercise, one could argue that the same form of religious exercise must also be protected when it is a for-profit corporation asserting the right.[96] Under this view, as long as the act is motivated by a religious belief that is sincerely held and the burden on the exercise would be substantial, the nature of the person engaged in the exercise should not be determinative.

However, evaluating the sincerity of the religious belief in a specific case would require an assessment of the indicia of the particular corporate claimant's stated religiosity. This assessment would involve some consideration of the corporate claimant's culture and identity. Organizational factors may indicate that the corporation has adopted certain religious beliefs.[97] For example, corporate charters, bylaws, board resolutions, mission statements, or other governing documents may expressly specify religious mandates or purposes for the corporation. The corporation might be organized as a "B corporation" or "benefit corporation" with a specific religious component built into its public-oriented purpose. Internally within the corporation, the religious identity may manifest in many different ways, such as work hours devoted to prayer, chaplains on staff, religious décor or artifacts at the worksite, and hours of operation limited to certain days. The corporation's culture among its members may specifically incorporate religious values in decision-making processes, in the treatment of employees, and in the definition and distributions of power within the organization. The corporation might choose to produce certain goods and services, and consciously refuse to produce or be affiliated with others, based on its religious principles. In its external marketing and branding, the corporation may hold itself out as having certain values that derive from its religious beliefs. It may make donations to religious charities or engage in acts of corporate

[96] *See* Conestoga Wood Specialties Corp. v. Sec'y of U.S. Dep't of Health & Human Servs., 724 F.3d 377, 402–03 (3d Cir. 2013) (Jordan, J., dissenting); Gaylord, *supra* note 56, at 648.

[97] *See* Thomas H. Jeavons, *Identifying Characteristics of "Religious" Organizations: An Exploratory Proposal, in* SACRED COMPANIES, *supra* note 80, at 79, 81 (discussing "basic aspects of an organization where it is important to ask of its 'religiousness'").

philanthropy designed to further religious purposes. In its public relations, the corporation may project a public image or make public statements that reveal its religious beliefs. While these patterns of conduct could risk public backlash or adverse reactions, the corporation that nonetheless maintains these patterns despite such consequences would appear to be a more credible claimant.

These indicia of the corporation's religious beliefs coincide with organizational theorists' schema of corporate culture and identity as discussed previously in Chapter 3 of this book. The visible artifacts of a corporation's culture reflect its underlying core values and beliefs, which in turn are generated by its deeper assumptions about the world. The total body of beliefs, knowledge, values, goals, norms, and assumptions constitutes the way of life within the organization and influences how an organization defines itself. When religious values permeate the various levels of culture and identity, the corporation itself can be understood as having a religious persona of its own that can persist even after key members leave or change their views. If the corporation's religious beliefs are built into the structure of the organization and are designed to ensure continuity of religious purpose even if individual members change over time, the corporate person carries its own religious identity, one that is not dependent on the religious beliefs of the human participants. This real entity dimension to corporate religious liberty rights was not explicitly endorsed in *Hobby Lobby*, yet it is not infeasible that corporations may attempt to utilize it as an avenue to claim religious liberty rights of their own in situations when key religious individual members have left the firm and the corporation's free exercise right cannot be tied to the right of particular individual constituents.

ARTIFICIAL PERSON ELEMENTS OF CORPORATE PERSONHOOD AND RELIGIOUS EXERCISE

Opponents of the real entity treatment of the corporation consider such analysis to be a form of corporate anthropomorphism, and they refute the idea that corporations should be treated as persons capable of claiming rights to religious freedom. As discussed in Chapter 2, many philosophers who deny the moral agency and personhood of corporations find no basis for holding corporations themselves morally responsible for their actions, nor for entitling them to claim moral rights. In their view, corporations lack many of the critical features of moral personhood such as the capacity for conscience, self-awareness, and emotion. If corporations are not real persons in and of themselves, they are undeserving of the moral deference that real persons are due. This perspective has ties to the artificial person view of the corporation, which is highly critical of the extension of any religious rights to the corporate entity.

Viewing the corporation as an artificial person or legal fiction significantly weakens the possibility for the corporation to claim the right of free exercise. If the corporation is simply a creature of law, its existence is a concession of the state, and we need give it only those rights that support its use as a legal tool to facilitate commerce and economic transactions. The free exercise right applies uniquely to human beings, not abstract fictional entities. It is designed to uphold the values associated with autonomy, conscience, and human dignity.[98] It recognizes that individuals should not be made unnecessarily to suffer the distress of being forced to choose between their deeply held religious convictions and compliance with the law. Rights of religious liberty are intimately connected to the needs of human beings to be free to engage in moral decision-making and religious practices that form integral parts of their self-identity and personhood.

According to the artificial person theory, none of these values and interests apply in the same way to corporations because they are not persons in any real sense. Their actions cannot be genuinely motivated by religious concerns because they do not have the capacity for mental and emotional states that constitute a true sense of conscience, or moral self-awareness.[99] As artificial constructs, it seems implausible that corporations possess any real spiritual dimension or soul. They do not pray, or worship, or observe sacraments as individuals do. "Religious belief takes shape within the minds and hearts of individuals, and its protection is one of the more uniquely 'human' rights provided by the Constitution."[100] The dissent in *Hobby Lobby* expressly endorsed this view of corporations in asserting that "the exercise of religion is characteristic of natural persons, not artificial legal entities,"[101] and that therefore corporations should have no claim to religious liberty rights.

The difficulty with this line of reasoning is that churches and religious nonprofit corporations are similarly artificial incorporated entities. They likewise do not themselves pray, or worship, or have the capacity for conscience. They do not possess the mental and emotional states that individuals do. Yet we afford them a special solicitude under the law to exercise religion and act in accordance with their religious precepts. One might argue that there is little reason to treat business corporations differently since they share the same incorporated status. Nonetheless, attempted distinctions are made between churches and business corporations on the basis of the latter's profit-making purposes. As previously discussed, however, the profit-making motivation alone does not provide an entirely satisfactory explanation for the differential treatment since many for-profit corporations can have other purposes too, including religious ones, and there is no inherent incompatibility between religious exercise and profit-making activity.

One of the main objections to granting religious exemptions to profit-making corporations is that corporate owners who seek such exemptions seem to want the

98 Gans & Shapiro, *supra* note 52, at 17 (statements of Gans); Corbin, *supra* note 82, at 281–82.

99 *See* Sepinwall, *supra* note 72, at 187–90; Sepper, *supra* note 58, at 1540 (explaining that conscience as a capacity for moral knowledge is "intimately connected to human nature").

100 Conestoga Wood Specialties Corp. v. Sebelius, 917 F. Supp. 2d 394, 408 (E.D. Pa. 2013).

101 Burwell v. Hobby Lobby Stores, Inc., 134 S. Ct. 2751, 2794 (2014) (Ginsburg, J., dissenting); *see also* Thomas E. Rutledge, *A Corporation Has No Soul – The Business Entity Law Response to Challenges to the PPACA Contraceptive Mandate*, 5 Wm. & Mary Bus. L. Rev. 1, 28, 31 (2014).

key benefits associated with the corporation's artificial personhood but they are unwilling to pay the costs. The law that creates corporations grants them the very advantageous feature of limited liability whereby shareholders are not personally liable for the debts of the business. The law places a veil between the corporation and its shareholders, allowing the corporation to stand as a separate artificial person to enter into contracts, own assets, incur debts, and otherwise transact business in its own name. Thus, the corporation is a distinct and separate legal entity with legal rights and duties that are different from those of the individuals who own and participate in the business. The corporate owners are permitted to stand apart from the corporation and to avoid liability for the corporation's debts and obligations. That liability shield, however, requires the owners to be careful to respect the separate nature of the corporate entity and treat it as a distinct legal person. They must maintain corporate formalities and avoid commingling personal funds with corporate funds. This normally poses no issue as owners dutifully stand behind the corporate veil to obtain the advantages of limited liability. But when religious owners argue that the corporation is not really a separate person for purposes of claiming religious liberty rights, the owners effectively seek to disregard the corporate veil and assert themselves as the real people whose religious rights are at stake. In insisting that legal burdens on the corporation's religious exercise are ultimately burdens on the exercise of their own religious beliefs, corporate owners no longer wish the corporation to be regarded as different from themselves.

Critics of corporate religious rights argue that corporate owners should not be allowed to claim the protection of the corporate veil to avoid personal liability but then discard the veil to claim religious rights. Owners who ignore the distinct legal existence of the corporation when it serves personal interests attempt to obtain all the benefits of the corporate form without accepting the costs.[102] The owners want to switch freely between corporate and individual status to gain the advantages and avoid the disadvantages of both positions. In the *Hobby Lobby* case, for example, the Green family presumably chose to operate their business in corporate form because they wanted the legal separation that comes from that designation in order to protect themselves financially. Having made that choice, they should not then be permitted to argue that they are one with the business for purposes of their religious beliefs. It is

[102] *See* Gans & Shapiro, *supra* note 52, at 22 ("[C]orporations cannot have their cake and eat it too, claiming all the special privileges given to corporations and all the fundamental, personal rights granted to individuals.") (statements of Gans); Kiel Brennan-Marquez, A *Business Can Exercise Religion, but Hobby Lobby Still Gets It Wrong*, BOS. REV. (July 7, 2014), http://bostonreview.net/blogs/kiel-brennan-marquez-hobby-lobby-for-profit-corporations-religion [https://perma.cc/3ZMJ-6V8A] ("[O]wners can't have it both ways. The corporate form can't be both a stout wall against shareholders' personal liability and a porous membrane that allows the beliefs of individual shareholders to pass through. Either owners are distinct from their corporations or they aren't."). The dissent in *Hobby Lobby* agreed: "By incorporating a business, however, an individual separates herself from the entity and escapes personal responsibility for the entity's obligations. One might ask why the separation should hold only when it serves the interest of those who control the corporation." *Hobby Lobby*, 134 S. Ct. at 2797 (Ginsburg, J., dissenting).

inappropriate to "pretend[] that the Greens and the corporation are one, unconflicted, fully unified being."[103] Several corporate and criminal law professors submitted an amicus brief in the *Hobby Lobby* case in opposition to the Green family's claim. They cited the fundamental legal principle that the corporation has and must maintain a separate and distinct identity, and they argued that transferring the Greens' religious identity to the corporation violates that principle.[104]

In related terms, one can argue that entering into business in corporate form is a choice, and it comes at a price. Entrepreneurs accept the benefits that come with operating as a corporation, including the advantage of limited liability, but then they can no longer insist on their right to raise religious objections to generally applicable laws. That is the result of creating a separate legal person under the law.[105] No one forces you to incorporate a business to engage in commercial activity. Once you do, however, you are subject to the restrictions and burdens of business regulation, and you must recognize that religious liberties have to yield to broader state interests. These views emphasize the artificial person aspect of the corporation. The corporation is a creature of law, and the law requires a division between shareholders and the artificial corporate person.

Even so, it is important to recognize that the law does not require a strict division all the time. "Separation for liability purposes does not require separation for all purposes."[106] For example corporate law recognizes that in the close corporation setting, there is more of an integration between the management of the business and its owners. In taxing the corporation, the IRS allows small S-corporations, which constitute the majority of for-profit businesses, to use pass-through tax treatment, ignoring the corporation's separate identity and signaling a unification of the business with its owners.[107] Commentators argue that the corporate veil, like the corporation itself, is an artificial construct of the law, and can mean whatever the law wants it to mean.[108] It does not have to be an immutable characteristic of the corporate form that dictates results in every case. It can be used to form a separation in some instances and not in others. The "conception of the company as a distinct entity is a conclusion of law, not one of fact, and one relevant only in its own particular context."[109] If the law decides to create a boundary between the corporate person and its owners that can be crossed in

103 Daniel J. H. Greenwood, *Neofeudalism: The Surprising Foundations of Corporate Constitutional Rights*, 2017 U. Ill. L. Rev. 163, 216.

104 Amicus Curiae Brief of Corporate and Criminal Law Professors in Support of Petitioners, at 3–8, 13–16, 22, Burwell v. Hobby Lobby Stores, Inc., 134 S. Ct. 2751 (2014) (Nos. 13–354 & 13–356), 2014 WL 333889. "Hobby Lobby . . . want[s] to argue, in effect, that the corporate veil is only a one-way street: its shareholders can get protection from tort or contract liability by standing behind the veil but the corporation can ask a court to disregard the corporate veil on this occasion." *Id.* at 14.

105 Mark, *supra* note 34, at 557–58. Rutledge, *supra* note 101, at 40–41.

106 Clark & Durham, *supra* note 64, at 258.

107 *See* Rienzi, *supra* note 28, at 97.

108 *See* Sepinwall, *supra* note 72, at 192.

109 Ross Grantham, *Commentary on Goddard, in* Corporate Personality in the 20th Century 65, 69 (Charles E. F. Rickett & Ross B. Grantham eds., 1998) (footnotes omitted).

certain situations to facilitate the enforcement of various rights, such as the religious liberty rights of an individual who owns a close corporation, there is nothing inherent in the nature of the corporation that would prevent that. The corporate form is flexible, enabling, and subject to contract; it is not fixed and unalterable. Shareholders can structure and operate it as they want for the purposes that they choose. Supporters of this flexibility contend that there is nothing wrong with using the benefits of incorporation for some purposes and not for others.[110]

To force those who choose to adopt the corporate form in order to take advantage of its limited liability feature to then forfeit their religious liberty rights in exchange for the privilege of incorporating potentially violates the doctrine of unconstitutional conditions. As discussed previously in the context of corporate political speech rights under the First Amendment, it is improper for the government to condition the receipt of state-conferred benefits on a waiver of fundamental rights to which one would otherwise be entitled. From this perspective, business owners should not have to trade away their rights to free exercise of their religious beliefs in order to secure the benefits of incorporating their business.[111]

However, many worry that granting corporate owners the advantage of limited liability, as well as the advantage of religious exemptions, compounds their competitive advantage in the market by not having to pay to comply with laws that other businesses do.[112] The potential for that competitive advantage may encourage the assertion of religious free exercise claims that are less than sincere in order to reap financial benefits. This gives for-profit corporations incentives to feign religiosity and file sham religious claims to obtain preferential treatment and avoid laws that impose costs on their operations.

These are empirical claims that may or may not bear out considering the costs associated with asserting religious liberty rights. While it is possible that corporations operating in accordance with religious principles may gain a competitive advantage by obtaining religious exemptions, it is also plausible that their religious practices cause them to suffer competitive disadvantages. This may be the case when corporations close their operations on Sundays, refuse to enter into potentially lucrative contracts because they involve activities that are contrary to their religious convictions (such as selling alcohol or tobacco), fail to attract qualified employees who are averse to the corporation's religious practices, or otherwise refuse to engage in profitable acts that their secular competitors, who are not constrained by religious demands, are willing to do. Corporations that follow religious practices may lose customers and suffer boycotts from large segments of the community that disagree with their religious practices.

110 Ahdar, *supra* note 70, at 12. "There is no need to be locked into a rigid either/or choice: either always a separate, distinct entity or always a mere aggregation of individual members." *Id.*

111 Steven H. Shiffrin, What's Wrong with the First Amendment? 140 (2016) ("The limited liability of shareholders is not designed as a favor to shareholders. It is calculated to encourage investment. Encouraging investment, however, need not and should not require the waiving of religious rights.").

112 *See* Mark Tushnet, *Do For-Profit Corporations Have Rights of Religious Conscience?*, 99 Cornell L. Rev. Online 70, 76–82 (2013).

It is true that corporations may assert disingenuous claims of religiosity, but that may not be a persuasive reason to deny religious exemptions to corporations altogether. Individuals, sole proprietorships, and partnerships can feign religious beliefs as well, but we do not render them ineligible to assert free exercise claims because of that risk. Instead, we evaluate their credibility and make reasoned judgments as to their sincerity in order to decide whether or not to uphold their claims. In free exercise cases, courts have always had to assess whether a claimant's religious beliefs are sincerely held.[113] Courts are no less capable of using their judgment to ferret out opportunists from sincere believers when the claimants are corporate owners than when they are sole proprietors.

The fear that corporations will assert fraudulent free exercise claims may be overblown because the cost of making such insincere religious claims can often turn out to be greater than the benefits. The negative market backlash of openly taking religious positions on issues of public concern can be harsh, and corporations have to be concerned about the reactions their religious actions may provoke among investors, customers, and employee candidates in the capital, consumer, and employment markets.[114] In our politically divisive times, it can be extremely damaging to a business to advocate an unpopular political or religious viewpoint that will alienate large segments of the population. That some corporate owners are willing to suffer significant adverse consequences for maintaining their religious beliefs may be a factor in establishing the devotion to their faith and the sincerity of their beliefs. The risk of negative public reaction may serve to dampen any urges to fabricate religious beliefs for the purpose of challenging business regulation. The likelihood that businesses will feign religious objections to gain an advantage in the marketplace does not seem exceedingly high when taking such actions may in fact badly backfire on the business.

RELIGIOUS EXERCISE RIGHTS AND ANTI-DISCRIMINATION LAWS

Even if corporate religious beliefs are genuine and sincerely held, critics of *Hobby Lobby* worry that there is no real stopping point for religious corporate owners to

[113] *See* Meese & Oman, *supra* note 53, at 293; John D. Moore, *The First Amendment Case for Corporate Religious Rights*, 16 Nev. L.J. 1, 38–39, 50–51 (2015). If we have irresolvable doubts about courts' ability to distinguish between genuine and false religious beliefs, then perhaps we should not be granting religious exemptions to anyone at all. *See* Sepinwall, *supra* note 72, at 197 n.119.

[114] *See, e.g.*, Stormans, Inc. v. Selecky, 854 F. Supp. 2d 925, 963 (W.D. Wash. 2012), *rev'd on other grounds sub nom.* Stormans, Inc. v. Wiesman, 794 F.3d 1064 (9th Cir. 2015) (noting that grocery store company faced organized boycotts and ongoing protests for refusing to comply with the contraceptive mandate based on religious beliefs); Mark Oppenheimer, *Few Resist the Temptation to Opine on Chick-fil-A*, N.Y. Times (Aug. 3, 2012), www.nytimes.com/2012/08/04/us/taking-sides-on-chick-fil-a-is-a-temptation-few-can-resist.html [https://perma.cc/7JDJ-3ZY7] (describing Boston and San Francisco mayors' attempts to discourage Chick-fil-A's business in their cities because of Chick-fil-A's support for a Biblical definition of marriage and its publicly expressed opposition to same-sex marriage).

raise objections to all types of regulation designed to protect others. In the context of employee health insurance coverage, corporate employers with religious convictions may argue that their beliefs prevent them from providing coverage for numerous items beyond contraceptives, including blood transfusions, psychiatric care, antidepressants, vaccinations, and illnesses related to alcohol or tobacco abuse.[115] More generally, corporate owners emboldened by *Hobby Lobby* may be more likely to challenge many other types of regulation, including anti-discrimination laws and public accommodation laws.

While opponents of *Hobby Lobby* predicted a proliferation of such challenges, to date there has not been the flood of litigation or the generous granting of religious exemptions to corporations that had been projected. With a few notable exceptions, religious corporate owners who have tried to resist the application of laws prohibiting discrimination in public accommodations on the basis of sexual orientation, for example, have not found significant success. In particular, small businesses that have raised religious objections to providing wedding services, such as flowers or photography, to same-sex couples have found their claims rejected in many states.[116] In such discrimination cases, the government's interests in eradicating the barriers to equal treatment of all citizens have taken priority over the religious free exercise rights of corporations and their owners.

Most recently in 2018, the Supreme Court in *Masterpiece Cakeshop, Ltd. v. Colorado Civil Rights Commission*, did uphold the free exercise right of a Colorado bakery owner who refused to bake a wedding cake for a gay couple because of his religious objections to same-sex marriage.[117] The case was controversial, and many people wondered whether it would extend the reasoning of *Hobby Lobby* to bolster the religious free exercise rights of corporations and their shareholders. As it turned out, the Court's holding was not a bold and sweeping endorsement of corporate or individual religious liberty rights, but a more balanced statement that was closely tied to the facts of the case.

Masterpiece Cakeshop Ltd. was a bakery business owned by Jack Phillips and his wife. Phillips, an expert baker and devout Christian who had owned the shop for twenty-four years, refused to create a wedding cake for Charlie Craig and David Mullins who had requested a cake for their wedding reception. Phillips offered to make other baked goods for the couple for other occasions, but he declined to create a wedding cake due to his belief that to do so would make him a participant in a

[115] Burwell v. Hobby Lobby Stores, Inc., 134 S. Ct. 2751, 2805 (2014) (Ginsburg, J., dissenting); Rutledge, *supra* note 101, at 16 n.74.

[116] *See, e.g.*, State v. Arlene's Flowers, Inc., 389 P.3d 543 (Wash. 2017), *cert. granted, judgment vacated, and remanded*, No. 17–108, 2018 WL 3096308 (U.S. June 25, 2018); Telescope Media Grp. v. Lindsey, 271 F. Supp. 3d 1090 (D. Minn. 2017), *appeal docketed*, No. 17–3352 (8th Cir. Oct. 30, 2017), Gifford v. McCarthy, 23 N.Y.S. 3d 422 (N.Y. App. Div. 2016); *see also* Frank S. Ravitch, Freedom's Edge: Religious Freedom, Sexual Freedom, and the Future of America 76–102 (2016).

[117] Masterpiece Cakeshop, Ltd. v. Colorado Civil Rights Comm'n, 138 S. Ct. 1719 (2018).

celebration that would be contrary to his sincerely held religious beliefs.[118] Craig and Mullins filed charges with the Colorado Civil Rights Commission alleging discrimination in violation of the state's anti-discrimination laws that prohibit businesses from denying goods or services to any customers on the basis of race, sex, disability, or sexual orientation, among other things. Phillips argued that requiring him to create a cake for a same-sex wedding would violate his constitutional right to free exercise of religion and his right to free speech by compelling him to express a message with which he disagreed. The Commission rejected his arguments and held that Phillips and the cakeshop violated the state's public accommodation laws. The Colorado state courts affirmed the ruling.[119]

In a 7–2 decision, the Supreme Court reversed the ruling and upheld Phillips' religious free exercise rights. Writing for the majority, Justice Kennedy laid out the important constitutional interests at stake on both sides. He wrote that "gay persons and gay couples cannot be treated as social outcasts or as inferior in dignity and worth" and that the "exercise of their freedom on terms equal to others must be given great weight and respect by the courts. At the same time, the religious and philosophical objections to gay marriage are protected views and in some instances protected forms of expression."[120] Courts must give fair consideration to religious freedom interests on the one hand, and to equality and dignity interests on the other. In Phillips' case, the Court found that the Colorado Civil Rights Commission did not demonstrate an impartial and neutral consideration of the respective claims, but showed "clear and impermissible hostility" toward Phillips' religious beliefs.[121]

In public hearings, the Commissioners had made disparaging comments about Phillips' beliefs, implying that religious beliefs and persons were not welcome in the public marketplace. One Commissioner called freedom of religion a justification for the worst forms of historical discrimination including slavery and the Holocaust, and described religion as "one of the most despicable pieces of rhetoric" that can be used "to hurt others."[122] The Commission also apparently had afforded entirely different treatment to three other bakers who had refused a customer's request to create cakes with images that demeaned or disapproved of same-sex marriages. In those instances, the Commission upheld the bakers' right to refuse service because

118 *Id.* at 1724. At the time of the request in 2012, same-sex marriages were not legally recognized in Colorado. That changed when the Supreme Court held in 2015 that state law bans on same-sex marriages were unconstitutional. *See* Obergefell v. Hodges, 135 S. Ct. 2584 (2015).

119 138 S. Ct. at 1725–27.

120 *Id.* at 1727.

121 *Id.* at 1729. The Court did not address Phillips' free speech claim, but Justice Thomas in his concurrence argued that Phillips' free speech claim should have been upheld because the creation of a wedding cake is expressive conduct. Justice Thomas noted that the Court has recognized many forms of expressive conduct, including nude dancing, burning the flag, and wearing a black armband. *Id.* at 1741–42 (Thomas, J., concurring). In Justice Thomas' opinion, forcing Phillips to make a custom wedding cake requires him to make a celebratory statement for an occasion that he believes his faith forbids, and this infringes on his free speech right. *Id.* at 1744.

122 *Id.* at 1729.

of what it deemed to be the offensive nature of the requested message. The Supreme Court found that, with no principled rationale for the difference in treatment between Phillips' case and that of the other bakers, the Commission was "neither tolerant nor respectful of Phillip's religious beliefs," and the Commission failed to judge his case "with the neutrality that the Free Exercise Clause requires."[123]

In framing its holding narrowly to deal with the specifics of Phillips' case, the Supreme Court appeared to acknowledge that it was saving for another day a broader determination of how to resolve clashes between the equality interests protected by anti-discrimination laws and the religious liberty rights of business owners: "The outcome of cases like this in other circumstances must await further elaboration in the courts, … recognizing that these disputes must be resolved with tolerance, without undue disrespect to sincere religious beliefs, and without subjecting gay persons to indignities when they seek goods and service in an open market."[124]

Given the limited nature of the *Masterpiece* holding and the Court's emphasis on balancing important fundamental rights, it does not appear that corporations and their owners will have broad latitude to claim religious free exercise rights to justify refusals to serve same-sex couples and other persons who are protected by public accommodation laws. Although many feared that *Hobby Lobby* would result in corporate religious rights trumping anti-discrimination laws, that does not seem to be the trend. Indeed, the Court in *Masterpiece* maintained that religious objections "do not allow business owners and other actors in the economy and in society to deny protected persons equal access to goods and services under a neutral and generally applicable public accommodation law."[125] Ironically, although the baker won in *Masterpiece*, for those people who worried that *Hobby Lobby* would be used by religious business owners to freely discriminate against certain customers, the Court's language gives them reason to be a little less anxious.

Interestingly, the Court's analysis in *Masterpiece* did not explicitly address the issue of corporate personhood, i.e., the bakery company's status as a person to claim a constitutional right to free exercise. In the lower court, the opinion of the Colorado Court of Appeals mentioned in a footnote that the "parties do not address whether for-profit entities like Masterpiece Cakeshop have free exercise rights under the First Amendment and … the Colorado Constitution."[126] Because the holding of the Court of Appeals against Phillips did not depend on the issue, the Court of Appeals chose to "assume, without deciding," that the cakeshop itself had free exercise rights.[127] In Phillips' brief before the Supreme Court, he stated in a footnote that

[123] *Id.* at 1731. Justices Ginsburg and Sotomayor disagreed, arguing that the comments of a few Commissioners did not justify reversing the judgment. *Id.* at 1749 (Ginsburg, J., dissenting).

[124] *Id.* at 1732; *see also id.* at 1724 ("[W]hatever the outcome of some future controversy involving facts similar to these, the Commission's actions here violated the Free Exercise Clause and its order must be set aside.").

[125] *Id.* at 1727.

[126] Craig v. Masterpiece Cakeshop, Inc., 370 P.3d 272, 289 n.13 (Colo. App. 2015).

[127] *Id.* at 290 n.13.

the "Free Exercise Clause protects Phillips and his closely held family business" and argued that "affirming Masterpiece's free-exercise rights 'protects the religious liberty of the humans who own and control' that family-owned company, which in this case is Phillips and his wife."[128]

Several corporate law professors disagreed and submitted an amicus brief in opposition to Phillips' claim. They cited the fundamental legal separation between shareholders and the corporate entity. They argued that Phillips should not be able to project his religious beliefs onto the company in order to enable the company to avoid complying with state public accommodation mandates to treat all patrons equally. The professors urged the Supreme Court to reject any ties between Phillips and the company that would allow the company to gain constitutional protection for his religious beliefs.[129]

The Supreme Court declined to engage in a discussion of the issue. Instead, the Court focused on Phillips' beliefs and conduct with no indication that the Court believed his religious free exercise claims were unconnected to what the cakeshop business was required to do. In other words, the Court's analysis verified that Phillips' religious liberty rights stemmed from his sincerely held religious beliefs, and a validation of those rights entitled his company to refuse certain business requests of customers on religious grounds. Although the Court's opinion included some references to the cakeshop as an entity (the "couple visited Masterpiece Cakeshop, a bakery in Colorado," "Masterpiece Cakeshop, Ltd., is a bakery," "the shop is subject to state public accommodations laws," "the Commission determined that the shop's actions violated the Act"),[130] the Court focused primarily on the beliefs and actions of Phillips personally. The opinion was replete with references to Phillips as an individual: "Phillips' religious beliefs;" "Phillips' conscience-based objection;" "he seeks to 'honor God through his work at Masterpiece Cakeshop;'" "the baker's refusal [was] based on his sincere religious beliefs and convictions;" Phillips could not "exercise the right of his own personal expression for their message . . . in a way consistent with his religious beliefs;" and the Commission's "inappropriate and dismissive comments show[ed] lack of due consideration for Phillips' free exercise rights and the dilemma he faced."[131]

The Court's attention on Phillips, acting in his capacity as the owner and decision-maker of the business, reflects an aggregate approach to the corporation

128 Brief for Petitioners at 38 n.6, Masterpiece Cakeshop, Ltd. v. Colorado Civil Rights Comm'n, 138 S. Ct. 1719 (2018) (No. 16–111), 2017 WL 3913762 (citing Burwell v. Hobby Lobby Stores, Inc., 134 S. Ct. 2751, 2768 (2014)).

129 Brief of Amici Curiae Corporate Law Professors in Support of Respondents at 6, Masterpiece Cakeshop, Ltd. v. Colorado Civil Rights Comm'n, 138 S. Ct. 1719 (2018) (No. 16–111), 2017 WL 5127303 (The corporation's constitutional claims "can succeed only if the company can claim Phillips's religious beliefs as its own. But Phillips and Masterpiece Cakeshop are not the same. They are not identical for purposes of corporate law, and they should not be deemed identical for purposes of First Amendment law.").

130 *Masterpiece Cakeshop*, 138 S. Ct. at 1723–24, 1726.

131 *Id*. at 1723–24, 1728–29, 1731.

that looks through the corporation and sees the human beings behind it. The rights of the company are protected to preserve the rights of the individuals who make up the corporation. The Colorado courts below used the same aggregate approach to hold the bakery corporation liable for discriminating against its customers Craig and Mullins. The courts found that Phillips' beliefs and actions were the foundation for the corporation's violation. The treatment of Phillips and his cakeshop company by the Colorado courts and the Supreme Court is consistent with the tendency to view private closely held corporations as extensions of the identity of their owners. The Supreme Court found no need to analyze the corporation's status separately because it perceived an equivalency of the corporation's personhood with that of Phillips.

In fact, Justice Thomas in his concurring opinion highlighted the character of the cakeshop business as a vehicle for Phillips to communicate a message about his faith: "even assuming that most for-profit companies prioritize maximizing profits over communicating a message, that is not true for Masterpiece Cakeshop. Phillips routinely sacrifices profits to ensure that Masterpiece operates in a way that represents his Christian faith. He is not open on Sundays, he pays his employees a higher-than-average wage, and he loans them money in times of need."[132] The references in the preceding sentence to "he" rather than to "the cakeshop" are telling, for they equate Phillips with his corporation and affirm the aggregate view of the corporate person. These comments also reflect a recognition that many different types of corporations can exist, some of which may be very closely aligned with the identity of their owners, and may be focused on other goals in addition to making profit.

Although the Supreme Court in *Masterpiece* did not speak directly to the free exercise right of the corporation as a person, Masterpiece Cakeshop and Phillips were both separate parties in the case, and the result of the holding, like that in *Hobby Lobby*, allowed the corporation itself to avoid compliance with a generally applicable law. If one were to interpret the case broadly, perhaps it may stand for the proposition that corporate entities themselves have religious liberty rights under the First Amendment.[133] However, corporations vary greatly in size, purpose, and practices, and the Supreme Court may not view its holding in *Masterpiece* as having broad precedential value in future controversies involving entirely different types of corporations seeking religious exemptions from public accommodation laws. In cases of alleged discrimination, the government's interest in ensuring the

132 *Id.* at 1745 (Thomas, J., concurring). Justice Thomas describes Phillips' business policies in language that is reminiscent of Hobby Lobby's practices: "Phillips also refuses to bake cakes containing alcohol, cakes with racist or homophobic messages, cakes criticizing God, and cakes celebrating Halloween – even though Halloween is one of the most lucrative seasons for bakeries. These efforts to exercise control over the messages that Masterpiece sends are still more evidence that Phillips' conduct is expressive." *Id.*

133 *See* Adam Winkler, *Masterpiece Cakeshop's Surprising Breadth*, SLATE (June 6, 2018), https://slate.com/news-and-politics/2018/06/masterpiece-cakeshop-grants-constitutional-religious-liberty-rights-to-corporations.html [https://perma.cc/XM8L-7J2G] (The "Supreme Court's decision in favor of the baker is also a victory for the corporation – one that may enable future businesses to assert that they too have been victims of religious discrimination.").

marketplace is open to all people on equal terms may take precedence over the religious objections made by some, but not all, business corporations. Given Justice Kennedy's carefully worded opinion stressing the need for a balancing of interests, the Court may have hinted that each case and corporation will be scrutinized for its specific facts and characteristics to properly resolve tensions between the fundamental constitutional rights of religious freedom and equal protection.

*****

The controversy over the capacity of corporations to exercise religious beliefs exposes the complexity of the nature, role, and purpose of corporations in society. The various arguments for and against corporate religious liberty rights reflect competing and complementary aspects of the corporate person. As in *Citizens United*, the Supreme Court majority in *Hobby Lobby* emphasized the role of the corporation as a collection of individual citizens, while the dissent focused on the nature of the corporation as an artificial creature whose features are defined by law. Notably lacking was any anthropomorphic suggestion that corporations could pray, worship, or exercise religion in an independent way. Corporations come in many different forms and sizes, with different purposes and goals. They may be incorporated churches, nonprofit religious corporations, small privately-owned businesses, or large publicly held companies. The urge to treat them all consistently because of their shared incorporated status is countered by the recognition that they are very different types of entities that serve different functions for the people who animate them. It is this variation that suggests the need for flexibility in according rights to the spectrum of entities that constitute corporate persons. The Supreme Court in *Masterpiece Cakeshop* seems to have emphasized the importance of accommodating various competing interests when resolving corporate constitutional challenges to business regulation. How broadly corporate religious liberty rights will be construed to apply to various corporate entities over time remains to be seen.

CORPORATIONS AND RACE

If corporations are persons who can possess their own speech for purposes of free speech rights, and who can form their own religious identity for purposes of religious liberty rights, might they also be capable of having their own racial identity for purposes of racial equality rights? There has been significant public discussion about corporate free speech and corporate religion, but another emerging topic involves the issue of corporate race.

The extent to which corporate persons may be described as having a race has become an important issue as modern society becomes increasingly more diverse and race relations grow more complex. There is a trend toward more liberal recognition of race with regard to corporations. Federal and state programs that certify companies as minority owned businesses entitled to a broad range of legal protections and government assistance affirm that businesses can be the victims of race discrimination. In upholding the rights of such companies under various constitutional and statutory provisions, some courts have held that race can be legally attributed to corporations in order to redress the harmful effects of racially discriminatory conduct.

Some might view this development as taking the personhood of corporations too far. To say that corporations are persons capable of possessing their own race seems to be an example of anthropomorphism at its extreme. But supporters of corporate racial identity maintain that permitting corporate entities to claim a certain race is simply to protect the racial equality rights of the underlying human participants within the corporation. In other words, for racial identity purposes, the corporation's race is equated with that of its human members.

This is not unlike the rationale of *Hobby Lobby* in upholding the religious exercise rights of corporations to protect the religious beliefs of the human owners. Ironically, as a political matter, politically conservative groups generally lauded the *Hobby Lobby* result, while more liberally minded citizens denounced the idea that corporations can have a religious identity; in the context of race, however, politically liberal groups generally favor the view that corporations, minority owned businesses in particular, can have a racial identity for purposes of claiming that they have been the target of racial discrimination. The dissonance in these positions was revealed in the government's oral argument before the Supreme Court in *Hobby Lobby*. Chief Justice John Roberts pointed out that several federal appellate courts have held that corporations as persons can assert racial discrimination claims, and he asked the U.S. Solicitor General (under the Obama administration) whether the government agreed with those cases. The Solicitor General acknowledged that corporations should be permitted to assert claims of racial discrimination, but he maintained that corporations should not be allowed to assert claims of religious freedom.[134] The government had difficulty making a convincing case that corporations are appropriately considered persons capable of claiming a certain race for purposes of challenging acts of racial discrimination, but not persons capable of claiming religious beliefs for purposes of challenging burdens on their religious exercise.

The Supreme Court itself has never squarely resolved the question whether corporations have standing to invoke constitutional and statutory protections against racially discriminatory conduct. Indeed, the closest the Supreme Court has come to addressing the issue was forty years ago in *Village of Arlington Heights v. Metropolitan Housing Development Corp.*[135] In that case, a nonprofit real estate development company sued local authorities in Illinois under the Fourteenth Amendment and the Fair Housing Act after the authorities denied the development company's petition to rezone land from a single-family to multi-family classification.

134 *See* Transcript of Oral Argument at 53–54, Burwell v. Hobby Lobby Stores, Inc., 134 S. Ct. 2751 (2014) (Nos. 13–354, 13–356), www.supremecourt.gov/oral_arguments/argument_transcripts/2013/13-354_3ebh.pdf [https://perma.cc/E8FC-GV99].

135 Village of Arlington Heights v. Metro. Hous. Dev. Corp., 429 U.S. 252 (1977).

The company alleged that the refusal to allow multi-family dwellings was due to the authorities' racially discriminatory motive to bar the development of federally subsidized, racially integrated low and moderate income housing in the area. In evaluating the standing of the company to bring such a race discrimination claim, the Supreme Court stated that "a corporation . . . has no racial identity and cannot be the direct target of the petitioners' alleged discrimination."[136] Yet this statement was merely dictum. The Court expressly admitted that it did not need to decide whether the company had standing to raise the race discrimination claim because the Court found that an individual plaintiff, a local black man who was a prospective tenant of the housing project, had the necessary standing to bring the claim.[137] Thus, although the Court's statement suggested that race cannot be attributed to corporations, the Court never directly grappled with the question whether the corporation is a person capable of experiencing harm from racial discrimination. The lower federal courts since the *Arlington Heights* decision have treated the Court's statement as surplusage and noncontrolling.

The social, political, and economic consequences of recognizing or denying corporate race can be significant. Billions of dollars are at stake in the award of contracts to minority business enterprises under federal and state programs that require the identification of a corporation's racial makeup in order to participate. To "racialize" corporations, or to assign a particular race to them, can have the effect of advantaging or disadvantaging corporations depending on the race that is attributed to them.[138] Social anthropologists contend that the process of racialization is an inescapable feature of American society; to racialize and categorize people on the basis of race "is a basic element of the social system and customs of the United States and is deeply embedded in the consciousness of its people."[139] If race "play[s] an important role in determining how individuals are treated, . . . their employment opportunities, . . . and whether [they] can fully participate in the social, political, and economic mainstream of American life,"[140] then any imputation of race to corporate persons will likewise affect how they are perceived and treated by others, what business opportunities are available to them, and which rights they are entitled to claim under the law.

There are many constitutional and statutory provisions that can potentially be invoked by corporations to assert rights to redress harms from racial discrimination. For instance, the equal protection clause of the Fourteenth Amendment, as well as federal statutes that prohibit discrimination on the basis of race in the making and

[136] *Id.* at 263.

[137] *Id.* at 263–64, 264 n.9.

[138] *See* Cheryl L. Wade, *Effective Compliance with Antidiscrimination Law: Corporate Personhood, Purpose and Social Responsibility*, 74 Wash. & Lee L. Rev. 1187, 1219 (2017).

[139] Audrey Smedley & Brian D. Smedley, *Race as Biology Is Fiction, Racism as a Social Problem Is Real: Anthropological and Historical Perspectives on the Social Construction of Race*, 60 Am. Psychologist 16, 22 (2005).

[140] *Id.* at 23.

enforcing of contracts, in the sale and purchase of property, in the extension of credit, and in the participation in programs receiving federal financial assistance, all serve as viable sources of racial equality rights for corporate persons. Federal and state statutes that provide a remedy for racial discrimination are designed to uphold constitutional rights to equality and fair treatment. A corporation with a certain racial identity that is denied the same opportunity to pursue a lucrative business contract, or buy a piece of property, or obtain a loan on equal terms as a corporation associated with a different racial identity, may have rights to claim that it has been treated in a discriminatory way due to racial animus.

Were we to focus exclusively on the artificial person elements of the corporate person, such claims of discrimination based on corporate racial identity might appear to make little sense. As a creature of statute existing only in contemplation of law, the corporation is not a real person with a physical body who can be said to possess a particular race or belong to any racial group. The loss of dignity and the suffering of insult resulting from treatment that is motivated by racial prejudice are deeply personal experiences that seem inapplicable to inanimate corporate entities. This viewpoint may have motivated the Supreme Court's statement in *Arlington Heights* denying the capacity of corporations to have a racial identity and to be the target of discriminatory conduct.

But such a narrow conception of the corporation as an artificial person obscures the fact that the corporate person consists of living natural persons. These individuals have fundamental rights that should not be diminished when they choose to join a corporation. They are entitled to protection when their businesses are discriminated against because of the race of the individual members. Supporters of this viewpoint argue that permitting discriminatory acts "merely because the injury is done to a corporation, rather than to a partnership or sole proprietorship, or to the corporation's constituents as individuals, inadequately deters discriminatory behavior and undermines the goals" of constitutional and statutory provisions designed to provide equal rights for all persons.[141] They contend that "the corporation, as representative of its constituents, should be able to claim a right to be free of race discrimination."[142]

Just as the Supreme Court in *Hobby Lobby* took an aggregate view of the corporate person for purposes of imputing the religion of the corporation's owners to the corporation to assert corporate religious exercise rights, the race of the corporation's owners might plausibly be imputed to the corporation in an analogous way to claim corporate racial equality rights. This is more likely to be feasible for close corporations where the members of the business are of the same race. Some commentators have suggested that corporate racial identity need not be derived solely from the corporation's owners, but could conceivably come from "the corporation's

141 Robert N. Strassfeld, Note, *Corporate Standing to Allege Race Discrimination in Civil Rights Actions*, 69 Va. L. Rev. 1153, 1180 (1983).

142 *Id.*

customers, managers, employees, or other agents, in addition to where the business is located, the communities it serves, and its principal activities and purposes."[143] This aggregate approach to the corporation's race underscores the extent to which corporations can be equated with their human participants.

From this point of view, there is no legal reason why corporate persons cannot be associated with particular racial identities to assert the right to be treated fairly. Corporations have standing as persons under the Fourteenth Amendment to claim equal protection rights. "It is not apparent why a corporation, although entitled to advance equal protection challenges based on inequality in taxation or regulation, should lack standing to complain of discrimination because of its activities or stock ownership based on racial grounds – the core of the equal protection clause."[144] Even if one acknowledges that the corporate person is a creature of law, it follows then that the law has the power to craft and define racial identity in corporations in furtherance of recognizing important legal rights and obligations. Just as the state can permit corporations to legally exist, the state can permit corporations to have racial character and can determine what the consequences of that designation will be, including authorizing corporations to bring legal claims to be free of racially discriminatory mistreatment.

Some scholars of race relations contend that race itself is a social construct, not a biological fact. "[R]ace is not an essence, something that is fixed, concrete, and objective,"[145] but rather "race is socially constructed at its core."[146] Under this view, differences in physical features and attributes are not as relevant as the social and cultural perceptions that are associated with a person's racial identity. "It is the culturally invented ideas and beliefs about these [physical] differences that constitute the meaning of race."[147] Commentators note that race is often attributed to places and things, such as racialized "white spaces" and "black spaces" where people perceive the boundaries between "white [versus black] neighborhoods, schools, workplaces, and restaurants, for example."[148] To suggest that "racialization does not depend on physical characteristics" or a physical body at all, "thereby mak[es] a corporation's racialization less implausible."[149] The corporation as an artificial person "can be black or possess some other race only if its race is a social product."[150] If racial identity is socially constructed by human interaction and social perceptions,

143 Richard R. W. Brooks, *Incorporating Race*, 106 COLUM. L. REV. 2023, 2077 (2006).

144 Hudson Valley Freedom Theater, Inc. v. Heimbach, 671 F.2d 702, 706 (2d Cir. 1982) (footnote omitted).

145 John O. Calmore, *Racialized Space and the Culture of Segregation: "Hewing a Stone of Hope from a Mountain of Despair,"* 143 U. PA. L. REV. 1233, 1236 (1995).

146 Brooks, *supra* note 143, at 2072; *see also* Jonathan Bailyn, *A Critical Race Theorist Account of Corporate Racial Standing*, 16 SCHOLAR 725, 728 (2014) ("According to racial constructionists, society—not biology—creates races.").

147 Smedley & Smedley, *supra* note 139, at 20.

148 Wade, *supra* note 138, at 1220.

149 *Id.* at 1219.

150 Brooks, *supra* note 143, at 2072.

then conceivably "[c]orporate persons [could] belong to socially constructed racial groups in ways that are similar to the assignation of race to flesh and blood persons."[151]

Proponents of corporate racial equality rights argue that corporations inevitably take on racial character, so the law's role in recognizing the standing of corporate persons to assert their racial character in legal claims is simply a reflection of reality.[152] For example, a corporation may purposefully seek to identify itself with a particular race in order to obtain various advantages afforded to minority business enterprises. It may want to affirmatively display a certain racial identity in order to more effectively reach a particular customer base, or to foster employee cohesion and loyalty, or to more visibly engage in activities that serve a specific community. In such cases, the corporation will willingly adopt a racial identity to further its goals and purposes. Other corporations, however, may try assiduously to avoid being associated with a race for fear that being identified as a minority business, for instance, will cause the corporation to be treated less favorably by potential customers, employee candidates, or contracting parties.[153] With regard to this latter situation, third parties at times may ascribe a particular race to the corporation, whether based on the race of its owners, employees, or otherwise, even if the corporation disagrees with this ascription and even if the corporation attempts to deny an association with the ascribed race. When third parties impute a racial identity to a corporation, they adjust their economic and social behavior toward the corporation based on its perceived race. "Based on their perception of its race, people may actively seek to do business with a corporation or shun it completely."[154] These outside perceptions of the corporation give it a racial character, irrespective of the corporation's own volition.

Thus, whether willingly or unwillingly, corporations can and do take on racial identities in fact based on the practices of individuals inside and outside of the corporation. In this manner, the racial character of corporate persons is not necessarily the creation of legislative fiat, but the unavoidable result of how the corporation is consciously or unconsciously displayed by its participants and how it is perceived by third parties. Because corporate persons thus have the capacity to acquire racial identities, they presumably should be permitted to exercise rights to redress injuries suffered on the basis of those racial identities.

If we are to base a corporation's racial identity on the race or perceived race of its human participants, we run into the familiar dilemma of trying to determine which participants count for purposes of ascribing race to the corporate person. Should we

151 Wade, *supra* note 138, at 1217.

152 *See* Strassfeld, *supra* note 141, at 1179–81.

153 *See* Brooks, *supra* note 143, at 2037–38 (noting that it may be "profit-maximizing for *some* black-owned businesses to organize their transactions under the veil of a black corporate personality, while others would find it optimal to clothe their transactions with a deliberate measure of racial ambiguity or anonymity").

154 *See* Strassfeld, *supra* note 141, at 1179.

look to the race of the corporation's owners, its key executives, its rank-and-file employees, its customers? If we impute the race of the corporation's owners to the corporation, as the Supreme Court imputed the religious identity of the corporation's owners to Hobby Lobby, must one hundred percent of the owners be of the same race, or would a majority be sufficient?[155] Could a corporation have bi-racial or multi-racial identities if it has an equal percentage of owners of different racial groups? If the race of the executives is considered, "how would the various offices be weighted? Would one minority CEO outweigh two nonminority vice presidents or vice versa? These questions demonstrate the theoretical problems."[156] Constructing definitive standards for what makes a corporation, for instance, legally black, or Asian, or any other race, requires difficult line-drawing that is bound to be vulnerable to criticisms of arbitrariness and underinclusiveness or overinclusiveness.

Despite these difficulties and the lack of instruction from the Supreme Court, the lower federal courts have developed their own approaches to determining the racial identity of corporate persons. Cases involving corporations that complain of injury from racially discriminatory treatment often turn on the issue of whether corporations have legal standing to assert constitutional and statutory rights to be free of racial discrimination. As the following sections explain, several federal circuits have held that corporations can bring such race discrimination claims. The courts have utilized at least four different theories to assign racial identities to corporations, or alternatively, to grant standing to corporations to assert discrimination claims regardless of the race of their individual members.

1 CORPORATE RACE VIA GOVERNMENT CERTIFICATION

One way corporate entities can be identified with a particular racial status is if they qualify under federal and state government programs as certified minority owned business enterprises. For example, the federal Small Business Act authorizes support for the extension of government contracts to eligible companies that identify as socially and economically disadvantaged small businesses. In enacting the statutory program, Congress found that some "persons are socially disadvantaged because of their identification as members of certain groups that have suffered the effects of discriminatory practices or similar invidious circumstances over which they have no control."[157] The statute's purpose in providing assistance to minority companies is to "promote the business development of small business concerns owned and

[155] *See* Brooks, *supra* note 143, at 2082 ("Perhaps a majority-share rule is the answer, assuming that a majority of the shares are held by individuals of a particular race or ethnicity.").

[156] Robert E. Suggs, *Racial Discrimination in Business Transactions*, 42 HASTINGS L.J. 1257, 1289 n.174 (1991).

[157] Small Business Act, § 2(f)(1)(B), 15 U.S.C. § 631(f)(1)(B) (2012). The statute states that "such groups include, but are not limited to, Black Americans, Hispanic Americans, Native Americans, Indian tribes, Asian Pacific Americans, Native Hawaiian Organizations, and other minorities." *Id.* at 15 U.S. C. § 631(f)(1)(C).

controlled by socially and economically disadvantaged individuals so that such concerns can compete on an equal basis in the American economy."[158] In order to qualify as an eligible business, the corporation must be at least fifty-one percent unconditionally owned by one or more socially and economically disadvantaged individuals, and its management and daily business operations must be controlled by such individuals.[159] "Socially disadvantaged individuals" are defined as "those who have been subjected to racial or ethnic prejudice or cultural bias because of their identity as a member of a group without regard to their individual qualities."[160] When a corporation certifies it is owned and controlled by such individuals for purposes of participating in federal contractual programs contemplated by the statute, the government recognition of the corporation as a minority owned business allows the corporation to take on a racial identity as a matter of law.

Various federal courts have affirmed that this approach to establishing the racial identity of a corporation is a valid method for creating standing for corporations to sue in their own right for race discrimination. For example, in *Thinket Ink Information Resources, Inc. v. Sun Microsystems, Inc.*, the Ninth Circuit held that a corporation that was certified under federal law as a minority owned business acquired a racial identity and could be the victim of discriminatory conduct based on its race.[161] Thinket was a technology services company certified by the U.S. Small Business Administration as a firm owned and operated by socially and economically disadvantaged individuals, eligible to receive federal contracts under the Small Business Act. All of the company's shareholders were black. Alleging that Sun Microsystems had deliberately refused to contract with Thinket because it was a minority owned business, Thinket sued Sun Microsystems under section 1981, which prohibits race discrimination in the making and enforcement of contracts.[162]

In deciding whether Thinket, as a corporation, had standing to assert discrimination claims under section 1981, the court acknowledged the Supreme Court's prior general observation in *Arlington Heights* that corporations have no racial identity and cannot be the direct target of discrimination. Nonetheless, the court described the *Arlington Heights* statement as "clearly dictum" and distinguished Thinket's situation due to its legal certification as a minority owned business.[163] "To receive certain governmental benefits, Thinket was required to be certified as a corporation

[158] *Id.* at 15 U.S.C. § 631(f)(2)(A).

[159] *See id.* at § 637(a)(4)(A), (B). If the corporation is publicly owned, at least fifty-one percent of the stock must be held by one or more socially and economically disadvantaged individuals. *See id.*

[160] *Id.* at § 637(a)(5). "Economically disadvantaged individuals are those socially disadvantaged individuals whose ability to compete in the free enterprise system has been impaired due to diminished capital and credit opportunities as compared to others in the same business area who are not socially disadvantaged." *Id.* at § 637(a)(6)(A).

[161] Thinket Ink Info. Res., Inc. v. Sun Microsystems, Inc., 368 F.3d 1053 (9th Cir. 2004).

[162] *See* 42 U.S.C. § 1981 (2012). The statute protects the "making, performance, modification, and termination of contracts, and the enjoyment of all benefits, privileges, terms, and conditions of the contractual relationship." *Id.* § 1981(b).

[163] *Thinket*, 368 F.3d at 1058 n.1.

with a racial identity; further, it alleges that it suffered discrimination because all of its shareholders were African-American. This is quite different from ... *Arlington Heights* where the corporate plaintiff had no particular racial identity."[164] Thus, the court concluded that when a corporation like Thinket has acquired a racial identity as a matter of law, it can be the direct target of discrimination, and the corporation is sufficiently within the statutory zone of interest to have standing to pursue a claim for race discrimination under section 1981.[165]

In similar fashion, the Fourth Circuit in *Carnell Construction Corp. v. Danville Redevelopment & Housing Authority* held that a corporation certified as a minority owned business under Virginia law could acquire a racial identity for purposes of establishing standing to bring a race discrimination claim under Title VI.[166] Carnell was a construction company hired to work on a large public housing venture for low-income residents in Danville, Virginia, that was funded in part by federal money from the U.S. Department of Housing and Urban Development. The relationship between Carnell and the local housing authority deteriorated as each party became dissatisfied with the other's performance, and Carnell's contract was not renewed. Carnell, whose sole owner and president was black, alleged that it was being mistreated on the basis of race and sued the housing authority under Title VI of the Civil Rights Act of 1964, which states that "[n]o person ... shall, on the ground of race, color, or national origin, be excluded from participation in, be denied the benefits of, or be subjected to discrimination under any program or activity receiving Federal financial assistance."[167] Relying on the Supreme Court's statement denying corporate racial identity in *Arlington Heights*, the defendant argued that Carnell was not a "person" within the meaning of the statute and that, as a corporate entity, it lacked race, color, or national origin. The Fourth Circuit viewed the *Arlington Heights* statement as "dictum" and "surplusage," and held that a corporation that "has been properly certified as [a minority owned business] under applicable law can be the direct object of discriminatory action and establish standing to bring an action based on such discrimination."[168] Because Carnell was properly certified by state law as a minority owned business based on the race of its sole shareholder and president, the court concluded that Carnell had a racial identity sufficient to place its race discrimination claims within the zone of interests protected by Title VI.[169]

164 *Id.* at 1059.

165 *Id.* at 1059–60; *see also* Org. of Minority Vendors, Inc. v. Ill. Cent. Gulf R.R., 579 F. Supp. 574, 588 (N.D. Ill. 1983) (Several black and Hispanic owned corporations that qualified as minority business enterprises under Department of Transportation regulations had standing to pursue race discrimination claims under section 1981 since it is possible that "some corporations, like the plaintiffs, which have been identified as minority business enterprises under federal regulations, do have a 'racial identity' and can be targets of discrimination.").

166 Carnell Constr. Corp. v. Danville Redev. & Hous. Auth., 745 F.3d 703 (4th Cir. 2014).

167 42 U.S.C. § 2000d (2012).

168 *Carnell*, 745 F.3d at 715.

169 *Id.* at 710, 715.

These cases illustrate the courts' reliance on law and government certification to give corporate persons their formal racial identity. Under this method, corporate race is defined by statute. If the corporation meets the conditions specified for minority owned status under applicable federal or state laws, the corporation has a legally recognizable racial identity, rendering it eligible for certain prescribed government benefits under the statute and giving it standing to complain when its rights are denied based on its race.[170] This approach to corporate race focuses on elements of the corporate person as both an artificial entity and an aggregate of its human members. As an artificial person or concession of the state, the corporation owes its existence and any other essential features, including its racial character if any, to the state, as it is defined by law. Yet laws that certify corporations as minority owned businesses look to the race of the corporation's owners and managers to determine whether the corporation qualifies for such status and possesses a particular racial identity. Thus, this method of identifying the racial status of the corporate person requires a dependence on certification statutes as well as an emphasis on the identity of the corporation's human participants.

One of the difficulties with using the government certification approach to establishing the race of corporations for purposes of corporate race discrimination claims is that statutory standards for certification may vary under federal and state law, as well as vary among different states. Differing requirements for certifying minority owned businesses can create inconsistent determinations as to whether corporations have a minority racial identity in one jurisdiction versus another. Moreover, statutory standards can change at the discretion of federal and state legislatures. To the extent the racial identity of the corporation is dependent on statutory standards, the racial status of the corporation presumably can suddenly change if the statute's requirements for certification are revised. While it might be unusual to say that a natural person's race can instantly change with a revision in the law, such a result would not be surprising for the corporate person if it must look to statutorily derived government certification measures to establish its racial character.

2 CORPORATE RACE IMPUTED FROM OWNERS

A second method of attributing race to the corporate person is by directly imputing the race of the corporation's owners to the corporation. This does away with the need

[170] To be precise, statutes that certify businesses as minority owned do not necessarily assign to the corporation a particular racial classification, but rather, a minority status. Theoretically, an Asian shareholder could own one percent of a corporation while the other fifty percent is owned by shareholders of other minority races, and the corporation would still be classified as a minority owned business under the federal statute. In such a case, the corporation may not have a single specific racial identity, but its statutory certification as a minority owned business gives it a minority racial status for purposes of asserting its right to beneficial and nondiscriminatory treatment. It is conceivable that minority status itself might be considered a form of racial identity. *See* Brooks, *supra* note 143, at 2077 & n.263.

to rely on any formal federal or state certification. Instead, courts simply look to the race of the corporation's human participants and allow the corporation to assert their racial identity. Many courts have utilized this approach to recognize the standing of corporations to bring race discrimination claims. In these cases, the corporation is solely owned by one shareholder, or it is closely held by a small number of shareholders who are of the same race. The courts impute the owners' race to the corporation to permit the corporation to sue when it suffers injury due to racial animus. In contrast to the artificial person view of the corporate person, this approach suggests that corporate racial identity is not the creation of law, but exists prior to and independent of the law. Equating the corporation with its shareholders, this approach adheres to an aggregate view of the corporate person.

For example, in *Howard Security Services, Inc. v. Johns Hopkins Hospital*, a federal district court held that a corporation wholly owned by a black individual could bring a section 1981 race discrimination claim against the defendant hospital for failure to award a security services contract to the corporation allegedly due to racial prejudice against the owner.[171] Arguing that the corporation itself has no race, the hospital maintained that the corporation cannot claim to be the victim of race discrimination. While the court acknowledged that the "[d]efendant's argument that corporations cannot be subjected to slavery and cannot have races and thus cannot be covered by the Thirteenth Amendment and § 1981 has a good deal of force," the court nonetheless chose to look through the corporate entity to see the shareholder himself.[172] "To deal with [the corporation] is, practically speaking, to deal with [the owner]."[173] According to the court, "[t]his is the clearest case for a 'black' corporation—100% owned by blacks and a close corporation."[174] Thus, the court allowed the corporation to identify as a black corporation for purposes of bringing its section 1981 claim.

Several federal courts of appeal have followed this approach to grant standing to corporations to assert race discrimination claims.[175] Most recently, in *Woods v. City of Greensboro*, the Fourth Circuit explicitly held that a corporation was not required

171 Howard Sec. Servs., Inc. v. Johns Hopkins Hosp., 516 F. Supp. 508 (D. Md. 1981).

172 *Id.* at 512–13.

173 *Id.* at 513.

174 *Id.* at 513 n.11; *see also* Ultimax Transp., Inc. v. British Airways, PLC, 231 F. Supp. 2d 1329 (N.D. Ga. 2002) (holding that a corporation whose sole shareholder, president, and CEO was black, and the majority of whose employees were black, had standing to assert a section 1981 claim based on racial discrimination directed at its owners and employees). Under such circumstances, "the racial identity that the parties and the Court assign to that corporation is an African-American or black racial identity." *Ultimax*, 231 F. Supp. 2d at 1338.

175 *See, e.g.*, Amber Pyramid, Inc. v. Buffington Harbor Riverboats, 129 F. App'x 292, 293–95 (7th Cir. 2005) (holding that a corporation owned by two black sisters assumed an imputed racial identity from its shareholders and had standing under section 1981 to sue for race discrimination); Bains LLC v. Arco Products Co., 405 F.3d 764, 770 (9th Cir. 2005) (holding that a trucking company owned by three Indian Sikh brothers "undoubtedly acquired an imputed racial identity" and established standing to pursue a section 1981 claim against the defendant for allegedly racially discriminatory mistreatment); Guides, Ltd. v. Yarmouth Grp. Prop. Mgmt., Inc., 295 F.3d 1065, 1072 (10th Cir. 2002)

to be officially certified by the government as a minority owned business in order to sue for race discrimination, but instead could establish an imputed racial identity stemming from the race of its owners.[176] The court found that a minority owned television network called the Black Network Television Ad Agency, which was owned by a husband and wife who were minorities, was not foreclosed from bringing a section 1981 claim against the city for denying their economic development loan allegedly because of racially discriminatory bias. Even though the corporation was not certified as a minority business, the court held that the owners' race could be imputed to the corporation for purposes of pursuing a race discrimination suit in its own right.[177]

To support the extension of race to the corporate person in this manner, some courts have invoked the Supreme Court's own cases that have allowed white owned companies to bring reverse discrimination claims challenging federal programs that set aside government contracts for minority owned businesses. For example, the Ninth Circuit in *Thinket* stated that the Supreme Court itself has "implicitly recognized that corporations can have racial characteristics by allowing white owned corporations to challenge contractor set asides on reverse discrimination grounds."[178] The Supreme Court's decision in *Adarand Constructors, Inc. v. Pena* upheld the right of a nonminority subcontractor company that was not awarded a contract for a federal highway project, even though it submitted the lowest bid, to challenge a federal affirmative action program that conferred contracting advantages on minority business enterprises and resulted in the contract being awarded to a minority owned company.[179] The Court emphasized that "any person, of whatever race, has the right to demand that any governmental actor subject to the Constitution justify any racial classification subjecting that person to unequal treatment under the strictest judicial scrutiny."[180] In entertaining the nonminority corporation's claim, the Court implicitly recognized that a corporation can be characterized as a person of a particular race with the right to object to unjustified

(holding that a company solely owned and operated by an Ethiopian immigrant had standing to assert discrimination claims under sections 1981 and 1982).

176 Woods v. City of Greensboro, 855 F.3d 639, 644–46 (4th Cir. 2017).

177 *Id.* at 641–46.

178 Thinket Ink Info. Res., Inc. v. Sun Microsystems, Inc., 368 F.3d 1053, 1058 (9th Cir. 2004) (citing City of Richmond v. J.A. Croson Co., 488 U.S. 469 (1989)). In the *Croson* case, the Supreme Court held that the city's set-aside program favoring minority owned companies was unconstitutional under the Fourteenth Amendment. The Court emphasized that "[t]he guarantee of equal protection cannot mean one thing when applied to one individual and something else when applied to a person of another color." *Croson*, 488 U.S. at 494 (quoting Regents of the Univ. of Cal. v. Bakke, 438 U.S. 265, 289–290 (1978)); *see also* Triad Assocs., Inc. v. Chi. Hous. Auth., 892 F.2d 583, 591–93 (7th Cir. 1989) (holding that a corporation owned by two white individuals had a cause of action under section 1985(3) for injuries suffered allegedly because of conspiracies motivated by racial animus); Holland/Blue Streak v. Barthelemy, 849 F.2d 987, 988–89 (5th Cir. 1988) (holding that a joint venture that was a majority white enterprise stated a claim under section 1981 for racially based reverse discrimination).

179 Adarand Constructors, Inc. v. Pena, 515 U.S. 200 (1995).

180 *Id.* at 224.

racial classifications by the government. Thus, despite the Supreme Court's earlier dictum statement in *Arlington Heights* denying the capacity of corporations to have any racial identity, the Court has permitted white owned corporations to complain of reverse discrimination, impliedly acknowledging that the corporate person is equivalent to its human owners who feel the injury of unequal treatment based on their nonminority racial status.[181]

Focusing in this way on the corporate person as an aggregate of its human members allows courts to look through the corporate form and see the individuals behind it. By imputing the race of those individuals directly to the corporation, courts have viewed corporations as persons that possess the capacity for racial identities, the potential to suffer legally cognizable harms from racially discriminatory acts, and the necessary standing to pursue causes of action to redress those racial harms.[182]

However, corporations must meet certain strict pleading standards to justify their claimed racial identity and their standing to bring race discrimination claims. They must explain why in each particular case it makes sense to impute the race of the

[181] Commentators have noted that racial standing for corporations has been a contested issue only when minority owned businesses are the plaintiffs bringing race discrimination claims. When nonminority firms sue to challenge set-aside programs that benefit minority companies, the courts seem to assume standing. In these cases, counsel defending set-aside programs that favor minority owned businesses would not argue that corporations cannot have racial identities or standing to bring reverse discrimination claims because to make such an argument would undermine the strategic position of their minority business clients who may themselves wish to bring race discrimination claims at some point. Suggs, *supra* note 156, at 1288 n.166.

[182] *See, e.g.*, Sec. & Data Techs., Inc. v. Sch. Dist. of Phila., 145 F. Supp. 3d 454, 465 (E.D. Pa. 2015) (citing precedent supporting the standing of corporations to bring section 1981 claims if they acquire an imputed racial identity by being owned and controlled by members of one racial group); Jones v. Culver Franchising Sys., Inc., 12 F. Supp. 3d 1079, 1085 (N.D. Ill. 2013) (holding two companies had section 1981 standing because they acquired an imputed racial identity through their members and allegedly were the target of racial discrimination); A.H. Emp. Co. v. Fifth Third Bank, No. 11 C 4586, 2012 WL 686704, at *5 (N.D. Ill. 2012) (holding corporation had standing to sue because it had the imputed racial identity of its owners); Major Tours, Inc. v. Colorel, 799 F. Supp. 2d 376, 392 n.9 (D. N.J. 2011) (noting that plaintiff companies have standing to bring race discrimination claims based on the race of their owners); Shah v. Am. Bottling Co., No. 07–1042, 2008 WL 718435, at *4 (C.D. Ill. 2008) (holding corporation acquired an "imputed racial social identity" sufficient for standing to sue under section 1981 based on the race of the sole shareholder); Ziegler v. City of Warren, No. 4:04CV1248, 2007 WL 509764, at *2, *5 (N.D. Ohio 2007) ("Because [p]laintiff [corporation] is considered a person, … it can also assume a racial identity … [B]ecause the only shareholder/employee of [p]laintiff [corporation] known by the Court is African American, the Court will assume its racial identity to be African American."); Florence Urgent Care v. Healthspan, Inc., 445 F. Supp. 2d 871, 877 (S.D. Ohio 2006) ("[W]here a corporation is owned and controlled by members of one racial group, it only comports with justice and common sense to conclude that such corporation could be the target of racial animus."); NDN Drywall, Inc. v. Custom Drywall, Inc., No. Civ. 04-CV-4706DSDSRN, 2005 WL 1324056, at *4 (D. Minn. 2005) (concluding that corporation had standing to bring section 1981 claim where the corporation was closely associated with its minority sole owner); Calderon v. Sw. Bell Mobile Sys., LLC, 390 F. Supp. 2d 714, 717 (N.D. Ill. 2005) (holding closely held corporation acquired an imputed racial identity from its majority stockholder, president, and operator, and corporation therefore had standing to pursue its section 1981 claim).

corporation's members to the corporation by showing, for example, that the corporation is solely owned by a single minority shareholder, or closely held by a few shareholders who are all of the same race, or perhaps held by numerous shareholders the majority of whom share a particular race. Courts have denied corporations standing to bring race discrimination claims when they do not sufficiently allege facts to establish the race of the corporation's owners, thus failing to justify the imputation of any race to the corporation.[183] It "only comports with justice and common sense to conclude that [a] corporation [can] be the target of racial animus" when the corporation has an identifiable racial character, which arises out of the racial characteristics of its members, particularly "where [the] corporation is owned and controlled by members of one racial group."[184] Without specific facts indicating the racial make-up of the individuals within the corporation, there are no grounds to ascribe any racial identity to the corporation as an aggregate of its members.

To determine the corporate racial identity, the focus for the most part has been on the corporation's owners, not on other corporate constituents such as employees or customers. Courts have held that a corporation cannot establish an imputed racial identity by arguing merely that it has a strong association with its minority employees or patrons.[185] The corporation must rely on the race of the owner or the majority shareholders to infuse it with a racial identity and to have standing to bring discrimination claims based on that racial identity.[186] This approach to ascribing race to the corporate person seems to bolster the view that protecting the corporation from racial discrimination is ultimately a means of protecting the rights of the shareholders whose race is the reason why the corporation has been subjected to discriminatory mistreatment.

183 *See, e.g.*, Cholla Ready Mix, Inc. v. Civish, 382 F.3d 969, 978 (9th Cir. 2004) (concluding that the plaintiff corporation has no viable section 1981 claim for race discrimination because it "fails to allege facts from which one could infer that [the corporation] has an imputed racial identity, for example the race of [the corporation's] owner"); Autolube Grp. LLC v. Delfin Grp. USA LLC, No. 2:13–2422-PMD, 2014 WL 5488400, at *5 (D.S.C. 2014) ("[W]ith respect to a 'racial' identity, . . . Plaintiff has set forth no allegations to establish a 'racial' corporate identity. Plaintiff has not alleged [for example] that it is owned entirely by shareholders of a single race."); New Louisiana Holdings, LLC v. Arrowsmith, No. 11 C 5031, 2012 WL 6061710, at *7–8 (N.D. Ill. 2012) (dismissing the corporate plaintiffs' race discrimination claims due to failure to allege adequately that corporate plaintiffs have a racial identity, where the complaint pleads no facts indicating who the sole owners or majority shareholders are).

184 *Florence Urgent Care*, 445 F. Supp. 2d at 877.

185 *See, e.g.*, Prestige Rests. & Entm't, Inc. v. Bayside Seafood Rest., Inc., No. 09–23128-CIV, 2010 WL 680905, at *7 n.9 (S.D. Fla. 2010) (noting that a corporation's claim "that it was discriminated against because of its patrons' race" does not establish a corporate racial identity); Contemporary Pers., Inc. v. Godiva Chocolatier, Inc., No. 09–00187, 2009 WL 2431461, at *1 (E.D. Penn. 2009) (rejecting a corporation's claim of an "imputed racial identity resulting from its strong association with its Hispanic and African-American employees").

186 *See Contemporary Pers.*, at *2 (holding that corporate imputed racial identity is appropriate "when *the owner, majority shareholders, and/or president are members of the specific class that is alleged to have been discriminated against*").

While the corporation therefore has standing to sue when it suffers business injury from racial discrimination, the individual shareholders themselves do not have standing to bring corporate claims. In section 1981 cases, for example, a corporation that has or would have rights under an existing or proposed contract can claim that it has been intentionally discriminated against on the basis of race in the making, performance, modification, or termination of the contract. When the corporation is the party to the contract, it is the corporation alone, not the individual shareholder, that has the legally cognizable interest to assert the discrimination claim, even though it is the race of the shareholder that has prompted the discriminatory treatment and that is the basis for the corporation's imputed racial identity.

In *Domino's Pizza, Inc. v. McDonald*, the Supreme Court affirmed this distinction between the shareholder and the corporate person. It held that a black shareholder who was the sole owner and president of a corporation, and who sued Domino's Pizza under section 1981 for breaching several contracts with his corporation allegedly due to racial animus toward him, had no standing to sue because he himself was not a party to the contract and therefore had no rights in his personal capacity.[187] Emphasizing the separate nature of the corporation, the Court cited "fundamental corporation and agency law" for the rule that a shareholder "has no rights and is exposed to no liability under the corporation's contracts."[188] The Court specified that because it was the corporate person that entered into the contract and allegedly suffered the injury to its contractual rights, the shareholder had no standing and could not claim that the corporation's rights accrued to him.[189] Courts have consistently held that individual owners do not have standing to bring section 1981 race discrimination claims when the corporation is the party to the contract, rather than the owners, although it is the race of the owners that supplies the corporation itself with the underlying imputed racial identity required to have such standing.[190]

On some level, this means that the view of the corporation as an aggregate of its members in the context of race operates unidirectionally. A corporation can claim

187 Domino's Pizza, Inc. v. McDonald, 546 U.S. 470, 479–80 (2006).

188 *Id.* at 477.

189 *Id.* at 476–80. The case was about the shareholder's attempt to assert the corporation's rights as his own, not the corporation attempting to assert the rights and acquire the race of the shareholder. The Court never addressed the issue of whether the corporation itself had standing to bring a section 1981 race discrimination claim because the corporation settled its claims and was not involved in the case. *See id.* at 473 n.1. Thus, the Court avoided making any direct statement about the capacity of corporations to acquire an imputed racial identity.

190 *See* Amber Pyramid, Inc. v. Buffington Harbor Riverboats, 129 F. App'x 292, 294–95 (7th Cir. 2005); Guides, Ltd. v. Yarmouth Grp. Prop. Mgmt., Inc., 295 F.3d 1065, 1072–73 (10th Cir. 2002); Gersman v. Grp. Health Ass'n., Inc., 931 F.2d 1565, 1567 (D.C. Cir. 1991); Searcy v. Hous. Lighting & Power Co., 907 F.2d 562, 565 (5th Cir. 1990); Jones v. Culver Franchising Sys., Inc., 12 F. Supp. 3d 1079, 1086–87 (N.D. Ill. 2013); A.H. Emp. Co. v. Fifth Third Bank, No. 11 C 4586, 2012 WL 686704, at *5 (N.D. Ill. 2012); Safety Sols., Inc. v. City of Chicago, No. 11 C 1305, 2011 WL 3652446, at *5–6 (N.D. Ill. 2011); Shah v. Am. Bottling Co., No. 07–1042, 2008 WL 718435, at *3 (C.D. Ill. 2008); Calderon v. Sw. Bell Mobile Sys., *LLC*, 390 F. Supp. 2d 714, 717 (N.D. Ill. 2005); Perez v. Abbott Labs., No. 94 C 4127, 1995 WL 86716, at *5 (N.D. Ill. 1995).

to be equal with its shareholders when it seeks to acquire the imputed racial identity of its shareholders for purposes of bringing race discrimination claims, but the shareholders cannot claim to be equal with the corporation when they seek to assert the rights of the corporation to redress injury from race discrimination. Focusing on the aggregate nature of the corporate person to impute the shareholder's race to the corporation seems feasible only for solely owned corporations, or closely held corporations with a few shareholders. Perhaps it is possible for even a large corporation with many shareholders to acquire the racial identity of its owners if they are all of the same race. However, it does not seem plausible that large corporations with numerous shareholders of diverse racial backgrounds could acquire a single racial identity for purposes of bringing race discrimination claims. If the Supreme Court were ever to take up the issue of corporate race, perhaps it would hold, analogously as it did in *Hobby Lobby* in the context of corporate religious rights, that corporations are capable of assuming the racial identity of their owners, but that this result is only viable when that identity can clearly be discerned from the race of the owners, which is likely to be possible only in the case of close corporations, not in large, publicly held companies with numerous diverse shareholders. Alternatively, as the following sections explain, the Court could endorse one of two other avenues that have been utilized to establish the standing of corporations to pursue race discrimination claims. These methods do not rely on the race of corporate owners at all.

3 CORPORATE RACE DERIVED FROM CORPORATE PURPOSE

Certain organizations are incorporated for the express purpose of protecting, promoting, or enhancing the interests of particular racial groups. When those organizations in the course of their operations suffer discriminatory mistreatment, they can assert discrimination claims based on the race of the class of people whose interests the organization is designed to serve.

For example, in *Hudson Valley Freedom Theater, Inc. v. Heimbach*, a New York nonprofit corporation brought a civil rights action against county officials for rejecting its application for public grant funds. The Hudson Valley Freedom Theater was organized specifically "to produce theatrical and artistic productions" that were designed to "reach and involve" and "reflect the cultural needs, aspirations and creativity of the Black and Hispanic communities" in the local area.[191] The Theater claimed that the denial of a grant to fund the production of several plays in the community was motivated by racial animus toward those minority groups. The district court held that the Theater lacked standing to bring the claim and dismissed the lawsuit because "a corporation, as a faceless creature of the state, may not assert

[191] Hudson Valley Freedom Theater, Inc. v. Heimbach, 671 F.2d 702, 703 (2d Cir. 1982).

claims of racial discrimination under the Fourteenth Amendment on its own behalf, and cannot be the 'target' of racial discrimination."[192]

On appeal, the Second Circuit disagreed and reversed the district court's ruling. Rather than being drawn into a discussion about whether a corporation is capable of having a race, the Second Circuit focused on the purpose for which the corporation exists. In this case, the Theater was specifically incorporated to further the cultural and artistic interests and development of the local minority community. The court found that such a racially oriented corporate purpose enables the corporation to assert certain rights against those who, for racially discriminatory reasons, "frustrat[e] specific acts of the sort which the corporation was founded to accomplish."[193] That the Theater's sole purpose was to serve the interests of a particular set of racial groups placed it "in a better position than anyone else to challenge discriminatory practices" resulting in unfavorable treatment.[194] Thus, the corporate raison d'etre provided the corporation with the necessary racial character to have standing to sue for racial discrimination, without the need to rely on the race of the corporate owners. Indeed, as a nonprofit corporation, the Theater had no shareholders whose race could be imputed directly to the corporation. Instead, the court allowed the corporation to derive its racial standing from its exclusive function to represent and benefit an identified racial group. A concurring opinion in the case emphasized that whether a corporation (as "a colorless corporate 'person'") "does or does not have a racial identity is irrelevant," so long as someone "with racially discriminatory intent, causes [the corporation] direct injury."[195]

A similar approach was taken by the Eighth Circuit in *Oti Kaga, Inc. v. South Dakota Housing Development Authority*, which held that a nonprofit corporation established and operated by Native Americans had standing to assert race discrimination claims under the Fair Housing Act. The corporation's "purpose [was] to acquire, construct, and operate rental housing" for Native Americans on a "Sioux Indian Reservation" in South Dakota.[196] The corporation sued the state housing authority for denying its request for tax credits and government funding allegedly due to race discrimination against the Native American community. The district court dismissed the claim on the grounds that "a corporation[] has no racial identity and cannot establish its membership in a protected class."[197] On appeal, the Eighth Circuit disagreed and held that the corporation had standing to proceed with its claim. Relying on the Second Circuit's reasoning in *Hudson Valley Freedom*

192 *Id.* at 704.

193 *Id.* at 706.

194 *Id.* The court maintained that it would be incongruous to "deny standing to the corporation because it 'has no racial identity and cannot be the direct target' of the discrimination, while at the same time . . . deny standing to the stockholders on the sound ground that the injury was suffered by the corporation and not by them." *Id.*

195 *Id.* at 708 (Pierce, J., concurring).

196 Oti Kaga, Inc. v. S.D. Hous. Dev. Auth., 342 F.3d 871, 875 (8th Cir. 2003).

197 *Id.* at 880.

Theater, the court focused on the purpose of the corporation to further minority interests. "The alleged discrimination has directly affected [the corporation's] economic interests and its ability to realize its corporate purpose. As such, [the corporation] is a logical and more effective adversary to combat the alleged discrimination."[198] The corporation's purpose to serve the interests of the Native American community gave it sufficient racial character to invoke the anti-discrimination provisions of the Fair Housing Act.

From this perspective, when the corporation's express purpose is to advance the interests of a particular racial group, the corporation can derive its racial standing from the individuals whom the corporation is established to serve. Rather than focusing exclusively on the race of those who own or control the corporation, this approach looks outside the corporate person to its external stakeholders to connect their race to the corporation. The corporation's intended customers, clientele, or beneficiaries of its efforts are the ones whose race attaches to the corporation. None of the corporation's owners or employees may be of the same race as that of the racial community the corporation is intended to assist, but that does not detract from the corporation's capacity to claim the race of its external stakeholders. The corporate person draws its racial standing from its identification with the particular racial group the corporation exists to benefit.

This manner of establishing corporate race works for both small and large corporations, unlike the method of imputing the corporate owners' race to the corporation, which presumably is feasible primarily for closely held corporations with one shareholder or a few shareholders of a single race. If a corporation can take on the racial identity of the distinct racial community whose interest it seeks to promote, then even a large corporation with numerous shareholders of different races could conceivably maintain its singular racial community identity for purposes of discrimination claims. When the corporation suffers discrimination because of racial animus toward that community, courts have held that the corporation falls within the "zone of interests" protected by the discrimination statutes and has standing to seek relief.[199]

While it seems this approach to attributing race to the corporate person applies most readily to nonprofit corporations that have the express purpose of furthering the interests of certain racial groups, it possibly could also extend to for-profit corporations that have adopted similar objectives. Corporations organized as "B corporations" or "benefit corporations," which are designed to promote a general or specific public benefit as well as to make profits, could presumably be eligible for this treatment. Such mission-driven businesses pursue both profits and certain social or moral goals. For certain corporations, these goals might include the advancement of the interests of particular racial communities that are socially or economically

198 *Id.* at 882. The court concluded that allowing the corporation to pursue its discrimination claims would further the purpose of the anti-discrimination provisions of the Fair Housing Act. *Id.*

199 *Id.* at 880.

disadvantaged. Such a public-oriented purpose could conceivably allow the corporation to invoke the race of the community it seeks to benefit and give the corporation racial standing for purposes of discrimination claims.

However, this raises the question of how prevalent the corporation's race-related purpose must be in relation to the corporation's other purposes, such as profit making. To what extent must the corporation's purposes be devoted to racial interests for the corporation to be able to claim a racial identity? If the corporation's purposes are divided equally between pursuing profits and furthering the interests of a racial community, would that be sufficient? Or must the corporation's predominant or majority purpose be dedicated to racial interests? How would the allocation of different corporate purposes be determined and weighed? Could a corporation, for example, plausibly state that seventy-five percent of its purpose is to promote racial interests, while the remaining twenty-five percent is assigned to profit making? Would the assignment and expression of the corporation's race-related purpose need to be explicitly articulated in the corporation's articles of incorporation, bylaws, and board resolutions? The complicated line drawing that is required to answer these questions raises the obvious difficulty with this approach to ascribing race to the corporate person. Moreover, the very determination of whether a stated corporate purpose actually has the effect of furthering the interests of a particular racial group involves subjective value judgments that are open to debate. Thus, this method of tying the racial identity of the corporate person to its stated purpose of benefiting racial groups raises challenges that can prevent its viability in certain circumstances.

4 CORPORATE RACIAL STANDING WITHOUT CORPORATE RACE

An alternative means of establishing corporate standing to sue for race discrimination abandons any attempt to impute a particular racial identity to the corporate person. Instead, the focus is on whether the corporation has suffered injury from racial discrimination directed against anyone with whom the corporation has a relationship. The foundation for this approach can be traced to early Supreme Court cases holding that a person can be injured by discriminatory conduct even if the person is not a member of a minority group. For instance, in *Sullivan v. Little Hunting Park, Inc.*, a white homeowner, who was expelled from his neighborhood park organization for renting a home to a black tenant and for protesting the organization's refusal to allow him to transfer his share of the park to the tenant, had standing to bring a race discrimination claim because he suffered injury allegedly in retaliation for trying to vindicate the rights of minorities under federal civil rights laws.[200] While the white homeowner was not a member of a protected

[200] Sullivan v. Little Hunting Park, Inc., 396 U.S. 229 (1969); *see also* Barrows v. Jackson, 346 U.S. 249 (1953) (holding that a white homeowner could raise Fourteenth Amendment objections to defend herself against efforts by another homeowner to enforce a racially discriminatory restrictive covenant that prevented her from transferring property to non-Caucasians).

racial minority, he still had standing to sue because he was being mistreated solely because of his association with someone of a minority race. Thus, a party need not be a minority to suffer harm from racial animus directed toward other individuals with whom the party has or seeks to have a relationship. From this perspective, any person, regardless of racial status, can challenge discriminatory treatment that injures the person's interests.

Several courts have adopted this line of thinking to allow corporations to bring causes of action for racially discriminatory acts without the need to find that the corporation itself has a race, so long as the corporation can point to injury that it has suffered due to the discrimination. Thus, the First Circuit in *Des Vergnes v. Seekonk Water District* held that a low-income housing development corporation had standing to sue a municipal water district under federal civil rights laws for denying the corporation's petition to have its land included within the water district allegedly due to a discriminatory intent to prevent low-income black individuals from moving into houses the corporation intended to build there.[201] The corporation argued that the water district's denial of its petition rendered the lots in its parcel of property less valuable and effectively punished the corporation for its willingness to contract with black individuals. Relying on the Supreme Court's reasoning in *Little Hunting Park*, the court acknowledged that one need not be a member of a protected racial class to invoke the federal civil rights laws. To effectuate the public policies embodied in such laws, the court concluded that "a person has an implied *right of action* against any other person who, with a racially discriminatory intent, interferes with his right to make contracts with non-whites … [or] injures him because he made contracts with non-whites."[202] Because the corporation's complaint adequately alleged that the water district's denial was racially motivated, the court held that the corporation had standing to bring its race discrimination claim even though the corporation itself had no particular racial identity, and even though the corporation did not name any specific member of the racially protected class who suffered discrimination.

The D.C. Circuit followed the same reasoning in *Gersman v. Group Health Ass'n, Inc.*, holding that a corporation had standing to bring a civil rights action against a customer that allegedly cancelled a contract with the corporation after the customer learned that one of the corporation's shareholders was Jewish.[203] The trial court dismissed the claim on the grounds that corporations as legally constructed entities have no racial or religious identity and cannot be the legally cognizable victims of discrimination. The D.C. Circuit disagreed and stated that "whether a corporation has a racial identity is not determinative of whether [it] has standing to bring a discrimination claim. Rather … if a corporation can suffer harm from

201 Des Vergnes v. Seekonk Water Dist., 601 F.2d 9 (1st Cir. 1979).

202 *Id.* at 14.

203 Gersman v. Grp. Health Ass'n., Inc., 931 F.2d 1565 (D.C. Cir. 1991), *vacated and remanded on other grounds*, 502 U.S. 1068 (1992) (mem.), *reinstated*, 975 F.2d 886 (D.C. Cir. 1992).

discrimination, it has standing to litigate that harm."[204] The court reasoned that the situation would be no different if non-Jewish shareholders owned the corporation and the customer ended the contractual relationship because the customer disliked the fact that the corporation had one single Jewish employee. In that case, the corporation would still suffer injury from the customer's discriminatory actions even though the corporation did not have predominantly Jewish owners or employees, or an imputed "Jewish identity."[205] The court also rejected any requirement that the corporation be incorporated expressly for the purpose of furthering the interests of a minority group. That the customer allegedly discontinued the contract with the corporation solely because an individual associated with the company was Jewish was sufficient to give the corporation standing to bring its discrimination claim for the injury it allegedly suffered.

This approach to corporate standing allows any corporation, even a "racially neutral" one, to pursue race discrimination claims when it "alleges that it was directly injured as the result of racial prejudice directed against a person with whom it has a relationship."[206] There is no need to analyze whether the corporation is officially certified as a minority owned business, or whether the racial composition of the corporation's owners, employees, or stakeholders is sufficient to establish an imputed corporate racial identity, or whether the corporation exists to serve the race-related purpose of furthering the interests of a specific racial group. The corporation has a cause of action, not because of a particular racial identity, but because it serves the purpose of discrimination law to permit corporations that have suffered actual harm as a result of racial discrimination to vindicate the rights that are protected by such laws.[207] As long as the corporation is a person that can suffer injuries cognizable under race discrimination statutes, it can seek a remedy for racially discriminatory acts aimed at others that have the effect of injuring the corporation. This manner of establishing corporate standing can be invoked for corporations of any size, whether large or small. Any corporation, regardless of the number or race of its shareholders, employees, or constituents, can be harmed when another party refuses to contract with the corporation out of racial bigotry toward any individual with whom the

204 *Id.* at 1568.

205 *Id.* at 1569.

206 Rosales v. AT&T Info. Sys., Inc., 702 F. Supp. 1489, 1497 (D. Colo. 1988); *cf.* Witte v. Zoological Soc'y of Phila., No. 06–3878, 2007 WL 433473, at *4 (E.D. Penn. 2007) ("[S]ection 1981 provides a remedy for any person or entity that has suffered actual harm as a result of racial discrimination, even if the discrimination was directed at a third party of a different race."). This expansive view of corporate standing has been adopted by several federal district courts to uphold the purposes of the federal civil rights statutes, regardless of the corporation's own racial identity. *See, e.g.*, John & Vincent Arduini Inc. v. NYNEX, 129 F. Supp. 2d 162 (N.D.N.Y. 2001) (holding that a corporation owned by two white shareholders had standing to bring a race discrimination claim against a customer that allegedly terminated a contract with the corporation in retaliation for the corporation's promoting a Hispanic employee to a supervisory position within the corporation).

207 *See* Coleman & Williams, Ltd. v. Wis. Dep't Workforce Dev., 401 F. Supp. 2d 938, 947 (E.D. Wis. 2005).

corporation has a current or anticipated relationship. This expansive view of discriminatory harm opens the door for more corporations to bring race discrimination claims when they suffer unequal treatment in business, regardless of the corporation's own racial affiliation.

*****

All the various ways of connecting the corporate person to a race for purposes of pursuing discrimination claims underscores the perception of corporations as separate persons who can suffer harm from unequal treatment. Whether it is because the corporation possesses the racial identity of the aggregate of its members, or because the corporation is capable of having a dedicated purpose to further racial interests, the corporation is viewed as a plausible claimant of racial equality rights.

As we have seen, the increasing extension of rights to the corporate person, be it in the context of corporate free speech, religious exercise, or racial equality, demonstrates the extent to which corporations are treated similarly to natural persons with fundamental interests that merit protection. The corporation as a person has status to claim important rights that flow from its own interests as an entity and that arise out of the interests of its members. When the corporation is perceived as having a very close link with its participants, as is the case in closely held corporations, we are more likely to attribute speech, religion, and race to the corporation.

The debates over corporate religion and race, like those involving corporate speech, reflect the many competing conceptions of the corporate person. Viewed as merely an artificial legal fiction, with no biology, sentience, or seeming spirituality of its own, the corporation seems unfit to claim a socially and legally recognizable religious or racial identity. Yet, as an association of individuals whose deepest beliefs and affiliations are connected to their religion or race, the corporation appears capable of serving as an extension of its members' own identities. The corporation is at once an independent entity, an aggregate of individuals, and a creature of the state. Its personhood is multifaceted. In the corporate religion and race cases, "we see the development of an image of the corporation as made up somehow of the people underlying it and simultaneously taking on some kind of status from the corporation as an entity. [The cases make little] sense under only one or the other of these [corporate personhood] theories; instead, the arguments depend on the ability to hold entity and aggregate stances simultaneously."[208]

Sometimes certain aspects of the corporation's personhood are more salient than others, and courts have appropriately focused more keenly on different aspects in varying circumstances. "[W]hile in some contexts the purposes for which the entity exists demands that its separateness be stressed, in others these purposes entail that we stress the role of the individuals joined in the common enterprise."[209] This is

[208] Gwendolyn Gordon, *Culture in Corporate Law or: A Black Corporation, a Christian Corporation, and a Māori Corporation Walk into a Bar . . .*, 39 SEATTLE U. L. REV. 353, 376 (2016).

[209] Grantham, *supra* note 109, at 69.

because the range of corporate organizations is vast. The nonprofit religious organization, the closely held minority business owned by a single shareholder, and the large publicly held corporation with thousands of shareholders are very different entities, but they are all incorporated organizations. They have different purposes, different needs, and different ways of interacting with their members and the public at large. They each have their own unique place in our cultural, political, and economic systems. Yet they share the same legal origin. The same law and social structure that facilitate the formation of Apple, Inc. also authorizes and fosters the formation of the local church on the corner and the small family restaurant owned by a husband and wife. The corporate form is flexible and enabling, affording its members broad opportunity to operate it in the manner they want, for the purposes they want.

As a result, we encounter a proliferation of different types of corporations lying along a spectrum of personhood. When legislatures and courts are confronted with the task of expanding or limiting the rights of these corporate persons, "[w]hat we see time and again is not the law's deference to some overarching conceptualization of the corporation and whatever logical consequences would flow therefrom, but rather a tailoring of rules and regulations to the particular business entity before it."[210] Absolutist positions arguing that corporations should always or should never be treated like natural persons, or that corporations of all types should be treated identically, do not account for the complexity of corporations. The multidimensional nature of the corporation and its continually evolving role in society require us to analyze corporate structure and function when determining whether and how our basic legal rights might apply to the many different types of corporations that exist along the continuum of corporate persons. These determinations are difficult, and the implications of treating certain corporations as persons whose speech, religion, and race are deserving of respect and protection are serious. The difficult issues of corporate rights and obligations will warrant careful analysis as our social, political, and legal systems evolve, and the types and purposes of corporations grow increasingly more diverse.

210 Colombo, *supra* note 53, at 191.

6

Abolishing Corporate Personhood

The topic of corporate personhood has generated disagreement and even dismay among a growing segment of the general public. Many people resist the notion that corporations can be considered persons for purposes of claiming constitutional rights. There is increasing concern about the expansion of corporate rights and corporate power in society. As discussed previously in Chapters 4 and 5, many people were outraged by the Supreme Court's decisions in *Citizens United* and *Hobby Lobby* to uphold corporate political speech rights and corporate religious exercise rights. The outrage stems from the belief that the rulings go too far in treating corporate persons with the same deference that is owed to natural persons. To say that the corporation is capable of engaging in speech and exercising religious beliefs, and is entitled to protection when it does so, appears to equate corporate entities with human beings. Viewing the corporation as a person with an entitlement to the same fundamental rights that belong to human individuals is regarded as a dangerous trend that gives corporations an elevated status they do not deserve. The mounting dissatisfaction with the idea that corporations can be considered persons for purposes of certain inalienable rights has galvanized some people to take action to roll back the status of corporations as persons under the law.

The last decade has seen dramatic growth among activist groups and community organizations that want to amend the United States Constitution to establish that the only persons who have constitutional rights are human beings, not corporations. Hundreds of grassroots organizations have worked to adopt local ordinances that reduce the political and economic power of corporations in their communities. In several states, officials at the state and municipal levels have supported these measures and are working to eliminate the doctrine of corporate personhood altogether. Members of Congress have introduced bills proposing amendments to the Constitution to reverse the *Citizens United* result and to abolish the personhood of corporations for purposes of all constitutional rights.

A social movement to address and attack corporate personhood has ebbed and flowed for many years, but it began to gain greater momentum after the *Citizens United* ruling. Participants in the movement believe that eliminating corporate personhood is the first step in abating what they regard as the increasingly coercive power wielded by corporations in the economic and political spheres of society. The overriding mission of these activist groups is to overthrow "corporate rule." I call them corporate abolitionists because they see their work as similar to that of the early abolitionists who demanded an end to slavery. One of their widely used slogans resonates with this theme: "Slavery is the legal fiction that a person is property. Corporate personhood is the legal fiction that property is a person."[1] The corporate abolitionists do not argue that large corporations must be more socially responsible or that we should adopt stricter laws to regulate corporate behavior and rein in corporate power. Instead, they believe the abolition of corporate personhood is an issue of human rights, like the abolition of slavery. They maintain that the whole institution is fundamentally wrong and must be eradicated if we are to have true democratic self-governance. In mobilizing their campaign to amend the Constitution, these activists hope to follow in the model of other social justice movements, like the suffragists and the civil rights activists, that successfully organized to demand reform.

The mission and methods of the corporate abolitionists are serious, and they have become very strategic in their efforts to move toward the complete revocation of the status of corporations as persons under the law. A book about corporate personhood would not be complete without some analysis of the impassioned effort to eliminate its legal effects altogether. This chapter looks carefully and objectively at this popular movement with an eye toward examining its goals, the organizations involved, the framing of their arguments, what their work has accomplished, and where their efforts are leading. It is important to understand what is at stake in the attempt to abolish corporate personhood from legal discourse entirely.

DISDAIN FOR CORPORATE PERSONHOOD AND POWER

Corporate abolitionists revile the dominance of corporations in modern society. They believe large corporations, with their vast concentrations of wealth and their enormous size, possess economic and political power comparable to government power.[2] Activists view multinational corporations as governing institutions whose presence permeates every aspect of "our lives, our government, our work, our health

[1] Molly Morgan & Jan Edwards, *Abolish Corporate Personhood*, 59 Guild Prac. 209, 214 (2002). In earlier works, I have examined the corporate abolitionist movement in the context of understanding the relationship between social movements and constitutional legal reform, as well as the legal source and maintenance of corporate power. *See* Susanna Kim Ripken, *Corporate First Amendment Rights After* Citizens United: *An Analysis of the Popular Movement to End the Constitutional Personhood of Corporations*, 14 U. Pa. J. Bus. L. 209, 224–44 (2011); Susanna Kim Ripken, Citizens United, *Corporate Personhood, and Corporate Power: The Tension Between Constitutional Law and Corporate Law*, 6 U. St. Thomas J. L. & Pub. Pol'y 285, 291–99 (2012). This chapter incorporates some of the analysis contained in those articles.

[2] Many scholars agree with this assessment of corporate power. *See, e.g.*, Kent Greenfield, The Failure of Corporate Law: Fundamental Flaws and Progressive Possibilities 4–5 (2006) (noting that

care and our food supply."[3] The economic power of these corporate entities unquestionably is significant. The largest corporations generate revenues that exceed the economies of many nation states.[4] They have the resources to drive out or acquire smaller businesses and eliminate competitive economic threats. They have access to tremendous amounts of cash, and they maintain control over substantial portions of earth's productive capacity.

Having control over such wealth produces unmatched political power. As discussed in Chapter 3, corporations are important players in the political system. Their role in lobbying government officials, in contributing to election campaigns, in exerting industry pressures on lawmakers and administrative agencies, and in heavily lawyering the rulemaking and enforcement processes, all allow corporations to "make changes to the political system itself that lock in lasting advantages for them and protect their dominance."[5] According to one member of Congress, "[t]oday there is virtually no element of the political landscape into which corporate influence has not intruded, and it is usually the strongest political force arrayed in any part of that landscape."[6] Anti-corporate activists believe that corporations' immense political influence threatens the integrity of our system of governance and renders it impossible for average citizens to have a meaningful voice in government.

Beyond their economic and political power, corporations also exert social and cultural power that has an impact on the desires, priorities, and behavior of consumers. Activists argue that corporate messaging plays a manipulative role in influencing our preferences, what we believe will make us happy, and how we view ourselves and others. This is a power that shapes our mindset and culture. So many aspects of our lives are governed by what corporations choose to do or not to do. Corporate decisions on what foods to produce, what products to manufacture, what services to offer, what research to fund, what drugs to market, what natural resources to use, what news to transmit, what forms of entertainment to make available, along with countless other fundamental corporate choices, directly impact our health, our work, our judgments, our activities, and the overall pace and quality of our lives. In these and other ways, corporations have profound effects on the basic structure and development of society.

In the view of corporate abolitionists, the prevalence and power of large corporations are a cause for deep concern because they serve only to corrupt our government

corporations are among the "largest and most powerful institutions in the world," wielding "the economic power of nations").

3 *About Us*, Alliance for Democracy, http://alliancefordemocracy.weebly.com/about-us.html [https://perma.cc/3HQS-UUUW].

4 *See* Joe Myers, *How Do the World's Biggest Companies Compare to the Biggest Economies?*, World Econ. F. (Oct. 19, 2016), www.weforum.org/agenda/2016/10/corporations-not-countries-dominate-the-list-of-the-world-s-biggest-economic-entities/ [https://perma.cc/G3QD-C3HQ].

5 Sheldon Whitehouse, Captured: The Corporate Infiltration of American Democracy, at xxii (2017).

6 *Id.*

and endanger our future. Activists contend that corporations "control the course and set the limits of public discussion, commercialize and debase our national consciousness, and manipulate mainstream public opinion. Everywhere the natural world is threatened. Yet people worldwide are exhorted to consume more and buy more in the name of 'progress' so big corporations can get bigger."[7] Activists believe the relentless pursuit of corporate profit is the greatest cause of political, economic, social, and ecological injury around the world. Although the corporation is subject to government regulation, the mighty grip that corporations have on the political system limits the government's ability to restrain the coercive power of corporations.

It was not always this way. The corporate abolitionists note that during the earliest years of corporations in America, states strictly limited corporations from gaining the kind of power they have today. As explained in Chapter 1, state legislatures historically granted special corporate charters to businesses on a case-by-case basis, and these charters typically went only to corporations serving a public function. Because a corporation derived its existence from the state, the state could restrict the powers of a corporation for the public interest. Laws kept corporate power in check out of fear that corporations, if left unbridled, would grow so large and amass such power that they would become oppressive and coercive.[8] When the Constitution was adopted, the Framers "took it as a given that corporations could be comprehensively regulated in the service of the public welfare."[9]

According to the corporate abolitionists, everything changed when the Supreme Court announced for the first time that corporations are persons under the Fourteenth Amendment. That was the tool corporations used to shift themselves "from the duty side of the line, where they're accountable to the people, to the rights side, where they get protection from government."[10] At that point, corporations were transformed into persons who could claim constitutional rights and compel the government to justify its regulations affecting corporate business activities. With this interpretation of the Fourteenth Amendment, corporations that had been subject to strict regulation of their operations became the bearer of rights to oppose legislation burdening their interests.

Activists call this the corporate "hijacking" of the Fourteenth Amendment, and they trace the roots and consolidation of corporate power directly to the concept of constitutional corporate personhood.[11] They blame corporate

7 Alliance for Democracy, *supra* note 3.

8 There was "[f]ear of encroachment upon the liberties and opportunities of the individual. Fear of the subjection of labor to capital. Fear of monopoly ... There was a sense of some insidious menace inherent in large aggregations of capital, particularly when held by corporations." Louis K. Liggett Co. v. Lee, 288 U.S. 517, 548–49 (1933) (Brandeis, J., dissenting).

9 Citizens United v. FEC, 558 U.S. 310, 428 (2010) (Stevens, J., dissenting).

10 Jan Edwards & Molly Morgan, *Abolish Corporate Personhood*, Reclaim Democracy (May 20, 2004), http://reclaimdemocracy.org/abolish-corporate-personhood/ [https://perma.cc/7K4V-NDQY].

11 *See* Doug Hammerstrom, *The Hijacking of the Fourteenth Amendment*, Reclaim Democracy (2002), http://reclaimdemocracy.org/wordpress/wp-content/uploads/2012/07/fourteenth_amendment_ham

personhood for allowing corporations over the last 130 years to gain one by one almost all the inalienable rights of human beings guaranteed by the Bill of Rights. In their view, *Citizens United* and *Hobby Lobby* continue the pattern of placing corporations in the same position as human beings for purposes of important constitutional and statutory rights. Although the majority opinions in *Citizens United* and *Hobby Lobby* did not explicitly rely on corporate personhood theories to justify their outcomes, corporate abolitionists contend that the unstated but key premise of those cases is that corporations are persons entitled to enjoy the same free speech and religious exercise rights as human individuals. Activists argue that these basic rights, combined with corporations' immense wealth and power, allow corporations to overpower individual citizens who consequently become second-class persons with little ability to oppose or resist corporate actions.[12] Many people fear that the corporate creation has now become more powerful than its human creators. This concern finds support in the work of some legal scholars who believe corporate rights threaten to undermine individual rights.[13]

Corporate abolitionists blame the Supreme Court for creating and entrenching corporate personhood in the law. They call the doctrine "illegitimate," a "fabrication," "fake constitutional law," and "unconstitutional folly."[14] They argue that the Court, an "unelected" body, "gave us corporate personhood," and "intentionally created this problem."[15] They maintain that the economic and political power of corporations is derived from corporations' status as legal persons, and corporate personhood is identified as the true "threat to authentic democratic self-

merstrom.pdf [https://perma.cc/TSL5-W5VE]. In line with this sentiment, one scholar calls the extension of the Fourteenth Amendment to corporations "one of the great perverse tragedies in legal history." William Quigley, *Catholic Social Thought and the Amorality of Large Corporations: Time to Abolish Corporate Personhood*, 5 Loy. J. Pub. Int. L. 109, 116 (2004).

12 *See* William Meyers, The Santa Clara Blues: Corporate Personhood versus Democracy 17–18 (2000), http://reclaimdemocracy.org/wordpress/wp-content/uploads/2012/07/santa_clara_blues.pdf [https://perma.cc/RZ78-XHY9]

13 *See* Tamara R. Piety, Brandishing the First Amendment: Commercial Expression in America 231 (2012) ("[Corporations'] power is already so great that they do not need the protection of the First Amendment. To the contrary, it is we who need protection from them."); Carl J. Mayer, *Personalizing the Impersonal: Corporations and the Bill of Rights*, 41 Hastings L.J. 577, 658 (1990) (The "extension of corporate constitutional rights is a zero-sum game that diminishes the rights and powers of real individuals.").

14 Jeffrey D. Clements, Corporations Are Not People: Why They Have More Rights Than You Do and What You Can Do About It 56 (2012); Greg Coleridge, *Gorsuch's Gory Expansion of Corporate Personhood*, By What Authority (Program on Corps., Law & Democracy, South Yarmouth, MA), Mar./Apr. 2017, www.poclad.org/BWA/files/2017/BWAMarchApril2017.pdf [https://perma.cc/N423-MQVW]; *Our Mission*, Free Speech For People, https://freespeechforpeople.org/our-mission/ [https://perma.cc/P5SX-ANF7].

15 Derek D. Cressman, When Money Talks: The High Price of "Free" Speech and the Selling of Democracy 149–50 (2016); Thom Hartmann, Unequal Protection: How Corporations Became "People" – and You Can Fight Back 322 (2d ed. 2010); Thom Hartmann, The Crash of 2016: The Plot to Destroy America – and What We Can Do to Stop It 207 (2013).

governance."[16] Indeed, activists portray corporations as being more than merely persons: "Corporations are now a sort of super-being: They can live forever, they cannot be jailed, they have no conscience—yet they also enjoy virtually all the rights that humans have."[17] "As long as superhuman 'corporate persons' have rights under the law, the vast majority of people have little or no effective voice in our political arena, which is why we see abolishing corporate personhood as so important to ending corporate rule and building a more democratic society."[18]

Corporate abolitionists say they are tired of trying to work within the existing legal structure to rein in corporate power with regulatory reform. Their sentiment is that it is futile to spend any more "strength, time, and hope" on pursuing "dead ends" such as "corporate responsibility, corporate accountability, corporate ethics, corporate codes of conduct, good corporate 'citizenship,' corporate crime, corporate reform, consumer protection, fixing regulatory agencies, or [helping] stakeholders."[19] These fixes do not address the real root of the problem. It is not corporate *behavior* that must be restricted, but corporate *status*. What the corporate abolitionists seek with their campaign to strip corporations of their status as persons is a transformation in the way corporations are viewed and treated in society so that corporations will always be regarded as subordinate institutions with no claim to inalienable rights. Activists believe the only way to accomplish this result is to take personhood away from corporations through a constitutional amendment.

In their call to action, corporate abolitionists view their work as similar to that of the historical abolitionists who successfully labored to end slavery, the suffragists who championed women's rights, the civil rights activists who opposed racial discrimination, and the American Revolutionaries who resisted political oppression in the name of democratic rule.[20] Corporate abolitionists believe that, like the abolition of slavery, the abolition of corporate personhood is supported by a moral imperative. They argue that the early abolitionists of the nineteenth century did not go to Congress to seek a Slavery Protection Act, or a Slavery Regulatory Agency, or a voluntary code of conduct for slave owners. The abolitionists viewed the institution of slavery as fundamentally and morally wrong, and therefore, "the whole thing had

[16] *Why Abolish All Corporate Constitutional Rights*, By What Authority (Program on Corps., Law & Democracy, South Yarmouth, MA), Nov. 2010, www.poclad.org/BWA/files/2010–11/BWANov2010.pdf [https://perma.cc/T3LD-UJXK].

[17] Doug Pibel, *Real People v. Corporate "People": The Fight Is On*, YES! Mag. (May 27, 2010), www.yesmagazine.org/issues/water-solutions/real-people-v.-corporate-people-the-fight-is-on [https://perma.cc/4B52-A787].

[18] Edwards & Morgan, *supra* note 10.

[19] Richard L. Grossman & Frank T. Adams, *Taking Care of Business: Citizenship and the Charter of Incorporation*, New Solutions, Spring 1993, at 7, 16; Cmty. Envtl. Legal Def. Fund et al., Model Brief of *Amici Curiae*, Preface (2003), www.ratical.org/corporations/demoBrief.pdf [https://perma.cc/8YWK-H6WZ].

[20] Kaitlin Sopoci-Belknap, Citizens United v. FEC: *Supreme Court Sides with Large Corporations*, Democracy Unlimited of Humboldt County (Feb. 28, 2010), www.duhc.org/profiles/blogs/citizens-united-v-fec-supreme [https://perma.cc/7GNE-E6DY].

to go."[21] In the same vein, corporate abolitionists insist constitutional corporate personhood must be dismantled in order to achieve democracy and equal rights. It is an all-or-nothing proposition. Through their push to amend the Constitution, the corporate abolitionists hope to "slay the dragon of corporate personhood once and for all."[22] Like other historical social movements that changed the culture to support a strategy to change the law, these activists stress the need for a grassroots effort to create a cultural shift in society favoring an amendment to the Constitution to limit constitutional rights to natural persons alone.

According to corporate abolitionists, the consequences of successfully abolishing the status of corporations as persons would be dramatic. They are confident that once corporate personhood is revoked, corporations will no longer be able to independently assert any constitutional rights. New laws and stricter regulation of corporate activity will be possible, and corporations will have no standing to challenge these laws. For example, without First Amendment rights, corporations could be prohibited from engaging in campaign spending and other forms of political activity. Without Fourth Amendment rights, government inspectors could more freely search corporate premises and seize corporate records to ensure compliance with various laws. Corporations could be prohibited from owning stock in other companies and prevented from becoming giant corporate conglomerates. Communities could ban corporations that exceed a certain size from operating in their towns and rely instead on local businesses and commerce. Corporations would once again be viewed as concessions of the government, subject to strict regulation and privileged to have only the limited rights the state chooses to bestow. The entire structure of society would be changed if corporations no longer dominated the political, social, and economic landscape. We could resume self-governance and "define our culture as we want to see it."[23] According to this viewpoint, the result of abolishing corporate personhood would be "a new flowering of freedom, democracy, and economic opportunity in America and around the world."[24]

PERSONHOOD THEORIES OF THE CORPORATION

It is clear from their rhetoric that the activists' preferred view of the corporation is in line with the artificial person or concession theory of the corporation. They insist that the corporation be regarded as simply a device created by the state, a concession of the government. The state defines the corporation's existence, the scope of its

21 Morgan & Edwards, *supra* note 1, at 213; *Why Abolish* All *Corporate Constitutional Rights, supra* note 16; *see also* Meyers, *supra* note 12, at 24 ("The abolition of corporate personhood is part of the abolition of slavery . . . This is not an optional campaign.").

22 Matthew Rothschild, *Corporations Aren't Persons: Amend the Constitution*, PROGRESSIVE, Apr. 2010, at 16, 20.

23 Doug Hammerstrom, *Why Bother with Corporate Personhood*, www.nancho.net/corperson/cpbother.html [https://perma.cc/K4XK-B7CQ].

24 Hartmann, UNEQUAL PROTECTION, *supra* note 15, at 296.

powers, and the limits of its activities. It is granted a charter by the state to operate for the lawful purposes permitted by the government and ultimately for the greater public interest. From this perspective, the corporation is merely a creature of law, an artificial, legal fiction. It is not, nor should it be analogized to, a real person. The corporation is an economic tool and nothing more.[25]

Corporate abolitionists reject the real entity theory of the corporate person, and they vehemently oppose language that anthropomorphizes corporations. They emphasize that corporations do not eat, sleep, dance, raise children, fight in wars, get sick, or lose loved ones. They argue that corporations have none of the truly essential elements that define the human condition. Corporate abolitionists commonly assert that corporations have no soul or conscience, no mental or emotional capacities, no internal moral compass or values. Corporations have no capacity for virtue or loyalty, nor are they designed for it. The corporation's sole objective is to pursue profit and externalize the costs of doing so on others.

Although corporate abolitionists resist any descriptions of corporations in human like terms, they interestingly and perhaps unwittingly have similar tendencies to speak of corporations in real person terms. They characterize corporations as "single-minded," and "determined." Corporations are "relentless pursuers of profit," with "appetites that are never satisfied." Corporations shrewdly plot to overpower citizens and undermine regulation. They seek to subvert the social order, corrupt our democratic system, promote irresponsible consumption, and brainwash society. Corporations are commonly referred to as self-interested "psychopaths" or "homicidal serial killers" holding little regard for others.[26] While activists maintain corporations have no virtues, feelings, desires, and beliefs, they routinely speak of "corporate greed," "corporate evil," and "corporate barbarity." Words such as "dominant," "diabolical," "tyrannical," and "pathological" appear often in the speeches and literature of the corporate abolitionists.

On some level, these descriptions draw on a view of corporations as more than merely an artificial legal fiction or inanimate tool. Rather, the corporation is portrayed as a driven, unrelenting person or being that makes deliberate choices to fulfill its desires in its own self-interest. Many people are comfortable making moral judgments about corporations because they believe corporations have obligations to act morally, honestly, and ethically. When corporations violate those expectations,

[25] *See* Clements, *supra* note 14, at 60–61, 67; Coleridge, *supra* note 14 ("Corporations are legal, subordinate creations of *We the People*. These artificial entities should receive only privileges, not rights, as authorized by the public.").

[26] *See* Joel Bakan, *Psychopaths, Inc.: On Corporate Personhood*, *in* THE OCCUPY HANDBOOK 353 (Janet Byrne ed., 2012); Bruce A. Dixon, *Time for a Corporate Death Penalty*, BLACK AGENDA REP. (June 9, 2010), https://blackagendareport.com/content/time-corporate-death-penalty [https://perma.cc/4GX9-H3KZ]. At times, corporations have even been described as living, albeit non-human, organisms: "Corporations function like retroviruses, taking over the rights and protections that we created for ourselves, and then using them against us, their human hosts." Greg Coleridge, *The System Isn't Broken, It's Fixed: Ending Big Money and Corporations in Our Elections*, 44 U. TOLEDO L. REV. 541, 553 (2013).

they become targets of blame and condemnation. Such feelings of moral blame would not be appropriate if directed to a merely inanimate object. Thus, invoking elements of the real entity aspects of the corporate person seems unavoidable even in the discourse of anti-corporate activists.

What is conspicuously missing from this activist discourse is any reference to the aggregate concept of the corporate person. Under the aggregate view, the corporation is more than a creature of law. Its existence depends on the aggregate of the actual human beings who underlie the corporate form. The justification for many of the Supreme Court's most controversial decisions regarding corporate constitutional rights has relied on the aggregate conception of the corporation as an association of the human individuals who make up the corporation. Those individuals are the ones whose rights are at stake. Under this view, the corporation is really the people who, by private contract, decide to participate together in an incorporated business. They do not lose their rights when they opt to operate their enterprise as a corporation. The Supreme Court has often looked through the corporation to the real people within and upheld the corporation's right as a means of upholding theirs.

Corporate abolitionists rarely mention or acknowledge the aggregate aspects of the corporation. Indeed, they often discount the aggregate view, if not reject it altogether. Holding steadfastly to the artificial person theory of the corporation, they argue that corporations "cannot exist by private arrangement."[27] They must be chartered by the state, and no amount of private contracting can form a legally recognized corporation. Corporate abolitionists disagree with the Supreme Court's view of the corporation as an aggregate of the human individuals who make up the corporation. Instead, they insist that a "corporation is not a person, nor is it an association or a group of people. A corporation is a creation of law, a *public* tool of economic policy."[28] Thus, corporate abolitionists have a very narrow theoretical vision of the corporation, one that focuses solely on the artificial person aspects of the corporation. This allows activists to argue that corporations are only what We the People say they are, nothing more and nothing less. Whatever privileges the legislature elects to extend to corporations are the prerogative of the state, and corporations have no independent basis for asserting any other rights. That the Supreme Court has treated corporations as independent persons or as representatives of their human members for purposes of constitutional rights is viewed by corporate abolitionists as deeply flawed and unsupportable. They believe now is the time for a popular uprising to undo this result. Their preferred method for doing so is to amend the Constitution to clarify that only human beings, not corporate entities, are persons entitled to constitutional rights. The movement, called "Move to Amend," seeks to abolish corporate personhood and invalidate all the fundamental constitutional rights that are currently afforded to corporations.

[27] Clements, *supra* note 14, at 60.
[28] *Id.* at 56.

MOVE TO AMEND

Many people reacted negatively when the Supreme Court in *Citizens United* invalidated strict campaign finance laws and upheld the First Amendment free speech rights of corporations to spend their money to support or oppose candidates in federal elections. Polls showed that a large majority of the public disfavored the ruling.[29] The Move to Amend campaign was launched to push for the adoption of a twenty-eighth amendment to the Constitution to declare that corporations are not persons entitled to any constitutional rights and that the spending of money is not political speech entitled to First Amendment protection.

Move to Amend is an outgrowth of several activist organizations that have been in existence for some time and have expressed a commitment to "ending corporate rule, and building a vibrant democracy that is genuinely accountable to the people, not corporate interests."[30] Nationwide, several hundred grassroots community-based groups have endorsed or joined the Move to Amend coalition. Many of these organizations are themselves extensive coalitions of other progressive groups that together create a national network of activists that support the campaign. The organizations include, for example, the Alliance for Democracy, the National Lawyers Guild, the Program on Corporations, Law & Democracy, Reclaim Democracy, and the Liberty Tree Foundation.[31]

Move to Amend activists have adopted the following petition as a centerpiece of their campaign: "We, the People of the United States of America, reject the U.S. Supreme Court's *Citizens United* ruling and other related cases, and move to amend our Constitution to firmly establish that money is not speech, and that human beings, not corporations, are persons entitled to constitutional rights."[32] Citizens are asked to sign the petition and endorse the effort to retract all constitutional rights from corporations. As of the time of this writing, approximately 460,000 signatures have been collected.[33]

The campaign engages in grassroots efforts to encourage cities and counties to pass official resolutions in support of amending the Constitution to abolish corporate personhood. Activists work with local organizations to draft resolutions for city

[29] *See* Dan Eggen, *Poll: Large Majority Opposes Supreme Court's Decision on Campaign Financing*, Wash. Post (Feb. 17, 2010), www.washingtonpost.com/wp-dyn/content/article/2010/02/17/AR2010021701151.html [https://perma.cc/7RQD-ZEDQ]. A recent survey indicated that most respondents support a constitutional amendment to effectively overturn *Citizens United*. *See* Ashley Balcerzak, *Study: Most Americans Want to Kill 'Citizens United' with Constitutional Amendment*, Ctr. Pub. Integrity (May 10, 2018), www.publicintegrity.org/2018/05/10/21739/study-most-americans-want-kill-citizens-united-constitutional-amendment [https://perma.cc/4SKF-2PGJ].

[30] *MTA Coalition*, Move to Amend, https://movetoamend.org/about-us [https://perma.cc/NGE7-FTZQ].

[31] *Endorsing Organizations*, Move to Amend, https://movetoamend.org/organizations [https://perma.cc/C3WR-EWNP].

[32] *Motion to Amend ~ Sign the Petition*, Move to Amend, https://movetoamend.org/motion [https://perma.cc/HFF4-695M].

[33] *Id.*

councils to adopt, as well as ballot initiatives for voting citizens to approve.[34] Move to Amend's goal is to create a groundswell of support at the municipal level in favor of amending the Constitution so that state legislatures and Congress will then be prompted to act. "When enough local communities have passed ordinances that directly challenge corporate personhood, state legislatures will begin to notice … [E]ventually the federal government will get on board."[35] Activists believe that the "[p]assage of a critical mass of [constitutional amendment] resolutions throughout the country will bring decisive pressure on Congress to finish the job."[36]

Move to Amend works alongside several other progressive groups with the goal of amending the Constitution and nullifying the *Citizens United* result. Organizations such as Free Speech For People, Common Cause, Public Citizen, People for the American Way, and American Promise, all support the adoption of a twenty-eighth amendment to the Constitution to curb the impact of corporate power on the political system. But tensions arise among these and other activist groups over the best strategies for accomplishing their common goal. Move to Amend is highly critical of other groups that promote a constitutional amendment that focuses primarily on campaign finance reform by forbidding corporations from spending money in political elections. While this strategy addresses the *Citizens United* result, Move to Amend and other corporate abolitionist groups believe it is weak and insufficient. In their view, revoking First Amendment corporate political speech rights to reverse *Citizens United* is a start, but not nearly enough to cut off the source of corporate power. Rather, they argue corporate personhood itself must be abolished, and any new constitutional amendment must explicitly affirm that corporations have no entitlement to *any* constitutional rights because they possess no standing as persons to claim them.[37]

Moreover, some activists believe that unions and nonprofit entities should be permitted to maintain their personhood status and that only for-profit corporations should be denied constitutional rights. However, other activist groups like Move to Amend contend that all corporate entities, whether nonprofit or for-profit, are strictly artificial persons created by the state, and none should be regarded as persons for any constitutional rights.[38]

Consequently, there is considerable disagreement over the language and scope of the proposed constitutional amendment, with some groups advocating a much more

34 *Pass a Local Resolution*, Move to Amend, https://movetoamend.org/pass-local-resolution [https://perma.cc/6ZLN-6MBR].

35 Hartmann, Unequal Protection, *supra* note 15, at 295–96.

36 Clements, *supra* note 14, at 153.

37 Move to Amend, The Path to the 28th Amendment: Strategic Plan to Pass the "We the People Amendment" to the United States Constitution 8–10 (2016), https://movetoamend.org/sites/default/files/move_to_amend_strategic_plan.pdf [https://perma.cc/24K3-V8WM].

38 *See* Move to Amend, *Why Non Profit Corporations Do Not Need (or Have) Constitutional Rights*, https://movetoamend.org/sites/default/files/non_profits_dont_need_constitutional_rights.pdf [https://perma.cc/QE4B-3K3F].

radical and progressive agenda, and others adopting a more mainstream and diplomatic approach.[39] In an effort to facilitate cooperation and consolidation, the American Promise group has recently begun a "Writing the 28th Amendment" program with the intent to build national consensus on effective language for a constitutional amendment.[40]

STATE AND LOCAL SUPPORT FOR ABOLISHING CORPORATE PERSONHOOD

The requirements for amending the Constitution are stringent. A proposed amendment requires approval from two thirds of Congress, and then three quarters of the states must ratify it. Alternatively, two thirds of the states can call a constitutional convention to consider the amendment and then three quarters of the states must ratify it.[41] Requiring such a supermajority of Congress and the states to agree on any issue poses a formidable challenge. Roughly 12,000 proposals to amend the Constitution have been introduced in Congress since the Constitution's ratification, but only twenty-seven have been adopted as constitutional amendments, ten of which comprised the Bill of Rights. In addition, although various states have filed hundreds of different petitions with Congress to call a constitutional convention to propose amendments, a convention has never occurred because the requisite supermajority of the states has never been met.[42]

The movement to end corporate personhood through a constitutional amendment has made inroads in various states and met with some degree of success. Move to Amend and other activist groups have aggressively engaged in grassroots efforts to prompt city councils and state legislatures to adopt resolutions urging Congress to propose a constitutional amendment eliminating the status of corporations as persons for purposes of constitutional rights.

Movement organizers claim that to date nineteen states have made some type of formal declaration in support of a constitutional amendment, whether through

39 *See* Joel Bleifuss, *Corporations Are Not People*, IN THESE TIMES (Sept. 19, 2011), http://inthesetimes.com/article/11937/corporations_are_not_people [https://perma.cc/7XVZ-ZYRK] (discussing contrasting strategies of different activist groups). Some anti-corporate activist groups believe the corporate abolitionist movement is not radical enough. They argue that attempting to eliminate corporate personhood through the constitutional amendment procedure is futile because it requires dependence on federal and state lawmakers who are members of a corrupt corporate political power system. Instead, some activists encourage civil disobedience and defiance of corporate rights, emphasizing the need to "become revolutionaries, not reformers." Cmty. Envtl. Legal Def. Fund, *Statement on Efforts to Amend the U.S. Constitution Following* Citizens United (Jan. 2012), https://celdf.org/wp-content/uploads/2015/08/CELDF-CITIZENS-UNITED-STATEMENT-JANUARY-17-2012.pdf [https://perma.cc/7AK8-F4UW].

40 *Vision/Mission*, AM. PROMISE, www.americanpromise.net/who_we_are#vision_mission [https://perma.cc/GR3R-2LNG].

41 U.S. CONST. art. V.

42 Roger C. Hartley, HOW FAILED ATTEMPTS TO AMEND THE CONSTITUTION MOBILIZE POLITICAL CHANGE 2–3 (2017).

official resolutions in the state legislature, ballot initiatives approved by voters in statewide elections, or formal letters to Congress signed by a majority of state lawmakers. Considering they will need thirty-eight states (i.e., three fourths of the states) to ratify the amendment, movement organizers claim that they are already half-way there.[43]

However, not all the nineteen states supporting a constitutional amendment have explicitly demanded an end to corporate personhood per se. Rather, many states merely advocate a constitutional amendment that would allow for stricter regulation of corporate spending in elections, thereby reversing the effect of *Citizens United*, but not suggesting that corporations should be stripped of standing as persons for purposes of all constitutional rights. For example, the Nevada legislature passed a joint resolution in 2017 that urges Congress to propose a constitutional amendment allowing the federal government and the states to regulate political contributions and expenditures. Although the recitals of the resolution describe *Citizens United* as a precedent that "harm[s] our democratic system of government," the text of the resolution contains no language condemning corporate personhood or calling for its abolition.[44] Similarly, the Maine legislature in 2013 approved a joint resolution declaring support for a constitutional amendment "regarding campaign finance that would reaffirm the power of citizens through their government to regulate the raising and spending of money in elections;" the language of the resolution does not refer to the personhood of corporations.[45] These and other states favor a constitutional amendment, but their focus is more generally on defining the scope of political speech rights, reforming campaign finance restrictions, and regulating corporate spending in elections, rather than targeting corporate personhood.

There are several states, however, that have explicitly raised concerns about corporate personhood and have expressed support for a constitutional amendment allowing only natural persons, not corporate entities, to claim constitutional rights. For example, the Illinois state legislature in 2013 passed a joint resolution calling on Congress "to propose and send to the states for ratification a constitutional amendment to overturn Citizens United" and "make clear that the rights of persons protected by the Constitution are the rights of natural persons and not those of corporations or other artificial entities."[46] Other states have utilized a direct written communication to Congress, rather than a state resolution, to express the same sentiment. For instance,

43 The nineteen states that appear to have indicated support for a constitutional amendment are California, Colorado, Connecticut, Delaware, Hawaii, Illinois, Maine, Maryland, Massachusetts, Montana, Nevada, New Jersey, New Mexico, New York, Oregon, Rhode Island, Vermont, Washington, and West Virginia. *See State and Local Support*, United for the People, http://united4thepeople.org/state-and-local-support-2/ [https://perma.cc/M3AW-WYXN]; Free Speech For People, 2017 End of Year Update 4, https://freespeechforpeople.org/wp-content/uploads/2018/03/2017-Annual-Report-.pdf [https://perma.cc/KYB8-Z45E].

44 S.J. Res. 4, 79th Leg. (Nev. 2017).

45 S.P. 548, 126th Leg., 1st Reg. Sess. (Me. 2013).

46 S.J. Res. 27, 98th Gen. Assemb. (Ill. 2013).

in 2012, a majority of state legislators in Connecticut signed and sent a letter to Congressional representatives in support of a constitutional amendment to overturn *Citizens United* and to "firmly establish that money is not speech and that human beings, not corporations, are persons entitled to constitutional rights."[47] These types of calls for a constitutional amendment contain personhood language highlighting the difference between corporations and human individuals.

At the local level, activists assert that approximately 800 cities and counties have approved resolutions and ballot measures calling for a constitutional amendment to revoke corporate personhood and/or authorize the regulation of corporate political spending. Chicago, Kansas City, Santa Fe, and Tucson are among the hundreds of cities that have formally expressed support for the constitutional amendment campaign in the last several years.[48]

One activist group called Wolf-PAC has focused on the alternative route to amending the Constitution: having two thirds of the states formally petition Congress to call a constitutional convention to amend the Constitution. To date, five states have officially adopted resolutions calling for a constitutional convention to propose an amendment to address corporate political spending and to overturn *Citizens United*.[49]

It is not entirely clear how long these various state and municipal resolutions, letters, and referenda remain in effect to express the sentiment of their respective decision-making bodies. Some may last indefinitely while others over time may no longer represent the state or locality's position and therefore require a renewed resolution by the state or city. For example, Illinois's joint resolution favoring a constitutional amendment was adopted in 2013. If it takes another ten years for the Move to Amend campaign to get a total of thirty-eight states to indicate support for the amendment, Move to Amend may not be able to still count Illinois as

47 Letter from Conn. Gen. Assembly to Conn. U.S. Representatives (May 1, 2012), https://org2.salsalabs.com/o/7003/images/CTStateRepstoFeds.pdf [https://perma.cc/A8C7-VL44]; *Connecticut Calls for Constitutional Amendment to Overturn Citizens United*, PUB. CITIZEN (Sep. 12. 2012), www.citizen.org/media/press-releases/connecticut-calls-constitutional-amendment-overturn-citizens-united [https://perma.cc/NY6S-JCT9].

48 *See Resolutions & Ordinances*, MOVE TO AMEND, https://movetoamend.org/resolutions-map [https://perma.cc/PC32-Y732]; *State and Local Support, supra* note 43; *2017 in Review*, AM. PROMISE, www.americanpromise.net/who_we_are#2017_year_end_report [https://perma.cc/RGF8-VQV7] ("800 cities and towns hav[e] passed local 28th Amendment resolutions.").

49 The five states are California, Illinois, New Jersey, Rhode Island, and Vermont. *See* David Guldenschuh, *Article V Progress Report*, ARTICLE V CAUCUS, http://articlevcaucus.com/news/article-v-progress-report-4/ [https://perma.cc/25QX-N4SC]. Some activist groups strongly oppose this approach because a constitutional convention has never been used before to propose amendments, and there are no settled rules or procedures to govern the convention once it is convened. They argue that the convention could potentially be unlimited in scope, might result in the elimination of other established constitutional rights, and runs the dangerous risk of producing a wholesale rewrite of the Constitution. *See* Common Cause, *U.S. Constitution Threatened as Article V Convention Movement Nears Success* (Feb. 2018), www.commoncause.org/wp-content/uploads/2018/03/Article-V-Memo-Feb-2018.pdf [https://perma.cc/4H43-2Q8Z].

a supporter state in the year 2029 if its resolution was passed in 2013.[50] In any case, corporate abolitionists claim there is currently significant popular interest nationwide to envision an amendment that would limit or eliminate constitutional rights for corporations, either specifically in the context of First Amendment political speech, or altogether for all rights enumerated in the Constitution.

FEDERAL SUPPORT FOR ABOLISHING CORPORATE PERSONHOOD

At the federal level, members of Congress have introduced various resolutions proposing a constitutional amendment. These resolutions address the status of corporations as holders of constitutional rights. One resolution, the "We the People Amendment," is the version endorsed by the Move to Amend campaign.[51] The resolution proposes a constitutional amendment providing that the "rights protected by the Constitution ... are the rights of natural persons only. Artificial entities, such as corporations, limited liability companies, and other entities ... shall have no rights under this Constitution" and the "privileges of artificial entities ... shall not be construed to be inherent or inalienable."[52] The intent of the resolution is to forbid *all* entities, whether for-profit corporations, nonprofit corporations, or unions, from claiming *any* constitutional rights. While some activists suggest that an exemption should be made for nonprofit organizations and unions, Move to Amend maintains that all corporate entities are created by state charter, and it "is not intellectually honest to attempt to create a constitutional exemption for the types of artificial entities that one likes but not for the ones one doesn't like ... Because only people have rights, and only people are people."[53] This proposed amendment seeks to eliminate more than merely the First Amendment political speech (i.e., political spending) rights of corporate entities. It targets all the rights corporations have ever gained under the Constitution and revokes the standing of corporations to claim any of them.

[50] The Illinois Legislative Glossary's definition of "resolution" states that a "resolution is merely to express the opinion of one or both houses ... [and] is typically temporary in character." *Illinois Legislative Glossary*, ILL. GEN. ASSEMBLY, www.ilga.gov/legislation/glossary.asp#R [https://perma.cc/CW5K-TSFZ].

[51] H.R.J. Res. 48, 115th Cong. (2017); *Move to Amend's Proposed 28th Amendment to the Constitution*, MOVE TO AMEND, https://movetoamend.org/wethepeopleamendment [https://perma.cc/5AFB-5KVM]. The resolution was introduced by Rep. Richard Nolan on Jan. 30, 2017. He has proposed the same resolution in the last two Congresses, but it did not gain approval. *See* H.R.J. Res. 48, 114th Cong. (2015); H.R.J. Res. 29, 113th Cong. (2013).

[52] H.R.J. Res. 48, 115th Cong. § 1 (2017). The proposed constitutional amendment would also require the government to regulate political spending in elections, and it would forbid the judiciary from equating the spending of money in elections with political speech protected by the First Amendment. *See id.* at § 2.

[53] Move to Amend, *Why Non Profit Corporations Do Not Need (or Have) Constitutional Rights*, *supra* note 38.

Another Congressional resolution is the "Democracy for All Amendment," which is endorsed by Free Speech For People.[54] The resolution proposes a constitutional amendment declaring that Congress and the states "may distinguish between natural persons and corporations or other artificial entities created by law, including by prohibiting such entities from spending money to influence elections."[55] The language of the proposed amendment is permissive, not mandatory. It does not call for the abolition of corporate personhood for all constitutional rights. Rather, it allows the government in its discretion to treat natural persons and corporate entities differently for purposes of regulating political spending. Move to Amend organizers and other corporate abolitionists are highly critical of this proposed amendment, calling it "a half-measure that – at best – takes us back to the pre-*Citizens United* era [where] corporations and the wealthy still dominated the political process."[56] They argue that merely overturning *Citizens United* or taking away corporate political speech rights is not enough. Instead, they believe that a complete revocation of corporate personhood under the Constitution is necessary to effectively address the problems associated with the power of corporations to influence not only politics and elections, but also the overall direction and well-being of society.

An alternative resolution addresses the meaning of personhood directly. The "People's Rights Amendment" proposes a constitutional amendment declaring that the rights protected by the Constitution are the rights of natural persons only, and the word "person" in the Constitution does "not include corporations, limited liability companies or other corporate entities."[57] The intent of the resolution is to establish that corporations are not persons entitled to claim any constitutional rights whatsoever. This is a broader approach that seeks to ensure only human individuals,

54 H.R.J. Res. 31, 115th Cong. (2017); S.J. Res. 8, 115th Cong. (2017). *The Democracy for all Amendment*, FREE SPEECH FOR PEOPLE, https://freespeechforpeople.org/the-amendment/democracy-for-all-amendment/ [https://perma.cc/58QC-ET5J]. The resolution was introduced by Rep. Theodore Deutch in the House on January 24, 2017, with an identical resolution introduced by Sen. Tom Udall in the Senate. The same resolution was introduced in the last two Congresses, but it failed to gain approval. *See* H.R.J. Res. 22, 114th Cong. (2015); S.J. Res. 5, 114th Cong. (2015); H.R.J. Res. 119, 113th Cong. (2014); S.J. Res. 19, 113th Cong. (2013). The resolution was debated in the Senate in 2014 and resulted in a Senate majority vote (fifty-four Senators) in favor of the resolution, falling short of the two-thirds majority (sixty-seven Senators) needed to pass. John Nichols, *The Senate Tried to Overturn 'Citizens United' Today. Guess What Stopped Them?*, NATION (Sep. 11, 2014), www.thenation.com/article/senate-tried-overturn-citizens-united-today-guess-what-stopped-them/ [https://perma.cc/J9PG-6JZW].

55 H.R.J. Res. 31, 115th Cong. § 2 (2017). The proposed constitutional amendment would also allow the government to regulate political spending in elections. *See id.* at § 1.

56 MOVE TO AMEND, THE PATH TO THE 28TH AMENDMENT, *supra* note 37, at 9.

57 H.R.J. Res. 88, 115th Cong. § 2 (2017). The resolution was introduced by Rep. James McGovern in the House on March 10, 2017. A similar resolution was introduced by Sen. Jon Tester in the Senate. *See* S.J. Res. 20, 115th Cong. (2017). The same resolutions were introduced in the last two Congresses but failed to gain approval. *See* H.R.J. Res. 23, 114th Cong. (2015); S.J. Res. 7, 114th Cong. (2015); H.R.J. Res. 21, 113th Cong. (2013); S.J. Res. 18, 113th Cong. (2013).

not corporate entities, are the holders of the rights guaranteed under the Constitution.

While all these resolutions have gained multiple co-sponsors in Congress, to date Congress has not passed any of these or other resolutions in favor of a proposed constitutional amendment limiting corporate constitutional rights. The corporate abolitionists are well aware of the uphill battle they face in Congress, but they continue to emphasize their grassroots efforts at the state and local levels to drive a nationwide popular movement that they believe Congress will eventually have to acknowledge. Drawing inspiration from social movements of the past that have effectuated transformational changes in society and the law, corporate abolitionists assert, "History shows that when the public is sufficiently aroused, actions that once seemed impossible can, in hindsight, seem inevitable."[58]

THE LANGUAGE OF CORPORATE PERSONHOOD

Critics of the corporate abolitionist movement suggest that activists are making too much ado about corporate personhood and blowing its significance out of proportion. Defenders of corporate rights often dismiss activists' attacks on corporate personhood with the reply, "Of course, corporations are not actually people. Everyone knows that." The statement implies that the clamor over the personhood status of corporations is unwarranted and exaggerates the significance of calling the corporation a person under the law. Courts have never said that corporations have rights because they are literally persons. Corporate personhood is a useful concept that allows corporations to enter into contracts, own property, and conduct business in the corporate name. Supporters of corporate personhood argue that activists' continual indictment of corporate personhood as the source of coercive corporate power and political dominance is misguided and unhelpful. While corporate abolitionists perceive corporate personhood as a treacherous weapon that threatens democracy and self-governance, those who disagree believe that corporate personhood is a red herring and that activists should stop fussing over it.[59]

Corporate abolitionists find it ironic that those who dismiss corporate personhood as "no big deal" also simultaneously argue that it is important not to abolish it because it is essential for the proper functioning of the legal system and the flow of commerce.

[58] Fran Korten, 10 *Ways to Stop Corporate Dominance of Politics*, YES! MAG. (Jan. 25, 2010), www.yesmagazine.org/people-power/10-ways-to-stop-corporate-dominance-of-politics [https://perma.cc/KZT6-FXWV].

[59] *See* Kent Greenfield, *In Defense of Corporate Persons*, 30 CONST. COMMENT. 309 (2015); Eric Posner, *Stop Fussing over Personhood*, SLATE (Dec. 11, 2013), www.slate.com/articles/news_and_politics/view_from_chicago/2013/12/personhood_for_corporations_and_chimpanzees_is_an_essential_legal_fiction.html [https://perma.cc/3AR2-DHFT]; *see also* Kent Greenfield, CORPORATIONS ARE PEOPLE TOO (AND THEY SHOULD ACT LIKE IT) 27–28 (2018) (arguing that "we should stop fighting corporate personhood" and instead adopt more pluralistic corporate governance structures that allow corporations to "behave more like people").

Activists contend that the practice of calling the corporation a person under the law has become more than a convenient fiction that facilitates commerce. They believe that attributing personhood to corporations suggests a moral equality and political commensurability between living persons and corporate entities that results in uniquely empowering corporations and disempowering human individuals.

Some legal scholars agree with this point. They reject the suggestion that personhood is not important. On the contrary, in their view, personhood matters, and it matters a lot.[60] Calling the corporation a person has substantial rhetorical power because of our deeply held belief that all persons are entitled to be treated equally, with dignity and respect. Our legal system is strongly committed to affording all people equal rights, and we generally condemn instances of discrimination among persons. When the corporation is viewed as a person, we are all the more inclined to afford it the same rights that are typically afforded only to human beings under the Constitution. Many believe that the personhood concept becomes misleading and dangerous at this point because it portrays the corporation as an embattled victim in need of protection from overbearing and discriminatory government power. Referring to corporations as persons invokes the cherished notions of autonomy, freedom, and fairness that are intrinsically associated with personhood. If the corporation is a person, then it is deserving of the rights that we as a civilized society extend to all those with that status. The idea that corporations are persons makes the establishment of corporate rights seem natural and self-evident.[61]

It is true that the Supreme Court did not explicitly rely on theories of corporate personhood as the justification for its holdings in *Citizens United* and *Hobby Lobby*. But a good chunk of the general public certainly seemed to perceive that personhood was the reason behind those decisions. The idea that corporations as persons must be afforded the same free speech rights and the same religious freedom rights as human beings is what prompted some of the strongest public opposition to those rulings.[62] Activists' attacks on corporate personhood arise from their belief that the personification of corporations is what gives corporations power in society. Reformers argue that "[w]hen we begin to insist that corporate money is not 'speech' and that corporations are not people, we begin to take back power."[63]

Much of this debate relates to the ability of language to reflect and to influence our beliefs and our perceptions of the world and reality. As discussed in Chapter 1,

60 *See, e.g.*, Tamara R. Piety, *Why Personhood Matters*, 30 CONST. COMMENT. 361 (2015).

61 *See id.* at 363, 384–85.

62 Shortly after the *Citizens United* decision, several members of Congress proposed a resolution to express disapproval of the case, specifically criticizing the Court for "treating corporations and living persons equally with respect to free speech rights under the First Amendment [and] effectively bestow[ing] on corporations aspects of personhood, which ... ensures that ... individual citizens ... must now compete against ... the vast resources of multibillion dollar, multinational corporations, thus diminishing the [free speech rights of] individual citizen[s]." H.R. Res. 1275, 111th Cong. (2010).

63 Clements, *supra* note 14, at 56.

the fact that we talk about corporations in the language of personhood is not insignificant. Language as a system of discourse conditions the way people think about things and interpret the world around them. Beyond merely reflecting societal views and values, language helps form them. The way we speak about corporations has a role in shaping our understanding of them and our judgments about them. Continually referring to corporations as persons may reveal certain perceptions of what corporations are or how they should be treated. But the practice of labelling a corporation a person may also nudge us toward viewing the corporation in a certain light and treating it in a certain way. We should not underestimate the power of words and language to influence thought and judgments. The vocabulary we use to characterize corporations affects the manner in which we perceive and relate to them. In this sense, labels matter.[64]

As mentioned in Chapter 3, postmodern philosophies view language as the medium through which our social world is constructed. Things around us become what they are and have their meaning as a result of the way we talk about them. To give something a name or a label, to speak about it in a particular way, and to verbalize a set of ideas around it, have powerful constitutive effects on what it becomes, how it is regarded, and why we treat it one way as opposed to another. "Language doesn't just describe; it creates, and partly constitutes, what it both describes and creates."[65]

If this is true, then centers of power within society have the profound ability to decide how our social reality is constructed because "anyone who controls discourse can make something exist, or disappear."[66] If you can control the direction of the discourse, you can shape the social world. Those who exercise power may allow some things to be said, but not others. Certain terminologies and communications may be endorsed, while other expressive forms are discouraged. "[T]hese controlled practices [give] rise to the discourse that guides meaning making within its boundaries."[67] This command over discourse can be particularly dangerous because "imbalances of power . . . allow some to define the reality in which others must live, creating the potential for exploitation and abuse."[68]

64 *See* Wm. Dennis Huber, *Law, Language and Corporatehood: Corporations and the U.S. Constitution*, 1 Int'l J. for Rule Law, no. 2, Dec. 2017, at 78, 79, 87. Some commentators have suggested that there may be benefits to discarding the corporate person terminology and replacing it with terms that do not invoke human personhood, such as "corporatehood" or "entity." *See id.* at 98; Gwendolyn Gordon, *Culture in Corporate Law or: A Black Corporation, a Christian Corporation, and a Māori Corporation Walk into a Bar . . .*, 39 Seattle U. L. Rev. 353, 393 (2016).

65 John R. Searle, Making the Social World: The Structure of Human Civilization 85 (2010) (describing language's role in constructing social reality). "[I]n human languages we have the capacity not only to represent reality, both how it is and how we want to make it be, but we also have the capacity to create a new reality by representing that reality as existing." *Id.* at 86.

66 Mary Jo Hatch with Ann L. Cunliffe, Organization Theory: Modern, Symbolic, and Postmodern Perspectives 13 (3d ed. 2013).

67 *Id.* at 43.

68 *Id.* at 14.

Perhaps this is in part why the corporate abolitionists so strongly condemn the terminology of corporate personhood. In their view, when the Supreme Court and those in power refer to the corporation as a person, they are attempting to control the discourse about corporations and their role in society. Judicial and legislative pronouncements that have the effect of categorizing corporations as persons continue the process of transforming and socially constructing corporate entities into persons with rights that, according to the corporate abolitionists, are intended only for human beings. Activists argue that this defines a reality in which corporations can use those rights to dominate and oppress individuals; activists want to change the flow of the discourse about corporations to create a different reality.

Those who are dismayed by corporate personhood also share a concern about the expressive function of legal language. As discussed in Chapter 1, expressive theories of law suggest that law does more than merely control or limit behavior. Law expresses certain beliefs and attitudes about societal values; it sends underlying messages and makes important statements that are understood by citizens.[69] Laws that send the wrong message or express the wrong values cannot be tolerated. For example, laws that are racially discriminatory are invalid under the Fourteenth Amendment because they tacitly communicate the abhorrent message that certain racial groups are inferior, disfavored members of society. Government policies that endorse a particular religion are invalid under the First Amendment's Establishment Clause because they impliedly signal to non-adherents that they are outsiders and that their religious beliefs are unwelcome in the community. Legal language is understood as expressing and endorsing particular value judgments. In a pluralistic civilized society, our goal is to ensure that our laws, as enacted by legislatures and interpreted by courts, send messages that are constructive, edifying, and ever reflective of our democratic ideals. The expressive function of legal language is said to be important because individuals can internalize a law's message and allow it to influence their judgments. Commentators argue that law can change people's beliefs and values, and consequently shape their preferred behaviors.[70]

In the context of corporate personhood, laws can signal certain judgments about the nature of corporations and then influence people's beliefs about them. Legal language that references the personhood and rights of corporations, whether through statutes or court decisions, may have expressive effects that send a message about the value we place on corporations. When the law announces a corporation is a person, or is entitled to the same rights as a human person, it makes

69 Alex Geisinger, *A Belief Change Theory of Expressive Law*, 88 Iowa L. Rev. 35, 40 (2002); Mark D. Rosen, *Establishment, Expressivism, and Federalism*, 78 Chi.-Kent L. Rev. 669, 681 (2003); Cass R. Sunstein, *On the Expressive Function of Law*, 144 U. Pa. L. Rev. 2021, 2024 (1996).

70 *See* Robert Cooter, *Expressive Law and Economics*, 28 J. Legal Stud. 585, 586 (1998); Alex C. Geisinger & Michael Ashley Stein, *Expressive Law and the Americans with Disabilities Act*, 114 Mich. L. Rev. 1061, 1062–66 (2016) (reviewing Richard H. McAdams, The Expressive Powers of Law: Theories and Limits (2015)).

a statement regarding the equality in status of corporations and human beings as holders of fundamental rights.

Although corporate abolitionists may not articulate their position in precisely these terms, it is these expressive and constitutive functions of law and language that seem to concern them so deeply. They worry that the legal doctrine of corporate personhood sends the message that corporations count fully as persons in our society, that they possess the worth of a person under the law, and that they deserve the same rights and respect that are accorded to natural persons. Corporate abolitionists argue that this is the wrong message to send. They believe the language of corporate personhood reflects an inappropriate valuation of corporations vis-à-vis human beings. When the Supreme Court announces in cases such as *Citizens United* that corporations should not be distinguished from individuals while engaging in certain activities like speech, corporate abolitionists contend such legal pronouncements disvalue human beings by improperly placing too much value on corporations.

There is often backlash and resistance when people perceive that law and legal language transmit signals that conflict with other evolving societal values. We see that backlash manifested in the popular movement to propose a constitutional amendment to abolish corporate personhood. Activists seek to stop the Supreme Court from continuing to send what they believe is the harmful message that corporate activity and individual activity are equally deserving of constitutional protection. They worry that such legal endorsements of corporate personhood cause people to internalize the notion that corporations are persons with the same constitutional status and entitlements. Corporate abolitionists want to reconstruct the law to change the way people talk and think about corporations with the hope that corporations can ultimately be removed from the category of persons altogether.

THE NEED FOR CORPORATE PERSONHOOD

While many people believe that corporations have too much economic and political power, and that something more should be done to regulate or limit the reach of corporate activity, not everyone agrees that taking all constitutional protections away from corporations is the answer. Some who sympathize with activists' concern over disproportionate corporate power in politics nonetheless believe that the attempt to pass a constitutional amendment abolishing corporate personhood is unwise and likely to cause more harm than good.

On one level, activists may be ignoring or minimizing the potential risks and negative consequences associated with eliminating the status of corporations as persons under the law. The Constitution was written to protect the people from overbearing government power. A person's ability to invoke fundamental rights under the Constitution provides an essential check on government abuse of power. In the absence of constitutional rights, the government has the potential to exercise control in oppressive ways. A constitutional amendment that terminates all constitutional rights for corporate entities could tip the scales in favor of government overreaching.

For example, if the corporation could claim no Fifth Amendment rights, the government might be able to freely take property from the corporation at any time without paying just compensation. The assets of the corporation would always be at risk of being confiscated. Knowing that corporate resources could be taken by the government whenever it wanted, investors would be far less likely to invest in corporate businesses. Drying up the capital markets that help to drive a healthy national economy could be an unfortunate consequence of revoking the constitutional rights of corporations.

Excluding corporations from the First Amendment's protection for freedom of the press could possibly have the unwelcome effect of undermining the free speech rights of media corporations. If freedom of press is a right enjoyed only by natural persons, not corporations, then the government could prevent the publication of newspapers or the broadcasting of news reports by media companies.

Without Fourth Amendment rights, corporations potentially could be subject to unreasonable searches and seizures of their property. The government could enter the corporation's premises to search and take corporate records without a warrant and without consideration for interference with its business activities or relationships. Records involving the corporation's business relationships with customers, suppliers, creditors, and employees would be subject to the government's unrestricted search and seizure power.

Taking away all corporate rights under the Constitution would mean that corporations charged with crimes would not be entitled to due process of law or a jury trial. If a corporation was acquitted of a crime, it could be tried again and again because it would have no claim to a constitutional right against double jeopardy.

If constitutional rights were stripped from all corporate entities, whether for-profit or nonprofit, then many organizations such as unions, churches, charities, universities, and small family businesses would lose their constitutional protections as well. The "We the People Amendment" advocated by the Move to Amend campaign would produce this result.

Corporate abolitionists argue that the loss of all corporate constitutional rights will not produce negative results because the human members of the corporate entity will retain their constitutional rights, and those individuals can always invoke their rights when necessary to protect their interests. So, even if "Apple is not a 'person' under the Constitution's due process clause," Apple's shareholders are real people who "do have due process rights not to have the value of their Apple shares turned over to the government without due process. Nothing . . . would prevent those real people from protecting their rights."[71] But how would those shareholders assert their due process rights if the government decided to take some of Apple's property

[71] Clements, *supra* note 14, at 171.

without due process? The activists' response is that the claim could "be brought by the corporation, if it is deemed to have standing by the Court to raise the rights of its shareholders."[72]

It is not entirely clear how this result would change or remedy the current framework that allows corporations to bring claims to assert constitutional rights. Requiring the corporation to prove that it has standing to raise the rights of its shareholders adds an extra layer of litigation to assert a due process claim the corporation would otherwise possess to make the very same substantive arguments. Constitutional rights have been extended to corporations in so many areas precisely because upholding the corporation's status to bring the claim ultimately protects the property or liberty interests of the underlying shareholders. Under the aggregate approach to corporate personhood, the rights of the corporation really boil down to the rights of its human members. In the Apple scenario, it seems likely that Apple would have standing to raise the rights of its shareholders if the government were to unreasonably search and seize Apple records, or take Apple's property without due process, or tax Apple in a discriminatory way. If so, then whether we say Apple can bring the claim directly or as a representative of its shareholders seems to make little substantive difference since the factual and legal arguments that would be made to prove the merits of the claims would be the same.

It appears that corporate abolitionists recognize that abolishing corporate constitutional rights can have detrimental effects on the interests of shareholders and others who participate in the corporate enterprise. This is why corporate abolitionists offer the possibility that, once corporate personhood is abolished, corporations would still be permitted to bring claims on behalf of shareholders to protect their interests. However, this road seems to lead to the same end result, i.e., corporations coming into court to complain of violations of constitutional rights. Therefore, it is plausible that abolishing the constitutional rights of corporations will not have as large an effect as activists presume since corporations will be able to simply assert the same constitutional challenges so long as corporations do so ostensibly as the representatives of their shareholders.

THE CONNECTION BETWEEN CORPORATE PERSONHOOD AND CORPORATE POWER

Activists have made corporate personhood the main target of their reform efforts, and their reasons for doing so are understandable. But there are also reasons to think that the popular movement to abolish corporate personhood may be somewhat misguided because it overstates the significance of corporate personhood as the origin of corporate power.

[72] Alternatively, the "claim could be brought by the shareholders as a class." *Id.*

Corporate abolitionists believe that the political and social power of corporations stems from their status as legal persons to claim constitutional rights. They blame the Supreme Court for giving corporations their personhood status when the Court in the late-nineteenth century held that corporations were persons entitled to claim equal protection rights under the Fourteenth Amendment. From that point on, corporations have steadily gained greater rights and correspondingly greater capacity to challenge laws that burden corporate interests. This is why activists believe the Supreme Court is ultimately responsible for the power and influence that corporations have today. They trace corporate power to the Court's 130 years of constitutional law jurisprudence establishing rights for corporations as persons under the Constitution.

The reality, however, is that constitutional analysis played only a partial role. "[C]orporations were already powerful institutional arrangements for governing [society and] the complex of individuals and things before they were given constitutional protections as persons."[73] The large railroad companies with their wealth and resources wielded enormous power long before the Supreme Court extended Fourteenth Amendment rights to them. It is a mistake to believe that the Court and constitutional law are entirely responsible for the rise of corporate power and influence in society. The legal personhood of corporations under the Constitution is not solely what created and consolidated corporate power. There were many other dimensions of the corporation's identity – its wealth, its longevity, its ability to absorb numerous individual participants into one body with a single-minded goal – that contributed to its empowerment.

A substantial part of what makes large corporations such a dominating force in the world today is their ability to accumulate such vast amounts of capital. The political, economic, and social power that comes from having money is undeniable. The capacity to make, keep, and spend that much money is not so much a function of constitutional law and one's legal standing as a person. It is a function of an economic system that embraces entrepreneurial enterprise, free markets, and capitalist values, and of a legal system and public policy framework that seeks to facilitate the implementation of those values.[74] The underlying economic and legal structures we have developed over time have the effect of promoting the formation and perpetuation of powerful corporate entities.

Our system of corporate law in particular makes this corporate empowerment possible. Corporate law doctrines allow corporations to be structured and operated in ways that enable exponential growth and unlimited life spans. Corporations can

[73] Joshua Barkan, Corporate Sovereignty: Law and Government under Capitalism 68 (2013).

[74] As one scholar stated almost a century ago, the "real danger that lies in the corporate organization is the fact that great accumulations of capital are by their very mass, tremendously powerful—and consequently capable of much mischief. Obviously, however, that is an incident of our economic structure and not a consequence of the [personhood of the] corporate entity." Max Radin, *The Endless Problem of Corporate Personality*, 32 Colum. L. Rev. 643, 658 (1932).

grow to an enormous size and exist perpetually. They are not generally constrained by legal restrictions on their wealth, size, or geographic reach. Nor are they held back by time limits on how long they can exist. They are given considerable freedom to operate for any lawful purpose, to make as much money as they can or want, and to spend it in whatever ways their duly elected managers deem best. Long-standing norms involving profit maximization, shareholder primacy, separation of ownership and control, and deference for the business judgment of corporate managers, have shaped the role that corporations play in our society.[75] The combination of these deeply entrenched corporate law doctrines and norms work together to cultivate an environment where corporations can achieve exactly what activists do not want corporations to have – enormous drive and power to accumulate and spend tremendous amounts of money – and thereby significantly influence our political and social systems.

What makes corporations so powerful then is not merely their personhood under the Constitution, but the features of our legal, economic, and cultural systems that facilitate the growth and proliferation of corporations and their large accumulations of capital. While judicial development and interpretation of constitutional law has played a role in elevating the legal status of corporations, our economic and business law frameworks have permitted and promoted corporate advantage and authority as well.

In some measure, this is a choice we have made. We have allowed these systems to flourish because we depend on the material goods only large corporations can provide. We live in a consumer world that wants, needs, and demands a wide selection of complex products and services at our disposal, for our convenience, at a good price, on a timely basis. These demands require the ingenuity, organization, and performance of countless corporations, without whose large-scale operations the unremitting desires of modern society would go unmet. Corporations provide goods and services that we would find it difficult to live without in our technological day and age. "Many of the things we buy are much more complicated to manufacture and bring to the marketplace than the products of an earlier generation . . . Individual producers, whether farmers, craftsmen, or professionals, can rarely satisfy the needs of the community."[76] The corporation enables human beings to accomplish, through concerted action, many things that no individual could achieve alone, free of many of the inefficiencies that plague bureaucratic government agencies. Because we need and want what corporations can provide, we have provided legal frameworks to foster their widespread existence and growth.

[75] *See* Ripken, Citizens United, *Corporate Personhood, and Corporate Power*, *supra* note 1, at 302–13 (discussing the direct connection between corporate power and corporate law doctrines and norms such as shareholder primacy, profit maximization, separation of ownership and control, business judgment rule, perpetual existence, and unlimited growth).

[76] Robert G. Kennedy, *Corporations, Common Goods, and Human Persons*, 4 AVE MARIA L. REV. 1, 27 (2006).

As a consequence, corporations proliferate, and they accumulate vast resources. With those resources comes power. With that power, corporations have a dominating presence in society. Their personhood stretches beyond a legal status on paper and becomes a real force that is akin to government power.

Thus, any efforts to curb corporate power or to address it in a meaningful way will have to involve more than terminating corporations' status as persons in the constitutional realm. Corporate personhood and power do not find their origin exclusively in constitutional law, but in the core fundamentals of the corporate law regime, and in the social and economic systems that animate corporate entities. The demands of our consumer culture facilitate the presence and power of corporations, and even our cultural perceptions of corporations give them a distinct social identity. In a complex way, the elements required to consolidate corporate power are embedded in the very structure of law, culture, and society itself. This suggests that a constitutional amendment to revoke the constitutional rights of corporations and reverse the effects of Supreme Court cases like *Citizens United* will not accomplish all that activists hope it will. Indeed, some of the corporation's most vocal critics acknowledge that "corporate power and malfeasance are not rooted in the Constitution, which is why excluding corporations from the benefits it confers can have only limited effects."[77] It is possible that "[e]ven were the [constitutional] amendment to pass, the Court could easily read its precedents to require little or no change in its doctrine."[78]

From this perspective, a constitutional amendment is not likely to dramatically diminish the power and influence of corporations because there will always still be the problem of corporate money. Money, like water, will always flow around obstacles and have its way. So long as corporations are authorized to accumulate immense stores of capital, that money will continue to have its influence. And so long as consumers want what corporations can provide, corporate presence will continue to endure.

Perhaps corporate abolitionists recognize all of this but feel they need to start somewhere. They know that passing a constitutional amendment to abolish the personhood of corporations under the Constitution faces long odds, but it presents a much more straightforward and clearly defined route than attempting to take on all of corporate law and our capitalist economic system as a governing structure. To otherwise address corporate power in the comprehensive manner that corporate abolitionists wish, they would need to challenge core corporate law doctrines and norms, as well as society's fundamental economic values and

77 Bakan, *supra* note 26, at 356.

78 Daniel J. H. Greenwood, *Neofeudalism: The Surprising Foundations of Corporate Constitutional Rights*, 2017 U. Ill. L. Rev. 163, 166; *see also* Adam Winkler, *Corporate Personhood and the Rights of Corporate Speech*, 30 Seattle U. L. Rev. 863, 872 (2007) ("Even if the courts were to permit the banning of corporate political speech entirely, corporate influence and power would not be substantially reduced ... The problem, in a nutshell, is corporate law.").

consumer preferences, and that is an entirely different battle that is much more difficult to wage. Focusing instead on corporate personhood gives activists a narrower target. Working to eliminate corporate constitutional rights seems to offer people a concrete, practical solution, a clear objective, and a method for fixing a political system they feel is broken. A message like "Stop Corporate Greed" is so general and amorphous that it is impractical. The call to amend the Constitution to "End Corporate Personhood," however, has appeal because it gives activists a precise and definitive goal, a specific path to take. It is something people believe they can take affirmative steps to try to accomplish. They view the abolition of corporate personhood as a viable and practicable solution to limit corporate power.

The shortcoming with this approach is that it focuses entirely on removing the legal personhood of corporations under the Constitution without addressing the other dimensions of the corporation's identity that continue to exist. The perceived personhood of the corporation is much more complex than just its legal status to claim rights under the Constitution. As the prior chapters of this book have explained, corporate personhood is a multidimensional phenomenon that can be analyzed from many different angles. It has legal, philosophical, moral, social, political, economic, and cultural implications. Revoking the corporation's legal personhood for constitutional rights will not make the other dimensions disappear. Personhood is more than a legal concept. Activists believe that the "dragon" of corporate personhood must be slain, but saying the corporation is no longer a person for purposes of constitutional rights will not by itself obliterate the many other non-legal reasons why corporations are regarded as persons in society. "Some may be tempted to jettison the idea of corporate personality entirely, but this is not a viable position. Ignoring the organizational persons that law, government, and society create will not make them go away."[79] Corporations are complex, multifaceted entities, and their perceived personhood arises from more than their legal status. Addressing the corporation's personhood and power requires us to ask tough questions about the economic, social, and political systems we have created for ourselves and how we want to order our priorities and values. Finding satisfactory answers to these questions, and deciding what changes, if any, we should make to the underlying structures that empower corporations is beyond the scope of this book, but it will likely require a much larger endeavor than seeking only to terminate the rights of corporations under the Constitution.

[79] Eric W. Orts, Business Persons: A Legal Theory of the Firm 243 n.72 (2013); *see also* Greenfield, Corporations Are People Too, *supra* note 59, at 211 ("Instead of responding to cases such as *Citizens United* and *Hobby Lobby* with cries of 'Corporations Are Not People,' we should be chanting 'Let's Make Corporations Human Again' or 'If Corporations Are People, They Should Act Like It.' More corporate personhood should be our goal, not our fear.").

THE ROLE OF SOCIAL MOVEMENTS IN INFLUENCING DISCOURSE AND LAW

Perhaps the movement to abolish corporate personhood can draw the nation into a broader conversation about those deeper questions. The drive to amend the Constitution may not be successful, but that does not mean it cannot be an effective instigator of an important dialogue about what role corporations can and should play in society. In this regard, the corporate abolitionist movement may be hoping to find the same success that other historic social movements have had in moving the needle of public opinion toward stricter regulation, despite a failure to obtain a constitutional amendment.

The organized women's movement of the 1970s accomplished this task. Although the movement failed in its effort to add the Equal Rights Amendment (ERA) to the Constitution to prohibit sex discrimination, the law today effectively operates as if the ERA had been adopted. Legislatures have enacted laws and the Supreme Court has interpreted the Constitution to forbid discrimination based on gender, leading many legal scholars commonly to describe the "failed constitutional amendment as a successful one."[80] Similarly, environmental activists never triumphed in securing constitutional protection for environmental sustainability. But they did succeed in motivating widespread concern for the environment and prompted the enactment of the substantial environmental regulatory system we now have in place, signifying "a transformation in American law that could be described as quasi-constitutional in scope."[81]

A social movement's failure to amend the Constitution does not necessarily spell failure to change societal values and, ultimately, to change how the Constitution is interpreted.[82] The amendment proposal process can be used as a political forum for expressing views and making arguments about what the Constitution does or should mean. Debate over whether to amend the Constitution can create a climate for

80 Reva B. Siegel, *Constitutional Culture, Social Movement Conflict and Constitutional Change: The Case of the de facto ERA*, 94 CAL. L. REV. 1323, 1332 (2006); William N. Eskridge, Jr., *Channeling: Identity-Based Social Movements and Public Law*, 150 U. PA. L. REV. 419, 502 (2001) ("[T]he women's movement ... was able to do through the Equal Protection Clause virtually everything the ERA would have accomplished had it been ratified and added to the Constitution."); David A. Strauss, *The Irrelevance of Constitutional Amendments*, 114 HARV. L. REV. 1457, 1476–77 (2001) ("Today, it is difficult to identify any respect in which constitutional law is different from what it would have been if the ERA had been adopted. For the last quarter-century, the Supreme Court has acted as if the Constitution contains a provision forbidding discrimination on the basis of gender.").

81 Cary Coglianese, *Social Movements, Law, and Society: The Institutionalization of the Environmental Movement*, 150 U. PA. L. REV. 85, 98 (2001); *see also* Jeannie Oakes et al., *Grassroots Organizing, Social Movements, and the Right to High-Quality Education*, 4 STAN. J.C.R. & C.L. 339, 353–58 (2008) (explaining how several social movements have had a dramatic impact on altering social practices, laws, and the interpretation of constitutional provisions).

82 *See generally* Hartley, *supra* note 42 (showing how failed attempts to amend the Constitution have successfully mobilized political change).

citizens to wrestle with important constitutional issues. Popular movements that oppose the status quo help to shape the way the Constitution is applied over time.[83] Although the Supreme Court, through controversial decisions like *Citizens United* and *Hobby Lobby*, plays a large role in generating and advancing debate over important social and political issues, popular movements that arise to dispute those decisions can play a significant role in doing so as well. Social movements, such as the women's rights movement, the environmental movement, the civil rights movement, or the labor movement, all help to apprehend and ignite social change. They provide input and anger, opinions and outrage, and in the process of contesting established constitutional understandings, they can have a voice in reforming the law.

Corporate abolitionists may find that achieving their ultimate objective to amend the Constitution is beyond their reach, but, in the process of trying, they can start and continue a public conversation about corporate personhood that is relevant. They have utilized the Move to Amend campaign to inform and educate people about the concept of corporate personhood, its history, and its implications. By targeting corporate personhood, activists have raised awareness about a concept that was largely of interest only to legal scholars for many years. Some of those scholars dismissed the concept as being indeterminate and irrelevant, recommending that we all stop ruminating over corporate personhood altogether. However, the disquietude over corporate personhood persists. It is a concept that is heavily laden with meaning, whether justified or not, for many people who worry about the scope and exercise of corporate power across the globe.

Recent Supreme Court cases like *Citizens United* and *Hobby Lobby*, which solidify corporate rights, have heightened public concern over the idea of treating corporations like persons with claims to fundamental rights of their own. Corporate personhood has become a topic of mainstream attention and a target of activists' ire. The movement to amend the Constitution has spawned important discussions about the meaning of corporate personhood and created a broader need for books like this one to explain and analyze its contours. In this regard, the corporate abolitionist movement has contributed to the discourse surrounding corporate personhood and power, and by affecting the discourse, may ultimately influence the direction of the law regarding corporate rights. Many social movements of the past have tried and failed to amend the Constitution, but they have nonetheless effectively altered how society and ultimately the courts interpret important constitutional issues. It remains to be seen whether the ongoing movement to change the way we currently view, treat, and protect corporations will accomplish its objective.

[83] *See* Jack M. Balkin, *How Social Movements Change (or Fail to Change) the Constitution: The Case of the New Departure*, 39 Suffolk U. L. Rev. 27, 28 (2005); Jack M. Balkin & Reva B. Siegel, *Principles, Practices, and Social Movements*, 154 U. Pa. L. Rev. 927, 928–29 (2006).

Conclusion

The place of corporations in our society and in our legal system has always been deeply ambiguous. Americans have a "long-standing love/hate relationship with the corporation" characterized by an "enthusiastic embrace of the corporation as an engine of opportunity and prosperity, and [a] simultaneous skeptical distrust of it as a source of corruption and driver of inequality."[1] The corporation is an extraordinarily useful instrument that can channel the collective energies of individuals to accomplish tasks that would be impossible for an individual to undertake alone. Corporations permeate almost every part of our lives, contributing to so many integral aspects of our existence, including our food, housing, healthcare, security, transportation, amusement, and communication needs. Through the production and distribution of innumerable goods and services, the corporation has revolutionized the way we live and offers every likelihood of further extending human possibility. Even so, the benefits produced by the corporation have come at a very high cost. Corporations have exposed us to unprecedented environmental hazards, worker alienation and exploitation, manipulative marketing, unsafe products, and financial scandals leading to market collapses that have had devastating rippling effects on people and communities worldwide. While the corporation would like to be viewed as "an engine of economic growth and a bulwark of democratic prosperity," it might also be legitimately described as "a potentially dangerous threat to that same democracy – a site of coercion, monopoly, and the agglomeration of excessive social, economic, and political power."[2] These concerns about corporate power are a factor driving the current popular movement to eliminate the status of corporations as persons under the Constitution.

We typically have ambivalent feelings about corporations because we desire all the material benefits they can provide, but we fear their power and their capacity to harm. This has led to competing public policies that seek to support and facilitate corporate activity while also trying to restrain and regulate it in the public interest.

1 Naomi R. Lamoreaux & William J. Novak, *Corporations and American Democracy: An Introduction, in* CORPORATIONS AND AMERICAN DEMOCRACY 1, 2 (Naomi R. Lamoreaux & William J. Novak eds., 2017).
2 *Id.*

Due to this ambivalence toward corporations, it has never been easy to decide how best to construct laws governing corporate actions.

In trying to determine which rights and duties are appropriate for corporate entities, we have often found ourselves implicitly addressing deeper questions about the nature, role, and purpose of the corporation. What exactly is the corporation and what is its reason for being? Is it a person, or something like a person, and is it prudent to treat it as other persons are treated under the law? Does the corporation exist for the benefit of a few or for the good of all in society? Although legal realists insist that we should not be wasting our time with such questions about the essential nature of corporations, the questions have an uncanny way of persisting, of seeping into our minds and refusing to be discarded. Perhaps this is due to our enduring preoccupation with the concept of personhood and our continual search for what it means to be a person, not just for groups, but for ourselves as individuals. Our judgments about personhood ineluctably have a way of affecting how we weigh the good and bad consequences of the legal rules we adopt to delineate individual and corporate rights and duties.

As this book has endeavored to demonstrate, the personhood of corporations is not a simple concept. It would be easy to call it a metaphor or a fiction and leave it at that. But that would fail to meaningfully address the very visible presence and identity of corporations in the world and the real social consequences that they have. It does not seem entirely fair to say that the corporation's personhood exists only in our imagination, that it serves only as an analogy, or that it occurs through a linguistic sleight of hand. It is true that the personhood of corporations is constructed and manufactured, but in some ways, it is also natural and unavoidable. We have engineered legal corporate personhood as a matter of expediency to serve certain legal purposes. However, we must also acknowledge that on some level it is inevitable that corporate bodies begin naturally to take on certain other personhood dimensions. Corporations have a palpable force and presence that have real and significant impacts on people and society. It may behoove us to acknowledge that corporations are the product of man and our culture, but we and our culture have also become products of the corporate world.

Certainly, it would not be wrong to say that the corporation is a collective of human beings without whom the corporation would arguably be an unanimated empty shell. Yet the corporation sometimes can have features and systems in place that produce independent corporate decisions and actions that are qualitatively different in kind from individual inputs. And so it appears the corporation, like so many other examples of human collectives, can become something larger than the sum of its individual parts. Nonetheless, corporations are not the equivalent of individuals, and this is an important distinction that should be respected.

Just as there is no single settled definition of individual personhood, there is no singular description of the character of the corporation that can capture the many dimensions of its perceived personhood. The corporation can be conceptualized in different ways depending on one's point of view. All of the various disciplinary perspectives shed light on different facets of the corporation as a person. Focusing on one aspect to the exclusion of the others risks oversimplification of complex social, economic, and political realities. The conflicting and coinciding conceptions of the corporation are not necessarily right or wrong, "neither true nor false but are only more or less helpful in calling attention to certain aspects of the phenomenon under study."[3] Each theory of the corporate person "has some validity and contributes to a better understanding of the full dimensions of a 'remarkably fluctuating reality.'"[4]

Personhood does not fit into a neat and tidy box. It is complicated, textured, and dynamic. People and societies change over time. Corporations change as well. As human collectives, corporations continually adapt and evolve to meet the demands and preferences of each generation. Our understandings of corporations and personhood are fluid and subject to adjustments as we experience changes in our circumstances, political structures, economic conditions, legal systems, beliefs, language, and culture. Our interactions with corporations bring about changes in them and us. How we perceive the personhood of corporations is affected by our engagement with them: "shifts in the nature of some of the most powerful institutions in our society have caused shifts in the way that persons relate to those institutions, and consequently shifts in the cultural meaning of personhood itself."[5] What a person is at any one point in time is an unfinished project, and so it is with the corporation. Conceptions of corporate personhood are bound to change over time, and matter in different ways for different issues. As the law both shapes and is shaped by the fluctuating factual realities of the corporate enterprise, the "law, like ourselves, is always in flux, always 'becoming.'"[6] The "ever-emergent quality of law" suggests that any attempted resolution of the controversy over corporate personhood will never be a final answer to the question: What is a corporation?[7]

Corporate personhood is not a unitary concept, and it raises issues that defy unitary treatment. Determining the legal rules by which corporate persons should be governed will necessarily involve a consideration of competing values and

3 W. Richard Scott, ORGANIZATIONS: RATIONAL, NATURAL, AND OPEN SYSTEMS 30 (5th ed. 2003). "[P]aradigms are not right or wrong, but they are predicated on the notion that certain questions are 'more important' and certain approaches to answering those questions are 'more useful.'" Pamela S. Tolbert & Richard H. Hall, ORGANIZATIONS: STRUCTURES, PROCESSES, AND OUTCOMES 162 (10th ed. 2009) (referring to Thomas Kuhn's views of paradigms).

4 Phillip I. Blumberg, *The Corporate Entity in an Era of Multinational Corporations*, 15 DEL. J. CORP. L. 283, 295 (1990).

5 Eric Guthey, *New Economy Romanticism, Narratives of Corporate Personhood, and the Antimanagerial Impulse, in* CONSTRUCTING CORPORATE AMERICA: HISTORY, POLITICS, CULTURE 321, 325 (Kenneth Lipartito & David B. Sicilia eds., 2004).

6 William T. Allen, *Our Schizophrenic Conception of the Business Corporation*, 14 CARDOZO L. REV. 261, 279 (1992).

7 *See id.*

a balancing of varying interests. "Human [and corporate] life is all about choices, and we cannot have it all. When important values come into conflict, the sensible approach is not to resolve ahead of time to pick one over the other."[8] Instead of dogmatically adhering to a particular theory of the corporate person that preferences one set of values over others in all circumstances, we should remain flexible and open to the many different conceptions of the corporation that highlight the corporation's diverse roles and multiple purposes. Corporations are multidimensional, and the law we construct to deal with them will need to be sensitive to their multifaceted nature as well. Understanding and accounting for the various dimensions of the corporation can help to shape public policies and legal rules that can effectively accommodate the complexity and the diversity of corporate organizations. A broad, multidimensional analysis allows for selective application of different conceptions of the corporate person, depending on the situation and the issues to be decided.[9]

At times, the process of legal decision-making will require difficult choices as different values and interests will be more pressing in some circumstances than others. The inevitable clash of values and theories can make construction of law difficult and can lead to inconsistent results. But corporations are complex, and they need complex rules. "[W]e must have law and that law must cover corporations. What more could we do, under such circumstances, than to construct a legal system that is as multifaceted—or, if one prefers, contradictory—as the reality it would presumably regulate?"[10]

The decisions we make today regarding corporate personhood, corporate rights, and corporate duties will necessarily be a function of our moment in history. The determinations represent our current understandings of corporations in their contemporary context. However, corporations, and our conceptions of them, are not static. It is to be expected that the compromises we reach in formulating rules to govern corporations may not last forever. Certain decisions that seem suitable for our society today may turn out to be less acceptable at a later time. Those who favor the status of corporations to claim all the rights of individual persons, and those who seek to abolish that status altogether, hold strong positions that will call for a certain amount of softening on both sides. In trying to reach consensus, the best that we can do is work toward "promoting and preserving an uneasy equilibrium, which is constantly threatened and in constant need of repair."[11] There will be much occasion for exercising sound judgment. As we strive to identity important values, balance competing interests, craft appropriate legal rules, and decide controversial

[8] Steven H. Shiffrin, What's Wrong with the First Amendment? 7 (2016).

[9] Susanna K. Ripken, *Corporations Are People Too: A Multi-Dimensional Approach to the Corporate Personhood Puzzle*, 15 Fordham J. Corp. & Fin. L. 97, 173 (2009).

[10] Alan Wolfe, *The Modern Corporation: Private Agent or Public Actor?*, 50 Wash. & Lee L. Rev. 1673, 1695 (1993).

[11] Isaiah Berlin, The Proper Study of Mankind: An Anthology of Essays 16 (Henry Hardy & Roger Hausheer eds., 1998).

corporate rights cases, we will have to use our best judgment in light of all that we know and understand about corporate persons and their reason for being.

The resulting resolutions may not always be consistent or logical. But, as Oliver Wendell Holmes observed, the life of the law really is not always about logic, but about experience. It is about making reasonable decisions based on the "felt necessities of the time, the prevalent moral and political theories, intuitions of public policy, avowed or unconscious,"[12] as well as the implicit beliefs we hold for the makings of a good society. The ideas that come from different disciplinary perspectives influence our beliefs and intuitions. Having a broad understanding of the multidimensional nature of corporations as persons from various disciplinary angles will help us to make important judgments about corporate matters on a more informed basis. In an effort to facilitate that broader understanding, this book has explored the unique contributions of different disciplines to illuminate the multifaceted nature of the corporation.

What is corporate personhood, and why does it matter? As the analysis in the preceding chapters has attempted to show, the answer to both of those questions is: It's complicated. The corporation is as complex as the human persons who animate it. Whether the corporation is, can, or should be considered a person is deeply contested. There are many different types of corporations and many different dimensions of personhood. The extent to which corporations and personhood can be sensibly combined for legal, economic, political, and moral purposes is not a settled matter. Perhaps it is simply a story in progress. It is a story about the unique relationship we have with corporations – organizations that fulfill both individualist and collectivist functions, that serve both private and public purposes, and that act both as property and person. Time will tell how the story will unfold. Our task will be to do our best to move the storyline ever toward an ideal balance between individuals and the vast array of corporate organizations that have become so central to our larger human narrative.

[12] O. W. Holmes, Jr., The Common Law 1 (Lawbook Exch. 2005) (1881).

Bibliography

Ahdar, Rex, *Companies as Religious Liberty Claimants*, 5 Oxford J. L. & Religion 1 (2016).

Albert, Stuart & David A. Whetten, *Organizational Identity*, *in* 7 Research in Organizational Behavior 263 (L. L. Cummings & Barry M. Staw eds., 1985).

Organizational Identity, *in* Revealing the Corporation: Perspectives on Identity, Image, Reputation, Corporate Branding, and Corporate-Level Marketing 77 (John M. T. Balmer & Stephen A. Greyser eds., 2003).

Alchian, Armen A. & Harold Demsetz, *Production, Information Costs, and Economic Organization*, 62 Am. Econ. Rev. 777 (1972).

Allen, William T., *Our Schizophrenic Conception of the Business Corporation*, 14 Cardozo L. Rev. 261 (1992).

Alschuler, Albert W., *Ancient Law and the Punishment of Corporations: Of Frankpledge and Deodand*, 71 B.U. L. Rev. 307 (1991).

Alvesson, Mats, *Organizational Culture: Meaning, Discourse, and Identity*, *in* The Handbook of Organizational Culture and Climate 11 (Neal M. Ashkanasy et al. eds., 2d ed. 2011).

American Law Institute, Principles of Corporate Governance: Analysis and Recommendations (1994).

Amicus Curiae Brief of Corporate and Criminal Law Professors in Support of Petitioners, Burwell v. Hobby Lobby Stores, Inc., 134 S. Ct. 2751 (2014) (Nos. 13–354 & 13–356), 2014 WL 333889.

Anderson, Elizabeth S. & Richard H. Pildes, *Expressive Theories of Law: A General Restatement*, 148 U. Pa. L. Rev. 1503 (2000).

Andrews, Kristin, *Beyond Anthropomorphism: Attributing Psychological Properties to Animals*, *in* The Oxford Handbook of Animal Ethics 469 (Tom L. Beauchamp & R. G. Frey eds., 2011).

Ashforth, Blake E., *Organizational, Subunit, and Individual Identities*, *in* The Oxford Handbook of Organizational Identity 79 (Michael G. Pratt et al. eds., 2016).

Ashkanasy, Neal M. & Charmine E. J. Härtel, *Positive and Negative Affective Climate and Culture*, *in* The Oxford Handbook of Organizational Climate and Culture 136 (Benjamin Schneider & Karen M. Barbera eds., 2014).

Avi-Yonah, Reuven S., *The Cyclical Transformations of the Corporate Form: A Historical Perspective on Corporate Social Responsibility*, 30 Del. J. Corp. L. 767 (2005).

Baddorf, Matthew, *Phenomenal Consciousness, Collective Mentality, and Collective Moral Responsibility*, Phil. Stud., doi:10.1007/s11098-016-0809-x (2016).

Bailyn, Jonathan, *A Critical Race Theorist Account of Corporate Racial Standing*, 16 Scholar 725 (2014).

Bainbridge, Stephen M., *Community and Statism: A Conservative Contractarian Critique of Progressive Corporate Law Scholarship*, 82 CORNELL L. REV. 856 (1997) (book review).

Bakan, Joel, THE CORPORATION: THE PATHOLOGICAL PURSUIT OF PROFIT AND POWER (2005).

Psychopaths, Inc.: On Corporate Personhood, *in* THE OCCUPY HANDBOOK 353 (Janet Byrne ed., 2012).

Baker, C. Edwin, *Commercial Speech: A Problem in the Theory of Freedom*, 62 IOWA L. REV. 1 (1976).

Scope of the First Amendment Freedom of Speech, 25 UCLA L. REV. 964 (1978).

Balcerzak, Ashley, *Study: Most Americans Want to Kill 'Citizens United' with Constitutional Amendment*, CTR. PUB. INTEGRITY (May 10, 2018), www.publicintegrity.org/2018/05/10/21739/study-most-americans-want-kill-citizens-united-constitutional-amendment [https://perma.cc/4SKF-2PGJ].

Balkin, J.M., *Some Realism About Pluralism: Legal Realist Approaches to the First Amendment*, 1990 DUKE L.J. 375.

Balkin, Jack M., *How Social Movements Change (or Fail to Change) the Constitution: The Case of the New Departure*, 39 SUFFOLK U. L. REV. 27 (2005).

The Proliferation of Legal Truth, 26 HARV. J.L. & PUB. POL'Y 5 (2003).

Balkin, Jack M. & Reva B. Siegel, *Principles, Practices, and Social Movements*, 154 U. PA. L. REV. 927 (2006).

Balmer, John M. T., *Corporate Brand Cultures and Communities*, *in* BRAND CULTURE 34 (Jonathan E. Schroeder & Miriam Salzer-Mörling eds., 2006).

Barkan, Joshua, CORPORATE SOVEREIGNTY: LAW AND GOVERNMENT UNDER CAPITALISM (2013).

Baron, Robert S., *So Right It's Wrong: Groupthink and the Ubiquitous Nature of Polarized Group Decision Making*, *in* 37 ADVANCES EXPERIMENTAL SOC. PSYCHOL. 219 (Mark P. Zanna ed., 2005).

Batchis, Wayne, THE RIGHT'S FIRST AMENDMENT: THE POLITICS OF FREE SPEECH & THE RETURN OF CONSERVATIVE LIBERTARIANISM (2016).

Bebchuk, Lucian Arye, *Foreword: The Debate on Contractual Freedom in Corporate Law*, 89 COLUM. L. REV. 1395 (1989).

Bell, Daniel, THE COMING OF POST-INDUSTRIAL SOCIETY: A VENTURE IN SOCIAL FORECASTING (1973).

Bellah, Robert N. et al., THE GOOD SOCIETY (1991).

Benson, Robert W., *How Many Strikes Do Big Corporations Get? The Petition to Revoke UNOCAL's Corporate Charter*, 55 GUILD PRAC. 113 (1998).

Berger, Peter L. & Richard John Neuhaus, TO EMPOWER PEOPLE: THE ROLE OF MEDIATING STRUCTURES IN PUBLIC POLICY (1977).

Berle, Jr., A.A., *The Developing Law of Corporate Concentration*, 19 U. CHI. L. REV. 639 (1952).

Berle, Jr., Adolf A., *Constitutional Limitations on Corporate Activity – Protection of Personal Rights from Invasion Through Economic Power*, 100 U. PA. L. REV. 933 (1952).

Foreword, *in* THE CORPORATION IN MODERN SOCIETY, at ix (Edward S. Mason ed., 1959).

THE 20TH CENTURY CAPITALIST REVOLUTION (1954).

Berle, Jr., Adolf A. & Gardiner C. Means, THE MODERN CORPORATION AND PRIVATE PROPERTY (1932).

Berlin, Isaiah, THE PROPER STUDY OF MANKIND: AN ANTHOLOGY OF ESSAYS (Henry Hardy & Roger Hausheer eds., 1998).

Björnsson, Gunnar & Kendy Hess, *Corporate Crocodile Tears? On the Reactive Attitudes of Corporate Agents*, 94 PHIL. & PHENOMENOLOGICAL RES. 273 (2017).

Blair, Margaret M., *Corporate Personhood and the Corporate Persona*, 2013 U. ILL. L. REV. 785.

Blair, Margaret M. & Elizabeth Pollman, *The Derivative Nature of Corporate Constitutional Rights*, 56 WM. & MARY L. REV. 1673 (2015).

Blau, Peter M. & W. Richard Scott, FORMAL ORGANIZATIONS: A COMPARATIVE APPROACH (1962).

Bleifuss, Joel, *Corporations Are Not People*, IN THESE TIMES (Sept. 19, 2011), http://inthesetimes.com/article/11937/corporations_are_not_people [https://perma.cc/7XVZ-ZYRK].

Blumberg, Phillip I., *The Corporate Entity in an Era of Multinational Corporations*, 15 DEL. J. CORP. L. 283 (1990).

Boudin, Louis B., *Truth and Fiction About the Fourteenth Amendment*, 16 N.Y.U. L.Q. REV. 19 (1938).

Bourdieu, Pierre, *The Force of Law: Toward a Sociology of the Juridical Field*, 38 HASTINGS L.J. 814 (1987).

Bratton, William W., *The Economic Structure of the Post-Contractual Corporation*, 87 NW. U. L. REV. 180 (1992).

Bratton, Jr., William W., *The "Nexus of Contracts" Corporation: A Critical Appraisal*, 74 CORNELL L. REV. 407 (1989).

Brennan-Marquez, Kiel, *A Business Can Exercise Religion, but Hobby Lobby Still Gets It Wrong*, BOS. REV. (July 7, 2014), http://bostonreview.net/blogs/kiel-brennan-marquez-hobby-lobby-for-profit-corporations-religion [https://perma.cc/3ZMJ-6V8A].

Brief of Amici Curiae Corporate Law Professors in Support of Respondents, Masterpiece Cakeshop, Ltd. v. Colorado Civil Rights Comm'n, 138 S. Ct. 1719 (2018) (No. 16–111), 2017 WL 5127303.

Brief for Petitioners, Masterpiece Cakeshop, Ltd. v. Colorado Civil Rights Comm'n, 138 S. Ct. 1719 (2018) (No. 16–111), 2017 WL 3913762.

Briloff, Abraham J., *LBOs and MBOs in the Takeover Alphabet Soup: Some Questions for Lawyers, Answers from an Accountant*, 15 J. CORP. L. 171 (1990).

Brodbeck, May, *Methodological Individualisms: Definition and Reduction*, *in* READINGS IN THE PHILOSOPHY OF THE SOCIAL SCIENCES 280 (May Brodbeck ed., 1968).

Brooks, Richard R. W., *Incorporating Race*, 106 COLUM. L. REV. 2023 (2006).

Brown, W. Jethro, *The Personality of the Corporation and the State*, 21 LAW Q. REV. 365 (1905).

Buccola, Vincent S. J., *Corporate Rights and Organizational Neutrality*, 101 IOWA L. REV. 499 (2016).

Buell, Samuel W., *The Blaming Function of Entity Criminal Liability*, 81 IND. L. J. 473 (2006).

Butler, Henry N., *The Contractual Theory of the Corporation*, 11 GEO. MASON U. L. REV., no. 4, Summer 1989, at 99.

Butler, Henry N. & Larry E. Ribstein, THE CORPORATION AND THE CONSTITUTION (1995).

Calmore, John O., *Racialized Space and the Culture of Segregation: "Hewing a Stone of Hope from a Mountain of Despair,"* 143 U. PA. L. REV. 1233 (1995).

Carrithers, Michael et al., eds., THE CATEGORY OF THE PERSON: ANTHROPOLOGY, PHILOSOPHY, HISTORY (1985).

Carruthers, Peter, INTRODUCING PERSONS: THEORIES AND ARGUMENTS IN THE PHILOSOPHY OF MIND (1986).

Chambers, Jr., Henry L., *Telescoping and Collectivizing Religious Free Exercise Rights*, 75 MD. L. REV. 392 (2015).

Chapple, Chris, THE MORAL RESPONSIBILITIES OF COMPANIES (2014).

Chemerinsky, Erwin, *The Most Important Decision of the Term*, TRIAL, May 2010, at 54.

Chen, Ronald & Jon Hanson, *The Illusion of Law: The Legitimating Schemas of Modern Policy and Corporate Law*, 103 MICH. L. REV. 1 (2004).

Chia, Robert, *Discourse Analysis as Organizational Analysis*, 7 ORGANIZATION 513 (2000).

Chirinko, Robert S. & Daniel J. Wilson, *Can Lower Tax Rates Be Bought? Business Rent-Seeking and Tax Competition Among U.S. States* (Fed. Reserve Bank of S.F. Working Paper Series, Paper 2009–29, 2010), www.frbsf.org/economic-research/files/wp09-29bk.pdf [https://perma.cc/AM84-8WHP].

Clark, Elizabeth A. & W. Cole Durham, Jr., *The Emergence of Corporate Religious Freedom*, *in* THE CHANGING NATURE OF RELIGIOUS RIGHTS UNDER INTERNATIONAL LAW 256 (Malcolm D. Evans et al. eds., 2015).

Clements, Jeff, Citizens United *and Corporate Personhood: Jeff Clements Responds to Kent Greenfield's Washington Post Op-ed*, FREE SPEECH FOR PEOPLE (Jan. 23, 2012), http://freespeechforpeople.org/node/315 [https://perma.cc/9HKD-SLNX].

Clements, Jeffrey D., CORPORATIONS ARE NOT PEOPLE: WHY THEY HAVE MORE RIGHTS THAN YOU DO AND WHAT YOU CAN DO ABOUT IT (2012).

Cmty. Envtl. Legal Def. Fund, *Statement on Efforts to Amend the U.S. Constitution Following* Citizens United (Jan. 2012), https://celdf.org/wp-content/uploads/2015/08/CELDF-CITIZENS-UNITED-STATEMENT-JANUARY-17–2012.pdf [https://perma.cc/7AK8-F4UW].

Cmty. Envtl. Legal Def. Fund et al., Model Brief of *Amici Curiae*, Preface (2003), www.ratical.org/corporations/demoBrief.pdf [https://perma.cc/8YWK-H6WZ].

Coates IV, John C., *Corporate Politics, Governance, and Value Before and After* Citizens United, 9 J. EMPIRICAL LEGAL STUD. 657 (2012).

Coates, John C. & Taylor Lincoln, *Fulfilling the Promise of* 'Citizens United', WASH. POST: OPINIONS (Sep. 6, 2011), www.washingtonpost.com/opinions/fulfilling-the-promise-of-citizens-united/2011/09/02/gIQAa4np7 J_story.html [https://perma.cc/2Q8 M-TEBM].

Coffin, Roger, *A Responsibility to Speak*: Citizens United, *Corporate Governance and Managing Risks*, 8 HASTINGS BUS. L.J. 103 (2012).

Coglianese, Cary, *Social Movements, Law, and Society: The Institutionalization of the Environmental Movement*, 150 U. PA. L. REV. 85 (2001).

Cohen, Felix S., *Transcendental Nonsense and the Functional Approach*, 35 COLUM. L. REV. 809 (1935).

Coleridge, Greg, *Gorsuch's Gory Expansion of Corporate Personhood*, BY WHAT AUTHORITY (Program on Corps., Law & Democracy, South Yarmouth, MA), Mar./Apr. 2017, www.poclad.org/BWA/files/2017/BWAMarchApril2017.pdf [https://perma.cc/N423-MQVW].

The System Isn't Broken, It's Fixed: Ending Big Money and Corporations in Our Elections, 44 U. TOLEDO L. REV. 541 (2013).

Collins, Jane L. & Walker N. Kahn, *The Hijacking of a New Corporate Form? Benefit Corporations and Corporate Personhood*, 45 ECON. & SOC'Y 325 (2016).

Colombo, Ronald J., THE FIRST AMENDMENT AND THE BUSINESS CORPORATION (2015).

The Naked Private Square, 51 HOUS. L. REV. 1 (2013).

Comment, *Law for Sale: A Study of the Delaware Corporation Law of 1967*, 117 U. PA. L. REV. 861 (1969).

Constantinescu, Mihaela, *Attributions of Moral Responsibility: From Aristotle to Corporations*, 62 ANNALS U. BUCHAREST PHIL. SERIES, no. 1, 2013, at 19.

Constantinescu, Mihaela & Muel Kaptein, *Mutually Enhancing Responsibility: A Theoretical Exploration of the Interaction Mechanisms Between Individual and Corporate Moral Responsibility*, 129 J. BUS. ETHICS 325 (2015).

Cooke, Robert A. & Janet L. Szumal, *Using the Organizational Culture Inventory to Understand the Operating Cultures of Organizations*, *in* HANDBOOK OF ORGANIZATIONAL CULTURE & CLIMATE 147 (Neal M. Ashkanasy et al. eds., 2000).

Cooter, Robert, *Expressive Law and Economics*, 28 J. LEGAL STUD. 585 (1998).

Copp, David, *The Collective Moral Autonomy Thesis*, 38 J. SOC. PHIL. 369 (2007).
Corbin, Caroline Mala, *Corporate Religious Liberty*, 30 CONST. COMMENT. 277 (2015).
Cormode, D. Scott, *Does Institutional Isomorphism Imply Secularization?: Churches and Secular Voluntary Associations in the Turn-of-the-Century City*, *in* SACRED COMPANIES: ORGANIZATIONAL ASPECTS OF RELIGION AND RELIGIOUS ASPECTS OF ORGANIZATIONS 116 (N. J. Demerath III et al. eds., 1998).
Cornelissen, Joep P. et al., *Bridging and Integrating Theories on Organizational Identity*, *in* THE OXFORD HANDBOOK OF ORGANIZATIONAL IDENTITY 200 (Michael G. Pratt et al. eds., 2016).
Cortright, S. A. & Ernest S. Pierucci, *Clearing Ground: Toward a Social Ethic of Corporate Management*, *in* RETHINKING THE PURPOSE OF BUSINESS 136 (S. A. Cortright & Michael J. Naughton eds., 2002).
Cressey, Donald R., *The Poverty of Theory in Corporate Crime Research*, *in* 1 ADVANCES IN CRIMINOLOGICAL THEORY 31 (William S. Laufer & Freda Adler eds., 1989).
Cressman, Derek D., WHEN MONEY TALKS: THE HIGH PRICE OF "FREE" SPEECH AND THE SELLING OF DEMOCRACY (2016).
Dan-Cohen, Meir, RIGHTS, PERSONS, AND ORGANIZATIONS: A LEGAL THEORY FOR BUREAUCRATIC SOCIETY (2d ed. 2016).
Danziger, Kurt, *Historical Psychology of Persons: Categories and Practice*, *in* THE PSYCHOLOGY OF PERSONHOOD: PHILOSOPHICAL, HISTORICAL, SOCIAL-DEVELOPMENTAL, AND NARRATIVE PERSPECTIVES 59 (Jack Martin & Mark H. Bickhard eds., 2013).
Davis, Joseph Stancliffe, ESSAYS IN THE EARLIER HISTORY OF AMERICAN CORPORATIONS (Vol. 2) (Lawbook Exch. 2006) (1917).
DeBow, Michael E. & Dwight R. Lee, *Shareholders, Nonshareholders and Corporate Law: Communitarianism and Resource Allocation*, 18 DEL. J. CORP. L. 393 (1993)
De George, Richard T., *Corporations and Morality*, *in* SHAME, RESPONSIBILITY AND THE CORPORATION 57 (Hugh Curtler ed., 1986).
Social Reality and Social Relations, 37 REV. METAPHYSICS 3 (1983).
de Tocqueville, Alexis, DEMOCRACY IN AMERICA (Harvey C. Mansfield & Delba Winthrop eds. & trans., Univ. of Chi. Press 2000) (1840).
Deiser, George F., *The Juristic Person*, 57 U. PA. L. REV. 300 (1909).
Dempsey, James, *Corporations and Non-Agential Moral Responsibility*, 30 J. APPLIED PHIL. 334 (2013).
Dennett, Daniel C., BRAINSTORMS: PHILOSOPHICAL ESSAYS ON MIND AND PSYCHOLOGY (MIT Press 1981) (1978).
Dewey, John, *The Historic Background of Corporate Legal Personality*, 35 YALE L.J. 655 (1926).
Dibadj, Reza, *Expressive Rights for Shareholders after* Citizens United?, 46 U.S.F. L. REV. 459 (2011).
Dixon, Bruce A., *Time for a Corporate Death Penalty*, BLACK AGENDA REP. (June 9, 2010), https://blackagendareport.com/content/time-corporate-death-penalty [https://perma.cc/4GX9-H3KZ].
Dodd, Senator Christopher S., Press Release, *Sen. Dodd Introduces Constitutional Amendment to Reverse Supreme Court Campaign Finance Ruling*, U.S. FED. NEWS, Feb. 25, 2010, 2010 WLNR 3913103.
Donaldson, Thomas, CORPORATIONS AND MORALITY (1982).
Drucker, Peter F., CONCEPT OF THE CORPORATION (rev. ed. 1972).
Dubbink, Wim & Jeffery Smith, *A Political Account of Corporate Moral Responsibility*, 14 ETHICAL THEORY & MORAL PRAC. 223 (2011).

Dunlavy, Colleen A., *From Citizens to Plutocrats: Nineteenth-Century Shareholder Voting Rights and Theories of the Corporation*, *in* CONSTRUCTING CORPORATE AMERICA: HISTORY, POLITICS, CULTURE 66 (Kenneth Lipartito & David B. Sicilia eds., 2004).

Eagles, Thad, Note, *Free Exercise, Inc.: A New Framework for Adjudicating Corporate Religious Liberty Claims*, 90 N.Y.U. L. REV. 589 (2015).

Easterbrook, Frank H. & Daniel R. Fischel, THE ECONOMIC STRUCTURE OF CORPORATE LAW (1991).

Edmonds, S. Chris, THE CULTURE ENGINE: A FRAMEWORK FOR DRIVING RESULTS, INSPIRING YOUR EMPLOYEES, AND TRANSFORMING YOUR WORKPLACE (2014).

Edwards, Jan & Molly Morgan, *Abolish Corporate Personhood*, RECLAIM DEMOCRACY (May 20, 2004), http://reclaimdemocracy.org/abolish-corporate-personhood/ [https://perma.cc/7K4V-NDQY].

Egan, Matt, *Wells Fargo Uncovers up to 1.4 Million More Fake Accounts*, CNN MONEY (Aug. 31, 2017), http://money.cnn.com/2017/08/31/investing/wells-fargo-fake-accounts/index.html [https://perma.cc/Y24F-Q5KT].

Wells Fargo Ups Its Customer Settlement to $142 Million over Fake Accounts, CNN MONEY (Apr. 21, 2017), http://money.cnn.com/2017/04/21/investing/wells-fargo-expands-customer-settlement/index.html [https://perma.cc/Q3LV-ZZ2E].

Eggen, Dan, *Poll: Large Majority Opposes Supreme Court's Decision on Campaign Financing*, WASH. POST (Feb. 17, 2010), www.washingtonpost.com/wp-dyn/content/article/2010/02/17/AR2010021701151.html [https://perma.cc/7RQD-ZEDQ].

Ehrhart, Mark G. et al., ORGANIZATIONAL CLIMATE AND CULTURE: AN INTRODUCTION TO THEORY, RESEARCH, AND PRACTICE (2014).

Elsbach, Kimberly D. & Janet M. Dukerich, *Organizational Identity and the Undesired Self*, *in* THE OXFORD HANDBOOK OF ORGANIZATIONAL IDENTITY 257 (Michael G. Pratt et al. eds., 2016).

Emerson, Thomas I., *Toward a General Theory of the First Amendment*, 72 YALE L.J. 877 (1963).

Epstein, Richard A., Citizens United v. FEC: *The Constitutional Right That Big Corporations Should Have But Do Not Want*, 34 HARV. J.L. & PUB. POL'Y 639 (2011).

Eskridge, Jr., William N., *Channeling: Identity-Based Social Movements and Public Law*, 150 U. PA. L. REV. 419 (2001).

Estes, Ralph, TYRANNY OF THE BOTTOM LINE: WHY CORPORATIONS MAKE GOOD PEOPLE DO BAD THINGS (1996).

Fama, Eugene F., *Agency Problems and the Theory of the Firm*, 88 J. POL. ECON. 288 (1980).

Fama, Eugene F. & Michael C. Jensen, *Separation of Ownership and Control*, 26 J. L. & ECON. 301 (1983).

Feldman, Daniel C. & Olivia Amanda O'Neill, *The Role of Socialization, Orientation, and Training Programs in Transmitting Culture and Climate and Enhancing Performance*, *in* THE OXFORD HANDBOOK OF ORGANIZATIONAL CLIMATE AND CULTURE 44 (Benjamin Schneider & Karen M. Barbera eds., 2014).

Finnis, John, *Corporate Persons II: Persons and Their Associations*, *in* 63 PROC. ARISTOTELIAN SOC'Y, SUPP. VOL. 267 (1989).

Fisch, Jill E., *The "Bad Man" Goes to Washington: The Effect of Political Influence on Corporate Duty*, 75 FORDHAM L. REV. 1593 (2006).

Measuring Efficiency in Corporate Law: The Role of Shareholder Primacy, 31 J. CORP. L. 637 (2006).

Flamholtz, Eric G. & Yvonne Randle, CORPORATE CULTURE: THE ULTIMATE STRATEGIC ASSET (2011).

Implications of Organizational Life Cycles for Corporate Culture and Climate, in The Oxford Handbook of Organizational Climate and Culture 235 (Benjamin Schneider & Karen M. Barbera eds., 2014).
Flynn, John J., *The Jurisprudence of Corporate Personhood: The Misuse of a Legal Concept, in* Corporations and Society: Power and Responsibility 131 (Warren J. Samuels & Arthur S. Miller eds., 1987).
Forsyth, Donelson R., Group Dynamics (6th ed. 2014).
Fort, Timothy L., *Business as Mediating Institution*, 6 Bus. Ethics Q. 149 (1996).
Frankfurt, Harry G., *Freedom of the Will and the Concept of a Person*, 68 J. Phil. 5 (1971).
Franzen, Giep & Margot Bouwman, The Mental World of Brands: Mind, Memory and Brand Success (2001).
Freeman, R. Edward, *A Stakeholder Theory of the Modern Corporation, in* Ethical Theory and Business 56 (Tom L. Beauchamp & Norman E. Bowie eds., 6th ed. 2001).
French, Peter A., Collective and Corporate Responsibility (1984).
The Corporation as a Moral Person, 16 Am. Phil. Q. 207 (1979).
Freund, Ernst, The Legal Nature of Corporations (Chicago, Univ. of Chi. Press 1897).
Friedman, Lawrence M., A History of American Law (2d ed. 1985).
Galanter, Marc, *Planet of the APs: Reflections on the Scale of Law and Its Users*, 53 Buff. L. Rev. 1369 (2006).
Gans, David H. & Douglas T. Kendall, *A Capitalist Joker: The Strange Origins, Disturbing Past, and Uncertain Future of Corporate Personhood in American Law*, 44 J Marshall L. Rev. 643 (2011).
Gans, David H. & Ilya Shapiro, Religious Liberties for Corporations?: Hobby Lobby, the Affordable Care Act, and the Constitution (2014).
Gaylord, Scott W., *For-Profit Corporations, Free Exercise, and the HHS Mandate*, 91 Wash. U. L. Rev. 589 (2014).
Gedicks, Frederick Mark, *"Substantial" Burdens: How Courts May (and Why They Must) Judge Burdens on Religion under RFRA*, 85 Geo. Wash. L. Rev. 94 (2017).
Geisinger, Alex, *A Belief Change Theory of Expressive Law*, 88 Iowa L. Rev. 35 (2002).
Geisinger, Alex C. & Michael Ashley Stein, *Expressive Law and the Americans with Disabilities Act*, 114 Mich. L. Rev. 1061 (2016).
Geldart, W. M., *Legal Personality*, 27 Law Q. Rev. 90 (1911).
Gibson, David, *Doing Good and Doing Well: Faith-Based Investing Converts the Skeptics*, USA Today (May 31, 2017), www.usatoday.com/story/news/nation/2017/05/31/faith-based-investing/102351062 [https://perma.cc/775N-P4RX].
Gibson, Kevin, *Toward an Intermediate Position on Corporate Moral Personhood*, 101 J. Bus. Ethics (Supp. 1) 71 (2011).
Gibson, Jr., Roger F., *Corporations, Persons, and Moral Responsibility*, 21 J. Thought, no. 2, Summer 1986, at 17.
Gierke, Otto, Associations and Law: The Classical and Early Christian Stages (George Heiman ed. & trans., 1977).
Political Theories of the Middle Age (Frederic William Maitland trans., Lawbook Exch. 2002) (1900).
Gill, Christopher, ed., The Person and the Human Mind: Issues in Ancient and Modern Philosophy (1990).
Gioia, Dennis A. & Aimee L. Hamilton, *Great Debates in Organizational Identity Study, in* The Oxford Handbook of Organizational Identity 21 (Michael G. Pratt et al. eds., 2016).

Gobé, Marc, EMOTIONAL BRANDING: THE NEW PARADIGM FOR CONNECTING BRANDS TO PEOPLE (2001).

Goodman, Michael F., ed., WHAT IS A PERSON? (1988).

Goodpaster, Kenneth E., CONSCIENCE AND CORPORATE CULTURE (2007).

Gordon, Gwendolyn, *Culture in Corporate Law or: A Black Corporation, a Christian Corporation, and a Māori Corporation Walk into a Bar* . . ., 39 SEATTLE U. L. REV. 353 (2016).

Graham, Howard Jay, *The "Conspiracy Theory" of the Fourteenth Amendment*, 47 YALE L.J. 371 (1938).

The "Conspiracy Theory" of the Fourteenth Amendment: 2, 48 YALE L.J. 171 (1938).

An Innocent Abroad: The Constitutional Corporate "Person," 2 UCLA L. REV. 155 (1955).

Grantham, Ross, *Commentary on Goddard, in* CORPORATE PERSONALITY IN THE 20TH CENTURY 65 (Charles E. F. Rickett & Ross B. Grantham eds., 1998).

Gray, John Chipman, THE NATURE AND SOURCES OF THE LAW (Roland Gray ed., Macmillan Co. 2d ed. 1921) (1909).

Green, David, MORE THAN A HOBBY (2005).

Greenawalt, Kent, *Religious Toleration and Claims of Conscience, in* THE RISE OF CORPORATE RELIGIOUS LIBERTY 3 (Micah Schwartzman et al. eds., 2016).

Greendorfer, Marc A., *Blurring Lines Between Churches and Secular Corporations: The Compelling Case of the Benefit Corporation's Right to the Free Exercise of Religion (with a post-*Hobby Lobby *Epilogue)*, 39 DEL. J. CORP. L. 819 (2015).

Greenfield, Kent, CORPORATIONS ARE PEOPLE TOO (AND THEY SHOULD ACT LIKE IT) (2018).

THE FAILURE OF CORPORATE LAW: FUNDAMENTAL FLAWS AND PROGRESSIVE POSSIBILITIES (2006).

In Defense of Corporate Persons, 30 CONST. COMMENT. 309 (2015).

Greenfield, Kent & Adam Winkler, *The U.S. Supreme Court's Cultivation of Corporate Personhood*, ATLANTIC (June 24, 2015), www.theatlantic.com/politics/archive/2015/06/raisins-hotels-corporate-personhood-supreme-court/396773 [https://perma.cc/FV24-LTS3].

Greenwood, Daniel J. H., *Essential Speech: Why Corporate Speech Is Not Free*, 83 IOWA L. REV. 995 (1998).

Neofeudalism: The Surprising Foundations of Corporate Constitutional Rights, 2017 U. ILL. L. REV. 163.

Grossman, Richard L. & Frank T. Adams, *Taking Care of Business: Citizenship and the Charter of Incorporation*, NEW SOLUTIONS, Spring 1993, at 7.

Guldenschuh, David, *Article V Progress Report*, ARTICLE V CAUCUS, http://articlevcaucus.com/news/article-v-progress-report-4/ [https://perma.cc/25QX-N4SC].

Guthey, Eric, *New Economy Romanticism, Narratives of Corporate Personhood, and the Antimanagerial Impulse, in* CONSTRUCTING CORPORATE AMERICA: HISTORY, POLITICS, CULTURE 321 (Kenneth Lipartito & David B. Sicilia eds., 2004).

Hacking, Ian, REWRITING THE SOUL: MULTIPLE PERSONALITY AND THE SCIENCES OF MEMORY (1995).

Hadani, Michael, Jean-Philippe Bonardi & Nicolas M. Dahan, *Corporate Political Activity, Public Policy Uncertainty, and Firm Outcomes: A Meta-Analysis*, 15 STRATEGIC ORG. 338 (2016).

Hadani, Michael & Douglas A. Schuler, *In Search of El Dorado: The Elusive Financial Returns on Corporate Political Investment*, 34 STRATEGIC MGMT. J. 165 (2013).

Hager, Mark M., *Bodies Politic: The Progressive History of Organizational "Real Entity" Theory*, 50 U. PITT. L. REV. 575 (1989).

Haji, Ish, *On the Ultimate Responsibility of Collectives*, 30 MIDWEST STUD. PHIL. 292 (2006).

Haliburton, Rachel, AUTONOMY AND THE SITUATED SELF (2014).

Hallowell, Billy, *Here Are 5 Christian Companies That Join Chick-fil-A in Publicly-Proclaiming Their Bible-Based Views*, BLAZE (Aug 2, 2012), www.theblaze.com/news/2012/08/02/here-are-5-christian-companies-that-join-chick-fil-a-in-publicly-proclaiming-their-bible-based-faith/ [https://perma.cc/9R7S-4XQN].

Hamilton, Sheryl N., IMPERSONATIONS: TROUBLING THE PERSON IN LAW AND CULTURE (2009).

Hammerstrom, Doug, *The Hijacking of the Fourteenth Amendment*, RECLAIM DEMOCRACY (2002), http://reclaimdemocracy.org/wordpress/wp-content/uploads/2012/07/fourteenth_amendment_hammerstrom.pdf [https://perma.cc/TSL5-W5VE].

Why Bother with Corporate Personhood, www.nancho.net/corperson/cpbother.html [https://perma.cc/K4XK-B7CQ].

Handy, Charles, *What's a Business For?*, HARV. BUS. REV., Dec. 2002, at 49.

Hansmann, Henry et al., *Law and the Rise of the Firm*, 119 HARV. L. REV. 1333 (2006).

Harris, Ron, INDUSTRIALIZING ENGLISH LAW: ENTREPRENEURSHIP AND BUSINESS ORGANIZATION, 1720–1844 (2000).

The Transplantation of the Legal Discourse on Corporate Personality Theories: From German Codification to British Political Pluralism and American Big Business, 63 WASH. & LEE L. REV. 1421 (2006).

Hart, H. L. A., ESSAYS IN JURISPRUDENCE AND PHILOSOPHY (1983).

Hart, Oliver, *An Economist's Perspective on the Theory of the Firm*, 89 COLUM.L. REV. 1757 (1989).

Härtel, Charmine E. J. & Neal M. Ashkanasy, *Healthy Human Cultures as Positive Work Environments*, *in* THE HANDBOOK OF ORGANIZATIONAL CULTURE AND CLIMATE 85 (Neal M. Ashkanasy et al. eds., 2d ed. 2011).

Hartley, Roger C., HOW FAILED ATTEMPTS TO AMEND THE CONSTITUTION MOBILIZE POLITICAL CHANGE (2017).

Hartman, Edwin, ORGANIZATIONAL ETHICS AND THE GOOD LIFE (1996).

Hartman, Edwin M., *The Commons and the Moral Organization*, 4 BUS. ETHICS Q. 253 (1994).

Hartmann, Thom, THE CRASH OF 2016: THE PLOT TO DESTROY AMERICA – AND WHAT WE CAN DO TO STOP IT (2013).

UNEQUAL PROTECTION: HOW CORPORATIONS BECAME "PEOPLE" – AND YOU CAN FIGHT BACK (2d ed. 2010).

Hasen, Richard L., PLUTOCRATS UNITED: CAMPAIGN MONEY, THE SUPREME COURT, AND THE DISTORTION OF AMERICAN ELECTIONS (2016).

Hasnas, John, *The Phantom Menace of the Responsibility Deficit*, *in* THE MORAL RESPONSIBILITY OF FIRMS 89 (Eric W. Orts & N. Craig Smith eds., 2017).

Should Corporations Have the Right to Vote? A Paradox in the Theory of Corporate Moral Agency, J. BUS. ETHICS, doi:10.1007/s10551-016-3172-0 (2016).

Hatch, Mary Jo, *Material and Meaning in the Dynamics of Organizational Culture and Identity with Implications for the Leadership of Organizational Change*, *in* THE HANDBOOK OF ORGANIZATIONAL CULTURE AND CLIMATE 341 (Neal M. Ashkanasy et al. eds., 2d ed. 2011).

Hatch, Mary Jo, with Ann L. Cunliffe, ORGANIZATION THEORY: MODERN, SYMBOLIC, AND POSTMODERN PERSPECTIVES (3d ed. 2013).

Hatch, Mary Jo & Majken Schultz, TAKING BRAND INITIATIVE: HOW COMPANIES CAN ALIGN STRATEGY, CULTURE, AND IDENTITY THROUGH CORPORATE BRANDING (2008).

Heider, Fritz & Marianne Simmel, *An Experimental Study of Apparent Behavior*, 57 AM. J. PSYCHOL. 243 (1944).

Held, Virginia, *Corporations, Persons, and Responsibility*, *in* SHAME, RESPONSIBILITY AND THE CORPORATION 159 (Hugh Curtler ed., 1986).

Helfand, Michael A. & Barak D. Richman, *The Challenge of Co-Religionist Commerce*, 64 DUKE L.J. 769 (2015).

Henn, Harry G. & John R. Alexander, LAWS OF CORPORATIONS AND OTHER BUSINESS ENTERPRISES (3d student ed. 1983).

Hess, Kendy, *The Unrecognized Consensus About Firm Moral Responsibility*, *in* THE MORAL RESPONSIBILITY OF FIRMS 169 (Eric W. Orts & N. Craig Smith eds., 2017).

Hess, Kendy M., *Because They Can: The Basis for the Moral Obligations of (Certain) Collectives*, 38 MIDWEST STUD. PHIL. 203 (2014).

The Free Will of Corporations (and Other Collectives), 168 PHIL. STUD. 241 (2014).

"If You Tickle Us...": How Corporations Can Be Moral Agents Without Being Persons, 47 J. VALUE INQUIRY 319 (2013).

The Modern Corporation as Moral Agent: The Capacity for "Thought" and a "First-Person Perspective," 26 SW. PHIL. REV., no. 1, Jan. 2010, at 61.

Hessen, Robert, IN DEFENSE OF THE CORPORATION (1979).

Editorial, *Creatures of the State? The Case Against Federal Chartering of Corporations*, BARRON'S NAT'L BUS. & FIN. WKLY., May 24, 1976, at 7.

Hightower, Jim, *Organize in 2012*, OTHER WORDS (Jan. 9, 2012), https://otherwords.org/organize_in_2012/ [https://perma.cc/W332-PL99].

Hindriks, Frank, *How Autonomous Are Collective Agents? Corporate Rights and Normative Individualism*, 79 ERKENNTNIS 1565 (2014).

Hilt, Eric, *Early American Corporations and the State*, *in* CORPORATIONS AND AMERICAN DEMOCRACY 37 (Naomi R. Lamoreaux & William J. Novak eds., 2017).

Holmes, Jr., O. W., THE COMMON LAW (Lawbook Exch. 2005) (1881).

Horwitz, Morton J., Santa Clara *Revisited: The Development of Corporate Theory*, 88 W. VA. L. REV. 173 (1985).

Horwitz, Paul, *The* Hobby Lobby *Moment*, 128 HARV. L. REV. 154 (2014).

Hovenkamp, Herbert, *The Classical Corporation in American Legal Thought*, 76 GEO. L.J. 1593 (1988).

Huber, Wm. Dennis, *Law, Language and Corporatehood: Corporations and the U.S. Constitution*, 1 INT'L J. FOR RULE LAW, no. 2, Dec. 2017, at 78.

Hurst, James Willard, THE LEGITIMACY OF THE BUSINESS CORPORATION IN THE LAW OF THE UNITED STATES 1780–1970 (1970).

INDEP. DIRS. OF THE BD. OF WELLS FARGO & CO., SALES PRACTICES INVESTIGATION REPORT (2017), https://assets.documentcloud.org/documents/3549238/Wells-Fargo-Sales-Practice-Investigation-Board.pdf [https://perma.cc/4JKQ-P382].

Ingber, Stanley, *The Marketplace of Ideas: A Legitimizing Myth*, 1984 DUKE L.J. 1.

INTERBRAND, *Best Global Brands 2017 Rankings*, www.interbrand.com/best-brands/best-global-brands/2017/ranking/ [https://perma.cc/QD6E-CDNT].

Isaacs, Tracy, MORAL RESPONSIBILITY IN COLLECTIVE CONTEXTS (2011).

Iuliano, Jason, *Do Corporations Have Religious Beliefs?*, 90 IND. L. J. 47 (2015).

Iwai, Katsuhito, *Persons, Things and Corporations: The Corporate Personality Controversy and Comparative Corporate Governance*, 47 AM. J. COMP. L. 583 (1999).

Janis, Irving L., GROUPTHINK: PSYCHOLOGICAL STUDIES OF POLICY DECISIONS AND FIASCOES (2d ed. 1982).

Jeavons, Thomas H., *Identifying Characteristics of "Religious" Organizations: An Exploratory Proposal*, *in* SACRED COMPANIES: ORGANIZATIONAL ASPECTS OF RELIGION AND RELIGIOUS ASPECTS OF ORGANIZATIONS 79 (N. J. Demerath III et al. eds., 1998).

Jensen, Michael C. & William H. Meckling, *Theory of the Firm: Managerial Behavior, Agency Costs and Ownership Structure*, 3 J. Fin. Econ. 305 (1976).

Johnson, Lyman, *Law and Legal Theory in the History of Corporate Responsibility: Corporate Personhood*, 35 Seattle U. L. Rev. 1135 (2012).

Johnson, Lyman & David Millon, *Corporate Law After* Hobby Lobby, 70 Bus. Law. 1 (2014/2015).

Joo, Thomas W., *The Modern Corporation and Campaign Finance: Incorporating Corporate Governance Analysis into First Amendment Jurisprudence*, 79 Wash. U. L.Q. 1 (2001).

Kadlac, Adam, *Humanizing Personhood*, 13 Ethical Theory & Moral Prac. 421 (2010).

Kahan, Dan M., *Social Influence, Social Meaning, and Deterrence*, 83 Va. L. Rev. 349 (1997).

Kant, Immanuel, Foundations of the Metaphysics of Morals (Robert Paul Wolff ed., Lewis White Beck trans., Bobbs-Merrill Co. 1969) (1785).

Keeley, Michael, *Organizations as Non-Persons*, 15 J. Value Inquiry 149 (1981).

A Social-Contract Theory of Organizations (1988).

Kennedy, Robert G., *Corporations, Common Goods, and Human Persons*, 4 Ave Maria L. Rev. 1 (2006).

Kim, Susanna M., *Characteristics of Soulless Persons: The Applicability of the Character Evidence Rule to Corporations*, 2000 U. Ill. L. Rev. 763.

Kish-Gephart, Jennifer J. et al., *Bad Apples, Bad Cases, and Bad Barrels: Meta-Analytic Evidence About Sources of Unethical Decisions at Work*, 95 J. Applied Psychol. 1 (2010).

Korten, Fran, *10 Ways to Stop Corporate Dominance of Politics*, YES! Mag. (Jan. 25, 2010), www.yesmagazine.org/people-power/10-ways-to-stop-corporate-dominance-of-politics [https://perma.cc/KZT6-FXWV].

Krannich, Jess M., *The Corporate "Person": A New Analytical Approach to a Flawed Method of Constitutional Interpretation*, 37 Loy. U. Chi. L.J. 61 (2005).

Kreiner, Glen E., *Organizational Identity: Culture's Conceptual Cousin*, *in* The Handbook of Organizational Culture and Climate 463 (Neal M. Ashkanasy et al. eds., 2d ed. 2011).

Kuhner, Timothy K., Capitalism v. Democracy: Money in Politics and the Free Market Constitution (2014).

Ladd, John, *Morality and the Ideal of Rationality in Formal Organizations*, 54 Monist 488 (1970).

Persons and Responsibility: Ethical Concepts and Impertinent Analogies, *in* Shame, Responsibility and the Corporation 77 (Hugh Curtler ed., 1986).

LaFollette, Hugh, *Introduction*, *in* The Oxford Handbook of Practical Ethics 1 (Hugh LaFollette ed., 2003).

Lakoff, George & Mark Johnson, Philosophy in the Flesh: The Embodied Mind and Its Challenge to Western Thought (1999).

Lakoff, Sanford A., *Private Government in the Managed Society*, *in* Private Government 218 (Sanford A. Lakoff with Daniel Rich eds., 1973).

Lambert III, Lake, Spirituality, Inc.: Religion in the American Workplace (2009).

Lamoreaux, Naomi R., The Great Merger Movement in American Business, 1895–1904 (1985).

Partnerships, Corporations, and the Limits on Contractual Freedom in U.S. History: An Essay in Economics, Law, and Culture, *in* Constructing Corporate America: History, Politics, Culture 29 (Kenneth Lipartito & David B. Sicilia eds., 2004).

Lamoreaux, Naomi R. & William J. Novak, *Corporations and American Democracy: An Introduction*, *in* Corporations and American Democracy 1 (Naomi R. Lamoreaux & William J. Novak eds., 2017).

Laski, Harold J., *The Personality of Associations*, 29 HARV. L. REV. 404 (1916).

Latham, Earl, *The Body Politic of the Corporation*, *in* THE CORPORATION IN MODERN SOCIETY 218 (Edward S. Mason ed., 1959).

Laufer, William S., CORPORATE BODIES AND GUILTY MINDS: THE FAILURE OF CORPORATE CRIMINAL LIABILITY (2006).

Lawrence, Paul R. & Davis Dyer, RENEWING AMERICAN INDUSTRY (1st paperback ed. 1984).

Laycock, Douglas, *Religious Liberty and the Culture Wars*, 2014 U. ILL. L. REV. 839.

Levitt, Justin, *Confronting the Impact of* Citizens United, 29 YALE L. & POL'Y REV. 217 (2010).

Lewis, Anthony, FREEDOM FOR THE THOUGHT THAT WE HATE: A BIOGRAPHY OF THE FIRST AMENDMENT (2007).

Linzey, Thomas, *Awakening a Sleeping Giant: Creating a Quasi-Private Cause of Action for Revoking Corporate Charters in Response to Environmental Violations*, 13 PACE ENVTL. L. REV. 219 (1995).

Petition to Attorney General of Delaware to Revoke Corporate Charters of WMX Technologies and Chemical Waste Management Inc., 52 GUILD PRAC. 116 (1995).

Lipartito, Kenneth & David B. Sicilia, *Afterword: Toward New Renderings*, *in* CONSTRUCTING CORPORATE AMERICA: HISTORY, POLITICS, CULTURE 343 (Kenneth Lipartito & David B. Sicilia eds., 2004).

Introduction: Crossing Corporate Boundaries, *in* CONSTRUCTING CORPORATE AMERICA: HISTORY, POLITICS, CULTURE 1 (Kenneth Lipartito & David B. Sicilia eds., 2004).

List, Christian, *What Is It Like to Be a Group Agent?*, NOÛS 1, doi:10.1111/nous.12162 (2016).

List, Christian & Philip Pettit, GROUP AGENCY: THE POSSIBILITY, DESIGN, AND STATUS OF CORPORATE AGENTS (2011).

Long, Norton E., *The Corporation, Its Satellites, and the Local Community*, *in* THE CORPORATION IN MODERN SOCIETY 202 (Edward S. Mason ed., 1959).

Lund, Christopher C., *Religious Liberty After* Gonzales: *A Look at State RFRAs*, 55 S.D. L. REV. 466 (2010).

Macfarlane, Alan, THE ORIGINS OF ENGLISH INDIVIDUALISM (1978).

Machen, Jr., Arthur W., *Corporate Personality*, 24 HARV. L. REV. 253 (1911).

Corporate Personality, 24 HARV. L. REV. 347 (1911).

Magid, Henry Meyer, ENGLISH POLITICAL PLURALISM: THE PROBLEM OF FREEDOM AND ORGANIZATION (AMS Press, Inc. 1966) (1941).

Maitland, Ian, *How Insiders Abuse the Idea of Corporate Personality*, *in* THE MORAL RESPONSIBILITY OF FIRMS 106 (Eric W. Orts & N. Craig Smith eds., 2017).

Mäkelä, Pekka, *Collective Agents & Moral Responsibility*, 38 J. SOC. PHIL. 456 (2007).

Maltz, Earl M., CIVIL RIGHTS, THE CONSTITUTION, AND CONGRESS, 1863–1869 (1990).

Manski-McCabe-Graves: 'Overrule the Court' Rally in Madison, DEMOCRACY SQUARE (Feb. 16, 2010), http://ds.liberalart.space/news/manski-mccabe-graves-overrule-court-rally-madison [https://perma.cc/TJ4 C-JB8 G].

Mark, Gregory A., Hobby Lobby *and Corporate Personhood: Taking the U.S. Supreme Court's Reasoning at Face Value*, 65 DEPAUL L. REV. 535 (2016).

Comment, *The Personification of the Business Corporation in American Law*, 54 U. CHI. L. REV. 1441 (1987).

Martin, Jack & Mark H. Bickhard, *Introducing Persons and the Psychology of Personhood*, *in* THE PSYCHOLOGY OF PERSONHOOD: PHILOSOPHICAL, HISTORICAL, SOCIAL-DEVELOPMENTAL, AND NARRATIVE PERSPECTIVES 1 (Jack Martin & Mark H. Bickhard eds., 2013).

Mason, Edward S., *Introduction*, *in* THE CORPORATION IN MODERN SOCIETY 1 (Edward S. Mason ed., 1959).

Mauss, Marcel, *A Category of the Human Mind: The Notion of Person; the Notion of Self* (W.D. Halls trans.), *in* The Category of the Person: Anthropology, Philosophy, History 1 (Michael Carrithers et al. eds., 1985).

May, Larry, The Morality of Groups: Collective Responsibility, Group-Based Harm, and Corporate Rights (1987).

Vicarious Agency and Corporate Responsibility, 43 Phil. Stud. 69 (1983).

Mayer, Carl J., *Personalizing the Impersonal: Corporations and the Bill of Rights*, 41 Hastings L.J. 577 (1990).

Mayer, David M., *A Review of the Literature on Ethical Climate and Culture, in* The Oxford Handbook of Organizational Climate and Culture 415 (Benjamin Schneider & Karen M. Barbera eds., 2014).

McAdams, Richard H., *The Expressive Power of Adjudication*, 2005 U. Ill. L. Rev. 1043.

The Expressive Powers of Law: Theories and Limits (2015).

McCall, Catherine, Concepts of Person (1990).

McCluskey, Martha T., *The Substantive Politics of Formal Corporate Power*, 53 Buff. L. Rev. 1453 (2006).

McConnell, Michael W., *Reconsidering* Citizens United *as a Press Clause Case*, 123 Yale L.J. 412 (2013).

McDonald, Michael, *The Personless Paradigm*, 37 U. Toronto L.J. 212 (1987).

McKenna, Michael, *Collective Responsibility and an Agent Meaning Theory*, 30 Midwest Stud. Phil. 16 (2006).

Meese, Alan J. & Nathan B. Oman, Hobby Lobby, *Corporate Law, and the Theory of the Firm: Why For-Profit Corporations Are RFRA Persons*, 127 Harv. L. Rev. F. 273 (2014).

Messieh, Nancy, 12 *Tech Companies That Offer Their Employees the Coolest Perks*, Next Web (Apr. 9, 2012), https://thenextweb.com/insider/2012/04/09/12-startups-that-offer-their-employees-the-coolest-perks/ [https://perma.cc/H2U7-X4DY].

Metzger, Michael B., *Corporate Criminal Liability for Defective Products: Policies, Problems, and Prospects*, 73 Geo. L.J. 1 (1984).

Meyers, William, The Santa Clara Blues: Corporate Personhood versus Democracy (2000), http://reclaimdemocracy.org/wordpress/wp-content/uploads/2012/07/santa_clara_blues.pdf [https://perma.cc/RZ78-XHY9].

Miller, Arthur S., *Corporations and Our Two Constitutions, in* Corporations and Society: Power and Responsibility 241 (Warren J. Samuels & Arthur S. Miller eds., 1987).

Miller, Darrell A. H., *Guns, Inc.:* Citizens United, McDonald, *and the Future of Corporate Constitutional Rights*, 86 N.Y.U. L. Rev. 887 (2011).

Millon, David, *Personifying the Corporate Body*, 2 Graven Images 116 (1995).

The Single Constituency Argument in the Economic Analysis of Business Law, in Law & Economics: Toward Social Justice 43 (Dana L. Gold ed., 2009).

Theories of the Corporation, 1990 Duke L.J. 201.

Moore, Geoff, *Corporate Moral Agency: Review and Implications*, 21 J. Bus. Ethics 329 (1999).

Moore, John D., *The First Amendment Case for Corporate Religious Rights*, 16 Nev. L.J. 1 (2015).

Morawetz, Victor, A Treatise on the Law of Private Corporations (Vol. 1) (Boston, Little, Brown, & Co. 2d ed. 1886).

A Treatise on the Law of Private Corporations other than Charitable (Boston, Little, Brown, & Co. 1882).

Morgan, Molly & Jan Edwards, *Abolish Corporate Personhood*, 59 Guild Prac. 209 (2002).

Morris, Paul et al., *Beyond Anecdotes: An Empirical Study of "Anthropomorphism,"* 8 Soc'y & Animals 151 (2000).

MOVE TO AMEND, THE PATH TO THE 28TH AMENDMENT: STRATEGIC PLAN TO PASS THE "WE THE PEOPLE AMENDMENT" TO THE UNITED STATES CONSTITUTION (2016), https://movetoamend.org/sites/default/files/move_to_amend_strategic_plan.pdf [https://perma.cc/24K3-V8WM].

Myers, Joe, *How Do the World's Biggest Companies Compare to the Biggest Economies?*, WORLD ECON. F. (Oct. 19, 2016), www.weforum.org/agenda/2016/10/corporations-not-countries-dominate-the-list-of-the-world-s-biggest-economic-entities/ [https://perma.cc/G3QD-C3HQ].

Naffine, Ngaire, *Who Are Law's Persons? From Cheshire Cats to Responsible Subjects*, 66 MOD. L. REV. 346 (2003).

Needleman, Martin L. & Carolyn Needleman, *Organizational Crime: Two Models of Criminogenesis*, 20 SOC. Q. 517 (1979).

Nelson, James D., *Conscience, Incorporated*, 2013 MICH. ST. L. REV. 1565.

Nesteruk, Jeffrey, Bellotti *and the Question of Corporate Moral Agency*, 1988 COLUM. BUS. L. REV. 683.

Law and the Virtues: Developing a Legal Theory for Business Ethics, 5 BUS. ETHICS Q. 361 (1995) (book review).

Law, Virtue, and the Corporation, 33 AM. BUS. L.J. 473 (1996).

The Moral Status of the Corporation: Comments on an Inquiry, 2 BUS. ETHICS Q. 461 (1992).

Nesteruk, Jeffrey & David T. Risser, *Conceptions of the Corporation and Ethical Decision Making in Business*, 12 BUS. & PROF. ETHICS J., no. 1, Spring 1993, at 73.

Neuborne, Burt, *Of "Singles" Without Baseball: Corporations as Frozen Relational Moments*, 64 RUTGERS L. REV. 769 (2012).

Nichols, John, *The Senate Tried to Overturn 'Citizens United' Today. Guess What Stopped Them?*, NATION (Sep. 11, 2014), www.thenation.com/article/senate-tried-overturn-citizens-united-today-guess-what-stopped-them/ [https://perma.cc/J9PG-6JZW].

Note, *Constitutional Rights of the Corporate Person*, 91 YALE L.J. 1641 (1982).

Note, *What We Talk About When We Talk About Persons: The Language of a Legal Fiction*, 114 HARV. L. REV. 1745 (2001).

Oakes, Jeannie et al., *Grassroots Organizing, Social Movements, and the Right to High-Quality Education*, 4 STAN. J. C.R. & C.L. 339 (2008).

O'Kelley, Jr., Charles R., *The Constitutional Rights of Corporations Revisited: Social and Political Expression and the Corporation After* First National Bank v. Bellotti, 67 GEO. L. J. 1347 (1979).

Olins, Wally, *How Brands Are Taking over the Corporation*, *in* THE EXPRESSIVE ORGANIZATION: LINKING IDENTITY, REPUTATION, AND THE CORPORATE BRAND 51 (Majken Schultz et al. eds., 2000).

Öncer, Ayla Zehra & Müge Leyla Yildiz, *The Impact of Ethical Climate on Relationship Between Corporate Reputation and Organizational Identification*, 58 PROCEDIA SOC. & BEHAV. SCI. 714 (2012).

Oppenheimer, Mark, *Few Resist the Temptation to Opine on Chick-fil-A*, N.Y. TIMES (Aug. 3, 2012), www.nytimes.com/2012/08/04/us/taking-sides-on-chick-fil-a-is-a-temptation-few-can-resist.html [https://perma.cc/7JDJ-3ZY7].

Orts, Eric W., BUSINESS PERSONS: A LEGAL THEORY OF THE FIRM (2013).

Theorizing the Firm: Organizational Ontology in the Supreme Court, 65 DEPAUL L. REV. 559 (2016).

Orts, Eric W. & N. Craig Smith, eds., THE MORAL RESPONSIBILITY OF FIRMS (2017).

Padfield, Stefan J., *The Silent Role of Corporate Theory in the Supreme Court's Campaign Finance Cases*, 15 U. PA. J. CONST. L. 831 (2013).

Patton, William & Randall Bartlett, *Corporate "Persons" and Freedom of Speech: The Political Impact of Legal Mythology*, 1981 WIS. L. REV. 494 (1981).

Peters, Ellen A., *Reality and the Language of the Law*, 90 YALE L.J. 1193 (1981).

Peterson, Dane K., *Deviant Workplace Behavior and the Organization's Ethical Climate*, 17 J. BUS. & PSYCHOL. 47 (2002).

Petriglieri, Jennifer L. & Beth A. Devine, *Mobilizing Organizational Action Against Identity Threats*, *in* THE OXFORD HANDBOOK OF ORGANIZATIONAL IDENTITY 239 (Michael G. Pratt et al. eds., 2016).

Pettit, Philip, MADE WITH WORDS: HOBBES ON LANGUAGE, MIND, AND POLITICS (2008).

Responsibility Incorporated, 117 ETHICS 171 (2007).

Phillips, Michael J., *Corporate Moral Personhood and Three Conceptions of the Corporation*, 2 BUS. ETHICS Q. 435 (1992).

Reappraising the Real Entity Theory of the Corporation, 21 FLA. ST. U. L. REV. 1061 (1994).

Phillips, Nelson & Cynthia Hardy, DISCOURSE ANALYSIS: INVESTIGATING PROCESSES OF SOCIAL CONSTRUCTION (2002).

Pibel, Doug, *Real People v. Corporate "People": The Fight Is On*, YES! MAG. (May 27, 2010), www.yesmagazine.org/issues/water-solutions/real-people-v.-corporate-people-the-fight-is-on [https://perma.cc/4B52-A787].

Piety, Tamara R., *Against Freedom of Commercial Expression*, 29 CARDOZO L. REV. 2583 (2008).

BRANDISHING THE FIRST AMENDMENT: COMMERCIAL EXPRESSION IN AMERICA (2012).

Why Personhood Matters, 30 CONST. COMMENT. 361 (2015).

Pilon, Roger, *Corporations and Rights: On Treating Corporate People Justly*, 13 GA. L. REV. 1245 (1979).

Plitt, Mark, Ricky R. Savjani & David M. Eagleman, *Are Corporations People Too? The Neural Correlates of Moral Judgments About Companies and Individuals*, 10 SOC. NEUROSCIENCE 113 (2015).

Pollman, Elizabeth, *Citizens Not United: The Lack of Stockholder Voluntariness in Corporate Political Speech*, 119 YALE L.J. ONLINE 53 (2009).

Constitutionalizing Corporate Law, 69 VAND. L. REV. 639 (2016).

Line Drawing in Corporate Rights Determinations, 65 DEPAUL L. REV. 597 (2016).

Reconceiving Corporate Personhood, 2011 UTAH L. REV. 1629.

Pollock, Frederick & Frederic W. Maitland, *Corporation and Person*, *in* ANTHROPOLOGY AND EARLY LAW 300 (Lawrence Krader ed., 1966).

PONTIFICAL COUNCIL FOR JUSTICE AND PEACE, VOCATION OF THE BUSINESS LEADER: A REFLECTION (4th ed. 2014), www.stthomas.edu/media/catholicstudies/center/ryan/publications/publicationpdfs/vocationofthebusinessleaderpdf/PontificalCouncil_4.pdf [https://perma.cc/LEL9-U8A7].

Poole, Ross, *On Being a Person*, 74 AUSTRALASIAN J. PHIL. 38 (1996).

Posner, Eric, *Stop Fussing over Personhood*, SLATE (Dec. 11, 2013), www.slate.com/articles/news_and_politics/view_from_chicago/2013/12/personhood_for_corporations_and_chimpanzees_is_an_essential_legal_fiction.html [https://perma.cc/3AR2-CHFT].

Post, Robert C., CITIZENS DIVIDED: CAMPAIGN FINANCE REFORM AND THE CONSTITUTION (2014).

Pratt, Michael G., *Disentangling Collective Identities*, *in* 5 RESEARCH ON MANAGING GROUPS AND TEAMS: IDENTITY ISSUES IN GROUPS 161 (Jeffrey T. Polzer ed., 2003).

Preda, Adina, *Group Rights and Group Agency*, 9 J. MORAL PHIL. 229 (2012).

Price, Nancy & David E. Delk, *Corporations Are Not People*, ALLIANCE FOR DEMOCRACY, www.theallianceforddemocracy.org/brochure.pdf [https://perma.cc/3WH3-HKXM].

Program on Corps., Law & Democracy, *Why Abolish* All *Corporate Constitutional Rights*, BY WHAT AUTHORITY, Nov. 2010, www.poclad.org/BWA/files/2010–11/BWANov2010.pdf [https://perma.cc/T3LD-UJXK].
Quigley, William, *Catholic Social Thought and the Amorality of Large Corporations: Time to Abolish Corporate Personhood*, 5 LOY. J. PUB. INT. L. 109 (2004).
Quinton, Anthony, *Social Objects*, 76 PROC. ARISTOTELIAN SOC'Y 1 (1976).
Radin, Margaret Jane, *Reflections on Objectification*, 65 S. CAL. L. REV. 341 (1991).
Radin, Max, *The Endless Problem of Corporate Personality*, 32 COLUM. L. REV. 643 (1932).
THE LEGISLATION OF THE GREEKS AND ROMANS ON CORPORATIONS (Tuttle, Morehouse & Taylor Press 1910).
Rafanelli, Lucia M., *A Defense of Individualism in the Age of Corporate Rights*, 25 J. POL. PHIL. 281 (2017).
Ravitch, Frank S., *Be Careful What You Wish for: Why* Hobby Lobby *Weakens Religious Freedom*, 2016 BYU L. REV. 55.
FREEDOM'S EDGE: RELIGIOUS FREEDOM, SEXUAL FREEDOM, AND THE FUTURE OF AMERICA (2016).
Redish, Martin H. & Howard M. Wasserman, *What's Good for General Motors: Corporate Speech and the Theory of Free Expression*, 66 GEO. WASH. L. REV. 235 (1998).
Rienzi, Mark L., *God and the Profits: Is There Religious Liberty for Moneymakers?*, 21 GEO. MASON L. REV. 59 (2013).
Ripken, Susanna K., *Corporations Are People Too: A Multi-Dimensional Approach to the Corporate Personhood Puzzle*, 15 FORDHAM J. CORP. & FIN. L. 97 (2009).
Ripken, Susanna Kim, Citizens United, *Corporate Personhood, and Corporate Power: The Tension Between Constitutional Law and Corporate Law*, 6 U. ST. THOMAS J. L. & PUB. POL'Y 285 (2012).
Corporate First Amendment Rights After Citizens United*: An Analysis of the Popular Movement to End the Constitutional Personhood of Corporations*, 14 U. PA. J. BUS. L. 209 (2011).
Risser, David Troup, *Power and Collective Responsibility*, 9 KINESIS 23 (1978).
Riva, Paola et al., *Humanizing Machines: Anthropomorphization of Slot Machines Increases Gambling*, 21 J. EXPERIMENTAL PSYCHOL. APPLIED 313 (2015).
Robbins, Stephen P. & Timothy A. Judge, ORGANIZATIONAL BEHAVIOR (17th ed. 2017).
Robinson, Zoë, *Constitutional Personhood*, 84 GEO. WASH. L. REV. 605 (2016).
Rodionova, Zlata, *World's Largest Corporations Make More Money Than Most Countries on Earth Combined*, INDEPENDENT (Sep. 13, 2016), www.independent.co.uk/news/business/news/worlds-largest-corporations-more-money-countries-world-combined-apple-walmart-shell-global-justice-a7245991.html [https://perma.cc/QBU5-RUYC].
Roe, Mark J., *The Shareholder Wealth Maximization Norm and Industrial Organization*, 149 U. PA. L. REV. 2063 (2001).
Rönnegard, David, THE FALLACY OF CORPORATE MORAL AGENCY (2015).
How Autonomy Alone Debunks Corporate Moral Agency, 32 BUS. & PROF. ETHICS J. 77 (2013).
Rönnegard, David & Manuel Velasquez, *On (Not) Attributing Moral Responsibility to Organizations*, *in* THE MORAL RESPONSIBILITY OF FIRMS 123 (Eric W. Orts & N. Craig Smith eds., 2017).
Rorty, Amélie Oksenberg, ed., THE IDENTITIES OF PERSONS (1976).
Rorty, Richard, PHILOSOPHY AND THE MIRROR OF NATURE (1979).
Rosen, Mark D., *Establishment, Expressivism, and Federalism*, 78 CHI.-KENT L. REV. 669 (2003).

Rosenberg, David, *The Corporate Paradox of* Citizens United *and* Hobby Lobby, 11 N.Y.U. J. L. & LIBERTY 308 (2017).
Rothschild, Matthew, *Corporations Aren't Persons: Amend the Constitution*, PROGRESSIVE, Apr. 2010, at 16.
Rovane, Carol, THE BOUNDS OF AGENCY: AN ESSAY IN REVISIONARY METAPHYSICS (1998).
Rowland, Wade, GREED, INC.: WHY CORPORATIONS RULE THE WORLD AND HOW WE LET IT HAPPEN (Arcade Publ'g 2012) (2005).
Rubin, Dale, *Corporate Personhood: How the Courts Have Employed Bogus Jurisprudence to Grant Corporations Constitutional Rights Intended for Individuals*, 28 QUINNIPIAC L. REV. 523 (2010).
Rucker, Philip, *Mitt Romney Says 'Corporations Are People,'* WASH. POST (Aug. 11, 2011), www.washingtonpost.com/politics/mitt-romney-says-corporations-are-people/2011/08/11/gIQABwZ38I_story.html [https://perma.cc/6LF6-BE5C].
Rutledge, Thomas E., *A Corporation Has No Soul – The Business Entity Law Response to Challenges to the PPACA Contraceptive Mandate*, 5 WM. & MARY BUS. L. REV. 1 (2014).
Sackman, Sonja A., *Culture and Performance, in* THE HANDBOOK OF ORGANIZATIONAL CULTURE AND CLIMATE 188 (Neal M. Ashkanasy et al. eds., 2d ed. 2011).
Samuels, Warren J., *The Idea of the Corporation as a Person: On the Normative Significance of Judicial Language, in* CORPORATIONS AND SOCIETY: POWER AND RESPONSIBILITY 113 (Warren J. Samuels & Arthur S. Miller eds., 1987).
Samuels, Warren J. & Arthur S. Miller, *Introduction: Corporate America, in* CORPORATIONS AND SOCIETY: POWER AND RESPONSIBILITY 1 (Warren J. Samuels & Arthur S. Miller eds., 1987).
Schall, James V., *The Corporation: What Is It?*, 4 AVE MARIA L. REV. 105 (2006).
Schane, Sanford A., *The Corporation Is a Person: The Language of a Legal Fiction*, 61 TUL. L. REV. 563 (1987).
Schein, Edgar H., THE CORPORATE CULTURE SURVIVAL GUIDE (new & rev. ed. 2009).
Schein, Edgar H., with Peter Schein, ORGANIZATIONAL CULTURE AND LEADERSHIP (5th ed. 2017).
Scherer, Andreas Georg, *Modes of Explanation in Organization Theory, in* THE OXFORD HANDBOOK OF ORGANIZATION THEORY 310 (Haridimos Tsoukas & Christian Knudsen eds., 2003).
Schneider, Benjamin & Karen M. Barbera, *Introduction, in* THE OXFORD HANDBOOK OF ORGANIZATIONAL CLIMATE AND CULTURE 3 (Benjamin Schneider & Karen M. Barbera eds., 2014).
Schragger, Richard & Micah Schwartzman, *Some Realism About Corporate Rights, in* THE RISE OF CORPORATE RELIGIOUS LIBERTY 345 (Micah Schwartzman et al. eds., 2016).
Scott, W. Richard, ORGANIZATIONS: RATIONAL, NATURAL, AND OPEN SYSTEMS (5th ed. 2003).
Scruton, Roger, *Corporate Persons, in* 63 PROC. ARISTOTELIAN SOC'Y, SUPP. VOL. 239 (1989).
Searle, John R., MAKING THE SOCIAL WORLD: THE STRUCTURE OF HUMAN CIVILIZATION (2010).
Selznick, Philip, LEADERSHIP IN ADMINISTRATION: A SOCIOLOGICAL INTERPRETATION (1957).
Sepinwall, Amy J., *Blame, Emotion, and the Corporation, in* THE MORAL RESPONSIBILITY OF FIRMS 143 (Eric W. Orts & N. Craig Smith eds., 2017).
Citizens United *and the Ineluctable Question of Corporate Citizenship*, 44 CONN. L. REV. 575 (2012).
Conscience and Complicity: Assessing Pleas for Religious Exemptions in Hobby Lobby's *Wake*, 82 U. CHI. L. REV. 1897 (2015).
Corporate Piety and Impropriety: Hobby Lobby's *Extension of RFRA Rights to the For-Profit Corporation*, 5 HARV. BUS. L. REV. 173 (2015).

Denying Corporate Rights and Punishing Corporate Wrongs, 25 BUS. ETHICS Q. 517 (2015).
Sepper, Elizabeth, *Taking Conscience Seriously*, 98 VA. L. REV. 1501 (2012).
Shapiro, Ilya & Caitlyn W. McCarthy, *So What If Corporations Aren't People?*, 44 J. MARSHALL L. REV. 701 (2011).
Shapiro, Robert J. & Douglas Dowson, Manhattan Inst., Corporate Political Spending: Why the New Critics Are Wrong (2012), www.manhattan-institute.org/pdf/lpr_15.pdf [https://perma.cc/L3ZM-UKQM].
Sherman, Steven J. & Elise J. Percy, *The Psychology of Collective Responsibility: When and Why Collective Entities Are Likely to Be Held Responsible for the Misdeeds of Individual Members*, 19 J. L. & POL'Y 137 (2010).
Shiffrin, Steven H., WHAT'S WRONG WITH THE FIRST AMENDMENT? (2016).
Siegel, Reva B., *Constitutional Culture, Social Movement Conflict and Constitutional Change: The Case of the de facto ERA*, 94 CAL. L. REV. 1323 (2006).
Sims, Ronald R. & William I. Sauser, Jr., *Received Wisdom, Groupthink, and Organizational Ethical Culture, in* RECEIVED WISDOM, KERNELS OF TRUTH, AND BOUNDARY CONDITIONS IN ORGANIZATIONAL STUDIES 373 (Daniel J. Svyantek & Kevin T. Mahoney eds., 2013).
Smedley, Audrey & Brian D. Smedley, *Race as Biology Is Fiction, Racism as a Social Problem Is Real: Anthropological and Historical Perspectives on the Social Construction of Race*, 60 AM. PSYCHOLOGIST 16 (2005).
Smith, Bryant, *Legal Personality*, 37 YALE L.J. 283 (1928).
Smith, Thomas A., *The Use and Abuse of Corporate Personality*, 2 STAN. AGORA 69 (2001).
Soares, C., *Corporate Versus Individual Moral Responsibility*, 46 J. BUS. ETHICS 143 (2003).
Solomon, Robert C., ETHICS AND EXCELLENCE: COOPERATION AND INTEGRITY IN BUSINESS (1992).
Somin, Ilya, *People Organized as Corporations Are People Too*, VOLOKH CONSPIRACY (Jan. 21, 2010, 5:12 PM), http://volokh.com/2010/01/21/people-organized-as-corporations-are-people-too/ [https://perma.cc/6GXF-P25 L].
Sopoci-Belknap, Kaitlin, Citizens United v. FEC: *Supreme Court Sides with Large Corporations*, DEMOCRACY UNLIMITED OF HUMBOLDT COUNTY (Feb. 28, 2010), www.duhc.org/profiles/blogs/citizens-united-v-fec-supreme [https://perma.cc/7GNE-E6DY].
Spicker, Stuart F., ed., THE PHILOSOPHY OF THE BODY: REJECTIONS OF CARTESIAN DUALISM (1970).
Stevenson, Jr., Russell B., *Corporations and Social Responsibility: In Search of the Corporate Soul*, 42 GEO. WASH. L. REV. 709 (1974).
Stolberg, Sheryl Gay, *Obama Turns Up Heat Over Ruling on Campaign Spending*, N.Y. TIMES, Jan. 24, 2010, at A18.
Stone, Christopher D., *Corporate Vices and Corporate Virtues: Do Public/Private Distinctions Matter?*, 130 U. PA. L. REV. 1441 (1982).
WHERE THE LAW ENDS: THE SOCIAL CONTROL OF CORPORATE BEHAVIOR (1975).
Strassfeld, Robert N., Note, *Corporate Standing to Allege Race Discrimination in Civil Rights Actions*, 69 VA. L. REV. 1153 (1983).
Stratman, Thomas & J. W. Verret, *How Does Corporate Political Activity Allowed by* Citizens United v. Federal Election Commission *Affect Shareholder Wealth?*, 58 J.L. & ECON. 545 (2015).
Strauss, David A., *The Irrelevance of Constitutional Amendments*, 114 HARV. L. REV. 1457 (2001).
Strine, Jr., Leo E., *A Job Is Not a Hobby: The Judicial Revival of Corporate Paternalism and Its Problematic Implications*, 41 J. CORP. L. 71 (2015).

Suchman, Mark C., *On Beyond Interest: Rational, Normative and Cognitive Perspectives in the Social Scientific Study of Law*, 1997 WIS. L. REV. 475.

Sugarman, Jeff, *Persons and Historical Ontology*, *in* THE PSYCHOLOGY OF PERSONHOOD: PHILOSOPHICAL, HISTORICAL, SOCIAL-DEVELOPMENTAL, AND NARRATIVE PERSPECTIVES 81 (Jack Martin & Mark H. Bickhard eds., 2013).

Suggs, Robert E., *Racial Discrimination in Business Transactions*, 42 HASTINGS L.J. 1257 (1991).

Summers, Robert S., *Pragmatic Instrumentalism in Twentieth Century American Legal Thought – A Synthesis and Critique of Our Dominant General Theory About Law and Its Use*, 66 CORNELL L. REV. 861 (1981).

Sunstein, Cass R., *On the Expressive Function of Law*, 144 U. PA. L. REV. 2021 (1996).

Sunstein, Cass R. & Reid Hastie, WISER: GETTING BEYOND GROUPTHINK TO MAKE GROUPS SMARTER (2015).

Szanto, Thomas, *Do Group Persons Have Emotions – Or Should They?*, *in* ANALYTIC AND CONTINENTAL PHILOSOPHY: METHODS AND PERSPECTIVES: PROCEEDINGS OF THE 37TH INTERNATIONAL WITTGENSTEIN SYMPOSIUM 261 (Sonja Rinofner-Kreidl & Harald Wiltsche eds., 2016).

Taylor, Henry O., A TREATISE ON THE LAW OF PRIVATE CORPORATIONS HAVING CAPITAL STOCK (Philadelphia, Kay & Brother 1884).

Teachout, Zephyr, CORRUPTION IN AMERICA (2014).

Teles, Steven M., THE RISE OF THE CONSERVATIVE LEGAL MOVEMENT: THE BATTLE FOR CONTROL OF THE LAW (2008).

Tergesen, Anne, *Financial Advisers Put Faith in Religion-Based Investing*, WALL ST. J. (Apr. 5, 2017), www.wsj.com/articles/financial-advisers-put-faith-in-religion-based-investing-1490363559 [https://perma.cc/C7JR-QCXH].

Thompson, Paul B., *Why Do We Need a Theory of Corporate Responsibility?*, *in* SHAME, RESPONSIBILITY AND THE CORPORATION 113 (Hugh Curtler ed., 1986).

Tissaw, Michael A., *The Person Concept and the Ontology of Persons*, *in* THE PSYCHOLOGY OF PERSONHOOD: PHILOSOPHICAL, HISTORICAL, SOCIAL-DEVELOPMENTAL, AND NARRATIVE PERSPECTIVES 19 (Jack Martin & Mark H. Bickhard eds., 2013).

Tolbert, Pamela S. & Richard H. Hall, ORGANIZATIONS: STRUCTURES, PROCESSES, AND OUTCOMES (10th ed. 2009).

Tollefsen, Deborah Perron, GROUPS AS AGENTS (2015).

Tosi, Henry L., THEORIES OF ORGANIZATION (2d ed. 1984).

Tribe, Laurence H., *The Curvature of Constitutional Space: What Lawyers Can Learn from Modern Physics*, 103 HARV. L. REV. 1 (1989).

Trumbull, Mark, *Can 'Occupy Wall Street' Really Get Money out of Politics?*, CHRISTIAN SCI. MONITOR (Oct. 14, 2011), www.csmonitor.com/USA/Politics/2011/1014/Can-Occupy-Wall-Street-really-get-money-out-of-politics [https://perma.cc/A2XT-D8UJ].

Tsuk, Dalia, *From Pluralism to Individualism: Berle and Means and 20th-Century American Legal Thought*, 30 LAW & SOC. INQUIRY 179 (2005) (book review).

Tucker, Anne, *Flawed Assumptions: A Corporate Law Analysis of Free Speech and Corporate Personhood in* Citizens United, 61 CASE W. RES. L. REV. 497 (2010).

Tur, Richard, *The 'Person' in Law*, *in* PERSONS AND PERSONALITY: A CONTEMPORARY INQUIRY 116 (Arthur Peacocke & Grant Gillett eds., 1987).

Tushnet, Mark, *Do For-Profit Corporations Have Rights of Religious Conscience?*, 99 CORNELL L. REV. ONLINE 70 (2013).

U.S. COMM'N ON CIVIL RIGHTS, PEACEFUL COEXISTENCE: RECONCILING NONDISCRIMINATION PRINCIPLES WITH CIVIL LIBERTIES (2016), www.usccr.gov/pubs/Peaceful-Coexistence-09-07-16.PDF [https://perma.cc/728R-TJX8].

U.S. Conf. of Cath. Bishops, *HHS Proposal Falls Short in Meeting Church Concerns; Bishops Look Forward to Addressing Issues with Administration* (Feb. 7, 2013), http://usccb.org/news/2013/13–037.cfm [https://perma.cc/TN87-EPWS].

Vacharkulksemsuk, Tanya et al., *Establishing a Positive Emotional Climate to Create 21st-Century Organizational Change, in* THE HANDBOOK OF ORGANIZATIONAL CULTURE AND CLIMATE 101 (Neal M. Ashkanasy et al. eds., 2d ed. 2011).

van Kleef, Gerben A. & Agneta H. Fischer, *Emotional Collectives: How Groups Shape Emotions and Emotions Shape Groups*, 30 COGNITION & EMOTION 3 (2016).

vanden Heuvel, Katrina, *Stanching the Flow of Corporate Dollars into Campaigns*, WASH. POST: OPINIONS (Nov. 8, 2011), www.washingtonpost.com/opinions/stanching-the-flow-of-corporate-dollars-into-campaigns/2011/11/04/gIQAy2cR1 M_story.html [https://perma.cc/G2LQ-QKU2].

Vargas, Michael, *The Next Stage of Social Entrepreneurship: Benefit Corporations and the Companies Using This Innovative Corporate Form*, BUS. L. TODAY, July 2016, www.americanbar.org/publications/blt/2016/07/01_vargas.html [http://perma.cc/JW2 L-MP5S].

Velasquez, Manuel, *Debunking Corporate Moral Responsibility*, 13 BUS. ETHICS Q. 531 (2003).

Velasquez, Manuel G., *Why Corporations Are Not Morally Responsible for Anything They Do*, 2 BUS. & PROF. ETHICS J., no. 3, Spring 1983, at 1.

Victor, Bart & John B. Cullen, *The Organizational Bases of Ethical Work Climates*, 33 ADMIN. SCI. Q. 101 (1988).

A Theory and Measure of Ethical Climate in Organizations, 9 RES. CORP. SOC. PERFORMANCE & POL'Y 51 (1987).

Vincent, Andrew, *Can Groups Be Persons?*, 42 REV. METAPHYSICS 687 (1989).

Vinogradoff, Paul, *Juridical Persons*, 24 COLUM. L. REV. 594 (1924).

Vischer, Robert K., *Do For-Profit Businesses Have Free Exercise Rights?*, 21 J. CONTEMP. LEGAL ISSUES 369 (2013).

Wade, Cheryl L., *Effective Compliance with Antidiscrimination Law: Corporate Personhood, Purpose and Social Responsibility*, 74 WASH. & LEE L. REV. 1187 (2017).

Walt, Steven & Micah Schwartzman, *Morality, Ontology, and Corporate Rights*, 11 LAW & ETHICS HUM. RTS. 1 (2017).

Watkins, J. W. N., *Methodological Individualism and Social Tendencies, in* READINGS IN THE PHILOSOPHY OF THE SOCIAL SCIENCES 269 (May Brodbeck ed., 1968).

Werhane, Patricia H., *Corporate and Individual Moral Responsibility: A Reply to Jan Garrett*, 8 J. BUS. ETHICS 821 (1989).

Corporate Moral Agency and the Responsibility to Respect Human Rights in the UN Guiding Principles: Do Corporations Have Moral Rights?, 1 BUS. & HUM. RTS J. 5 (2016).

PERSONS, RIGHTS, AND CORPORATIONS (1985).

Werhane, Patricia H. & R. Edward Freeman, *Corporate Responsibility, in* THE OXFORD HANDBOOK OF PRACTICAL ETHICS 514 (Hugh LaFollette ed., 2003).

Whetten, David A. & Peter Foreman, *An Organizational Identity Lens for Organizational Climate Scholarship, in* THE OXFORD HANDBOOK OF ORGANIZATIONAL CLIMATE AND CULTURE 443 (Benjamin Schneider & Karen M. Barbera eds., 2014).

White, James Boyd, *How Should We Talk About Corporations? The Languages of Economics and of Citizenship*, 94 YALE L.J. 1416 (1985).

JUSTICE AS TRANSLATION: AN ESSAY IN CULTURAL AND LEGAL CRITICISM (1990).

Whitehouse, Sheldon, CAPTURED: THE CORPORATE INFILTRATION OF AMERICAN DEMOCRACY (2017).

Winkler, Adam, Citizens United, *Personhood, and the Corporation in Politics, in* CORPORATIONS AND AMERICAN DEMOCRACY 359 (Naomi R. Lamoreaux & William J. Novak eds., 2017).

Corporate Personhood and the Rights of Corporate Speech, 30 SEATTLE U. L. REV. 863 (2007).

Masterpiece Cakeshop's Surprising Breadth, SLATE (June 6, 2018), https://slate.com/news-and-politics/2018/06/masterpiece-cakeshop-grants-constitutional-religious-liberty-rights-to-corporations.html [https://perma.cc/XM8 L-7J2 G].

"Other People's Money": Corporations, Agency Costs, and Campaign Finance Law, 92 GEO. L.J. 871 (2004).

WE THE CORPORATIONS: HOW AMERICAN BUSINESSES WON THEIR CIVIL RIGHTS (2018).

Wolfe, Alan, *The Modern Corporation: Private Agent or Public Actor?*, 50 WASH. & LEE L. REV. 1673 (1993).

Wolfe, Christopher J., *"An Artificial Being": John Marshall and Corporate Personhood*, 40 HARV. J.L. & PUB. POL'Y 201 (2017).

Wolff, Martin, *On the Nature of Legal Persons*, 54 LAW Q. REV. 494 (1938).

Wolgast, Elizabeth, ETHICS OF AN ARTIFICIAL PERSON (1992).

Yener, Müjdelen et al., *The Effect of Ethical Climate on Work Engagement*, 58 PROCEDIA SOC. & BEHAV. SCI. 724 (2012).

Yosifon, David G., *The Public Choice Problem in Corporate Law: Corporate Social Responsibility After* Citizens United, 89 N.C. L. REV. 1197 (2011).

Zolt, Eric M., *Tax Deductions for Charitable Contributions: Domestic Activities, Foreign Activities, or None of the Above*, 63 HASTINGS L.J. 361 (2012).

Index